The Psychology of Emotion

Second Edition

K. T. STRONGMAN
Psychology Department, University of Exeter

JOHN WILEY & SONS
Chichester · New York · Brisbane · Toronto

CAMROSE LUTHERAN COLLEGE
Library

Library of Congress Cataloging in Publication Data:

Strongman, K. T.
  The psychology of emotion.

  Bibliography: p.
  Includes index.
  1. Emotions. I. Title.
  BF531.S82 1978   152.4   77-26618
  ISBN 0 471 99624 6 (cloth)
  ISBN 0 471 99625 4 (paper)

Typeset by Preface Ltd., Salisbury, Wiltshire.
Printed in Great Britain by
Unwin Brothers, The Gresham Press, Old Woking, Surrey

For Lara and Luke

Preface to First Edition

In spending some years teaching an advanced undergraduate course on the psychology of emotion, I increasingly felt the need for a book which gathered together some of the very different approaches which have been made to the subject. Our knowledge of emotion has been gained in diverse ways; it is discussed in most areas of psychology and, indeed, permeates the whole subject. This inevitably means that its study within a single course is difficult—the relevant sources and their evaluations are spread very widely throughout the psychological literature. The present book is an attempt to simplify matters by drawing together and comparing representative examples of the better thought and research on emotion. In that it presupposes some knowledge of psychology, the book is not directed at the beginning student. It is meant for the second or third year undergraduate who wises to gain a more specialized knowledge of the subject.

Although the basic aims of the book are to provide a broad coverage of emotion and to suggest guidelines for its study and research, it is not completely unbiased. It quite self-evidently reflects two fundamental viewpoints. First, emphasis is laid on research which is reasonably sound methodologically, and on theory which is reasonably well anchored to such research. Second, there is more than a faint leaning towards the behavioural (although not necessarily behaviouristic) approaches to the subject. In spite of this, it should be simple enough for the reader who is antipathetic to these types of analysis to skim over them or miss them out altogether. In any case, he should certainly forgo the last few pages of the book. However, I make no apologies for such biases, since I believe them to lead to research strategies which are important to the overall study of psychology.

Finally, I would like to express my gratitude to all those who have tolerated my vagaries during the writing of this book. In particular, I thank my friends and colleagues Philip Wookey and Robert Remington for their help, advice, and encouragement, and my wife, Thelma, without whose support I should never have finished.

Acknowledgments

The author wishes to acknowledge the cooperation of the following for granting permission to reproduce diagrams from their publications:

Academic Press, Inc.
Figures 4 and 5 (M. Arnold, Ed., *Feelings and Emotions*, Academic Press, New York, 1970, pp. 10–11.

American Psychological Association
Figure 11 (V. H. Denenberg, *Psychol. Rev.*, 1964, **71**, 235–351). Copyright 1964 by the American Psychological Association and reproduced by permission.

McGraw-Hill Inc. and Appleton-Century-Crofts
Figure 7 (from *Physiological Psychology*, 3rd edn. by G. T. Morgan ©1965 McGraw-Hill Inc., adapted from *Bodily Changes in Pain, Hunger, Fear and Rage* by W. B. Cannon, published by Appleton-Century-Crofts).

NEW York Academy of Sciences
Figure 3 (D. Bindra, 'A unified interpretation of emotion and motivation', *Ann. New York Acad. Sci.*, 1969, **159**, p. 1073).

Preface to Second Edition

There were a number of reasons why I welcomed the opportunity to produce a second edition of *The Psychology of Emotion*. Naturally, since 1973 more research on various aspects of emotion has been carried out, and some of the more important parts of this have been included in this new edition. Also, there were a number of errors of omission in the first edition which I hope have now been rectified. Doubtless, there are still some ideas and research findings which have been forgotten, although I have tried to keep these to a minimum. Similarly, there were some parts of the original edition which both hindsight and critical comment tell me to have been poor. It was a relief to attempt to improve them.

More important than new research findings, there have been a number of recent publications which, in my opinion, have somewhat changed the direction of research and theory in emotion. Broadly speaking, a greater emphasis has been placed on analysis of cognitive factors in emotion and on the significance of emotional expression and recognition. In large measure this is due to the work of Izard, reflecting ideas and approaches which I suspect will become very influential. In consequence, I felt it necessary to allow these new emphases to partly replace the rather behavioural orientation of the first edition.

Finally, since the publishers have allowed me a few more words in this edition, I have been able to expand some sections of the book a little. This was particularly enjoyable in dealing with the chapter on theories of emotion, which is now more representative of the many directions which these have taken. Also, I have been able to include an entirely new chapter on the phenomenology of emotion—a subject too often neglected by experimental psychologists and yet which can have much to offer.

To sum up, the aims of the second edition are precisely the same as those of the first. It is merely that I have attempted to realize them in slightly different ways.

Contents

1

Introduction

As it is commonly conceived, emotion is bound up with feeling. Were you to produce an off-the-cuff definition of the term, it would probably make some reference to subjective feelings. Go on stage further and consult a dictionary, and yet again the word feeling would be prominent. For example, the *Shorter Oxford English Dictionary* defines emotion (in psychology) as a 'mental feeling or affection, distinct from cognitions or volitions'. Clearly, one thing we mean if we use the word emotion is personal, subjective feeling. We describe this feeling as pleasant or unpleasant, mild or intense, transient or long lasting, and as interfering with or enhancing our behaviour.

In his *Dictionary of Psychology*, Drever (1952) is a little less subjective in his definition. He describes emotion as a complex state of the organism involving widespread bodily changes. Mentally, this is accompanied by strong feelings and impulses to behave in particular ways. He has added two more ingredients to the mixture—bodily states and behaviour. To return to your off-the-cuff definition, it may well have included some reference to physiological changes, such as an increased pulse rate, or sweating, a feeling of palpitations or trembling. Or it may have referred to some behaviour such as fighting or running, or to some strained facial expression. Emotion, then, also involves physiological and behavioural change; again, such change may vary along several dimensions—it may, for example, be great or small, acute or chronic, we may enjoy it or we may not.

To take the exercise one stage further, were you to define a specific emotion, such as anger or fear, you might well begin your definition with some phrase like: 'It is when . . .' or 'Yesterday, I was . . .'. In other words, you would escape the definition by giving an example, and that example would describe some environmental situation that you had experienced.

Emotion is feeling, it is a bodily state involving various physical structures, it is gross or fine-grained behaviour, and it occurs in particular situations. When we use the term we mean any or all of these possibilities, each of which may show a wide range of variation. This points to the major difficulty which besets the academic study of the subject. Different theorists have taken different starting points. Any theory of emotion or any empirical research on emotion deals only with some part of the broad meaning that the term has acquired. Some theorists stress psychological factors, some behavioural, some subjective. Some deal only with extremes, some say emotion colours all behaviour. There is no consensus of opinion; at present emotion defies definition. It is impossible to make conclusive statements about the whole subject merely from ideas or research in only one of its aspects. And these aspects are often too disparate to attempt more than the slightest synthesis. At best we can perhaps suggest that some of the areas of study which make up emotion can be usefully and cogently reduced to others. For the moment, I will not add to the confusion by producing my own definition of emotion. Most of this book will be concerned with describing emotion rather than defining it. The aim is to give the reader more connotations to the word than he has at present.

FOUNDATIONS OF THE STUDY OF EMOTION

Leeper (1965) puts forward an interesting hypothesis to account for the rationalist, commonsense doctrine of the emotions which was generated by the early philosophers. Briefly, this doctrine contrasted reason and emotion by proposing that man is basically knowing and rational, but to achieve this must minimize his baser, emotional elements. Reason was equated with choice and emotion was regarded as an inbuilt response to significant environmental stimuli—we hear the roar of the lion, feel afraid and run, rather than coolly and rationally shooting it between the eyes.

Leeper argues that there are parallel trends in everyday thought about emotion and in its pre-scientific study. He suggests that these trends come from the emphasis which is usually laid on palpable factors in any new field of study. He describes palpable factors as tangible, highly invariable, and showing close relationships between cause and effect. He believes that stress on such factors led pre-scientific thought to focus on conscious, intense emotions, particularly those capable of strongest expression. Also, emotion (as a process underlying behaviour) was viewed as having its effects mainly by increasing the intensity and duration of primitive behaviours such as fighting, and as producing socially irresponsible actions.

Leeper suggests further that much of present-day scientific thought is still caught in this basic philosophy. For example, despite Freud, there is not much credence given to possible unconscious emotions. Emotions are still often thought of only as strong experiences, and it is mainly the negative ones which receive attention. Emotions continue to be regarded as fundamentally opposed to realistic, adaptive functioning.

Although the rationalist philosophy of the emotions began with Plato and Aristotle, it received its fullest expression by Descartes in the seventeenth century. Descartes' was the extreme dualistic philosophy, separating mind and body. In animals, he thought that there is simply an environmental input and a bodily output. In man, reason (or choice) intervenes. Emotions (or passions) were vital to his viewpoint since he thought of them as changing the flow of animal spirits, the basic determinants of action. Descartes suggested that there are six primitive emotions: admiration, love, hate, desire, joy, and sadness. These combine to produce the introspective feelings which we regard as emotion. However, he also drew attention to the place of physiology and bodily functions in emotion. He regarded overt emotional behaviour as the result of instinctive attempts at achieving suitable responses to given environmental conditions.

Descartes believed emotions to have four main functions. They cause: (1) the appropriate flow of animal spirits in the body; (2) the body to be held ready for the various environmental goal objects which come its way; (3) the soul to desire these objects, which nature has already told us are of use; and (4) a persistence of the desire for these objects.

Descartes regarded the actual course taken by the emotions as beginning with an object in the environment which, via the sense organs and nerves, creates an impression on the pineal gland. This causes the soul to apprehend the stimulus and also causes the animal spirits in the brain and nerves to become active. These spirits act on the pineal gland to convert the feeling which is already there into a passion (emotion). Thus Descartes distinguishes between passions (in the soul), bodily commotion (in the viscera) and action (overt movement). However, although his view of emotion is considerably more sophisticated than previous ideas, and although he lays much emphasis on emotion as basic to behaviour, the problem of the relation between emotion and reason (and also between mental and bodily factors in emotion) is still very apparent. His theory of emotion can be summarized as suggesting that emotion intervenes between stimulus and response, causing the response to be less rational than it otherwise would have been.

After Descartes, the next significant discussion of emotion is to be found in Darwin's *Expression of the Emotions in Man and Animals* (1872). He stressed overt action as the biologically significant aspect of emotion and emphasized the importance of causative environmental stimulation. Also, of course, his theory of evolution pointed to the continuity between man and animals with respect to emotion, as well as in every other way. Shortly following this, James (1884) brought together the ideas of Descartes and Darwin and with a neat reversal of the commonsense view produced what was effectively the first psychological theory of emotion. James' theory will be discussed at length later, but, in summary, he suggested that the perception of emotional stimuli leads both to visceral reactions and to overt muscular reations. The feeling of these reactions (i.e. cortical feedback from them) *is* the emotional experience. We hear the lion roar, run, and then feel afraid. James' theory was important in that it pointed to a relationship between emotional stimuli, emotional behaviour, and emotional experience. In fact, it is James who provided the obvious and necessary stimulus to academic thought about emotion. He removed the emphasis from considerations of how emotion might function.

MODERN APPROACHES TO EMOTION

Since James, the experimental and theoretical work on emotion has diversified considerably. Bindra (1970) provides a concise breakdown of the various experimental approaches. These have been clearly related to emotion as feeling, emotion as response, and the stimuli which produce emotion. (1) Emotional experience (or recognition); this refers to emotion as subjectively reported by man and as inferred by him about other men and about animals. (2) Emotional arousal; referring to changes in internal bodily process, i.e. visceral, somatic, and neural function, as produced by environmental stimuli. (3) Emotional action; referring to overt response patterns, obvious behaviour. (4) Emotional stimuli; here the stress has been on the stimulus features of the physical or social environment that produces (1), (2), and (3). This last line of attack carries an immediately obvious problem, its implicit circularity; it is difficult to define emotional stimuli independently of emotional responses. However, it has led to two research strategies. First, one aimed at finding what stimuli will produce a given range of emotional responses. And second, the selection of a particular stimulus pattern and a determination of what responses this will elicit under various organismic conditions, such as hormonal change.

Theoretically, the aim over the last 80 years or so has been to define emotion and to find a place for it in behaviour theory. Bindra again provides a cogent analysis of the three major approaches which have developed. The most common of these specifies emotion as a *unique* process. However, ideas on the workings of this process have taken many forms. As we have seen, James (1884), for example, viewed it as a 'feeling' of bodily changes stemming from a perception of an 'exciting' fact. Wenger (1950) regarded it as visceral reaction, Cannon (1927) as neural thalamic impulses which are generated by the release of cortical inhibition. Or Arnold (1950) regarded it as an appraisal in the brain of sensory stimuli, resulting in an 'emotional attitude' which produces the 'emotional experience', and Lindsley (1951) as behavioural activation due to arousal of the brain-stem reticular formation. There are many such theories, some of which will be discussed in detail later. However, none has gained general acceptance. This is probably because the idea of emotion as a single process cannot cater for all the data which have been gathered from empirical studies. And the studies themselves have been concentrated on very different aspects of emotion.

Emotion has sometimes been analysed as an intervening variable, anchored to observable stimuli and responses. McDougall's (1928) instinct theory, for example, posits an 'emotional impulse' which links stimuli and responses. Or Brown and Farber (1951) describe emotion within a Hullian framework. The third approach has the advantage of immediately fitting emotion into general behaviour theory. It explains all emotional phenomena without any theoretical recourse to emotion; a single set of processes are hypothesized to account for emotion, for motivation, and for perception. Bindra (1969) and Leeper (1965) provide examples of such theories. If the theories which adopt this broad strategy can be judged as 'good' theories (see below) they are perhaps to be preferred, since they make considerable gains in parsimony. However, this remains to be seen.

The more recent theories of emotion can also be analysed in terms of their main emphasis. Such a breakdown points to at least five major approaches. (1) Emotions as conscious experiences, differentiated subjectively (for example the psychoanalytically oriented theories). (2) Emotions as psychological states, emphasizing either the autonomic nervous system and/or the limbic system (for example Lindsley; Arnold). (3) Emotions as representing inadequate adaptation (for example Plutchik). (4) Emotions as motivational (for example Leeper). (5) Emotions as one aspect of behaviour (for example Millenson).

Finally, an even broader analysis, and one which will be used in this book, is simply into those theories which are primarily cognitive, those which are primarily physiological, those which are primarily behavioural, and, to some extent, those which are primarily experiential.

It should be clear from what has been said so far that rather than simplifying the layman's view of emotion, modern academic psychology complicates it even further. Theory and research have stemmed from and developed the many intuitive meanings which emotion already has. More complexity is added to this increasingly complex picture by each line of enquiry appearing in several contexts. Most aspects of psychology are relevant to emotion. As will be explained below, it is hoped that the structure of this book will aid understanding of these various areas and approaches. However, before this, mention must be made of some more general issues. First, there is a brief description of what characterizes a good theory; in considering emotion it is necessary to evaluate many theories. There will follow a discussion of some problems which should be borne in mind in any appreciation of emotion. Some of these are germane to particular approaches such as the physiological or behavioural. Others occur with regularity across the whole sphere of emotion, and indeed throughout much of psychology.

THEORY

To some extent any theory must be formal. It should employ terms with rules that tie them together. In turn, these rules should be defined or related to empirical events. The theory should account for and reduce these empirical events in a simplified manner and to a more simplified form. Many theories of emotion can be judged as reasonably successful in this respect (for example Izard; Plutchik; Millenson), although they are often lacking in a formal structure (for example Schachter). Perhaps the most important aspect of any theory is the degree to which it is anchored to an empirical base. Only thus can it be tested. A theory which is untestable is surely of less value than one which has been tested and proved wrong. So, any theoretical constructs should be linked semantically to empirical constructs. The empirical constructs themselves are mainly the descriptions of behaviour and of the situations in which it occurs. It is here that many theories of emotion are lacking (for example Arnold; Hillman). They are too speculative and couched in terms which are often too nebulous to lead to clear prediction. One problem is that, as has already been pointed out, descriptions of emotion and of emotion-producing stimuli are very often made in quite disparate ways. Theories then become correspondingly difficult to compare. (Compare, later Arnold's cognitive/physiological theory with Millenson's behavioural model or Duffy's activation theory, for example.)

Whatever is referred to by the constructs of a theory, these must be a combination of economy and complexity. A theory should describe empirical relationships which already obtain and yet also explain both them and other possible relationships. It must be adequate in its formal structure and yet well grounded empirically. Essentially, it represents a compromise, but a compromise from which predictions can be made. Ultimately, the strength of a theory lies in its predictive power. Some theories of emotion are so broad as to predict almost anything (for example Leeper). Others hardly move any distance from the empirical observations on which they are based, and hence predict little (for example Davitz). As will become obvious, there is room for a good theory of emotion which takes into account all of its various overtones, although Izard has perhaps gone some way in providing this.

SOME BASIC PROBLEMS

At present, there are no right or wrong answers to the problems discussed below. Although they are pressing and important to the study of emotion, they have tended to be dealt with in idiosyncratic and arbitrary ways. Each investigator produces equally good solutions and an equally cogent supportive argument. For this reason they are problems about which the reader should for the most part draw his own conclusions.

Terminology

Within the literature on emotion many terms are employed quite freely. Their usage is inconsistent and they are seldom adequately defined. Not least of these is 'emotion' itself. Other words which have high association value but which nevertheless denote little are 'feeling', 'affect', and 'emotionality'. A similar lack of precision surrounds terms which refer to specific emotions, jealousy, fear, love, anger, for example (and particularly anxiety). To concentrate on 'emotion', it has sometimes been defined, for example, as a state of the organism which affects behaviour, and sometimes more directly as a response. When defined as a state, it is sometimes regarded as mentalistic and sometimes as physiological. When defined as a response, it is sometimes seen as physiological and sometimes as behavioural. The particular everyday connotation of emotion which has provided the starting point for any one theorist or researcher has led to an individualistic and biased definition. Occasional inconsistencies are even evident *within* as well as between those who study emotion.

At this point, I do not wish to add to extant definitions. When words such as feeling and affect are found in this book, it will be made clear whose usage is being followed. Otherwise they will be avoided. For the most part, the term emotion will itself be used broadly. In this way it is hoped that the reader will build up a general concept of emotion; and one which in fact reflects its everyday usage. It clearly does embody many different aspects at many levels of function. It is a large part of a complex subject.

Levels of discourse

The problem of the various levels of discourse to be found in the psychology of emotion has already been described. It devolves from the continuing division of emotion into experience, behaviour, physiological substrates, and eliciting stimuli. Those who study emotion have their own preference for the terms in which they can most comfortably converse and presumably in which they regard emotion as most appropriately expressed. They may be restricted to one of the above types of discourse or they may be happy to handle them in combination. Whichever way, it is frequently difficult to compare the work and ideas of various researchers.

Subsuming the type of problem to be discussed here under the rubric of levels of discourse is perhaps mistaken, since it implies that some 'levels' are higher (more worthy) than others. This in itself must be an arbitrary matter, since each level brings its own problems. Whether one believes the advantages to outweigh the disadvantages is ultimately a matter of personal predilection (or, in other terms, depends on one's past history of reinforcement).

The problems of regarding emotion primarily as a matter of personal experience are the most self-evident; they concern the validity and reliability of data. It is many years since the introspectionist approach to psychology was thrown into disrepute. It would perhaps be a retrograde step to make it respectable once more. This is not to suggest that the subjective report of 'how a person is feeling' or of what emotion he is experiencing may not provide useful information, but rather that as a datum it cannot stand alone. We cannot place reliance on verbal report from one time to the next. It may be mistaken or aimed at pleasing. We cannot know whether one man's 'anger' is the same as his brother's. Results from any studies of emotion which stress subjective experience should be regarded as no more than indicative, as productive of hypotheses which can be more rigorously tested. On the other hand, phenomenological accounts of emotion should not be cast aside too easily. They may have much which is of use to the conventional scientific psychologist.

Problems which are an integral part of any discussion of emotional stimuli can also be quickly dealt with. How can we know that a stimulus is 'emotional' without finding that it leads to 'emotional behaviour'? It is difficult to define the stimulus independently of the response. For example, common-sense or intuition (i.e. everyday observation) tells us that if we jostle someone in the street he is likely to become angry, that is, he may shout at us or perhaps hit out. More systematic observations may confirm us in this belief. We would happily maintain our hypothesis until we met the man who ignored our jostling or who ran from it. Is jostling no longer an anger-producing stimulus? Did our man 'feel' anger but not show it in the usual way (statistically speaking)? Does jostling also act as a fear stimulus? It is difficult to break the circle between stimulus and response. Of course, if a definition of emotional stimuli can be made independently of the responses which they produce, then these problems fade away. But this has not usually been done. It is similar to the problem which, for example, has faced learning theorists in their considerations of punishment (see, for example, Azrin and Holz 1966).

Research and theory into the physiology of emotion has produced a vast literature, but has been beset by the insoluble problem of reductionism. As will be seen in Chapter 3, the physiological approach to emotion has been focused largely on the possible emotional functions of the autonomic nervous system (ANS) and the central nervous system (CNS)—mainly the limbic system. Subjectively, the reason for this emphasis is easy to see. For example, we can 'feel' our pulse rate increase and our face become red when we are experiencing what we have been taught to call anger. However, if this approach is taken too far, then psychology (as the study of behaviour) becomes reduced to physiology. It is conceivable that this is all to the good, though there are many psychologists who would not agree. Clearly, psychology can gain much from physiology, and physiological fact may well lead to useful behavioural predictions. Basically, there are two important questions which require an affirmative answer before we can argue that a reductionist approach is justified: (1) *Can* we reduce whatever we are studying to another level? (2) It is useful to make this reduction? In the study of the physiology of emotion these questions have usually received scant attention. The physiology has often been far removed from behaviour, and the physiological speculations have frequently been far removed from physiological fact. And, of course, there are the inevitable problems which vitiate most attempts to compare results from psychological and physiological studies of emotion—essentially different languages are being used and different experimental techniques followed. Emotion can be *studied* physiologically, but as this is but one of its many aspects, it is unlikely that there could be any justification for reducing it entirely to this level.

Finally, there is a large body of work on emotion in which the main emphasis or level of discourse is on overt behaviour. Such work can have the advantages of increased objectivity. It is methodologically 'purer' to deal with observable behaviour than with more hypothetical experiences or feelings. However, this level of discourse is often criticized for oversimplifying complex problems. Internal feelings which we 'know' subjectively to exist are disregarded and little notice paid to physiological changes. The behavioural approach is good from the viewpoint of sound investigation, but may seem to give less than the whole picture. On the other hand, it may be that ultimately we shall be able to make any necessary predictions about emotion solely in terms of emotional behaviour. Whether there is any underlying feeling state which is in some way determining the overt behaviour may be immaterial if we can specify the external determinants of the state. We can then jump from environmental stimuli to overt behaviour. Such would be the standpoint of the more confirmed behaviourist. However, it is just as germane to argue that understanding of emotion would be incomplete without any descriptions of the subjective experiences it involves.

Animals or humans—artificiality

Studies of emotion have been carried out on a large variety of species—from mice to man—and the primary emphasis has by no means been on human investigations. The reasons for (what at first sight might seem to be) the surprisingly large number of animal studies in this field are quite straightforward. In fact, they are just slightly more obvious than those that apply in many other areas of psychology. The first is rooted in the problem of artificiality. Are human 'laboratory' emotions, emotions at all? It is notoriously difficult to evoke human emotion in a laboratory setting, even with powerful, intense stimuli. The subjects' responses are tempered by the situation. In passing, it is worth noting that this idea brings out the 'language problem'. For example, we can say that the laboratory nature of a study will change the stimuli used from what they would otherwise have been in real life. They become fresh stimuli evoking new responses. Or we can say that the subject 'knows' that it is only an experiment and cuts down the tenor of his reactions accordingly. Either way, however, the result is artificiality.

The most obvious way around this problem is to use stimuli which are intense or powerful enough to produce responses which approximate to our everyday observations of emotion (although there is some circularity in this argument). Alternatively, the subjects may be so completely deceived that they are unaware that they are taking part in an experiment. The ethical objections to each of these solutions are immediately apparent. The other possibility is to use infrahuman subjects. Here, any objection that artificiality will lead to distorted results is weakened, particularly if laboratory-raised animals have been used; their 'natural' home is the laboratory. With such subjects a much closer control can be legitimately exercised over their emotional behaviour, making it that much more likely that its determinants will be found.

However, many psychologists would question the validity of using animal subjects at all in the study of emotion. Are 'animal' emotions emotion? They might argue that animals do not have emotions, or if they do then they may be so different from human emotion as to make comparison fruitless. Such an attitude would be most likely to be held by those who view emotion primarily at an experiental level. How can we meaningfully speak of the subjective experiences and feelings of animals? Conversely, it can be argued that if the determinants of emotion can be elucidated by well-defined and methodologically sound animal studies, then they will lead to hypotheses which will be more easy to test at the human level. So the argument twists on, and it is for the individual to reach his own conclusions. However, it should be noted that if the decision is to be against the validity of animal studies of emotion, then a vast amount of well-conceived and well-conducted research is rendered somewhat pointless. That much of the present book depends upon evidence from investigations of emotion using animal subjects shows the direction of my own views. It is possible to concede the usefulness of animal research without arguing that it will answer all questions.

The relationship of emotion to other fields of study

The difficulty in defining emotion and the problem of its general breadth as a concept have led it to overlap considerably with some of the other equally wide concepts with which psychology abounds. Three in particular will be met frequently in this book: drive, motivation, and arousal. Each of these will be briefly discussed below, but for the reader who is interested in them in more depth, a good starting point is provided by Bolles (1967) for drive and motivation and Bindra (1959) for arousal.

In some form or another the concept of motivation has existed for as long as man has been attempting to account for his own behaviour. It makes no reference to experience or to any behavioural fact, but is used as a *hypothetical* cause of behaviour. It is conceived of as a force which lies behind behaviour and which therefore aids in our understanding of it. Although not an essential construct in explanations of behaviour, motivation has tended to appear in most accounts of behaviour and has frequently led to highly productive investigations.

An attempt to give a firm theoretical and empirical basis to motivation is embodied in the idea of drive, taking over as it did from instinct. Like instincts, drives were first seen as basic to motivation, as a way of objectifying the subjective, and as of biological importance. These three qualities were itemized as a result of the idea that drive has a solid physiological foundation (in bodily need). If this were in fact the case, then the concept of motivation would become less hypothetical than it is. From these hopeful if vague formulations four main lines of research developed. (1) Hunger and thirst were studied as central dynamic states, not just as stimuli. (2) It was demonstrated that animals become more active with increases in biological need, i.e. drives have general energizing effects. (3) Evidence accrued to support the idea of specific hungers. (4) Drive strength was measured. Although each of these avenues of research provided interesting information in its own right, it did not lead to any generally acceptable definition of drive. Instead there were many definitions, each of which could be objected to in some way. Some were too loose and others too tight; sometimes drive was regarded as a stimulus, sometimes as a central state.

At this point in the development of the drive concept, two further problems came to light. (1) How many drives are there? There may be just one which has a general effect, or there may be many. Should we invoke a new drive to account for every new sort of behaviour which is observed? (2) Do drives add to the direction of behaviour, or to its energy, or to both?

In the midst of this confusion, Hull (1943) gave drive a much firmer theoretical basis. Briefly, he related it to physiological need and viewed it as similar to, but independent of, habit. He regarded it as energizing behaviour, and when it was reduced, as reinforcing behaviour. He saw it as nonspecific and nondirectional. Recent evidence concerning these and other defining characteristics of drive point to it as a not very robust concept. However, Hull's formulations were the most far-reaching, and so when the term is used in the present text it will be in the Hullian sense.

The other concept which inevitably keeps popping up within this book is that of arousal (or activation). Some psychologists (for example Duffy 1941) altogether replace 'emotion' with 'arousal'. This is yet another hypothetical construct, and one which is closely related to drive. Various theorists (for example Duffy 1951; Bindra 1969; Lindsley 1951) believe the basis of drive to be the hypothetical physiological state of arousal. The fundamental suggestion is that the diffuse projection system in the reticular formation of the brain enhances the reception of specific stimuli and thus serves to influence any learning that is occurring at the time. Although, like drive, arousal is a heavily used concept, hard evidence to support it is not aboundant. This state of affairs is worsened by the theoretical structure on which the concept of arousal is built. This depends on the notion that for a behavioural task of a given complexity there is an optimum level of arousal for optimal performance. Thus is derived the notorious inverted U-shaped function relating arousal to performance. The main problem integral to this idea is that of the whereabouts on the arousal curve of a particular behavioural performance. Is it approaching the optimal level or retreating from it? Overall, we are ignorant of any individual response patterning in arousal and there is little evidence for any individual differences.

Although there is little empirical support for the validity of a unitary concept of arousal, it is frequently used in accounts of emotion. It is often accepted that emotional behaviour occurs with high levels of arousal and that different emotions enjoy different positions on the arousal continuum. If physiological arousal involves pushing the sympathetic nervous system into action, then this is a reasonable idea, but it does not account for all emotional behaviour. A necessary condition for emotion to occur must be an aroused organism, but arousal need not imply emotion. A similar set of physiological changes may be seen in hard physical exercise. The general view adopted here is that arousal as a unitary concept is not very useful, particularly to our understanding of emotion. It is difficult to define and awkward to measure. As will be seen, people differ in their physiological response patterns and different situations may have similar or different physiological effects.

THE STRUCTURE OF THE BOOK

The various problems described above have led to the particular form taken by the present book. Essentially it is a compromise, but one which it is hoped will put the psychology of emotion into some sort of perspective. As so much of the area is characterized by theories or models, Chapter 2 presents a number of these in summary form. Although many of these appear again in greater detail in their specific contexts later in the book, some points of criticism and some attempts at coordinating comments are made. Mainly, they are collected together to give some idea of the development of theoretical viewpoints of emotion and to allow the reader a comparative basis for evaluating them.

Following Chapter 2 are four chapters which each emphasize a different approach to the study of emotion: physiological, cognitive, behavioural, and phenomenological. After these are three further chapters which deal with the study of emotion as it cuts across psychology. These are emotional development, the social psychological approach to the expression and recognition of emotion, and abnormal emotion. Throughout the seven basic chapters an attempt is made to present the major empirical facts and wherever possible to fit these into the existing theories. Also, where appropriate, critical comment is made. Finally, Chapter 10 offers a brief overview and some implications.

Although the coverage of the major topics within this book is fairly complete, or at least representative of the main work which has been done, not every aspect of the study of emotion is dealt with. For example, only very brief mention is made of the psychoanalytic approaches to emotion, or of the ethological work on human sex and aggression. The prime reason for such omissions is that these approaches are properly covered elsewhere and have very little to offer the present analysis. The major aim of the remainder of this book is to present a balanced view of research into emotion, be it theoretical or empirical

2

Theories of Emotion

There are many theories of emotion. They stem from various fundamental assumptions, they stress different problems, and they can be distinguished both in the degree of their formality and in the degree to which they are anchored to empirical fact. The present chapter contains straightforward summaries of some of these theories. No evidence will be presented either for or against them and they will be neither evaluated nor criticized. The aim is to provide some idea of the breadth of thought which has been put into theorizing about emotion. Also, it is intended that this chapter may be used as a comparative reference guide to representative aspects of the many approaches which have been made to the subject. To describe all theories of emotion would necessitate a book in itself, so the number has been restricted. Those included have been chosen either because they are centrally important to modern thought in emotion and/or because they illustrate the breadth of the subject. Many of the theories which are described here will be analysed in greater detail later in the book. There, when appropriate, they will also receive criticism. Others, judged to be of less importance, will only be encountered in this chapter and the interested reader should study the references given for a fuller exposition of these.

Any sample of theories of emotion could be organized in a number of ways—according to the type of approach or emphasis which they take, their chronological order of appearance, the extent of their influence, and so on. Whichever way is followed leads to some confusion. The plan used here was devised to minimize such confusion and to allow similarities and differences between the theories to be seen as easily as possible. The earlier theories are arranged in rough chronological order and the more recent are gathered into a broad classification according to the type of approach on which they depend and the assumptions which they share. There are examples of theories which highlight arousal, motivation or physiological mechanisms, those which stress behaviour, those which stem from the psychoanalytic and experiential traditions, those which emphasize cognition, and finally those which could be termed grand theories, since they combine a number of approaches and even in some cases relate emotion to personality theory.

As will be seen, the divisions are not always distinct. There are a number of reasons for overlap between them. First, the confusion inherent in some theories makes them difficult to categorize. Second, some theories place equal emphasis on more than one aspect of the subject, making classification somewhat arbitrary. When this is the case and where there are obvious grounds for comparison, it will be indicated. Finally, the theories to be described differ from one another in their breadth of approach, some being very narrow and biased, others broad and all-inclusive.

When reading the summaries which follow, it is worth keeping in mind the problems mentioned in Chapter 1. It is here that they will first become evident.

EARLY THEORIES

W. James (the James–Lange theory)

The James–Lange theory of emotion is probably the most famous of all in that it generated a lasting controversy amongst psychologists. Also, it has acted as a stimulus for many more recent theories and a great deal of research (see Chapters 3 and 4). The theory is usually attributed to James and to Lange since it was put forward separately by each (James 1884; Lange 1885), although James was its main and clearest exponent.

James began by limiting his field of consideration to those emotions which have 'a distinct bodily expression', He was attempting to distinguish between mental processes which have no obvious physiological concomitants and those in which straightforward, easily observable changes occur. He suggested that the everyday way of regarding these grosser emotions is: (1) we mentally perceive some fact, (2) this produces some mental affect (called the emotion), and (3) this in turn produces the bodily expression. His view was the converse of this:

'... the bodily changes follow directly the PERCEPTION of the existing fact, and that our feeling of the same changes as they occur IS the emotion'.

(1884, p. 189; italics and capitals his)

So, for example, rather than face some public performance to which we are unused, *at this point we become anxious* and then have 'butterflies in the stomach', tremble and stutter; in James' terms we face our public performance, have 'butterflies', tremble and stutter, and *as a result feel anxious*. He was therefore (as have so many emotion theorists in lesser ways) making a *volte face* on what had gone before, the nub of his theory resting on the notion that the visceral discharges associated with some environmental situation actually lead to the emotion as we know it.

The argument which James used to support this theory can be reduced to a few main points; it was based largely on introspection. He asserted that any sensation has extremely complex physiological manifestations and that these are all felt, some obviously, some more obscurely. He suggested that we imagine some strong emotion and then try to push from our consciousness all of the feelings of the bodily symptoms associated with it. He maintained that if we do this successfully there will be nothing left; we shall have completely exorcized

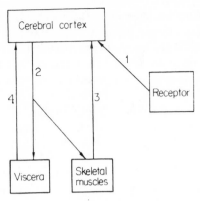

Figure 1. Diagrammatic representation of the James—Lange theory. Arrows show direction of function

the emotion. Finally, he cited many examples of how everyday situations lead directly to these complex, strong (bodily) feelings (seeing a friend peering over the edge of a cliff, for example) and argued support of his case from the idea of how easy we find it to classify both abnormal and normal behaviour according to bodily symptoms.

The James–Lange theory can best be summarized as in Figure 1. This simply represents in diagrammatic form the way in which emotions are experienced as James saw it. (It is worthwhile to compare this figure with Figure 2, which represents the Cannon–Bard theory in a similar way.)

The main point of James' theory then is that afferent feedback from disturbed organs produces the feeling aspect of emotion. The implication is that the cortical activity which comes from this feedback is the actual feeling and that the conscious awareness of this feeling is the emotion itself. Izard (1972) reminds us of an important point about James' view of emotion, that is that as well as emphasizing the role of the viscera in emotion, he also afforded a similar role to the voluntary muscles. In so doing he laid the groundwork for a search for general bodily patterns and facial expressions in emotion.

Overall, James may be fairly said to have produced the first theory which assumed the existence of discrete emotions, these having an instinctive basis and being separable from certain feelings. Thus, for example, stimuli which come from colours and sound lead to nonemotional feelings on a pleasant/unpleasant dimension, and equally nonemotional feelings of interest/excitement may come from intellectual activity. These points have all had an influence on more modern theories of emotion.

W. B. Cannon (the Cannon–Bard theory)

Cannon's ideas were the first of any note to appear after those of James. His approach usually took the form of a criticism of James (see Chapters 3 and 4) and then a statement of an alternative theory (1915; 1927; 1931; 1932). At different times, Cannon's theory has been referred to as a thalamic theory, the first of the emergency theories, or as a neurophysiological theory. This last gives the clue as to why it is often described as the Cannon–Bard theory, since much of the experimental work on which it was based was carried out separately by Bard (for example 1928; 1934; 1950).

Cannon's attack on James will be left for Chapter 4. For now it is enough to say that he based his own theory on evidence (for example Bard 1928; Cannon and Britton 1927; Head 1921) which could be best interpreted as suggesting that the neurophysiological side of emotional expression is subcortical, or, more particularly, thalamic. He argued that all emotions depend on a similar chain of events. An environmental situation stimulates receptors which relay impulses to the cortex. The cortex, in turn, stimulates thalamic processes which act in particular patterns corresponding to particular emotional expressions. Cannon believed that nothing more specific is required than that the neurons in the thalamus be 'released'. He maintained that the nervous discharge from the thalamus has two functions, first to excite muscles and viscera and second to relay information back to the cortex. Thus in Cannon's words:

'... *the peculiar quality of the emotion is added to simple sensation when the thalamic processes are aroused'.*

(1927, p. 119; italics his)

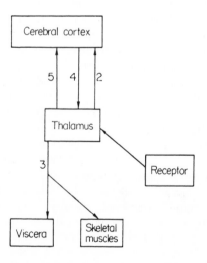

Figure 2. Diagrammatic representation of the Cannon–Bard theory. Arrows show direction of function

This implies that when the thalamus discharges, we experience the emotion at almost the same time that bodily changes occur.

Cannon's theory of emotion is diagrammatically summarized in Figure 2. Basically, Cannon brought into regard the importance of the thalamus and in so doing produced some cogent arguments against James, although these have since been seriously questioned. However, as will be seen later, the neurophysiological picture is far more complicated than Cannon painted it. At least he drew attention to the neurophysiology of emotion and hence acted as the progenitor of much research and theory.

W. McDougall

McDougall (1910; 1923; 1928) attempted to distinguish between emotions and feelings, an endeavour made somewhat similarly by a few of the more Gestalt-based European psychologists (for example Klages 1950; Krueger 1928). His theory also depended on some basic biological considerations (compare with Plutchik's theory). McDougall believed that the capacity to approach beneficial goals is fundamental to psychology and that all behaviour stems from seeking food and escaping or avoiding noxious stimuli. He argued that what we call emotions and feelings occur as adjuncts to these basic processes; they come from the way in which we perceive our environment and our various bodily changes.

McDougall proposed that two feelings—pleasure and pain—modify all of our goal-directed behaviour. However, he also regarded man as more complex than this; man is cognitive and has expectations, he fuses together many experiences and has odd concentrations of feelings. McDougall suggested that it is these cognitions that set man apart from other organisms and direct that he no longer alternates between pleasure and pain but continually ranges over a complexity of feelings. McDougall believed that through everday usage these complex feelings have become known as the various emotions. He then argued that in fact these are not 'real' emotions and that science would profit if the term were not used in their description (see Duffy for a similar argument).

As is well known, McDougall put instincts foremost in his accounts of psychology, seeing them as providing the impetus for all thought and action. He also argued that all instincts have knowing, feeling, and striving components, with some emotional excitement in evidence as well. Doubtless depending to an extent on James and Cannon, he suggested that this emotional facet of instinct is reflected by discrete visceral and bodily changes. He also felt that emotions can be distinguished from the cognitive processes which go with them. McDougall was implying that perception triggers emotion. For example, an organism might perceive a threatening stimulus; this would provoke it both to flee and to feel fear, the whole process reflecting a basic survival need or instinct. But McDougall is by no means clear how the instrumental and emotional aspects of such reactions become connected, and in his descriptions usually made little precise reference to the matter of bodily responses or cognition.

McDougall's schema for emotion proper began with a statement that throughout the evolution of man goals became more specific and goal-directed behaviour became more specialized. The result was more precise and particularized bodily adjustment. The experience of each of these well-differentiated strivings gave the clear quality of a 'primary emotion'. If two or more of these main bodily reactions conflict, from the experiential point of view this results in '. . . the secondary or blended emotions' (1928), such complexities as shame or reproach.

McDougall also compared complex feelings (not really emotions) with emotions proper (whether primary or secondary). He suggested three main points of comparison. (1) Complex feelings are conditioned by success or failure in our strivings and therefore colour any subsequent impulse that may be similar. 'True' emotions are quite independent of this. They are simply what makes each impulse distinctive and so do not affect any later strivings. (2) McDougall believed that complex feelings were restricted to man since they depend for their appearance on the development of cognition. Real emotions must, however, have appeared much earlier on the evolutionary scale. (3) Finally, named complex feelings such as hope and anxiety are not entities. They just reflect ill-defined ranges of experience and feelings in which there is no blending. Conversely, McDougall viewed each primary emotion as long lasting; it is '. . . an enduring feature of the mental structure of the organism' (1928). Each emotion is only associated with desire and therefore, unlike complex feelings, conflicting desires may produce blends of emotion. Allowing that this was a very subjective analysis, it is possible to appreciate what McDougall was suggesting by comparing, in an everyday sense, the behaviours that tend to accompany 'complex feelings' of anxiety and hope with those that occur with 'true' emotions of, say, fear and curiosity.

J. W. Papez

After Cannon, Papez's (1937) theory of emotion was the next to have a neurophysiological basis. His starting point came from the idea that in lower vertebrates there are anatomical and physiological connections on the one hand between the cerebral hemisphere and the hypothalamus, and on the other between the cerebral hemisphere and the dorsal thalamus. These relationships become further elaborated in the mammalian brain. Papez believed emotion to be mediated by such cortico-hypothalamic interconnections.

Papez stated simply that emotion implies behaviour (expression) and feeling (experience or subjective feeling), and quoted Bard's (1929) results as showing that emotional expression depends on the hypothalamus. But he viewed the cortex as being necessary for the mediation of subjective emotional experience. And further, he suggested that emotional expression and emotional experience are phenomena which can be dissociated from one another in man. Papez also provided a general anatomical picture of the possible structures involved in a corticothalamic mechanism of emotion. Since by now this is a somewhat dated view, it is not worth describing in detail. However, Papez believed that his hypothesized circuits could account for emotion as arising either from psychic (cortical) activity or hypothalamic activity.

Finally, Papez suggests three routes that might be taken by afferent connections from the receptors after they have arrived at the thalamus. He termed these the 'stream of movement', 'stream of thought', and 'stream of feeling', these names presumably reflecting their possible function.

Clearly, Papez's theory depended heavily on neurophysiologizing. However, it was couched in terms such that it could account for the apparently different origins of emotion, for emotion felt and emotion expressed, and for the emotional colouring which seems to be present in many other nonemotional experiences.

J. B. Watson

Watson (1929; 1930) provided the first of the clearly behaviourist theories of emotion. However, he stressed the physiological aspects of emotion as well as the behavioural. Thus:

'An emotion is an hereditary "pattern-reaction" involving profound changes of the bodily mechanism as a whole, but particularly of the visceral and glandular systems'.

(1929, p. 225; italics his)

Given this definition, Watson went on to distinguish between emotional and instinctive reactions. He did this by asserting that an emotional stimulus shocks an organism into a state of chaos, at least for a brief period of time. So, to Watson, emotions were disorganizing.

On the basis of observational work with children, Watson postulated that there are three types of fundamental emotional reaction—fear, rage, and love. However, he maintained that such words often cause confusion and that it might therefore be better to term them X, Y, and Z. He suggested that the X (fear) dimension is caused by: (1) sudden removal of support from an infant, (2) loud sounds, and (3) mild but sudden stimuli when an infant is just falling asleep or awakening. Typical responses are breath-catching, hand-clutching, eye-closing, lip-puckering, and crying. He viewed the Y (rage) dimension as caused by 'hampering an infant's movements'. Responses to this include crying, screaming, body-stiffening, limb-slashing, and breath-holding. Finally, he saw the Z (love) dimension as caused by any gentle manipulation, particularly of the erogenous zones of the body, responses to which include smiling, gurgling, and cooing. Watson believed each of these patterns of reaction to be built in and evident from birth.

Watson's main contributions to the study of emotion were to offer this three-dimensional theory and to place emphasis on behavioural rather than on internal states and feelings. This, and his classic study with Rayner (Watson and

Rayner 1920) on Little Albert, proved to be the foundation on which later behavioural conceptions of emotion have been built (see Chapter 5). In the way in which Watson was the general father of behaviourism, so he was the particular father of the behaviourist approaches to emotion.

General points

The five theories of emotion discussed so far might by now be reasonably described as the classical theories. Perhaps the most interesting point about them is that they contain in one form or another most of the ideas and concepts which can be found in the more modern theories and models. This will become clear throughout the remainder of this chapter. For now, these ideas can be listed quite simply. Some or all of the early theorists: (1) saw emotion as a system which both affects and is affected by other systems; (2) saw both similarities and differences between the various emotions; (3) viewed some emotions as fundamental or primary and others as derived or secondary, hinting at a nature/nurture division; (4) tended to suggest that emotions have ranges of intensity which change their quality when beyond certain levels; (5) viewed emotions as energizing or motivational in their effects; (6) in occasionally stressing voluntary muscle involvement and the expressive side of emotion, hinted at the possibility of emotional control. This final point has obvious therapeutic implications and will be explored in detail in Chapter 8.

Even though the theories of emotion which appeared in the first part of this century now inevitably look a little naive, they clearly provided the foundation for present views. Also, by being concerned with such a large range and variety of behaviours, feelings, cognitions, and physiological changes, they highlighted the enormous complexity of emotion. With one or two not especially noteworthy exceptions, the more recent theories of emotion have added to this complexity.

THEORIES BASED ON MOTIVATION, AROUSAL, AND/OR PHYSIOLOGY

E. Duffy

Duffy has expressed her view of emotion many times (for example 1934; 1941; 1962), but probably put it best in her 1941 paper, which she began:

'For many years the writer has been of the opinion that "emotion", as a scientific concept is worse than useless'.

This sets the scene perfectly, for Duffy tries to explain away emotion rather than to account for it, her argument being couched in terms of a behaviourally oriented activation theory. Her views on activation in general can be read in *Activation and Behaviour* (1962).

Duffy's first (1934) reason for suggesting that the term emotion be dropped from scientific usage was that it had been used mainly to refer to the extreme end of a continuum of behaviour, but one which anomalously involved a sharp noncontinuation between emotion and nonemotion. She argued that a behavioural continuum and discrete categories of behaviour are likely to have different underlying constructs. Duffy preferred the idea that emotional phenomena are separate aspects of responses in continua.

In 1941, Duffy developed her argument further. She suggested that emotion as it is commonly conceived refers to how we feel and act towards a situation which we expect to be important; our expectations may be positive or negative. So, we shall feel angry and perhaps afraid only if we are blocked from attaining some goal. Duffy hypothesizes that such a state of emotion must involve a change in energy level; excitement represents a higher energy level and depression a lower energy level. Energy level itself is dependent on the stimulus situation. It will increase either when we are blocked or when a block is removed; conversely, there is a decrease only when a goal is so effectively blocked that we give up altogether.

Duffy then widened her argument to include the idea that all behaviour is motivated. She suggested that without motivation there would be no activity, and that what is called emotion simply represents an extreme of motivation, i.e. energy. But, she then posed the rhetorical question, how do we know when behaviour is extreme enough to be called emotional? Her answer was that there is no criterion for this, since emotion-producing behaviour does not differ in kind from other behaviour—to Duffy other responses follow the same principles. In her terms, *all* responses are adjustive responses which enable the organism to adapt.

From Duffy's standpoint, the second characteristic of emotion as commonly conceived is that it is disorganizing (see Leeper). However, she thought that this apparent disorganization is a function of behaviour which occurs at very high or at very low energy levels. This is not a function of 'emotion', since disorganization is also found at energy levels not extreme enough to be normally called emotions, for example the stammer of an enthusiastic child or the double fault of the overinvolved tennis player. This, of course, is representing emotion in terms of the hypothetical inverted U-shaped function relating arousal to performance (see Chapter 1).

Finally, Duffy set out to deal with what she regarded as the commonly proposed fact of its conscious awareness (see Mandler). We tend to feel that our conscious experiences of emotion are different from our conscious experiences of anything else. Duffy argued that such a conscious awareness involves awareness of the environmental situation which leads to the emotional state, awareness of bodily changes, and awareness of a set for response in the situation. Duffy maintained that these factors also make up any nonemotional state of consciousness.

To summarize, Duffy breaks down emotion (and in fact all behaviour) into changes in: (1) level of energy, (2) organization, and (3) conscious states, and suggests that each of these occurs on a continuum. The final stage in her argument is that it is meaningless to try to study emotion at all, because it is something which '. . . has no distinguishing characteristics' (1941). Instead, she suggests that *any* response should be considered according to its energy level (activation), how well it maintains goal-direction (organization/disorganization), and the environmental situation in response to which it occurs. Duffy's is a theory of nonemotion.

D. B. Lindsley

Lindsley's theory of emotion first appeared in 1950 and 1951. More recently (1957; 1970) he has extended it to broader aspects of behaviour. Essentially, it is similar to Duffy's theory in that it is based on the concept of arousal. However, it is expressed in neurophysiological rather than behavioural terms.

Lindsley's (1951) theory depended on his belief in five empirical findings. These are summarized below, although it should be borne in mind that some doubt has been cast on them by more recent thought and empirical work. (1) In emotion, the electroencephalogram (EEG) is characterized by desynchronization, i.e. alpha-blocking or activation. (2) EEG activation can be produced by stimulation of the brain-stem reticular formation, or of the sense modalities. (3) Synchrony is restored and EEG activation is abolished by destruction of the basal diencephalon. (4) The behaviour which occurs, at least in cats, if lesions appropriate to (3) above are produced is described by Lindsley as being opposite to that which is usually seen in emotional arousal. It is apathy, somnolence, etc. (5) Overlapping the cortically arousing EEG mechanism is that of the basal diencephalon, which is the substrate for the objective part of emotional expression.

Although Lindsley (1957; 1970) has added some empirical support to these basic points and has also revised some of the details of his theory, the fundamental idea remains the same: arousal/motivation mechanisms underlie emotion. He suggests that the mechanisms of arousal are the brain-stem reticular formation interacting with the diencephalic and limbic systems via the ascending reticular activating system. He also maintains that the limbic systems control emotional expression and emotional and motivational behaviour. He regards emotion as being expressed in three ways: (1) through cortical channels, for example thought, worry, anxiety (cortical arousal); (2) through visceral channels, for example sweating, crying, in fact ANS function (cortical, diencephalic, and brain-stem arousal); (3) through somatomotor channels, for example facial expression, muscle tension (somatomotor arousal).

Lindsley is a wide-ranging neural arousal theorist. Although his research and theory are important to emotion, he also takes in such phenomena as sleep, wakefulness, alerting, attention, selective attention, vigilance, and, of course, motivation. Such is the postulated ubiquity of function of the descending and ascending reticular systems, and of those other CNS structures with which they interact.

P. T. Young

Young's (1961) theory is unusual in that it is relatively modern, American, and yet somewhat isolated; it differs both in conception and language from many of the other theories described here. Although he leans heavily on the concept of arousal, Young distinguishes it from what he terms an hedonic dimension. He seems to be the last of the hedonic philosophers, although simultaneously an experimental psychologist.

Young does not speak of emotion *per se,* but rather of affective processes and an hedonic continuum. He regards affective processes as varying in sign, intensity, and duration. Thus, if naive organisms develop approach behaviour, he postulates that an underlying positive central affective process is at work; similarly, a negative affective process underlines withdrawal responses. Further, he suggests that affective processes can vary from maximally positive intensity to maximally negative—as shown by the development of preferences. And lastly, he maintains that affective processes can differ in duration. Young views these affective processes as spread along an hedonic continuum which ranges from extremely negative through an area of indifference to extremely positive. Hedonic changes can occur in either direction, and from time to time may even be in opposition. This schema leads to four possible types of affective change: increasing positive, decreasing positive, increasing negative, and decreasing negative. (In some ways this is similar to Millenson's behaviourist ideas.)

Young proposes that affective processes are quite distinct from sensory processes and that their essential role is motivational, having a regulatory influence on behaviour. He postulates a series of principles and functions concerning affective processes. First the principles. (1) Stimulation has affective as well as sensory consequences. (2) Affective arousal points the organism towards or away from a stimulus. (3) Affective processes lead to motives. (4) The strength of a recent motive is related to various aspects of previous affective arousals (duration, intensity, frequency, and recency). (5) Motives also depend on learning—affective processes determine what will and will not be learned, but learning itself is simply practice, neurobehavioural change due to exercise. (6) Affective processes can be conditioned—we learn 'how to feel' in given situations. (7) Affective processes exert their regulatory function by influencing choice. (8) The final principle is very wide-ranging—neurobehavioural patterns themselves follow a pattern of organization which maximizes positive affective arousal and minimizes negative affective arousal.

Young suggests that effective processes have four main functions. (1) They activate, by provoking action. (2) They sustain and terminate behaviour. (3) They regulate behaviour (as to whether or not it will develop or continue). (4) They organize, in that they determine the formation of neurobehavioural patterns which usually become learned.

Essentially, Young is speaking of pleasantness and unpleasantness rather than emotion. These are affective processes arranged on an hedonic continuum which itself has an arousal function. The affective processes accompany all behaviour to some degree and themselves work according to a set of underlying principles, and in turn exercise various influences on behaviour.

D. Bindra

Bindra (1968; 1969) puts forward an up-to-date neurophysiological theory of emotion, or more strictly, of emotion and motivation. He suggests that both emotional and motivational phenomena can best be accounted for in terms of one construct, that of the central motive state (CMS).

Bindra begins by denying that any useful distinction can be made between emotion and motivation, and speaks instead of 'species-typical', biologically useful actions. He suggests that such actions are an interaction between environmental stimuli (which he terms incentives) and physiological change. (Evidence in support of this contention is reviewed, for example, in Glickman and Schiff 1967.) Bindra believes this interaction to take place in the brain and to involve joint environmental and physiological action on a common group of neurons. He maintains that this produces a CMS; this is not in itself a drive but is simply a functional change in neurons which needs *both* an environmental stimulus and a physiological change before it will occur. Thus, for example, physiological hunger and the sight, smell, and taste of food are not by themselves enough to produce a CMS; they must occur together.

The hypothetical notion of how a CMS produces a species-typical action is shown in Figure 3. A CMS is thought to increase the probability of a response to certain environmental stimuli by altering the effectiveness of the sensory input—shown as 'selective attention' in the figure. Or a CMS may increase the likelihood of a particular action by altering neural discharge to appropriate autonomic and somatic motor sites—'motor facilitation' or 'response bias'. Bindra argues that this scheme is equally apposite to considerations of both emotion and motivation. This leads him to the view that many words traditionally used in discussions of emotion and motivation can be replaced by common terms. For example, CMS instead of emotion or emotional state and motive or motivational state; physiological condition instead of emotional predisposition and drive.

Two further aspects of Bindra's CMS ideas are worth summarizing. (1) He believes that CMSs can be classically conditioned. Their nature depends on the actual physical state and environmental stimuli involved in this conditioning stimulus and the unconditioned stimulus (incentive). (2) Bindra asserts that the CMS can be used to resolve many of the long-enduring problems in the study of emotion. For example, the occurrence of emotion has often been thought to depend on external stimuli, whereas that of motivation has been seen to depend on internal stimuli. CMS analysis puts these together and implies that the traditional distinction has been drawn because of a difference in the value of the determining conditions—a very wide environmental stimulus can create an emotional CMS, whereas physiological states for motivational CMSs are very

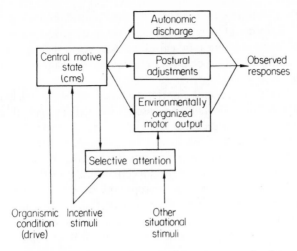

Figure 3. Bindra's central motive state mechanism (taken from Bindra 1969). The figure shows two ways in which the hypothetical CMS can bring about species-typical action. (1) Via organismic conditions and incentive stimuli from the environment, i.e. selective attention. (2) Via effects on sensory and motor mechanism, i.e. motor facilitation or response bias

specific. To take another example, emotional behaviour has often been thought of as disorganized (but see Leeper) and motivational behaviour as organized. Bindra argues that both types of behaviour can be organized or disorganized depending on when they are observed during individual development. Thus a lack of experience with a particular environmental stimulus will lead to disorganized responding. However, he also suggests that motivational patterns start early on in development and occur frequently, whereas emotional patterns occur less frequently and involve more unusual situations. In this sense, he views motivation as organized and emotion as disorganized, but there seems to be little justification for this in terms of the CMS.

General points

Although the four theories described in this section differ in the degree to which they emphasize physiological mechanisms of emotion, they have a number of points in common. They each put emotion on a sort of continuum, be this of arousal, activation, motivation, or pleasantness, and in so doing bracket emotion together with motivation. Given the usual awkwardness of deciding where one is on an arousal curve, and in this case of deciding where emotion begins and all else finishes, the implication is that the concept of emotion should be done away with altogether. Indeed, Duffy states this overtly, and Bindra replaces both emotion and motivation with central motive state. Lindsley almost casts emotion out as well, although not quite, and Young, even though allowing for more subtleties in emotion than the other three theorists, is basically speaking in terms of an all-embracing pleasantness/unpleasantness continuum.

Enough is now known about emotion to render the approach exemplified by these theorists neither pertinent nor useful. As will be seen throughout the remainder of this book, emotion is very rich, complex, and subtle, and appears to be subjectively, cognitively, and behaviourally different from other experiences and acts. Even if emotion often does involve extremes of arousal, it would seem cavalier to throw out the concept entirely for this reason. Nothing would be achieved by this, either conceptually or empirically. On the other hand, the theories discussed here are useful in that they help to draw attention to the physiological bases of emotion and to point to some of the problems of arousal with which the more general theorist of emotion has to contend.

BEHAVIOURAL THEORIES

H. F. Harlow and R. Stagner

It is difficult to categorize Harlow and Stagner's (1933) theory of emotion. It was quite clearly based on a conditioning model and owed much to Watson's behaviourism, and yet retained overtones of Cannon's physiologizing while maintaining a distinction between feelings and emotions. Briefly, they suggested that at the root of emotion are unconditioned affective responses (central physiological changes experienced as feelings). All emotions occur through becoming conditioned to these responses. The effect of this is to modify the original unconditioned affective state in two ways: (1) the range of eliciting stimuli is widened; (2) the violence of the original responses is dampened.

Harlow and Stagner made a number of extensions of their theory. (1) They suggested that although the basic emotional states are feelings, emotions may also reflect other conscious states. (2) Feelings are controlled thalamically, and sensations cortically. (3) Emotions are not innate; Harlow and Stagner simply suggested that there are unconditioned responses from which emotions develop. They believed the innate part of emotion to be the 'four fundamental feeling tones, pleasure, unpleasantness, excitement and depression'. (4) Emotion is distinct from feeling in that in emotion there is cognition of the outside situation. We feel things in such a way that they are connected to external stimuli. To return to the nature/nurture question, we are born with the capacity to feel but have to learn the various emotions.

Finally, Harlow and Stagner suggested a behaviouristic way in which the various emotions become differentiated from the original amorphous mass of feeling states. They argued, via introspective analysis, that the emotion labels which we attach to various experiences simply reflect our cognitions of the external stimuli involved and the meanings which they have for us. Any name which becomes appropriate to describe an affective state must therefore result from social conditioning. Harlow and Stagner viewed fear and rage, for example, as basically the same states. However, the situation which brings them about is one of threat, and if it is appropriate to attack then we call the state rage, whereas if it is appropriate to run we call it fear.

To summarize, Harlow and Stagner suggested that there are innate, undifferentiated, basic feelings. Emotions are the conditioned form of these which we learn to refer to in particular ways. The feelings, the emotional conditioning, and the social learning of labels are each mediated cortically and subcortically.

J. R. Millenson

Millenson (1967) provides the closest approximation to a modern behaviourist theory of emotion, although he himself admits it is no more than a model. It is rooted in Watson, owes much to Plutchik, and is inspired by Estes and Skinner's (1941) experimental paradigm for studying conditioned emotional behaviour (see Chapter 6).

Millenson's model rests on the fundamental proposition that emotional changes, which he believes come about through a process of classical conditioning, either enhance or suppress other, nonemotional behaviour. He argues that: (1) some emotions differ only in intensity; and (2) some emotions are basic and others are compounds of these. From this Millenson produces a three-dimensional system to describe all emotion, each dimension representing variations in emotional intensity. Dimension 1 is terror, anxiety or apprehension, such emotions sometimes suppressing and sometimes facilitating operant behaviour. Dimension 2 is made up of elation or pleasure, which enhance operant behaviour. Dimension 3 is anger; this facilitates some operant behaviour and leads to a greater likelihood of attack and destruction. Clearly, these dimensions are close to Watson's X, Y, and Z factors.

Millenson suggests that more complex emotions develop from mixtures of these three dimensions, which he regards as primary. For example, we feel 'guilt' if we steal a book. In Millenson's terms, such behaviour would possibly lead to both positive (possession of the book) and negative (being caught) consequences. This is psychological conflict, which Millenson views as often underlying our more complex emotional reactions. Also, he argues that at the human level emotional reactions often become complex due to the very involved history of conditioning and reinforcement which we all have. Occasionally, great changes can be wrought in the mass of interrelated reinforcers which are controlling our behaviour at any time. For example, a friend may die, or we may suffer a loss of status. In either case we have suddenly been deprived of many reinforcers. We label our emotional reaction to this as sorrow. This argument leads Millenson to an interesting conjecture concerning a possible difference between human and animal emotion. He suggests that we may well be correct in believing certain emotions (such as sorrow) to be essentially human. There are simply no conditions in the infrahuman world which are complex enough to produce them—it is not necessarily that animals are incapable of them.

Hence, Millenson's view of emotion is extremely behaviouristic. He concerns himself with little more than observable behaviour and the environmental conditions which he believes to control it. In this singlemindedness, Millenson's ideas are unique amongst the more recent formulations of emotion.

J. A. Gray

Gray (1971) also puts forward a theory of emotion in the behavioural tradition. As will be seen in later chapters, it is a theory which in its conceptualization has relevance to the development of emotion and in its ramifications for abnormal emotion.

Gray views emotion as comprising three distinct systems, each of which is grounded in relationships between reinforcing stimuli and response systems. (1) When *approach* predominates, the reinforcing stimulus is a conditioned stimulus for reinforcement or nonpunishment. (2) When *behavioural inhibition* predominates, the reinforcing stimulus is a conditioned stimulus for punishment or nonreward. (3) When the *fight/flight* system predominates, the reinforcing stimulus is unconditioned punishment or nonreward.

Gray arrives at this conceptualization of emotion via a useful and cogent analysis of innate fears and early conditioning (see Chapter 7) and an initial distinction of emotional states in the common language. He is taking the position that emotions are internal states which are mainly caused by external events (an idea which endorses that of Weiskrantz 1968) and distinguishes them from drive. When the relationships between external events and emotional states become confused, then pathological reactions result. This leads Gray to a pertinent discussion of anxiety and neurosis, psychosis and depression. However, as Mandler (1976) points out, it is a discussion which leads Gray into problems in accounting for sex and hunger, for example. He describes feeling sexy as nonemotional and love by contrast as emotional. Whilst not wanting to deny that love involves emotion, it can surely be argued that sexual arousal is also emotional, as might be extreme hunger or thirst as well.

General points

The three behavioural theories or models of emotion described here clearly have much in common. Equally clearly, they owe their derivation to Watson, although they go much further than his primitive theory. Of course their greatest point in common is that they dwell almost entirely on behaviour, and then tend to view emotion as dependent on the nature of reinforcing stimuli and the complexities of classical conditioning. That it is possible to conceptualize some aspects of emotion behaviourally is beyond dispute, a point to which Chapter 6 below attests. However, whether or not it is appropriate to do this is another question. By now, there is an impressive array of evidence and thought pointing to the significant role of cognitive functions in emotion (see Izard, Mandler and Schachter for example) which it would seem inapposite to ignore. Also, whether or not one assigns a causal role to cognitions and subjective experiences in emotion, they surely exist, and consequently attempts should be made to understand them if we are to obtain a full picture of emotion. A purely behavioural analysis, for all the scientific rigour which it promotes, does not permit this and is perhaps therefore somewhat wanting.

PSYCHOANALYTIC AND EXPERIENTIAL THEORIES

D. Rapaport (psychoanalytic theory)

Rapaport (1950) provides a good general introduction to the psychoanalytic approach to emotion. The reader who is interested in pursuing this line of study will find worthwhile analyses of the Jungian idea of emotion in Hillman (1961; 1970) and of the neoFreudian in Arieti (1970).

As one might expect, Rapaport's first major point is that the Freudian concept of emotion is unclear. On some occasions, Freud considered affects to be *a* or *the* form of psychic energy; on others, he viewed affect as an implied attribute of other psychoanalytic concepts. Hence: '. . . affects regulated from the unconscious are defined as discharge processes of energies of instinctual origin' (Rapaport 1970, p. 29).

Rapaport considers that the old problem of the time sequences involved in feeling and the expression of emotion (see James and Cannon) detracted from the possible idea that 'felt' emotion and physiological changes are both the result of some common variable. Naturally, any investigation of this underlying variable would be difficult, since in Freudian terms it is concerned with the unconscious. For Freud, emotions may be psychic energies or they may be discharge processes associated with these energies, but either way one is squarely within the murk of the unconscious and its instinctual origins. Psychoanalytic theory is not concerned with possible sequences of emotional events. Perception occurs and therefore anything might happen; the emotion 'felt', or the bodily process, or both, or neither.

In his account of the psychoanalytic theory of emotion, Rapaport continues by drawing attention to some of the neo-Freudians and showing how their views on emotion differ from Freud's original ideas. For example, he mentions Brierley (1937) as concluding that affect is some kind of tension phenomenon which leads to an inner and outer discharge. Brierley also believed affect to show what will happen to the basic impulse. According to Rapaport, this notion is in accord with Freud's idea of pleasantness and unpleasantness. These are the conscious parts of decreasing and increasing tension. And further, Rapaport draws from Federn (1933; 1936) to demonstrate the importance of conflict theory in the psychoanalytic consideration of emotion. Affect, or emotions, result when different drive cathexes are in conflict. (A cathexis is an amount of psychic energy which is associated with some idea which may be held by a person.)

This is but a taste of the psychoanalytic theories of emotion. To summarize, as far as this is possible, they assert that the substrates (psychic processes) underlying emotion are unconscious and that affects have been variously viewed as psychic energies, discharge processes of psychic energies, and manifestations of instinctual conflict. It is best to let this discussion rest here, since if it is taken any further the writer will become more lost that the reader no doubt already is.

M. Pradines

A résumé of some of Pradines' ideas has been included for comparative purposes. His work (1958) has become more generally available in translation (Begin and Arnold; see Arnold 1968). Pradines theorizes first in the tradition of distinguishing between feelings and emotions, and second in that of regarding emotions to be disorganizing. Also, in that it is concerned with what is adaptive and maladaptive, Pradines' theory of emotion has biological overtones. However, it is expressed in nonbiological, nonbehavioural terms.

To understand Pradines' ideas on emotion, it is first necessary to appreciate what he means by sentiment. This depends on his assertion that perception occurs not only intellectually but also via various affective states. He views these affective states both as complex feelings and as simple feelings of pleasure and pain. Sentiments involve complex mental images of possible pleasure and pain. But also, sentiment has the effect of breaking down feeling and making the power to act (which is part of feeling) autonomous. In addition, Pradines considers sentiment to be a complex feeling because it can absorb strong energies which are aroused by the associations attached to any perceptions. Thus, sentiment can be a simple sensory feeling or a complex feeling following perception.

Pradines argues that sentiments, like perception, are regulators of action; they adaptively guide our actions towards specific objects. In this way he distinguishes sentiments from tendencies, the latter being (unobjective) inclinations which are not tied to specific circumstances. Sentiments, on the other hand, are very much dependent on objective circumstances, which he suggests might give them their agreeable nature; circumstances change. Any stability in sentiment must come from the stability of the object to which it is attached.

Pradines believes that psychologists have often been misled into their ideas on emotion through their observations of disordered sentiments, and it is here that we come to his ideas on emotion. He regards emotion as one of four ways in which sentiments can become disorganized, the others being via what he terms fixation, passion, and inversion; these are not worth elaboration here. Pradines maintains that emotions are disruptive in that they reduce sentiments to little more than reflex. Emotions are simply sentiments in extreme, explosive, crisis form. So any situation may produce some sentiment in us (for example anger) without necessarily leading to an emotional outburst.

The key to Pradines' theory lies in the imagination. He suggests that it is through imagination (and belief) that memory images become more affective and active. Both sentiments and emotions spring from imagination, pointing to the adaptive nature of the one and the maladaptive nature of the other. Pradines asserts that it may be that something is imagined as experienced, expected, and then becomes reality. If so, we may react to it in an extreme but simple and effective way. Such an emotional action will squash the more gentlemanly and adaptive sentiment which would otherwise have occurred. 'Emotion is a mental and motor disaster experienced by the subject who is its victim' (Pradines 1958, p. 721; Arnold 1968, p. 200).

J. Hillman

Although basically a Jungian analyst, Hillman (1960) gives what is arguably the fullest nonexistential but nevertheless phenomenological account of emotion. He bases his theory on Aristotle's four causes.

1. *Efficient cause.* Hillman argues that the stimuli which might cause emotion, that is, which function as efficient causes, are either representations, conflicts, and situations or those with a physiological basis, such as arousal instinct, constitution, or energy. He integrates these with the idea of the symbol, which he characterizes as a mixture of inner and outer, conscious and unconscious representations. Thus a situation will arouse emotion if it is perceived symbolically. 'Emotion is thus the symbolic apprehension of the subjective psyche . . .' (1960, p. 253).

2. *Material cause.* In dealing with material cause, Hillman asks the question: what is the stuff of emotion? and then applies six criteria used since Aristotle to establish evidence for the existence of material cause. He concludes from this analysis that material cause in emotion is energy. To be able to say that emotion is present, there must be gross bodily changes plus representations of these in consciousness. At the same time, however, emotion *is* the body as it is experienced here and now. The body becomes the material cause of emotion and the order of its energy is a person's homeostatic balance.

3. *Formal cause.* The formal cause of emotion must be its essential defining qualities, that which distinguishes it from all else. In Hillman's view this is the psyche, emotion being its total pattern, a combination of expression and inner states. Thus up to this point in his theory, Hillman has symbol and form corresponding to each other and only occurring when there is energy.

4. *Final cause.* Aristotle's concept of final cause can be viewed as the purpose or goal of something or simply as the end of some operation. Hillman reconciles these two possibilities by suggesting that the finish of any emotional process is an achievement; this is its purpose. Such an achievement need not be final in time. Hence, in Hillman's view, emotion can be an event in which the

final cause is contemporaneous with the efficient, material, and formal causes. The final cause of emotion is its value which comes about through change, particularly if this change leads to survival or improvement. One is immediately led to ask how emotional change can be distinguished from any other sort of change. In answer, Hillman argues that distinction can be made using the idea of transformation. Emotion is the transformation of conscious representations in terms of symbolic reality; it is a transformation of energy, of the whole psyche.

This still does not amount to a clear statement of the possible value of emotion; when is emotion good? Hillman is even less clear on this matter than on others. He suggests that *true* emotion (not just deep feelings or concentrated willing, or abortive emotion) always achieves its purpose; it is always good. Its results on the other hand may be good or bad, although emotion itself is always an improvement of some sort. This is somewhat of a miasma through which it is difficult to pick a way.

In summary, then, Hillman argues that the efficient cause of emotion is the symbolic perception of the objective psyche, the material cause, or body, of emotion is energy, the formal cause, or essence, of emotion is the total pattern of the psyche (or soul), and that the final cause or value, of emotion is change or transformation, which is always and inevitably good.

J.-P. Sartre

Sartre (1948) provides the most complete account of emotion that there is from the existential viewpoint. He argues that the emotional subject and the object of the emotion are inextricably bound up. Emotion is a manner of apprehending the world. For example, if a man believes that his wife is losing interest in him, then he sees his every action in terms of what he should do about this. If he fails in his attempts, then again his perceptions are coloured.

A second important point of Sartre's theory is that he believes emotion to involve a transformation of the world. If paths to particular goals are blocked or too hard to follow, then a man will try to change the world. If he cannot deal with the world as it is, he might be able to if it is changed. The impetus for making this emotional transformation of the world comes simply from the impossibility of solving the problem with whatever is already available.

Emotion then to Sartre is an attempt to make a qualitative change in an object, to give it an altogether new quality without changing it substantively. Directed by consciousness, the body changes its relationship with the world—and the world is suddenly seen with new qualities. Sartre is not, of course, saying that emotions change the world in reality; the real, external world is as static as ever. Rather, emotions create a magical transformation.

Although Sartre's ideas are analysed in more detail in Chapter 5, at this point an example might help. Sartre states that if a man is afraid and runs away from the source of his fear, then he is usually reckoned to be behaving rationally. However, Sartre maintains that this is not rational behaviour. In his terms, the man is not running to gain shelter, security or protection, but because he cannot 'annihilate (himself) in unconsciousness'. His fear and running away bring about a magical change in the world so that the dangerous object, with which he can deal in no other way, is negated. It is as if by running away in fear he is pretending that he is in a world in which the dangerous object does not exist. So, as Sartre views it, fear is consciousness magically negating or denying something which substantively and dangerously exists in the external world.

In developing his tentative theory of emotion, Sartre also makes the point that simple behaviour is not, and can never be, emotion. Emotion always involves a qualitative transformation of the world. He argues that there are some behaviours which at first sight look to be emotion, the pretence of anger or joy for example. But he characterizes these as spurious or false emotions. He urges that real emotion is always accompanied by a belief. In his terms, a person uses his will to give new qualities to objects in the environment and then believes these qualities to be real. So to be defined as real, an emotion must be experienced; it is not something which can be stopped if it is wished to, or which can be cast off because it is unpleasant. Also, Sartre regards the physiological concomitants of emotion as the phenomena of the type of belief just described. It is these that can be used to distinguish between false and real emotion. Thus, although a man can stop running, he cannot stop tembling.

Finally, in this description it is worth making the point that Sartre suggests that not all emotions are fully fledged. Subtle emotions can give momentary glimpses of the unpleasant or the excellent. These are dim intuitions which are nevertheless full of potential and give a vague sense of disaster or of something very good. Sartre views the social world as full of such potentials; it is always edging on the magical.

General points

The types of theory exemplified in this section could not contrast more strongly with the behavioural theories considered above. The psychoanalytic and phenomenological theories are concerned with a conceptual analysis of emotional experience and abound with terms such as consciousness, will, and even, in Sartre's case, magic. They are dealing with nonobservables and cannot be considered to provide the basis of scientific investigation.

Nevertheless, it can be argued that theories which deal with emotional experience have their place. For example, as will be seen in the cognitive theories which are to be described next, a great deal of emphasis is placed on the idea that emotion involves an appraisal of significant stimuli. This is a process which it is believed occurs almost instantaneously. It may be that Hillman, Sartre, and the other theorists reviewed here are attempting to speculate about what such a process might involve. Also, to return to a point made earlier, whether or not the subjective and cognitive aspects of emotion are given a causal role to play, merely for the sake of completeness there is some room for theories which attempt to come to grips with them. But it must be remebered that such attempts do not lead to anything which approximates conventional scientific endeavour.

COGNITIVE THEORIES

N. Bull

Although involving a straightforward modification of James' ideas, Bull's (1951) theory of emotion is unique in its central concern with motor behaviour. However, it also has enough of a cognitive orientation to be best included within this section. Bull's pivotal idea is that emotion is mediated by an attitude of preparedness to respond, to cry or to run for example. She views this as an involuntary motor attitude which leads to a series of incomplete movements which occur in invariant sequences. Such incomplete motor sequences are latent, being dependent on predispositions which come from neural organization.

Bull suggests further that not only is there a motor or bodily readiness but also a mentally oriented awareness, this being the emotion as it is experienced. Emotion is then *reduced* by action, especially if this action is consummatory. Bull regards emotion as occurring only when the individual is less than fully aware of the motor aspects of his readiness to respond. The argument is that when the individual is fully aware of the possibility of a complete sequence of motor behaviour then he gets a feeling of purpose and does not therefore experience emotion.

Bull's theory of emotion, then, lays great stress on motor action but also implies that consciousness or cognition sets limits on emotion, almost by default. Thus if a person consciously realizes the full implications of a potential motor sequence, no emotion is possible. Whereas if he is less than fully aware, then the sequence of motor behaviour is fragmentary or incomplete and emotion is experienced.

P. V. Siminov

Although Siminov's (1970) theory of emotion is brief and simple, it is described here since it reflects a similar approach to that of Leventhal (below); it is presented directly in terms of information theory. Siminov begins with a definition of what he calls negative emotion:

$$E = -N(I_n - I_a)$$

where emotion equals need times the difference between the necessary information and the available information. In this context, information is the possibility of reaching a goal due to a particular communication. Thus, if an organism cannot organize itself appropriately through lack of information, then the nervous mechanism leading to negative emotions starts to act. Siminov suggests that this has three main implications. (1) 'Dominant' reactions occur—i.e. previously neutral stimuli begin to be reacted to, and ineffectual (as regards any usual goals) activity is maintained. (2) This ineffectual activity leads to physiological changes typical of emotion. (3) The emotions themselves have a strong physiological activating influence. Consequently, if this mechanism becomes active, then some habitual response must have been disrupted.

Siminov views positive emotions in a similar way. When an organism's needs are satisfied it is emotionally quiescent, but if there is a surplus of information over and above that which is necessary for this satisfaction then positive emotion is the result. In the terms of the formula, $I_a > I_n$. Such positive emotions endure in the same way as do negative emotions and may facilitate behaviour.

Finally, Siminov suggests that emotions may be classified by taking into account: (1) the strength of the need; (2) the extent of the information deficiency or redundancy; and (3) the specificity of the action which is aimed at satisfying the need. He believes that it is only when 'action at a distance' is necessary (i.e. defence or struggle rather than just pleasure or displeasure brought about by immediate contacts) that emotions proper are seen. Thus he is viewing emotion from a standpoint which involves information theory directly and motivation by implication.

H. Leventhal

Starting with the general cry that to understand emotion fully it is important to come to terms with subjective experience, Leventhal (1974) proposes an information-processing model of emotion. He states that such a model must integrate four mechanisms or systems. (1) An interpreting mechanism which turns on emotional reactions. (2) An expressive system, feedback from which will define the subjective quality of emotion. (3) An instrumental action system. (4) A bodily reaction system which maintains the instrumental system. In this statement it seems that Leventhal is simply emphasizing in information-processing terminology the same points that many others have stressed before him; namely, that a theory of emotion should take account of how emotion is instigated, and deal with its subjective, behavioural, and physiological aspects.

In an attempt at the suggested integration, Leventhal proposes a two-phase model of emotion. In the perceptual/motor phase he suggests that the cognitions which promote emotion and expressive reactions are necessary for feedback to occur, and in its turn the feedback is necessary for subjective feelings. He argues that this process must involve an appraisal of meaning and hypothesizes that this is achieved by two types of decoder. The first is an automatic, built-in decoder and the second a discrepancy decoder which is involved in sorting out discrepancies from a person's expectations.

Leventhal is therefore arguing for the presence of innate perceptual mechanisms which are sensitive to particular features of stimuli—the usual feature analysers of information-processing models. These instigate feelings *before* expressive reactions can occur. However, he does not see these feelings as falling into precise categories of emotion, but as merely being positive or negative. More specific emotional discriminations occur later and involve feedback from the expressive and autonomic systems. All of which can be automatic or deliberate, but only with a contribution to subjective feeling when it is automatic (a point with which Izard 1972 would disagree).

The second component of emotion according to Leventhal is that which is concerned with action. He argues that the overt activity involved and any associated autonomic and visceral activity are clearly separated from feeling states. He makes this point to the extent of saying that the action system will detract from feeling; if a person is aware of his actions then he will be less aware, or even unaware, of his feelings. But, to have the best of both worlds, his final point is that if action and the feeling state which preceeds it are closely associated, then the action may enhance the feeling.

Leventhal is concerned with the promotion of theoretical development on three fronts. (1) The analysis of innate distinctive cues to emotion. (2) A theory of expectancies and their confirmation and disconfirmation. (3) A theory of emotional meaning. Although his model of emotion is couched in a language which is not especially familiar to theorists, when it is translated it is not arguing for anything particularly new. However, perhaps the most important aspect of Leventhal's ideas is the stress which he lays on emotional expression, thereby endorsing the views of a number of recent influential works on the subject.

S. Schachter

This brief section on Schachter is included since no collection of summaries on the influential theories of emotion would be representative without his name. However, much of Schachter's contribution is through a cunningly devised series of experimental situations and the interpretation of the results which they have produced (see Chapter 4).

For an overview of Schachter's ideas the best sources are Schachter (1959; 1964; 1972). He develops what he terms a cognitive/physiological view of emotion. In fact, however, he suggests that emotional states are mainly determined by cognitive factors, a suggestion made by others before him (for example Ruckmick 1936), but not developed so far. He argues that emotional states are characterized by a general arousal of the sympathetic nervous system (SNS) and that from state to state this may differ slightly in its pattern. He maintains that we interpret and classify these states by clues from the situation which brought them about and also from our typical mode of perception. Physiological arousal occurs and is given its precise direction by our cognitions of what brought it about.

This formulation led Schachter to make three propositions. (1) If an individual is physiologically aroused but cannot explain why, or what caused the arousal, then he will give his state a name and react to it in whatever cognitive way is open to him. Thus any *one* state could be labelled in many ways depending on the individual and his situation. (2) If an individual is physiologically aroused and has an entirely reasonable explanation of this available, it is improbable that he will entertain any alternative cognitive accounts. (3) The third proposition involves approaching the theory from the opposite direction. If from time to time an individual experiences the same cognition, he will only describe his feelings as emotions if he is also in some state of physiological arousal. Hence, Schachter's basic idea is that emotions are controlled through a very close interrelationship and interaction between physiological arousal and cognitive appraisal.

M. B. Arnold

Arnold's theory of emotion has been developing for more than three decades (see, for example, 1945; 1960; 1968; 1970a; 1970b) and has appeared as a mixture of phenomenology, cognition, and physiology. It depends on the assumption that we can gain most knowledge about brain function in emotion (which to Arnold is of fundamental importance) by a cognitive analysis. This will enable us to identify the physiological mediation of the process running from perception to emotion and action.

Arnold's cognitive analysis of emotion depends very much on the construct of appraisal. She suggests that we immediately, automatically, and *almost* involuntarily evaluate, with respect to ourselves, anything that we encounter. As long as no other appraisals interfere, this leads us to approach anything appraised as 'good', to avoid what is 'bad', and to ignore what is 'indifferent'. When we have a 'good' object we may well reappraise it and on the basis of this perhaps alter our behaviour. So Arnold regards appraisal as complementing perception and producing a tendency to *do* something. When this tendency is strong it is called emotion, although to Arnold all appraisals at least have the status of affective experiences.

Arnold suggests that in most new experiences memory is at the basis of our appraisals (the exceptions are 'simple' experiences such as taste or pleasure/pain). Anything new is evaluated in terms of our past experiences. She argues that the new object also evokes a memory of the *affect* associated with the previous experience. These affective memories are relivings of our past appraisals. Arnold regards them as continually distorting our judgment and therefore to be guarded against.

The final link in the appraisal chain comes from our imagination. Before we act, Arnold believes that the situation plus any relevant affective memories lead us to guess at the future. We imagine whether what will happen will be good or bad for us. Our appraisal then becomes dependent on memory plus expectation. From this we devise a plan of action which involves various possibilities for coping with the situation; we choose which is the best. It is worth pointing out again that Arnold suggests that this whole complex process of appraisal *may* well occur almost instantaneously.

For the most part, the remainder of Arnold's theory is concerned with hypothetical neural pathways which may mediate the hypothetical appraisal processes. These will be discussed in Chapter 3 (see also Chapter 4 for discussion of Arnold's theory). However, she also distinguishes between feeling and emotion. Emotional action patterns arise from positive or negative appraisals of perceived or imagined objects, whereas feeling action patterns are viewed as resulting from appraisals of something which may be either beneficial or harmful for our functioning. Although drawing this distinction, Arnold regards the hypothetical sequence of events involved in feeling as being much the same as that for emotion. For example, if I am sitting in a comfortable chair enjoying an amicable discussion, I may well be driven away if a pneumatic drill starts up in the roadway outside. Here is involved perception of the situation, appraisal, feeling, and finally a desire for action; just the same as if I had perceived a situation which had led me to be afraid and run away (emotion).

Arnold also discusses deliberate actions, which involve neither feeling nor emotion. Thus, I may sit writing this summary of Arnold's ideas on emotion without any desire to do so. Any pleasure comes when it is finished, not from the fairly mechanical progression of physically writing one word after another. Each successive word has no special attraction for me. If I were to express any emotion at all in the situation it would occur because I had had a period of difficulty in expressing myself, or alternatively had just completed a fluent two thousand words.

Arnold regards such deliberate action as: (1) making up the bulk of our everyday behaviour; (2) involving what we could call rational judgment; and (3) that which distinguishes us from the animals. So we judge situations both in terms of short-term (emotional) possibilities and long-term, more abstract, goals. And we often relinquish the former, which seem more immediately attractive, for the latter, which are better for us in the long run. Animals do not have this capacity; they can only make immediate, emotional appraisals. With her distinction between emotional action patterns and deliberate action patterns, Arnold believes that in reality she is separating emotion and will. In fact, she is nicely maintaining the traditional rationalist doctrine.

R. S. Lazarus

Basically, Lazarus stresses the importance of cognitive factors in emotion. However, in addition to this, he also considers the significance of factors which stem from biological and cultural perspectives (see Lazarus 1966; 1968; Lazarus *et al.* 1970). Lazarus suggests that although concepts of emotion exist in psychology and are important in the description and classification of behaviour, they are not necessarily much use in its explanation. This idea bears comparison with those of both Duffy and Leeper. Lazarus asserts that the development of the concept of emotion has been hampered by difficulties in description and classification. Since there is no one thing to which emotion can be meaningfully and unequivocally said to refer, Lazarus suggests that it is a 'response syndrome'. This is a directly drawn medical analogy, with emotions viewed as having causes, symptoms, and a number of courses. In Lazarus' view, the overall pattern of relationships between causes, symptoms, and courses permits the descriptive use of the word emotion and also allows the possibility of classification.

As already mentioned, Lazarus dwells on biological and cultural aspects of emotion. But he finds them lacking. He maintains, for example, that emphasis has shifted away from the role of the viscera and other such peripheral 'biological' structures in emotion and has moved towards more central mechanisms. Even within the CNS, the emphasis has been on the evolutionarily more primitive subcortical structures. He argues, however, that these structures have themselves undergone evolutionary change, as have cortical structures, and that they also play an important part in our cognitive functions. Similarly, Lazarus believes that cultural influences on emotion can be just as easily stressed. He suggests that culture affects emotion in four ways: (1) through the manner in which we perceive emotional stimuli; (2) by directly altering emotional expression; (3) by determining social relationships and judgments; (4) by highly ritualized behaviour such as grief. Should we stress the evolutionary, biological viewpoint or the cultural? Lazarus believes that this problem can be resolved by taking a more individual, cognitive perspective.

To Lazarus we are evaluators; we evaluate each stimulus that we encounter, with a view to its personal relevance and significance. Lazarus regards this as cognitive activity with emotion as part of it. Hence:

'. . . each emotional reaction . . . is a function of a particular kind of cognition or *appraisal*'.

(Lazarus *et al.* 1970, p. 218; their italics)

Lazarus recognizes emotional reactions at three levels, the behavioural, the physiological, and the cognitive or subjective. He views each of these as important in its own right and suggests that the particular pattern which may obtain between them is a distinguishing feature of emotion.

Lazarus extends his ideas with the suggestion that we have dispositions to search for and respond to or attend to particular stimuli, and that these dispositions shape our interaction with the environment. Our cognitive appraisal of these stimuli produces the emotional response. The stimuli themselves are constantly changing and we are continually 'coping' with them; so our cognitions alter, as do our emotional reactions. Lazarus (1966; 1968) argues that there are two sorts of coping process. We may deal with threat or harm by direct action, the urge to which he regards as an important part of emotion. Since the success or failure of this direct action constantly fluctuates, our cognitive evaluations and hence our emotional reactions also fluctuate. Lazarus terms the second type of coping 'reappraisal' This is solely cognitive, involving no direct action. We may reappraise from positive to negative or negative to positive, and may do so realistically or distortedly. We (and animals) appraise and reappraise all incoming information, each twist and turn of which is shown in emotional reactions.

Lazarus realizes that he has only presented the outlines of a cognitive theory of emotion and that there must eventually be some attempt to point to the detailed cognitive aspects of any individual emotional response. He suggests, however, that a cognitive/phenomenological approach, linked with biological and cultural considerations, will have the effect of putting emotion back into the forefront of psychology.

Averill *et al.* (1969) put a slightly different perspective on Lazarus' basic views. They describe emotion as a complex response system made up of three subsystems. (1) Stimulus properties. They argue that a stimulus may be influenced by the response which is made to it. So an emotional response may be a stimulus in its own right, which helps to add to the quality of emotion. (2) Appraiser subsystem. The brain appraises and evaluates stimuli, the primary appraisal reducing the stimulus array to a unitary concept such as threat and the secondary appraisal being appropriate for coping behaviour. (3) Responses. These are categorized into cognitive, expressive, and instrumental, which are poorly correlated. Here, cognitions are being viewed as defence mechanisms, expressions are mainly facial, and instrumental responses are seen as symbols which signal the presence of affect. In this context they also speak of operators which are complex goal-directed acts, and conventions which are culturally determined operators.

The emotional response system can interrupt and modify ongoing behaviour and is self-contained. Hence Averill *et al.* suggest that emotions can only be distinguished through their eliciting conditions, their patterns of response, and via any developmental changes—not through their structure.

General points

The theories which are grouped together in this section have various origins. This can be seen in the differential stress they accord to analyses of motor responses, the processing of information, perception, motivation, and physiological reactions in emotion. However, the point which binds them together is that they each give cognition a crucial role to play in emotion—a role which is sometimes causal, sometimes not. It is this which gives the theories a richness which is not often seen in the theories discussed so far.

The idea which most often occurs in the cognitive theories of emotion, whether it is explicit or implicit, is appraisal. This is a process of cognitive evaluation, usually regarded as virtually instantaneous, which the cognitive theorists believe to be a necessary component of emotion. Thus, in stressing cognition they are not trying to come to terms with emotional experience, but less ambitiously endeavouring to speculate about the cognitive mechanisms which they believe to mediate emotion. Whether cognitive mediation *is* a necessary idea in an understanding of emotion remains to be seen. However, it can be said that in recent years the theories which take cognition into account have been more influential than those which do not (particularly those of Arnold and Schachter). This influence is also felt from the even broader theories which are described in the next section, all of which have a place for cognition as well as for many other processes.

THE GRAND APPROACH

R. W. Leeper

Leeper (1948) put forward a strong argument against the idea of emotions as having a disorganizing influence on behaviour (see Chapter 4). He maintained instead that emotions pervade all behaviour by organizing and motivating it. More recently (1963a; 1963b; 1965; 1970), he has added considerable refinement to this basic idea.

Leeper (for example 1970) suggests that emotions act as motives since they are mildly aroused most of the time. They control our behaviour without our awareness. He argues that emotions give behaviour (and mental activity) its goal-directedness in, for example, allowing us to choose between alternatives, or solve problems, or endure sanctions to obtain a reward. He believes that the traditional emphasis has been antipathetic to the view of emotions as motives since they have been studied in ways indicated by everyday considerations. As mentioned in Chapter 1, psychologists have given most attention to extreme and sensational (therefore highly noticeable) aspects of emotion. At present, however, Leeper sees the idea of emotions as motives creeping, almost insidiously, into psychological theorizing, often without appearing as a formal statement.

The most recent idea extended by Leeper (1970) is that emotions function not only as motives, but also as perceptions. By this he means that emotions are cognitive in that they convey information to the organism. In fact, they are perceptions, perhaps long standing, of situations. Again, Leeper suggests that this view is breaking with tradition. He suggests that, in the past, motivation and perception have been regarded as distinct. He puts forward arguments to explain this dichotomy similar to those which he uses to account for the division between emotions and motives.

Leeper develops his ideas with the assertion that emotional motives depend for their function on a similar mechanism to that of the more obvious physiologically based motives. He believes that there are 'emotional mechanisms' which function through signals that indicate the favourability of environmental circumstances. These mechanisms act like reflexes.

These developing ideas on emotion have sprung from two aims. Leeper has attempted to dispel the more traditional view of emotion as disorganizing, chaotic, and interfering in its effects on behaviour. Also, he maintains that emotion is an active force involving motivation and perception, which organizes, sustains, and directs behaviour. The implications of Leeper's ideas for the control of emotion and therapy will be discussed in Chapter 9.

K. H. Pribram

Pribram's ideas concerning emotion overlap with many other theories. He begins from a neurophysiological viewpoint, takes into consideration ideas of appraisal (see e.g. Arnold) and motivation (see e.g. Leeper), and develops a cognitive/information theory position (see e.g. Siminov). Originally, Pribram (1970; Miller *et al.* 1960) regarded emotion as Plans, these being '. . . neural programs which are engaged when the organism is disequilibrated'. Pribram states that, normally, motivationally based Plans change because they are carried out, but if their execution is blocked then emotion results. Whether this emotion closes or opens the organism to more input (and Pribram allows both capacities), the Plan involved is stopped. When a Plan is held up in this way for a long period, then 'regression' tends to occur. Pribram (Miller *et al.* 1960) goes on to argue that emotional expression is more primitive and basic than rational behaviour, although emotions need not be expressed at all. Thus, there are emotional Plans as well as motivational Plans, both of which are altered by experience. Pribram (1970) maintains that this idea of emotions as Plans brought with it too many problems. As an alternative, he speculates about feelings rather than emotions.

Pribram distinguishes between the 'objective' world of sense data and the subjective world of feelings, and proposes that where we have no evidence which will allow us to construct the objective world then we must rely on the subjective. In other words, if we have no good evidence that we are faced with something which we can see, hear, smell, taste, or touch, then we must be feeling it inside. These feelings Pribram describes in his usual capitalized way as 'Feelings as Monitors'. He develops good, empirically based neurophysiological arguments to support such subjective feelings and affirms that this viewpoint is more fruitful than his previous idea of Plans.

We do not plan to be happy or sad or angry; rather, Pribram suggests, we simply *feel* happy or sad or angry. We construct Plans and implement them. They may be very easily executed, or they may fail, miserably or otherwise. We evaluate or appraise their success, and this process of appraisal is monitored, i.e. it is felt. Thus Feelings as Monitors are regarded as Images not Plans. Plans are merely constructed within the matrix that Images provide. A final contribution (and slight confusion) to the language of emotion suggested by Pribram is that 'go' Plans equal motivations and 'no-go' Plans equal emotions.

In summary, Pribram's most recent suggestion is that the study of emotion will benefit by distinguishing between feelings and emotions, and then concentrating on the former. Feelings are Monitors and Images are appraisals of the degree of success attached to the execution of Plans. The Plans themselves may allow the organism to go ahead, in which case they are motivational, or they may be blocked, in which case the organism is thwarted and we have emotion. Although expressed in a somewhat idiosyncratic language, Pribram's theory of emotion is quite similar to Arnold's: basically, it is cognitive/phenomenological in nature and yet it draws on neurophysiological evidence for empirical support.

R. Plutchik

Although comparatively recent, Plutchik's theory of emotion has evolved over a number of years (see, for example, 1962; 1965; 1966; 1970). In his later formulation (1970) he begins as others have done by outlining what any theory of emotion should do and how some of the previous theories have not lived up to this. He suggests that his own theory, essentially biological in nature, does not have these shortcomings.

Plutchik regards emotion as multidimensional, the dimensions being those of intensity, similarity, and polarity. Any emotion can vary in its intensity (for example between pensiveness and grief); any emotion varies as to its degree of similarity to any other emotion (for example joy and anticipation are more similar than loathing and surprise); and all emotions are polar (for example disgust is the opposite of acceptance).

Plutchik represents these three dimensions in the form of a model shown in Figure 4. Vertically, on the inverted cone in this figure intensity is represented, whereas each section portrays a primary emotion. Figure 5 shows a cross-section through the cone, with the area in the centre denoting the conflict which Plutchik believes to be involved in mixed motives.

In developing his ideas, Plutchik discusses the problem of the language used in any analysis of emotion. He maintains that we normally use everyday, subjective language of the sort employed in the figures to describe emotion. However, he suggests that there are two other possible sorts of language—a purely descriptive one based on behavioural observation, and a functional one

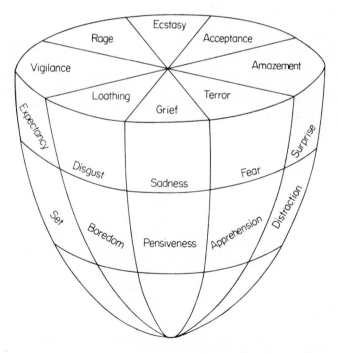

Figure 4. Plutchik's three-dimensional model of emotion
(taken from Arnold 1970).

based on the adaptive function of what the organism does. Hence, in Plutchik's terms, we may be experiencing joy or ecstasy, whilst behaviourally we are mating or possessing and functionally we are reproducing. He argues that the functional/adaptive language is the best to use when discussing emotion, since he views it as varying along the same three dimensions (i.e. intensity, similarity, and polarity) as a number of basic adaptive functions. Adaptively speaking, an organism can protect, destroy, reproduce, deprive, incorporate, reject, explore or orient: four pairs of what Plutchik regards as opposites which can vary in intensity and in similarity to one another. Clearly, a behavioural language could also be generally applicable, and a subjective one could only be used with humans (and with caution). However, Plutchik prefers his adaptive language, simply viewing emotion as a bodily reaction of one of the types mentioned above.

Overall, Plutchik regards subjective feelings as sufficient conditions for emotion, but not necessary; in other words, a person may have an emotion but be unaware of it. By the same token, physiological changes are necessary but not sufficient for emotion to occur. They can come about through exercise, for example, in which emotion is not involved.

Emotion to Plutchik is a patterned bodily reaction which has its correspondent underlying adaptive processes which are common to living organisms. Primary emotions are short-lived and usually triggered by external stimuli and there are frequently mixtures of physiological and expressive patterns. It is therefore only possible to infer discrete patterns approximately.

This is a very broad, biological definition of emotion and as such is perhaps of limited use. But Plutchik suggests that it has a number of important implications: (1) emotion involves a prototypical adaptation; (2) emotion involves cognition; (3) emotion involves evolution; and (4) from a different viewpoint, emotion should be studied by specially devised methods—some of which Plutchik suggests.

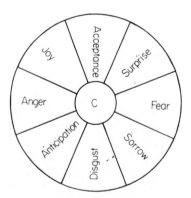

Figure 5. A cross-section through Plutchick's emotional solid (taken from Arnold) 1970)

S. S. Tomkins

Tomkins (1962; 1963) speaks of affect rather than emotion and provides a broadbased and ingenious but somewhat idiosyncratic theory. This means that his theory is not well related to others, although it did provide some of the impetus for Izard's (1972) approach; an approach which, by contrast, is better, fuller, and more easily linked to empirical findings.

Tomkins argues that the affect system is primary, that is, it has innate determinants and interacts with the drive system (which is secondary or learned) to give drive its urgency. Further, he suggests that affect has no necessary constraints in time or intensity and hence gives it insatiable and very changeable aspects. At the outset, then, he is suggesting very strong links between emotion and motivation.

Like Izard, Tomkins argues that affects are mainly reflected in facial responses, the feedback from which, if it is selfconscious, can be rewarding or punishing. There are organized patterns of facial response which are innate and which are triggered by subcortical mechanisms in the central nervous system. He does not deny that affect is also reflected in bodily responses, but simply regards these as less significant than facial expression.

Like many other theorists who aver that there is a strong innate component to emotion, Tomkins lists what he regards as the eight primary affects. These are: interest/excitement, enjoyment/joy, surprise/startle, distress/anguish, disgust/contempt, anger/rage, shame/humiliation, and fear/terror. He postulates that the instigation of these affects is dependent on the rate of neural firing in the central nervous system, arguing appropriately enough that this rate may increase, decrease, or remain steady. He regards these rate changes or lack of them as actually promoting emotion and argues further that any such change or steady rate may be punishing or rewarding, presumably depending on the external situation, but nevertheless serve to meet any contingencies.

The final point of Tomkins' theory which should be mentioned now is that the instantaneous responses which he believes to occur to the sources of affect require a feedback mechanism. From this he argues that it is very rare for a person to gain precise control over his emotional state.

Tomkins' theory of emotion is very widely based, ranging from a conceptual analysis of motivation to physiological possibilities, and stressing the importance of innate factors. Although an interesting theory it is very speculative, does not relate well to most other theories, and, apart from some work on the facial expression of various primary emotions, is not well anchored to empirical data.

G. Mandler

In his recent and extremely well-argued book, Mandler (1976) offers a summary statement of what he terms a system of emotion. He humbly suggests that he is not putting forward a theory, but is less ambitiously discussing the parameters involved in emotion. However, his ideas are of sufficient status and cogency to warrant inclusion in this section.

In Mandler's view the three integral aspects of emotion are *arousal, cognitive interpretation,* and *consciousness.* He refers to undifferentiated arousal as the perception of activity in the sympathetic nervous system. Conditions for its presence depend on cognitive interpretation, particularly with respect to interruption and blocking. It has the functions of maintaining homeostasis and of the seeking of information.

Cognitive interpretation involves structures which promote innate reactions to events, plus evaluations of perceptions of self. Mandler argues that expressive movements produce automatic cognitive reactions which are altered by reinterpretation. The experience of emotion and emotional behaviour result from an interaction between autonomic arousal and cognitive interpretation. Arousal gives the visceral quality and intensity of emotion and cognitive interpretation provides a category for the experience Mandler also argues that emotional experience occurs in consciousness and outputs from this are coded appropriately into conventional language.

In some detail, Mandler goes into the means and the effects of interaction between arousal and cognitive interpretation. His general thesis is that autonomic nervous system arousal sets the stage for emotional behaviour and experience. The quality of the emotion then comes from meaning analysis which is engendered by arousal, the general situation, and cognitive state. From this point on there are outputs to both consciousness and action.

Arousal, Mandler argues, can be produced in two ways: first by preprogrammed release from the ANS, and second that which is mediated by meaning analysis which makes mental stimuli into ANS releasers. Thus Mandler is speaking of a continuum from innate to experiential factors. Any perceived input from arousal leads to automatic meaning analysis. This generates a search for structures that can assimilate input, its analysis plus perception of arousal. If the search is successful it stops, and the particular structure is put into consciousness.

Without going into too many of the complexities which Mandler introduces at this stage of the argument, summary can be made by saying that *continuous feedback* is involved. Hence environmental stimuli lead to cognitive interpretations which lead to perception of arousal which leads to emotional experience which leads to perception and evaluations of the experience which changes the original cognitive interpretation, and so on.

An essential aspect of Mandler's view of emotion concerns the analysis of meaning. He argues that the complexity of inputs in emotion makes emotion very rich, its meaning being given by the structure of the input and its relation to other inputs and existing mental structures.

Mandler makes two interpretations of the interaction between cognition and arousal in meaning analysis. In the *passive* view emotion is given by the total relational network from the two sets of structures. For example, an interaction between the autonomic arousal perception and the evaluation of a situation as positive and joyful gives the feeling of joy. In the *active* view, which Mandler believes to be more appropriate, the inputs from either system are fed into existing structures based on past experience and innate factors. Of course, both systems may operate and the same set of events may act as arousal releasers and have to be cognitively evaluated.

In a little more detail, Mandler suggests that structures give analyses of inputs and initial identification of emotion. These are stored, meaning analysis gives further interpretation, and then arousal is produced which, with cognitive appraisal of the situation, gives a specific emotional reaction. He argues further that a hierarchy of meaning nodes could give various effects, from repression to virtually any emotional experience, all depending on past experiences. So, whether or not an input leads to emotional experience depends on whether or not an arousal switch is triggered, which itself depends on a particular meaning analysis of the input.

Finally, a brief description must be given of Mandler's complex analysis of the role of consciousness in emotion. He makes the necessary point that events in consciousness are unique and sensitive indicators for the individual but are not open to the observer. Therefore any consideration of consciousness must needs be speculative. Mandler suggests that some emotions may *only* be experienced in consciousness and also that many of the determining functions of emotion may occur in consciousness. And finally, Mandler argues that emotional consciousness develops from basic processes which involve both arousal and cognition.

Although Mandler is tentative and unpretentious about his ideas on emotion, it is quite clear that he has constructed the beginnings of a far-reaching theory or system of emotion which has many implications. Within it are all the usual considerations and facets of the more recent and grander theories of emotion. And perhaps most interestingly, it provides a place for the role of consciousness in a context of ideas and data which derive from conventional science.

C. E. Izard

In what is the most complete and elegant discussion of emotion to have appeared for many years, Izard (1972) puts forward an all-embracing theory of emotion. The details of this theory are intricate and will be examined at length in Chapter 4, although Izard's influence on the present book is not restricted to that one chapter. For now, a summary of his theoretical viewpoint will suffice.

Izard's theory has grand aims. (1) To account for the great complexity of emotion. (2) To deal with neural activity, glandular, visceral, and psychophysiological responses, subjective experience, expressive behaviour, and instrumental responses. (3) To provide a framework within which to look at innate and learned characteristics of emotion and patterns of emotional–cognitive–motor responses. (4) To fit in with a general theory of behaviour.

Izard regards emotion as one of five interrelated subsystems of personality and as made up of nine fundamental innate and unique emotions, which produce the main human motivational system. These emotions are: interest, enjoyment, surprise, distress, disgust, anger, shame, fear, and contempt. He maintains that these emotions are discrete, subjectively and in neurochemistry and behaviour, but that their particular discretion comes from feedback from facial and bodily activity.

In Izard's view, the emotional elements of personality themselves form an interrelated system, which through certain innate influences may be organized hierarchically. There is apparent polarity between some pairs of emotions and certain regular relationships between others. All of which can combine to become like traits and personality patterns. Also, *all* emotions have some common characteristics. They are noncyclical, have unlimited generality and flexibility as motivators, and influence drives and other personality subsystems.

Izard's great stress on the importance of facial expression in emotion will be discussed later. For the present, it is important to see how this fits in with his general analysis of the emotional process. He suggests that emotion is made up of three intertwined components: neural activity, facial–postural activity, and subjective experience. Also important are two auxiliary systems: the reticular arousal system which amplifies and attenuates emotion, and the visceral system which helps to prepare the ground for emotion and also to sustain it. And the general emotion process usually functions in an integrated way with the cognitive and motor systems, personality depending on the balance between the three.

Izard describes three person–environment interactions and five intra-individual processes which he believes can activate emotion. Person–environment interactions: (1) Obtained perception; this follows stimuli from selective activity of the receptors or sense-organs. (2) Demanded perception, in which an environmental/social event demands attention (the basic orienting reflex for example). (3) Spontaneous perception, which is the indigenous activity of a perceptual system.

Intra-individual processes: (1) Memory, which may be obtained (active), demanded (reminded), or spontaneous (indigenous cognitions). (2) Imagination. (3) Proprioception of facial–postural or other motor activity, taking the form of habitual striate action, spontaneous striate action, or motor responses for adaptive behaviour. (4) Endocrine and other autonomic activity which affects neural or muscular mechanisms of emotion. (5) Spontaneous activity of any or all of the neuromuscular systems.

Izard affirms that once emotion has been instigated, its further phases depend on the site and nature of the original activity. There is no fixed number or order to these phases and very many possible mechanisms and interactions are involved. Without going into the details of exactly how, Izard implicates perception, efferent neural transmission, brain-stem reticular arousal system, hypothalamus, facial–postural patterns, feedback, limbic cortex, endocrines and viscera, cardiovascular and respiratory systems, subjective experience, and emotion–cognition–motor interaction.

Finally, Izard suggests that for any given emotion there are three levels. (1) Electrochemical or neural activity which for the fundamental emotions is innate. (2) Efferent aspects of emotional activity innervate striate muscle involved in *facial–postural* patterning; patterning which normally give cues and information to the individual and to the observer. (3) For cues to be useful there must be *feedback* to the association areas of the brain, although an awareness of this process is not inevitable. It can be interfered with in many ways. However, if it is normal it generates the subjective experience of emotion, which in itself is independent of cognition.

There are a number of points which Izard suggests follow from this conceptualization. If feedback is distorted (and hence nonveridical), then so will be awareness. Each level of emotion has particular functions which any analysis must take into account. A given emotion is a subsystem of the overall emotional system and thus has all the qualities of the whole system. And, in conclusion, the emotional system has changed with evolution and also changes with individual development. Even at the adult level, various requirements must be met for subjective experience to be of a specific fundamental emotion. For example, facial expression or memory must be true to the original neural message; the neural message must travel via innate neural pathways; and the face–brain feedback of memory images must be full enough to give a true representation of facial patterns.

GENERAL CONCLUSIONS

Having now described some thirty theories of emotion, representing all conceivable psychological approaches to the subject, and varying in their spheres of influence, it remains to draw out any common threads that there might be. First, it would seem reasonable to discard theories which suggest that emotion should not exist as a discrete topic but as merely one aspect of arousal. These theories only seem to typify a state of quiescence, or perhaps a disenchantment with research into emotion which existed some years ago. And they are clearly untypical, although having the saving grace of drawing attention to the role of physiological arousal in emotion. Linked to this, of course, is a long history of ideas which intertwine emotion with motivation.

Arguably the main common ground between most theories of emotion is the explicit or implicit belief that discrete emotions and emotional expressions and emotional experiences exist—a point made with some force by Izard (1972). This seems to be so whether emotion is viewed primarily as a response or as a motivational process. Then it commonly follows from the idea of discrete emotions that some of these are primary (perhaps innately determined) and others are secondary (learned combinations of the primary emotions).

Other points in common were also shared by the early theories of emotion and have changed little in the half century or so since these appeared. Thus emotion is still regarded by most theorists as a system which affects and is affected by other systems, and emotions are usually conceived of as varying in range and intensity. Also the implication is often made that the control of emotion is possible, a point which has obvious importance in therapy (see Chapter 9).

Finally, in the most recent theories to be considered, which I suspect will soon prove to be the most influential to date (particularly those of Mandler and Izard), two interesting developments may be seen. First, increasing importance is being laid on the expressive side of emotion, especially when this is facial rather than postural. This is reflected in a recent proliferation of work (see Chapter 8) as well as ideas. This emphasis harks back to the enormous influence that James has had on emotion. Second, the role of consciousness in emotion is beginning to be explored as it relates to arousal and cognition via hypothetical feedback mechanisms. If such analyses lead to the development of techniques which allow something more than speculation about consciousness, they could be crucially important not only to an understanding of emotion but also to psychology in general.

Each of the points mentioned above is made in a context in which emotion is viewed as an integral system of the normally functioning individual, a system which interrelates with other systems and which is necessary to the development of personality. So, rather than being given a back seat or even kicked out altogether, emotion is now being granted far more of a central position.

Finally, although it is not incumbent upon psychologists to take account of everyday experience or to make sense of the common language, it seems appropriate when this does happen as part of their more academic endeavours. This is clearly the case when emphasis is laid on facial expression and consciousness in accounting for emotion, for it is these two aspects which seem to be basic at the everyday level.

3

The Physiology of Emotion

From the subjective viewpoint, it seems clear that different emotions involve distinct bodily changes. It is therefore appropriate that many investigations have been made into the physiological substrates of emotion. However, from its inception, this approach has been bedevilled with problems. Although there is an immense body of relevant research, its techniques and findings are so diverse as to make systematization awkward to impose and conclusions difficult to draw.

There are three basic research strategies within physiological psychology. (1) The most common of these involves the making of lesions in some part of the nervous system and observing any effects that these might have on behaviour. The lesions may be very restricted in extent or may be complete transections or ablations. As will be discussed below, this strategy can lead to great difficulty in the interpretation of any data which derive from it. (2) The second method is that of electrical or chemical stimulation. This type of technique has long been used to record changes in the ANS. However, since the development of a technology which allows the chronic implantation of electrodes, it has also been much used in CNS measurement. (3) The final strategy is fundamental to psychophysiological research (see below). It involves the recording of ongoing changes in such peripheral physiological measures as respiration, heart rate, etc. Each of these research methods has produced a wealth of data. Although this has often shown remarkably little consistency, it has been used as a basis for many theories and models of emotion and for much general physiologizing.

Naturally, physiological studies of emotion often employ behavioural measures. Although the independent variable in such studies is usually physiological, it is always the resultant changes in behaviour which must be of interest. There are two types of behavioural measure of emotion commonly taken in physiologically based studies. The more frequent, and more naive, is the direct behavioural description of 'typical' emotional reactions, usually in infrahuman subjects. For example, fear in cats is thought to be indicated by freezing or by dashing away, rage by violent lashing, arching movements, thrusting, jerking, snarling, biting, and so on, pleasure by purring. Although such anthropomorphic measures appear to be simple, on occasion they have been developed into complex systems. Brady and Nauta (1953), for example, describe a six-component rating of emotionality, including resistance to handling, vocalization, startle and flight, urination and defecation.

The other behavioural measures used in physiological studies of emotion are considerably more sophisticated. They derive largely from techniques designed to study conditioned emotional responding (CER) and active and passive avoidance. Briefly, the CER technique is based on the indirect recording of the 'emotional' influences of signalled uncontigent stimuli as these affect some ongoing operant baseline. Active avoidance involves the making of a (fear-motivated) response in the presence of a neutral stimulus to avoid some forthcoming aversive stimulus. Passive avoidance can be defined as learning to avoid some aversive stimulus by *not* making a response. (See Chapter 6 for a full exposition of behavioural measures of emotion.)

The first of the behavioural measures mentioned above points to two of the problems encountered in this field. In many studies, although the physiological manipulations are reasonably sophisticated, the behavioural observations are naive, poorly controlled, and somewhat subjectively judged. Also, such studies frequently use infrahuman subjects. The difficulty in extrapolating from animals to man has already been discussed. In the search for the physiological substrates of emotion, it is even more of a difficulty. Presumably, the precise functions of, and interconnections between, various parts of the nervous system differ from species to species.

A more fundamental set of problems are an inherent part of studies involving CNS ablation and stimulation. There are a number of technical difficulties: how to separate the brain into distinct areas, how to determine the precise location and extent of a particular lesion, how to confine a lesion or an electrical or chemical stimulation to a given area, to mention but a few. Also, there is the question of localization of function. The majority of studies of emotion which have dwelt on the CNS depend on this concept. Its meaning, however, is difficult

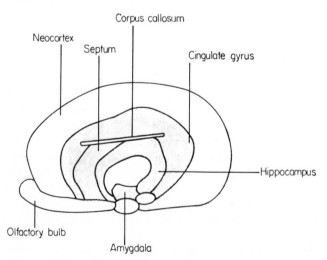

Figure 6. Diagrammatic representation of the limbic system (shaded areas)

to pin down. The implication is that some structurally well-defined area of the brain is (causally) responsible for some well-defined behavioural function. This cannot be so. At best we can say that some area of the brain may be a necessary condition for the occurrence of some behaviour; it cannot be a sufficient condition. Also, even to this extent, we cannot say that function is localized until we understand how the system works, which at present we do not. What can we say if, on removing one area of the brain or stimulating another, we achieve

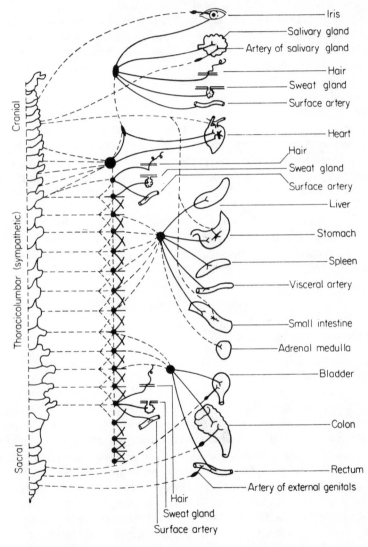

Figure 7. Diagrammatic representation of the autonomic nervous system and the bodily structures that it serves (taken from Morgan 1965)

certain behavioural effects? No more than that these parts are necessary to that function. Too little is known about the precise function of the CNS to determine the neurophysiological extent of our manipulations. It may be that the interconnections within the CNS are such that a stimulus or lesion in one area may produce unexpected changes in behaviour. This, of course, could indirectly affect whatever behavioural measure we might be taking. The picture is complicated in at least three other ways. (1) There are large individual differences in behavioural reaction. (2) The effects of a particular ablation may only become apparent under certain criterial conditions. (3) There is some evidence for mass action in the brain, or of a degree of equipotentiality between various areas. At present, there appears to be no solution to this set of problems. However, they should be borne in mind when evaluating the research and theory to be found in this chapter. Most of this research relies unquestioningly on a belief in localization of function.

Those interested in the physiology of emotion have naturally followed diverse paths to the subject. These have frequently been dictated by that part of the nervous system which the investigator believes to be of particular importance. Hence, there is much pertinent information to be found in studies of the ANS, the subcortex, and the cortex. The present chapter will cover these approaches systematically and will also include mention of research involving glandular function and neurochemistry. Wherever possible, fact will be presented before theory.

Finally, it may be useful to refer to Figures 6 and 7. They represent in simplified form the structural relationships in the nervous system. Much of the text which follows concerns the functional relationships (of emotion) which are hypothesized to cut across these.

PERIPHERAL MECHANISMS

Psychophysiological measures

Psychophysiology is the term which has come to be used to describe the study of peripheral measures of ANS activity, such as respiration or cardiovascular change. It is appropriate to begin a consideration of the physiology of emotion by discussing such responses, since they are basic to the influential James–Lange theory. Initially, the psychophysiological approach looks promising; if there are physiological concomitants of emotion, then introspectively they would seem to be reflected in our breathing or blood flow or sweating, and so on. Subjectively, we can *feel* such changes; when we are angry or afraid, our breathing may become fast and shallow or we may sweat more profusely. Or, for example, the physiological changes which occur when we engage in some vigorous sport are superficially similar to those which stem from emotion-producing stimuli, but they 'feel' different bodily. Also, it might be expected that any peripheral changes would perhaps occur in orderly patterns corresponding to the various emotions. However, a somewhat disappointing picture has emerged. With a few important exceptions, psychophysiological measures have not produced evidence for any clear patterns. At first sight this seems odd, since, intuitively, peripheral feedback would seem relevant, if not crucial, to our experiencing of emotion. With hindsight, however, it is perhaps less surprising. Psychophysiology relies quite heavily on the idea of general arousal, indeed it is one of the main sources of evidence for its existence. As mentioned in Chapter 1, although arousal is a subjectively reasonable concept, it leads to notoriously imprecise predictions about behaviour or physiological function. Bearing in mind these difficulties, some of the main psychophysiological measures and the results which they have led to will be briefly discussed. The interested reader is referred to Grossman (1967) and Sternbach (1966) for good overall reviews of psychophysiology, and to the CIBA Foundation Symposium on Physiology, Emotion and Psychosomatic Illness (1972) for a discussion of recent specific developments in the physiology of emotion.

Circulation

Circulation and the circulatory system are important both to the everyday maintenance of bodily function and to any emergency which may arise. There are two equally significant mechanisms involved. (1) The heart, pumping; this may change both in rate and strength and is regulated by central reciprocal links between the parasympathetic and sympathetic nervous systems (PNS and SNS). (2) The relative dilation or constriction of the blood vessels; dilation increases the blood which is available to a particular area and results in a consequent constriction elsewhere. The main measures are blood pressure and pulse rate. Although circulatory changes are correlated with behavioural changes, for example in the patterns of sleep and waking or in reaction to sudden, intense stimuli, we cannot use them to discriminate between the various emotions (for example Landis 1925, but see Lacey and Lacey 1970 below for a possible exception to this). However, cardiovascular changes may represent changes in general arousal. Also, although some circulatory disorders are clearly psychosomatic (for example eczema), there is no evidence for particular dysfunctions stemming from particular emotional problems.

Galvanic skin response

Galvanic skin response (GSR) refers to the electrical resistance of the skin to the flow of electromotive current. Skin resistance (or its reciprocal, skin conductance) fluctuates constantly, but any strange or novel stimulus superimposes immediate although transitory changes on these fluctuations. Much research using this measure (as with other psychophysiological measures) is concerned with techniques for recording, and although very important is of little relevance here (see Sternbach 1966). As regards emotion, the problem hinges on whether *all* new, sudden or intense stimuli lead to particular emotional reactions or whether these changes in the electrical activity of the skin just reflect general activation. The GSR allows little differentiation between emotions. There are only poor relationships between changes in skin reactivity and (1) the intensity of the stimuli which produced them, (2) reports of emotional reactions, and (3) distinctions between pleasant and unpleasant emotions.

Respiration

The rate and depth of breathing must be quite directly and closely related to our basic needs. Yet again, this indicates that respiration should provide a fair measure of general arousal. By the same token, respiratory changes would appear likely to accompany any emotional reactions, but as with the other psychophysiological measures, no study has successfully used respiratory changes to distinguish between emotions or even between emotional and non-emotional situations. The only exception to this is in two early studies by Felecky (1914; 1916), who reported correlations between measures of respiration and six imagined emotions. However, the research was method-ologically inadequate and the results have never been replicated.

Other peripheral measures

The remaining psychophysiological measures present essentially the same picture as that given by circulation, skin resistance, and respiration. Muscle potential, for example, providing an index of muscular tension, also simply reflects general alertness or arousal (for example Jacobson 1932; 1951), but no relationships are seen with specific emotions. An early exception to this general rule was seen with gastrointestinal activity and various biochemical measures. Brunswick (1924), for example, showed there to be a loss of gastrointestinal tone during a number of emotional reactions, fear, envy, disappoint, etc. Distress, surprise, and startle had the opposite effect of augmenting it.

Electrical activity of the brain

Although the electrical activity of the brain is clearly not a peripheral response like respiration or muscle potential, it is included here because it is often measured peripherally, and recorded as the electroencephalogram (EEG). When a person is at rest or relaxed, the brain is characterized by regular 10 per second waves of electrical activity (alpha). This rhythm tends to disappear with the input of sensory stimulation. This is usually termed alpha-blocking; it seems to depend on the novelty of the stimulus and, in fact, may rapidly habituate. (See Coles 1970; Lindsley 1951.)

As with the psychophysiological measures, arousal has a prominent part to play in the thinking of those investigators concerned with EEG activity. For example, it is argued that anxiety may produce nonspecific arousal and in so doing activate electrical activity in the brain (for example Darrow et al. 1946). Also, the stimulation of the brain-stem reticular formation elicits cortical arousal (Moruzzi and Magoun 1949) and the general autonomic and somesthetic responses which tend to accompany emotion (Ranson and Magoun 1939). Such relationships led to Lindsley's (1951; 1970) activation theory of emotion, which is couched sheerly in terms of cortical arousal. Although this theory seems superficially good sense, to be viable it would require fine shadings of cortical arousal; at the moment there is no evidence for these. Also, as with other psychophysiological measures, there is no evidence for relationship between specific emotional reactions and cortical EEG.

Darrow's (1947; 1950) approach also involved EEG. He proposed that particular cortical arousal results from nonsynchronized electrical activity across many cortical neurons. In some way this summates and thereby cancels many of the (electrical) potential differences, so producing the fast, low-amplitude electrical activity characteristic of arousal. Darrow suggests that this could lead to 'cortical anxiety'. He regarded the other emotions as characterized by alpha waves from synchronized rather than desynchronized activity. There are three main problems with these ideas. (1) It is difficult to see why anxiety should be afforded pride of place. (2) It is odd that an emotion such as rage should be viewed as having the same EEG correlates as relaxation—subjectively and behaviourally they could not be further apart. (3) It is strangely anthropomorphic to regard the cortex as anxious.

Relationships between the ANS and CNS—response patterning

From what has been said so far, it can be seen that work involving psychophysiological measures of emotion has not produced definitive results. However, there is one tenuous line of evidence which looks more promising. This will be described in greater detail. Most of the work in this area has shown only a generalized psychophysiological response to any emotion-producing stimuli. However, Wolf and Wolf (1947) carried out extended observations of a man with a gastric fistula. They found that there were two types of gastric change with emotional disturbance. (1) With reported anxiety and the wish to escape there was a reduction in the output of acid, vascularity, and gastric motility. (2) With reported anger and resentment there was an acceleration of gastric functions. This was the first evidence for any form of physiological response patterning in emotion.

The discovery of epinephrine and norepinephrine (adrenalin and nor-adrenaline) reinforced the idea of physiological response patterning. Both increase systolic blood pressure, but epinephrine by increasing cardiac output and norepinephrine by increasing vascular resistance. These differences led Ax (1953) to devise an ingenious study, the results of which clearly show physiological differentiation between emotions. When connecting subjects to a polygraph recorder, he made them afraid or angry either by handling them roughly and criticizing them or by 'accidentally' giving them mild electric shocks, becoming alarmed himself, and hinting at danger. He found a rise in diastolic blood pressure, muscle potential, and in the number of increases in skin conductance; and a fall in heart rate. These effects were all more extreme in the anger than in the fear condition. Also, skin conductance and respiration rate both rose more in the fear condition. The fear pattern was similar to that which follows an epinephrine injection, the anger like that which follows a norepinephrine injection. The only study to directly confirm Ax's results is Schachter's (1957). Any further attempts, including those of Lacey (1950; 1956) and Lacey and Lacey (1958), although demonstrating that there are various autonomic response patterns, have not shown that any of these correlate with particular emotional responses. However, Lacey and Lacey's (1970) more recent work rests on a far more sophisticated and definitive approach to the psychophysiology of emotion than that of any previous work. Their research depends on the fundamental idea that organs innervated by the ANS are important to emotion and that the various phenomena which they mediate can be brought together by the concept of arousal. Also, they suggest that ANS reponses are usually regarded as effector events which may be modified by the CNS. However, they point out that ANS responses are also different and affect brain function accordingly.

Lacey and Lacey emphasize the cardiovascular system. They suggest that this provides negative feedback to the CNS, which causes *inhibitory* electrophysiological effects. They quote many studies which show increases in heart rate and blood pressure to cause electrophysiological change— notably those of Bonvallet (for example Bonvallet and Allen 1963). Briefly, the argument is for an inhibitory CNS mechanism which produces an inhibitory control of the duration and course of internally and externally stimulated muscular, autonomic, and cortical responses. This hypothesized area (centred on the nucleus of the *tractus solitarius*) is involved with autonomic function and has many cardiovascular afferents. Impulses from this region should suppress any emotional (cortical, motor, autonomic) activity. For example, stimulation of the aortic carotid sinus stops the sham rage usually shown by decorticate cats (for example Baccelli *et al.* 1965).

Lacey and Lacey reevaluated the hypertension (chronic high blood pressure) and tachycardia (chronic high pulse rate) seen in acute emotion as attempts to inhibit an internal 'turmoil' rather than as an index of arousal. Hence, any decrease in blood pressure and pulse rate should lead to an absence of CNS inhibition leading in turn to a corresponding increase in excitation. A test of this proposal involves: (1) a demonstration, following a steady state, of experimental conditions which would *decrease* hypertension and tachycardia whilst other psychophysiological measures are reflecting changes typical of the SNS; (2) an evaluation of whether or not decreases in cardiovascular activity lead to increased behavioural efficiency.

Lacey and Lacey offer four lines of experimental evidence. (1) Lacey *et al.* (1963) gave subjects a series of tasks. Cardiac deceleration was produced by those tasks which required subjects to pay attention to the stimuli. Others which required concentration (for example mental arithmetic) led to cardiac acceleration. A combination of both types of task produced intermediate changes in heart rate. Broadly speaking, 'cognitive' tasks led to a rise in heart rate and 'perceptual' tasks to a fall. Other psychophysiological measures did not reflect this pattern but simply showed the usual arousal. (2) Lacey and Lacey (1970) extended this work in reaction time (RT) studies. They found a systematic deceleration in heart rate during the warning signal. This was accompanied, for example, by wide variation in respiratory responses and preceded by an early, immediate, and transient accleration in heart rate. These heart-rate changes were intensified in more highly motivated subjects. If the actual RT stimulus was omitted, the deceleration continued (subject 'searching' for the target), and with a longer fore-period, the heart decelerated to much the same level but took longer to do so. Also, the greater the deceleration in heart rate, the faster the RT. (3) The third line of evidence uses Walter et al.'s (1964) CNVs, a measure of negative EEG variation reflecting the readiness of a subject to respond (RT). Lacey and Lacey (1970) found that the greater the cardiac deceleration, the greater the CNV; this was also related to speed of reaction. (4) Finally, there is some external support. To quote but one example of this, Israel (1969) related cardiovascular change to cognitive style. He regarded people as either levellers (those who make global judgments, do not attend to detail, etc.) or sharpeners (those who do attend to detail). On appropriate tasks, the heart beat of sharpeners decelerated more than that of levellers, a difference not reflected in other psychophysiological measures.

Lacey and Lacey have a more productive approach to the psychophysiology of emotion than have many other investigators. They emphasize the cardio-vascular system. They regard this as a specific and delicate response mechanism which does more than just reflect nonspecific arousal. Within a general arousal there appears to be some response patterning and perhaps the possibility of emotional differentiation.

Psychosomatic disorders

Since psychosomatic disorders are closely linked to physiological dysfunction and have often been studied with psychophysiological measures, it is appropriate to consider them now. However, it should be borne in mind that some of the discussion which follows is predicated on a consideration of anxiety (see Chapter 9).

Psychosomatic disorders have medical, organic symptoms, but an aetiology closely bound up with psychological variables. Although there have been many models and definitions of psychosomatics, most of them include specific reference to emotional disturbance (particularly anxiety), since the symptoms are seen in structures innervated by the ANS, the stomach, bronchioles, and skin, for example. (Instances of the more common disorders are asthma, peptic ulcers, and hypertension.) However, it should be said at the outset that it is impossible to determine the extent of the emotional involvement, the degree to which emotion is a causative factor. Sternbach's (1966) view is that *all* illness is psychosomatic, but that some diseases have more obvious emotional aspects than others.

There have been many explanations offered for psychosomatic illness. For example, one viewpoint is that, biologically, emotions have come to energize us for survival. Nowadays, however, violent physical responses gain social disapproval. Hence, we experience emotion from physiological change, but have no opportunity to discharge our energy behaviourally. Organic changes persist and pathology results. Alternatively, it has been argued that psychosomatic disorder results when physiological responses in emotion are either too great or too small. This leads to excessive or inadequate adaptation. Finally, from the psychoanalytic viewpoint, it is said that if a person regresses for example, the inappropriate emotions associated with an earlier stage in his development lead to specific symptoms and pathology results.

These various ways of accounting for psychosomatic disorder can be categorized into two major groups, the biological and the psychological. A more detailed example will be given of each of these and the work of Grinker will be covered, since he has done much to aid our understanding of psychosomatic disorder, both conceptually and as regards measurement. Moreover, his views rely heavily on the notion of anxiety. (For a full summary of theories of psychosomatics see Buss 1966.) To end this section, the work of Lader (1972) will be considered in detail, since he forges close links between psychophysiology and psychosomatic disorder.

The biological theory of psychosomatics most relevant to emotion suggests that patterns of autonomic reactivity are inherited. This is based largely on the work of such as Lacey et al. (1963) and Lacey and Lacey (1958), which shows consistent individual variation in automatic reactivity. They demonstrate that there are hierarchies of autonomic reactivity which are maintained whatever the stress might be. Of course, it could be that such differences are learned. But Mirsky (1958) showed fairly conclusively that physiological overreactivity, which is probably inherited, is an important determinant of ulcer formation.

There are many psychological theories of psychosomatic disorder, but they can be exemplified by Mahl (1950). He points to the importance of fear (anxiety) in this context, and sees it as usually preventing the expression of behaviour. For example, a conflict between dependency and anxiety will lead to ulcers, between anger and anxiety to hypertension, and fear of separation or crying in children will lead to asthma. Mahl's theory is specific to ulcers and is based on studies with dogs, monkeys, and students. For instance, he compared students who were to sit an examination later in the day with those who were not. He found more free hydrochloric acid in the 'anxious' than the 'nonanxious' group. Confirmation of this comes from Brady's (1958b; 1963) studies on 'executive' monkeys. Monkeys were studied in pairs, one being trained to respond to shock for both of them. Only the executive monkey developed ulcers. Although this work is open to alternative interpretations (Seligman 1975), it is still reasonable for Mahl to suggest that acute anxiety leads to sympathetic dominance and therefore a decrease in stomach acid, but that in chronic anxiety the parasympathetic nervous system becomes dominant and acid is secreted. This is supported by research which shows that acid is only secreted after prolonged anxiety. To account for some individuals developing ulcers and others not, such a theory must also depend on the inheritance of physiological dispositions.

In making observations during World War II, Grinker and Spiegel (1945) showed that, in the field of battle, moderate anxiety facilitated performance. On the other hand, excessive anxiety resulted in inefficiency. Perceptions were distorted and the men became overreactive. They described this as tending to lead to psychological and physical regression and dependency, which often became intensified towards the end of stressful stimuli. Various post-war studies (for example Harrower and Grinker 1946) confirmed these observations. Grinker also developed a test of stress tolerance which provided an index of the capacity to tolerate stress and recover from it.

Grinker (1966) argues that he chose to measure anxiety because it is ubiquitous and because it spirals; in his terms, inadequacy leads to inadequacy.... He regards mild anxiety as a useful signal for threat, but extreme anxiety as leading to a great disorganization in behaviour. He suggests that psychopathological defences often develop against this extreme anxiety. Thus he regards anxiety as a fundamental mover in behaviour. He believes this to be evident in any form of therapy; when defences are penetrated, there is the underlying anxiety. Grinker *et al.* (1961) go further and say that anxiety as a feeling indicates that an individual is moving into or out of a depression; any other factors are mere defences against the presence of anxiety. The problem is worsened if we attempt to provide an external cause for our anxiety but cannot; it then becomes impossible to explain it away by calling it fear.

Although he basically regards anxiety as a danger signal, Grinker also views it as being associated with many interrelated but often individualistic somatic processes. As the anxiety increases, so the somatic components become more diffuse. Anxiety also colours interpersonal behaviour with inexplicable feelings of the foreboding of danger or disintegration. The basic problem as Grinker sees it is that we are all prone to anxiety, but we need to establish what makes this proneness become realized.

At the start of his work, Grinker was unable to find freely anxious people, so he had to manufacture anxiety. He did this in terms of four phases: alertness, apprehension, free anxiety, and panic, the last two being seen as neurotic or pathological. His first studies were conducted on the liver (for example Persky *et al.* 1950; 1952). Substances which needed to be broken down in the liver were injected and a measure taken of the amount of hippuric acid secreted. The rapidity and degree of the breakdown were used as an index of the extent of the anxiety. As anxious patients were treated, so the amount of hippuric acid which they secreted fell. Grinker (1953) then moved on to an analysis of what he called 'system anxiety', i.e. he attempted to break down anxiety into its parts. He gradually developed what he believed to be reliable measures. These were based on: (1) observing patients diagnosed as anxious and developing specific verbal descriptions of their various degrees of anxiety; (2) interviewing the patients and taking statements as to their levels of anxiety; (3) having the patients rate their own anxiety. After this, anxiety was manipulated individually, this being determined by what the interviewer had found to be most likely to disturb the patient. The best method was usually to block dyadic communication. There were various problems with this technique—ranging from the anxiety produced by the comparative strangeness of the experimental set-up and the consequent difficulty in the first few stages of the experiments to the slowness involved in the experimental production of anxiety. Also, it is ethically impossible to subject someone to anxiety-provoking experiences for more than two to three hours, and, of course, responses such as anger and depression were also often unwittingly invoked.

Grinker's analysis points to the possibility of anxiety having a central place in the aetiology of psychosomatic disorders. Initially, there was excitement over Alexander's (1950) idea that there are specific emotional factors involved in degenerative diseases not associated with bacterial infection—such as migraine. Thus, if people suffer from a particular emotion for a long time then psychosomatic symptoms will develop. However, Grinker (1966) argues that it has been long observed that various psychosomatic diseases do *not* have specific emotional aetiologies, but instead ones that are characterized by specificity of response. Hence, he suggests that the main causative factor is likely to be anxiety. Grinker (1953) also proposes that it is the individual conditioning of responses in the young organism that is critical in psychosomatics, rather than specific emotional constellations.

Grinker has clearly made a considerable contribution both to the study of psychosomatic disorders and to the study of anxiety, but again it is obvious from this description of his work that he is dealing with an obscure, nebulous concept that he can do little to clarify.

More recently, Lader (1972) provides an extremely thorough analysis of the relationships between psychophysiology and psychosomatic disorder, in which he emphasizes arousal and response specificity rather than anxiety. His starting point is with the idea that both psychophysiological investigation and psychosomatic medicine assume a psychophysical parallelism—the assumption of a simultaneity of function rather than causal links. This promotes investigation of the relationships between behavioural and physiological events. Hence, within the framework of psychosomatics, it would not be said that anxiety causes tachycardia, but rather that verbal reports of anxiety accompany tachycardia, both in response to the same stimulus.

Lader argues that two main concepts relate psychophysiology and psychosomatics—arousal and response specificity. He suggests that arousal helps our understanding by functioning as a construct between physiological measures and any concomitant emotions, with heightened arousal being a necessary condition for the experience of emotion. This will be reflected in any psychophysiological measure, but to be meaningful this must also be consistent with self-reports and observed changes in behaviour. Of course, Lader cannot deny the low intercorrelations which obtain between measures of arousal, but suggests that in using psychophysiological measures of arousal it is important to make clear distinctions between individuals, within individuals on one occasion, within individuals on different occasions and within individuals on any one occasion under different conditions.

The idea of psychophysiological response specificity is central to understanding psychosomatic dysfunction, since it gives a theoretical basis for the variation in vulnerability of physiological systems from person to person. In support, Lader mentions Lacey's ideas on three types of response stereotypy (see also Fehr and Stern (1970) below). There are: (1) intrastressor stereotypy, in which each subject shows a similar psychophysiological response pattern to a repeated stimulus; (2) interstressor stereotypy, in which some subjects show similar response patterns to different stimuli; and (3) situational stereotypy, in which response patterns are related to the type of stimulation rather than to idiosyncracies of subjects.

These ideas lead to the view that different somatic processes play different roles in different types of behaviour. This is related to an analysis of psychosomatic disorder with the notion of symptom specificity, namely, that the particular physiological mechanism involved in some somatic complaints (in some psychiatric patients) is especially susceptible to activation by stress.

From this discussion of the functions of arousal and response specificity Lader proposes a model of the psychophysiological basis for psychosomatic disorder. This is represented in Figure 8.

In the terms of this model, environmental stimulation (unconditioned or conditioned) interacts with individual factors to produce general arousal. Appraisal follows, and a specific emotion is experienced. These interactions may be conscious or unconscious, and the emotions may therefore be rational or irrational.

Lader calls upon four factors to account for the individual response patterns in the concomitant psychophysiological changes. (1) Emotion is partly

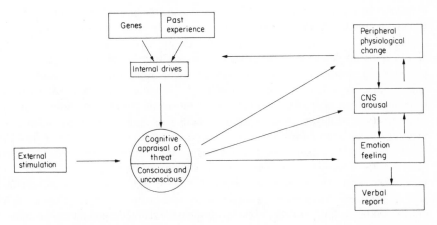

Figure 8. Lader's model of the psychophysiological basis of psychosomatic disorder.

dependent on previous experience and physiological patterns vary according to the emotion. (2) Individual differences in responses to emotionally neutral stimuli are also very variable. (3) There are individual differences in the intensity of physiological responses; bodily systems are differentially involved. (4) The awareness of peripheral changes varies from bodily system to bodily system, hence there is differential feedback from these systems.

The final step in the argument inevitably brings in a discussion of severe or chronic environmental events. In Lader's view, these interact with internal factors and produce high arousal and intense emotion. The physiological changes which accompany this may be morbidly severe in one bodily system. Also, there is a loss of adaptive responses when arousal is very high. All of which becomes self-perpetuating. If this process goes on for long enough, then anatomical changes occur and psychosomatic illness appears.

There is a reasonable amount of empirical support for these carefully conceived ideas of Lader's which clearly have important therapeutic implications (see Chapter 9), particularly if they are considered in conjunction with the work of Miller (e.g. 1969) and others on the operant conditioning of autonomic reponses, and biofeedback in general. Why, for example, should not *any* bodily disorder be capable of control in this way?

Peripheral theories of emotion

As was seen in Chapter 2, *James'* (1884) theory of emotion was the first to be couched in psychological rather than philosophical terms. It was also the first of the 'peripheral' theories. Before James, organisms were thought only to react emotionally after having reacted cognitively. James reversed this in saying that emotion (as felt experience) occurs after visceral discharge and feedback from motor responses; we feel 'happy' because we are laughing. In its inherent untestability, James' theory was not satisfactory. On the other hand, in stressing the significance of the viscera it had a far-reaching effect.

In that he regarded the thalamus as the seat of the emotions, Cannon (1927) based his theory more on the CNS than did James. Cannon regarded the thalamus as exerting a continuous inhibitory control which is lifted when emotional stimuli arrive at the cortex. Impulses then released by the thalamus proceed via autonomic motor nerves for behaviour and to the cortex for emotional experience. The research which led to this theory and the various points which can be levelled against it will be discussed later. More importantly, however (see Mandler 1962), Cannon made five major criticisms of James' views. (1) The artificial production of visceral changes does not seem to lead to emotion. (2) There is no evidence for any visceral response patterning in emotion. (3) Visceral organs have little sensitivity; any feedback they give could hardly be used to differentiate emotion. (4) If the viscera are surgically separated from the nervous system by sympathectomy or vagotomy, then emotional behaviour still occurs even though no visceral responses can be made.

(5) The viscera only react slowly. Emotion could only occur at least one second after external stimulation. Subjectively, it seems to be faster than this.

On the basis of empirical research, Schachter (for example 1964) has effectively argued against Cannon's points (1), (2), and (3) above, at least as they refer to the general role of the viscera in emotion, rather than especially in vitiating James (see Chapter 4). This work clearly shows that the viscera are a necessary, but not sufficient, condition for the occurrence of emotion. Also, Mandler (1962) argues that points (4) and (5) are accounted for by the fact that after the initial formation of emotional behaviour it may become conditioned to external stimuli, and therefore may occur either before visceral change or without its intervention (see Chapter 6).

Two more recent theories also bear on the James–Cannon controversy. Like James, *Wenger* (1950) equated visceral responses with emotion, but also suggested how these could function in 'hypothetical robot'. To get away from James' introspectionist sort of approach, he concentrated very much on behaviour. He regarded emotional 'states' as in fact emotional 'complexes', which he saw as explaining why we usually have no language which is adequate to describe them. Wenger also suggested that our perception of an emotional stimulus depends on the pairing of conditioned and unconditioned stimuli, following which the arousal of the ANS leads to visceral responses. These in turn lead to drive stimuli which Wenger regarded as perceptions of visceral action. Appropriately enough, the end point in this chain is overt (muscular) response and verbal report.

The essential difference between James' and Wenger's theories is that James' is introspective and therefore essentially untestable. Wenger does at least emphasize behaviour. However, there is a lack of sophistication in his theory; it is a general mixture of behaviouristic and nonbehaviouristic elements, whilst still pointing to the role of the viscera. Some introspective influence remains in that the intervening variable 'drive stimulus' determines both skeletal response and verbal report. It is from the latter that Wenger infers feelings.

If Wenger's theory bears comparison with James', then Freeman's (1948) dynamotor theory was dependent on Cannon's. He suggested a concept of 'neuromuscular homeostasis' pointing to a rapprochement between central and peripheral mechanisms. He regarded emotional experiences as 'peripheral meaning structures'. These come from two sources which interact cortically: proprioceptive impulses from learned responses, and unlearned thalamic reactions. Freeman is proposing a combination between proprioceptive stimuli and hypothalamic processes. This allows him the experimental aspects of emotion via proprioception but keeps emotional behaviour distinct from this. This is different from Cannon's view in that the latter postulated distinct physiological substrates for the two. However, Freeman's theory suffers from the same lack of sophistication as Wenger's, given the complexities of more recent physiologically based findings.

Fehr and Stern (1970) put forward the latest argument for a renewed emphasis on the periphery in studying the physiology of emotion. Moreover, they suggest that the original James–Lange theory still has much to recommend it. James spoke of 'primary feelings', 'immediate reflexes', and 'secondary feelings'. Fehr and Stern maintain that primary feelings and immediate reflexes might *now* be seen as hypothalamic discharges which inhibit the cortex and excite the ANS (the importance of the hypothalamus to emotion will be seen later). Secondary feelings are perhaps given by afferent feedback from the periphery. This is a similar idea to that of Lacey and Lacey (1970). However, Fehr and Stern deny that there is afferent feedback from the periphery. They argue that behaviour can be produced such that it looks like emotion, but without involving visceral mechanisms. Although this may be so, afferent feedback may still occur in 'real' emotion. They also point out that with peripheral feedback cut out there may still be primary feelings and immediate feelings to the object in question. However, as Mandler (1962) suggested, these may be learnt.

Fehr and Stern discuss many recent investigations which lend support to the importance of the periphery in emotion. For example, Hohmann (1966) described the reactions of 25 adult males with lesions in the spinal cord as being consistent with James' theory. Their reported experiences of feelings of anger, sex, and fear were decreased. Hohmann showed that although apparently emotional behaviour might still be seen in these patients if and when it is appropriate, no *feelings* are involved.

As might be expected, Fehr and Stern lay most emphasis on the evidence supporting differential physiological responses to different stimuli. Following Lacey and Lacey (1958), they suggest that there are three aspects to this research, these depending on the type of stereotypy involved. (1) They name the first situational stereotypy. Distinct psychophysiological response patterns are related to various empirical conditions, particularly those which simulate various emotions. (2) For a given stress, a given individual shows a reproducible psychophysiological response pattern (intrastressor). (3) The response pattern for one stressor is similar to that for others (interstressor). This clearly supports Cannon rather than James. But Fehr and Stern argue that all the *different* stress situations which have been studied in this context possibly have fear or anxiety as a common factor. They maintain that any study in this field can be interpreted in this way.

Finally, as an example of Fehr and Stern's argument, it is worth mentioning their reservations concerning Sherrington's (1900) and Cannon's (1927) demonstrations of emotional responses in spinal dogs and sympathectomized cats which are often quoted against James. They dismiss this work since: (1) in both the spinal dogs and sympathectomized cats a number of possible pathways from the periphery were not severed; (2) the work was methodologically deficient; and (3) the responses studied may have been as much instrumental as emotional.

Overall, Fehr and stern put forward a plea, which is endorsed here, that the periphery should not be ignored in any physiological consideration of emotion.

The James–Lange theory was sound insofar as it is now clear that the viscera are necessary to emotion. Also, Fehr and Stern's ideas are important to other peripheral theories of emotion (see Goldstein 1968 for a review of these). At present, the significance to emotion of peripheral physiological mechanisms would seem difficult to deny. However, it should not be forgotten that much of the basic work involving psychophysiological measures (including EEG) assigns to them no more than a vague reflection of general arousal and a very complex role in possible response stereotypy, important though this is to a consideration of psychosomatic disorder.

INTERMEDIATE MECHANISMS

In heading this section, the term intermediate is used very broadly. There have been some recent approaches to the physiology of emotion which concentrate directly on neither peripheral nor central mechanisms. Their methodology differs from that of the more usual research strategies, but their results have relevance for the general physiological bases of emotion.

The endocrines and the ANS

The most interesting recent study of the interrelationships between the endocrine systems, the ANS, and emotion has been made by Brady (for example 1962; 1970a; 1970b). His investigations combine standard physiological and behavioural research strategies. Like many others before him, he distinguishes between feelings or affects and emotional behaviour. He bases this distinction on the localizability of the main effects or consequences of the phenomena. Hence, he regards emotional behaviour as part of a class of interactions which have their main effects within the organism. He also suggests that feeling has many subclasses, but that emotion is simply a change, an abrupt immediate disruption in the interaction between the organism and its environment (the nature of this change is examined a little more closely in Chapter 6).

Brady argues that feelings are associated with autonomic, visceral, proprioceptive, and endocrine activity, and quotes many studies as showing such interoceptive events acquiring discriminative control over behaviour (for example Katkin and Murray 1968). He regards any variation in, or proliferation of, feelings as limited only by the conditioning history of the organism and the complexity of the environment. However, he suggests that there is interoceptive participation in some effective response patterns. This does not mean that it is a defining characteristic of emotional behaviour. For Brady, like others who have a behavioural orientation, the defining quality of emotional behaviour is that it is characterized by abrupt changes in an organism's interaction with its environment. This leads Brady to a directly behavioural analysis of emotion, but with an overriding interest in its psychophysiological and hormonal correlates.

Brady, and others working with a similar viewpoint, has followed three strategies. (1) There has been interest in cardiorespiratory changes which result from acute and chronic emotional stress. Such changes have been found mainly in the results of studies involving behavioural conditioning, but ranging from aversive control with physiological stimuli (for example De Toledo and Black 1966) through those including few aversive elements (for example Belanger and Feldman 1962) to those showing transient, situational-bound effects (for example Ross *et al.* 1962). (2) Brady (1970a) describes a long series of his own studies concerned with visceral–alimentary and endocrine changes; these are more permanent than the cardiorespiratory effects. (3) Finally, some studies have related gastrointestinal and infectious disease to emotional stress. For example, Sawrey and Weisz (1956) produced gastric lesions in rats by placing them for 30 days in a chamber where to get food and water they had to cross an electrified grid floor. Brady (1970a) reviews such studies, which in fact involve the experimental analysis of psychosomatic disorders (see above). It is worth noting that a major difficulty in this area comes from the frequent irreversibility of effects that might be produced.

Brady's own studies are of monkeys incarcerated in a complex restraining apparatus. They can be given food, water, and footshock. They have access to a hand-operated lever, visual and auditory stimuli can be presented to them, and samples of blood and urine collected. Everything is automized, allowing straight-forward studies using the CER paradigm or conditioned avoidance, but making it a fairly simple matter to take psychophysiological measures.

Brady's general findings are succinctly summarized in his 1970 papers. Firstly, they demonstrate relationships between autonomic–endocrine activity and emotional behaviour. For example, there is an increase in the output of the pituitary–adrenocortical system during the acquisition of a CER. Some studies have used a Sidman avoidance procedure. The restrained monkey is given foot-shock every 20 seconds unless it presses the lever to postpone the shock for 20 seconds. This procedure is associated with large increases in corticosteroid levels. Brady suggests that such findings simply reflect the general arousal which is induced by these 'emotional' situations. The time course of steroid and visceral changes has been well observed in these studies. Brady has also shown the importance of the organism's previous history in determining these reactions, behavioural and autonomic–endocrine activity again being closely related.

Brady's investigations point to many interdependent autonomic and endocrine systems as providing broad patterns of change during more prolonged emotional responding. He speculates that there may be a relationship between such physiological activity and broader aspects of emotion, 'mood' or 'affective dispositions' for example. He argues that if autonomic–endocrine response patterning can be established in relation to behaviour, then this will be useful in the analysis of many internal consequences of emotion.

In that it provides some further evidence for physiological response patterning in emotion, Brady's approach is interesting. Also the work which it has led to is difficult to fault. However, this evaluation is tempered by the relative artificiality of the experimental procedures on which the approach depends and by the gulf between Brady's relatively sophisticated theorizing behaviourally and physiologically and his speculations about concepts such as mood.

Intercranial electrical stimulation (ICS)

Apart from the traditional stimulation of various parts of the brain simply to see what behavioural effects this might have, brain stimulation has also been used as punishment, reward, and motivation. Its motivating effects seem to be related to emotion. Delgado *et al.* (1954) and Miller (1958) have carried out many studies on the aversive effects of intercranial stimulation. In a typical experiment, cats would receive electric shock through a grid floor. They could terminate this by. turning a wheel. Once this response had been satisfactorily learned, the foot-shock would be substituted with electrical stimulation of the CNS through implanted electrodes. Such studies show that animals learn avoidance responses based on CNS stimulation just as fast as those based on external shock. This lends support to the hypothesis that in avoidance learning fear rather than pain is the motivating agent, as it is thought to be in studies involving external aversive stimulation.

The much quoted studies on reward are those of Olds and Milner (1954) and Olds (1955; 1958). Here, an animal, usually a rat, learns to press a bar in a Skinner box solely to receive intercranial electrical 'reinforcement'. This can evidently act as a very powerful drive. With an appropriate electrode placement as many as 2000 responses per hour for 15–20 hours have been observed. This rate picks up again after a sleep. This shows that intercranial self-stimulation may be more rewarding than food, water or sex. Also, with an optimal placement of electrodes, there are very fast rates of acquisition and extinction. The acquisition of responses leading to other, external, rewards may be equally fast, but not so rates of extinction. On the other hand, extended partial reinforcement schedules need much more training; this may mean that self-stimulation is rewarding only when it is activating a structure relevant to some other drive.

Olds has demonstrated the importance both of the positioning of the intercranial electrode and of the characteristics of the shock which it delivers. For example, shock intensity is more important than frequency. There is an inverted U type of relationship between shock intensity and rate of bar-pressing. Of more importance to the present discussion is the locus of the shock. In general, ICS in the neocortex is not rewarding and may be aversive. The most rewarding sites are in the limbic system and its associated areas. There seems to be one main dorsal and one main ventral reward area, although in some locations stimulation can have both rewarding and punishing effects, the lateral and posterior parts of the hypothalamus for example. Thus, self-stimulation studies support the idea (discussed below) that the limbic system is at the physiological core of emotion.

Delgado (1970) describes a recent and important technological development in this field. He argues, with good foundation, that the neurophysiological correlates of emotion may be found more simply with experimental manipulations that disturb the phenomenon in question as little as possible. He suggests that a move in this direction can be made with remote stimulation of the brain with radio waves, whilst recording brain activity telemetrically. So, any subjects are behaving freely. Two research strategies are developing from this basic technique. (1) Using cats, monkeys, and chimpanzees, a programmed electrical stimulation of the brain has been found to alter behaviours such as pupillary contraction, food intake, grooming, aggression, and general instrumental behaviour. (2) A two-way 'communication' has been effected with the brains of people suffering from disorders of the temporal lobe. With the EEG continuously monitored, correlations between electrical activity and behaviour have been observed.

As Delgado points out, this is a very new field but it could have far-reaching theoretical and therapeutic ramifications. The type of study described here is based on the general 'localization of function' view that the brain contains groups of functionally related neurons which give experiences the positive or negative bias which typifies each emotion. This will determine the emotional stage. Delgado suggests that there is an anatomical and functional differentiation between two groups of neural structures, one related to emotional 'timing', the other to behavioural performance. His results to date support this hypothesis and are suggestive concerning the emotional functions of certain brain areas. In the future, this technique and the hypotheses to which it has given rise could easily assume central importance in the search for the physiological substrates of emotion.

Intercranial chemical stimulation

A technique which has recently been gaining in importance for the study of the physiology of emotion involves the intercranial administration of drugs. In most cases, this procedure simply has reversible effects on function without causing any permanent structural damage. It is therefore useful in delineating the general relationships between the CNS and behaviour. However, in a review of this field, Grossman (1970) points to two problems which have yet to be solved. First, it is difficult to determine precisely either the extent or the rate of diffusion of a drug through the brain. Second, but just as important, the way in which the drug acts is often unknown. For example, it may either affect behaviour directly and/or because abnormal conditions are created at that point where it is injected. Of course, appropriate control groups could, and should, be used to take account of these types of confounding influence.

There has been a great deal of work on carbachol, which is parasympathetic-like in action. Grossman (1963), for example, injected it into the amygdaloid complex of cats. The initial reaction was generalized seizures and convulsions, but the EEG gradually became more normal. Everyday behaviour was relatively unchanged except that the animals remained vicious and unhandleable. In some cases this effect was still in evidence after five months. Similar studies with rats have demonstrated altered reactions to punishment, thus making it difficult to establish CERs and passive avoidance responses. Grossman mentions several studies (for example Grossman 1964; Kelsey and Grossman 1969) which show the involvement of two separate components in the septal region. Carbachol injections cause a radical slowing down of avoidance learning, but not to the same extent if they are given after asymptotic performance. Of course, this *may* be a motivational rather than an emotional effect. Also, injections of atropine (which acts as a cholinergic block and has effects similar to those of epinephrine) into the same area facilitate avoidance behaviour.

Many similar effects on emotionality have been shown with carbachol injections into the hypothalamus and preoptic areas, the thalamus, and the caudate nucleus. But more interesting are the reactions which follow injections into the lower brain areas. For example, an injection of carbachol into the brain-stem reticular formation leads to agitation, and inhibition of avoidance responses, reactions which gradually adjust to repeated injections. However, similar injections in the midbrain produce, for example, a marked hyperactivity to all stimuli but no lowering of the threshold to them. This effect does not show habituation. Also, although eating and drinking are quite normal, the aquisition of appetitively based responses is considerably impaired.

Some of the studies on spreading cortical depression are also of interest in the context of intercranial chemical stimulation. This technique involves the permanent implantation of cannulae into the skull (usually of rats) such that they can be used to inject small amounts of chemicals (for example potassium chloride) directly on to the surface of the cortex. This functionally depresses cortical activity, the time sequence of the effects being in proportion to the strength of the chemical solution. This technique has mainly been used in the study of the memory trace (for example Bures and Buresova 1960; Russell 1967). However, it has also led to evidence which points to classical conditioning being mediated subcortically (for example Ross and Russell 1967). This has received some support from studies involving surgical rather than chemical decortication (for example Oakley and Russell 1968). If, as is suggested in Chapter 6, conditioned emotional responses come about through a process of classical conditioning, these results have clear significance for the physiology of emotion. They imply that the cortex may be concerned in emotion on some basis of mass action rather than specific localization of function. Such a possibility should modify any evaluation that is made of the more traditional work on the CNS and emotion.

These then are just a few examples of the recent studies and findings based on intercranial injections. Although the techniques cannot yet be said to have clarified our knowledge of the physiological substrates of emotion, they are providing information. As is often the case with a technique which has obvious possibilities, there has been a somewhat hasty proliferation of research. Results therefore tend to be complicated and confusing. This is largely due to: (1) possible species differences, (2) differential responses to different drugs, and (3) the lack of relevant comparative control conditions.

Neurochemistry and emotion

In his review of work on the neurochemistry of emotion, Kety (1970) divides it into two major fields of study: (1) that concerned with peripheral biochemical changes which are related to a possible central emotional state; (2) that concerned with those changes in brain biochemistry which are related to emotion. Peripheral changes have received rather more attention (see earlier), but Kety concentrates on central changes.

This approach gained its impetus from recent Swedish work which indicates the specific locale of those neurons which contain monoamines (mainly norepinephrine and serotonin), and also traces their connection with other parts of the brain. The amines are concentrated at the end of the axons of these neurons and seem to be acting as CNS transmitters. The neurons involved connect mainly with the hypothalamus and the limbic system. This indicates that they probably relate to autonomic control in the hypothalamus and *possibly* relate to emotion in the limbic system. Also, many of the fibres that contain norepinephrine and serotonin pass through the neocortex; Kety suggests that they *may* be important to arousal or learning or consolidation.

Work on the neurochemistry of emotion began with the discovery of lysergic acid diethylamide and of its interactions with serotonin in inhibiting the action of smooth muscle. It seemed as though one function of serotonin was the direct control of mood (see Chapter 4). In addition to this, Kety's (1970) interest was fired by the possible importance of norepinephrine. This will be briefly discussed to exemplify the influence of amines on emotional behaviour. For instance, Thierry *et al.* (1968) showed that severe and mild stress induce the synthesis and use of norepinephrine in the brain. And Reis and Fuxe (1969) demonstrated an increase in norepinephrine when rage occurred in cats electrically stimulated in the amygdala or with brain-stem lesions. And drugs which promote or inhibit norepinephrine also promote or inhibit rage.

Kety (1966) suggests that drugs which alter man's emotions also affect the amines in a way which indicates that they are involved in emotion. Reserpine, for example, often depresses those who take it to combat hypertension. And anti-depressants have the opposite effects on norepinephrine. Of course, depression is only one aspect of emotion, but such results are suggestive. Kety (1970) becomes more speculative when considering electroconvulsive shock (ECS), which is sometimes effective in the treatment of depression but which has an un-known method of operation. Kety proposes that ECS may be effective because it persistently stimulates the brain synthesis of norepinephrine. Animals given ECS twice per day for one week showed a significantly greater turnover of norepinephrine than controls for at least 24 hours after the final shock. Kety suggests that ECS may substitute for rapid eye movements or paradoxical sleep and that both act to build up norepinephrine in the brain. These arguments imply that at least one of the amines is involved in depression and may provide the mechanism whereby antidepressant drugs and ECS have their effects.

Kety does not maintain that neurochemistry is the final answer to the analysis of emotion. The research to date is only suggestive. He believes, however, that the amines in the brain possibly provide a system which is 'sluggish, coarse and diffuse' but which parallels the sensory–motor system. He regards it as more primitive and crude, but based on survival. It may therefore be influencing all behaviour rather than just emotion.

CENTRAL MECHANISMS

The subcortex

That various subcortical CNS structures are important to the physiology of emotion is axiomatic. However, their precise function and interrelationships in this respect are confusing. This is reflected in both fact and theory. At the lowest level of the CNS, the *spinal cord* and *medulla* provide the first information. Animals with transected spinal cords show some autonomic emotional behaviour, but animals with cuts just above the cord and the medulla show far better integrated autonomic responses—presumably because the medulla probably controls circulatory and respiratory functions.

The *brain stem* (that area above the medulla and below the cerebrum) is more interesting. Studies involving decerebration (i.e. brain-stem transection) tend to rely on observations rather than experimentation and to concentrate on behaviours such as rage in dogs (for example Goltz 1892). Decerebrate animals display some emotion. However, this is usually poorly coordinated and poorly directed (for example Kelly *et al.* 1946). The general rule seems to be the lower the brain-stem transection the poorer the behavioural integration. However, even if it occurs at the highest level, the resultant behaviour is never fully integrated. This suggests that individual emotional responses may be regulated in the lower brain stem, but that the cortex is necessary for their integration. As will be seen later, evidence at the cortical level is regarded as supporting this idea.

The subcortical structures most implicated in emotion are the *hypothalamus* and *thalamus*. The classic study was that of Dusser de Barenne (1920), who found that decorticate animals (i.e. with the hypothalamus and thalamus intact) showed violent rage in response to trivial stimuli. This led to the term 'sham rage'. Results of lesion studies are well exemplified by Bard (1928), who confirmed that the threshold for rage is lowered after decortication (pointing to the inhibitory function of the cortex). However, he also demonstrated that a complex emotional reaction was evident only when the hypothalamus was left intact. The general emotional reactions of decorticates do not tend to be directed towards the source of stimulation. This may be partly due to the increased hyper-sensitivity which is thought to result from the removal of the forebrain.

Evidence on possible hypothalamic involvement in emotion also comes from studies of electrical stimulation and lesions rather than complete transections. Hess (1936; 1949; 1954), for example, has attempted to chart the behavioural responses of cats to systematic electrical stimulation of the diencephalon. His results suggest the presence of distinct systems which mediate attack, defence, and flight. In general, electrical stimulation of the hypothalamus produces rage; its destruction should therefore lead to a decrease in emotional behaviour. This was partially borne out by Brady (1960; 1962), for example, with posterior lesions. He also showed, however, that medial lesions may lead to well-integrated but very savage rage and ferocity. And Bard (1950) suggested that emotional behaviour in animals that have been electrically stimulated in the hypothalamus eventually returns to normal.

Work involving the thalamus is even more complex and confusing. For example, stimulation of the posteroventral nucleus elicits a range of emotional activities described as anything from anxiety to attack or defence. And stimulation of the dorsomedial nucleus leads to fear (behaviours such as crouching). Clearly, the thalamus is well positioned to perform a subcortical integrative function, particularly of afferent input, and there is a wealth of early clinical data bearing on its importance to emotion (for example Dana 1921). Such evidence led to Cannon's usefully straightforward thalamic theory of emotion. However, as mentioned earlier, there would seem to be two main objections to Cannon's theory. (1) The complete removal of the thalamus does not affect the rage reactions of decorticate animals—it is only removal of the posterior and ventral parts of the hypothalamus which does this. (2) Removal of the thalamus should produce a permanent rage reaction, which it does not. In spite of these objections to Cannon's theory, the thalamus must be involved in emotion to some extent. There are also two difficulties in interpreting any experimental evidence which bears on these issues. It should be noted in fact that these difficulties are of general application to this area of research. (1) The thalamus has extensive projections which make it very awkward to confine lesions or electrical stimulation to specific nuclei. (2) The thalamus has important sensory functions. This makes it difficult to separate effects due to a change in emotional capability from those which might be due to changed sensory function. General perception might be altered for example.

To summarize, the subcortex has an important part to play in emotion. This has been indicated with studies involving either complete transections or preparations (experimentally in animals, clinically in humans), lesions or stimulation. The functions and projections of the subcortex are so complex that the overall pattern becomes very confusing. However, in general terms, the higher the position of a subcortical structure within the CNS, the more important to emotion it appears to be. This culminates in the hypothalamus and thalamus.

The cortex and the limbic system

Although there is little doubt that subcortical structures of the CNS are important to the mediation of emotion, it is equally clear that they *alone* do not account for all the facts. The cortex must be involved, particularly those parts of it (i.e. mainly the limbic system) which are interconnected with subcortical areas. For example, general decortication has three main effects on emotion. (1) There is a lowered threshold to those stimuli which usually produce emotion—the organism becomes overreactive. (2) There tends to be little direction to emotional responses—they are very generalized. (3) The timing of the emotion is changed—it has an unusually rapid onset and offset. These effects point to the cortex as having an inhibitory influence on emotion, which is of course removed when the cortex is removed.

The boundaries of the limbic system are ill-defined and, somewhat like national boundaries, change from time to time. The most recent formulations include all the *allocortical* and *juxtallocortical* parts of the cerebrum. These are the phylogenetically older areas of the neocortex. Structurally, they are both simpler and distinct from the remainder. These areas are formed by: the cingulate, retrosplenial and hippocampal gyri, the island of Reil, the operculum, and that part of the fronto-temporal cortex which is not neocortex; also included are the olfactory bulb and tubercle, the diagonal band of Broca, the septal area, the prepyriform and preamygdaloid complex, and the hippocampal formation. Finally, the amygdaloid complex is also usually subsumed under the general limbic system heading. This is solely for the sake of functional convenience, since it is actually subcortical. Much of the literature on the limbic system is concerned with its important olfactory functions. However, the main usefulness of this work to the study of emotion has been to point to the extensive inter-connections within the limbic system.

Lateral limbic system

From the research viewpoint, the lateral limbic system can be divided into five major structural possibilities. These will be discussed in turn.

1. *Temporal lobe*. It is in the area of the temporal lobe that Klüver and Bucy (1937; 1938; 1939) first made their observations which led to the coining of the term Klüver–Bucy syndrome. They made lesions in the temporal lobe involving the hippocampus, amygdala and pyriform and fronto-temporal cortex. This made previously aggressive monkeys tame, active, hypersexual, and very oral, a finding which was supported by Bard and Mountcastle (1948) and Bard (1950), who first ablated the neocortex, leaving the limbic system intact. This produced tame, placid, emotionally unresponsive animals. They then produced an increase in emotionality by ablation of the amygdaloid complex and/or cingulate gyrus, suggesting that these areas may have inhibitory functions.

2. *Amygdaloid complex*. As mentioned above, some studies (for example Bard and Mountcastle 1948) show there to be an increase in emotional activity following amygdaloid lesions. Others do not (for example Schreiner and Kling 1953). Similarly equivocal findings obtain for aggression and dominance. At this point it is perhaps worth reemphasizing the general idea outlined in the introduction that it is virtually impossible to ascertain from one study to the next whether or not the lesions involved were in precisely the same places. The

possibility that they were not can always account for discrepancies in results. However, each of the studies on the amygdaloid complex shows some effect, which suggests that this area is sensitive for emotional reactivity, without being more specific. This is supported by recent studies involving more sophisticated measurements than the behavioural observations characteristic of the earlier research. For example, Schwartzbaum (1960; 1965) has shown amygdaloid lesions not to interfere with the acquisition of simple discriminations, but to block the formation of CERs and nonreinforced response suppression (see Chapter 6). Also, animals wih such lesions are relatively insensitive to changes in reinforcement conditions.

3. *Amygdala–hippocampus.* Both Smith (1950) and Walker *et al.* (1953) carried out studies involving lesions in the amygdala *and* the hippocampus. These produced the tameness and docility part of the Klüver–Bucy syndrome without the hypersexuality and orality. There appeared to be only a *temporary* reduction in emotional reactivity. Stimuli needed to be far more intense to produce the usual fear or rage.

4. *Hippocampus.* Electrical and chemical stimulation of the hippocampus facilitates emotional responses and autonomic reactions similar to those which are found during normal emotion (MacLean 1954; 1957). Also the hippocampus influences hormonal mechanisms which may affect emotional behaviour. Whether they have been based on naive or sophisticated experimentation, the results of the many studies of hippocampal influences do not lead to any firm conclusions. For example, at the observational level, Orbach *et al.* (1960) showed monkeys with hippocampal lesions to be highly ferocious, and Mirsky (1960) showed no changes in the social rankings of monkeys with such lesions and described them as being less fearful of man. Similarly, at the more formal level, Pribram and Weiskrantz (1957) showed hippocampal lesions to lead to a decrement in active avoidance responses acquired pre-operatively, although Isaacson *et al.* (1967) showed rats with such lesions to acquire an avoidance response faster than control animals and to be more resistant to its extinction. On the other hand, most studies show hippocampal lesions to produce deficits in passive avoidance (for example Isaacson and Wickelgren 1962) and CER responding (for example Brady and Hunt 1955).

All hippocampal studies are difficult to interpret, since lesions and stimulation in this area may have many other effects which could indirectly influence emotional behaviour—such effects could be sensory, motor or motivational. Also, in few studies have the lesions been restricted precisely to the hippocampus; surrounding structures may have been damaged, which again clouds the issue.

5. *Fronto-temporal cortex.* Fulton *et al.* (1952) show that ablation of the fronto-temporal cortex leads to much of the Klüver–Bucy syndrome, but excluding orality and hypersexuality.

Reading between the lines of the mass of research findings on the lateral limbic system, it can be tentatively concluded that lesions in this area reduce emotional reactivity, especially where fear and rage are concerned.

Cingulate gyrus

In neodecorticate animals, removal of the cingulate gyrus has effects similar to those following ablation of the hippocampus and amygdala—a *rise* in emotional reactivity. In normal animals, removal of the cingulate gyrus *lowers* the threshold for fear or rage (for example Bard and Mountcastle 1948). But Pribram and Fulton (1954), for example, show such changes to be only temporary. Also, some studies (for example Kennard 1955) report an immediate but transient increase in emotionality following bilateral damage to the cingulate gyrus—there is an increased aggression and viciousness.

Lesions in the cingulate gyrus have often been used in attempts to combat clinical problems of anxiety neurosis and obsession (see Fulton 1951), but reports of such work obscure as much as they clarify. There is the usual problem of ensuring that *only* this area has been damaged and also that of the notorious inadequacy of behavioural testing by many clinicians. However, there have been a few well-conducted analyses of post-lesion behavioural changes. For example, Lubar (1964) showed that rats with cingulate lesions learnt passive avoidance better than normal rats, but were worse at active avoidance. Fortunately, such results have led subsequent work in the direction of greater precision in the siting of the lesion.

Septal region

Much of the experimental work on the septal region has been concerned with avoidance behaviour. Its beginnings can be found in Brady and Nauta (1953; 1955) and Brady (1958a; 1958b; 1960), who made lesions in the ventral portions of this area. Their general findings were quite clear, namely, increases in general emotional reactivity and in the startle response to loud auditory stimuli. But these effects disappeared within a few weeks, behaviour reverting to normal. In the longer term, there is improved performance in the acquisition of active avoidance responses but interference with these same responses if they have been acquired pre-operatively. Performance is impaired whenever appetitive responding is involved. Also, Harvey *et al.* (1961) found general post-septal lesion impairment of CER behaviour. This complex picture is further complicated by equivocal results from passive avoidance studies (see Grossman 1967 for a fuller discussion).

Four possible explanations of the observed changes in avoidance behaviour following septal lesions have been suggested. (1) King (1958) argues that septal lesions result in emotional hypersensitivity. However, this is unlikely, since Brady (1960) showed that any hypersensitivity soon wears off. (2) The weakening of the crouching reflex to electric shock *could* lead to faster active avoidance responses (for example Krieckhaus *et al.* 1964). Perhaps this is so; crouching *may* be a good index of emotional sensitivity. (3) The septal area may be partially in control of motivation; food and water intake are affected by septal lesions. Although this could account for some of the behavioural effects which have been observed, possible changes in drive states would not explain all. (4) Finally, on the basis of many studies showing inappropriate responding in appetitive discrimination following septal lesions, McCleary *et al.* (1965) suggest that behaviour may increasingly perseverate since the lesion has destroyed the mechanism which usually suppresses over responses to non-reinforced or punished stimuli. Which of these explanations, if any, is correct it is impossible to judge.

Frontal lobes

Although the frontal lobes are mainly neocortex, they are clearly implicated in emotion. There is a straightforward anatomical and functional relationship between them, the limbic system proper, and the relevant subcortical structures. Also, there are no obvious sensory or motor functions mediated by the frontal lobes and they do receive most of the hypothalamic connections to the cerebrum.

The basic work on the frontal lobes began with Ferrier (1875), who carried out frontal ablations in monkeys. This changed their 'character' and 'disposition'. Via the work of such as Fulton (for example 1951), who showed the frustrational responses of chimpanzees to nonreward disappear after frontal ablation, this eventually led to the development of the clinical technique of frontal lobotomy. Many thousands of lobotomies have been carried out. Analysis of these (for example Rylander 1939; 1948) leads to the conclusion that approximately half the cases result in lowered anxiety. However, many individuals also show post-operative intellectual inpairment. Different investigators stress the efficacy of the ablation of different areas in the frontal lobes. No further conclusions can be drawn. With the increasing use of drug treatment, interest in frontal operations has declined. The frontal lobes are important to emotion, but how important or in what way is unknown. Arnold (1950) suggests that they are concerned with the sympathetic side of emotion, and (1970a; 1970b) with emotional appraisal (see Chapter 4). But some studies have found (for example Kennard 1955) an increase in emotional responsivity after lobotomy, rather than the more common decrease.

Conclusions

It is as difficult to summarize the results of the more traditional work on the role of the CNS in emotion as it was to summarize evidence from psychophysiological investigations. Much of the work has been reasonably sophisticated on the physiological side, but there is always the problem of the precise locations and ramifications of the lesions or stimulations. Also, no study has produced unarguable evidence in support of localization of function, although most have simply assumed its existence. On the side of the dependent variable, behaviour, the problem has been the usual one of striking a balance between artificiality and the lack of methodological expertise. It is not easy to fault those studies which have taken measures of avoidance learning or CERs, but how relevant are they to emotion as it is commonly conceived? (See Chapter 6 for a discussion of this.) On the other hand, many behavioural measures taken following CNS manipulation have been little more than observational. Can we rely on the observers? Was their reliability checked? Has the investigator given a precise behavioural definition of 'ferocity' or 'pleasure', etc? All too often these questions can only be answered in the negative.

We are left in the position of knowing that various subcortical structures, particularly the hypothalamus and thalamus, and perhaps the brain-stem reticular formation, together with parts of the cortex, the limbic system, and frontal lobes, are all implicated in emotion. But how exactly they are implicated, or what the functional relationships are between these structures, at the moment cannot be said. Often it is even impossible to say that they are necessary to emotion, simply that they are implicated.

Central theories of emotion

The remainder of this chapter will be taken up with a discussion of six physiological theories of emotion that rely at least as much on hypotheses concerning the CNS as the ANS. The first two are the only truly 'cortical' theories of emotion. The second two have been included to give an idea of recent physiological theorizing in emotion. And the last two represent the more traditional, grander approach to theory.

Papez (1937; 1939) and *MacLean* (1949; 1970) are the two major cortical theorists of emotion. Papez can be discussed briefly. Basically, he suggested that emotional expression and emotional experience may be dissociated and that the experiental aspects require cortical mediation. The physiological details of the theory are not worth describing, since they are not supported by empirical data. From this starting point, MacLean suggests that the limbic system in particular integrates emotional experience, although the effector mechanism is probably the hypothalamus. He gives two reasons for this: (1) the limbic system has extensive subcortical connections; (2) it is the one part of the cortex which has visceral representation. This accords with the extensive olfactory functions of the limbic system. MacLean argues that olfaction is of prime importance to motivation in lower animals, from food-seeking to obtaining sexual partners. He suggests that although the sense of smell is no longer involved to the same extent in more advanced organisms, their emotional behaviour may be mediated by the same mechanisms.

MacLean regards the hippocampus and amygdala as having especial significance for the subjective side of emotion. However, as was seen above, much recent empirical evidence simply gives the general indication that the cortex has a critical, complex, but ill-defined role to play in emotion. So, unlike Papez, MacLean does not attempt to trace specific cortical pathways for emotion to follow. All the structures in the limbic system seem in some way to be involved in emotion, but *no* specific mechanisms have been found which mediate particular emotional patterns.

Melzack and Casey's (1970) recent view of emotion rests on the assumption that emotion is so complex as to be virtually inseparable from any other aspects of behaviour. To this extent, rather than providing a theory of emotion, they do away with the necessity for one.

Melzack and Casey are primarily interested in an analysis of pain. They use this to establish some principles which they suggest may account for the main characteristics of emotion. They illustrate their three-part analysis with the example of tickling young children. (1) There is a *sensory input* which involves emotion—for tickling this is light, repetitive touching. (2) Emotion is always characterized by a high level of *arousal* which in itself has an affective tone and is partially dependent on stimulus intensity. To extend the example, at high intensity tickling becomes unpleasurable and provokes escape reactions. (3) There are *central mediating processes* (perhaps similar to Arnold's appraisals) which are in fact our experience and imagination. The tickle becomes unpleasant if delivered by a scowling stranger.

Although Melzack and Casey regard emotion as complex, their theory is so broad as to either imply that emotion is simple, or to suggest that it is indistinguishable from nonemotion—most behaviour must have as its components input, arousal, and central components. To this extent, Melzack and Casey's theory is inadequate. It is based on a mixture of concepts drawn from physiological and phenomenological approaches. It is very difficult to find a firm empirical foundation for concepts such as arousal and central mediating processes. It is hard, if not impossible, to use this theory to make any concrete predictions.

Stanley-Jones (1970) also provides an example of a recent physiologically based theory of emotion, but one which is even more woolly than Melzack and Casey's. He regards love and hate as the two primary emotions. Physiologically, he imagines these to be rooted in lust and rage, which can be used to describe the two primitive emotional reactions of decerebrate animals. Stanley-Jones believes that such animals can express but not feel. Clearly, this can never be more than a belief.

He defines rage as the physiological response of a decerebrate animal, or of a man 'in the solitude of his own company'. It is primarily sympathetic and is characterized by blind, immediate, transient reactions with no cortical control. Its bodily expressions are muscular and cardiovascular, and the affective component, if it occurs, is hate. If rage becomes directed outwards, then it is termed aggression. Lust, on the other hand, Stanley-Jones views as a state which results from decerebration which is followed by a reduction to spinality. The limbs become rigid and the genitals engorged. A similar pattern is seen in spinal man. There is no apparent affective component and it is parasympathetically controlled.

Having established this background, Stanley-Jones turns to what for him is the crux of the emotions, the hypothalamus. He regards the crucial function of the hypothalamus as its homeostatic control over behaviour. Connections of the SNS to the posterior hypothalamus and the PNS to the anterior allow the possibility of balanced controls such as glucostasis, thermostasis, and emotional homeostasis. Stanley-Jones argues that the biological origins of the human emotions of love and hate are to be found in the fundamental mammalian defences against heat and cold. This may be described as a *thermostatic* theory of emotion. He suggests that the autonomic centres in the hypothalamus for the SNS and PNS seem to be almost identical to those for temperature control. Also, *both* are reversed in cold-blooded animals, and finally, in some cold-blooded animals, thermostasis is the main control of behaviour. This theory accounts for the immediacy of our emotions—thermal responses could not occur at long range but can only be of use immediately, although of course they could become conditioned.

Up to this point, Stanley-Jones' theory is no worse than many others. Although somewhat speculative at times, it has reasonably firm empirical roots. Hereafter, however, it strays in unjustifiable directions. To take two examples, consider Stanley-Jones' ideas on guilt and will. He regards guilt as expressed by blushing, parasympathetic vasodilation, and sees it as mutually exclusive with lust; there are many obvious sexual examples. When we feel guilty he suggests that parasympathetic lust is being blocked by sympathetic fear. He supports this by pointing out that this 'ethical' sense of guilt is lacking in mania and after leucotomy, but is prominent in psychotic depression. Finally, and without going into more detail, it is perhaps best to allow Stanley-Jones to speak for himself about the will. It is difficult to see what such a comment can do for the physiology of emotion or indeed for the study of emotion in general.

'It has long been known that the principal determinant of human behaviour is emotion, that when the emotions and the intellect are in competition for control of the will, it is usually the emotions that win'.

(1970!)

Gellhorn. Over many years, Gellhorn has made a huge contribution to our knowledge of the physiological bases of emotion. His work, however, both in research and theory, seems to have often been passed over by other investigators. Examples may be seen in Gellhorn (1964), Gellhorn and Loufbourrow (1963), and more particularly and more recently in Gellhorn (1968). The latter gives a good introduction to his erudite approach to the subject and provides a statement of his general theory.

Gellhorn suggests that the basis of emotion is the integration of somatic and autonomic activities, as modified by neurohumours (chemicals liberated at the nerve endings) and hormones, into what he terms ergotropic and trophotropic activities. The former are work-directed and the latter rest-directed. When one of the two systems becomes excited the other is correspondingly diminished, this balance being independent of the stimuli which bring it about. Gellhorn cites the example of the inhalation of carbon dioxide. This increases ergotropic excitability and raises the spindle threshold in the caudate nucleus. This spindle is a series of nervous potentials lasting for a few seconds, and is regarded as a good indicator of trophotropic reactivity. A similar effect is seen if the ergotropic part of the hypothalamus is increased in excitability (for example by electrical stimulation). On the other hand, the spindle threshold in the caudate nucleus drops if the organism receives barbiturates, chlorpromazine or a lesion in the posterior hypothalamus. Also, Gellhorn suggests that both ergotropic and trophotropic effects can be brought about by manipulations of the thalamic reticular system, septum, anterior hypothalamus, and medulla—the continuous balance between the two supposedly reflecting emotional reactivity.

Gellhorn evaluates any work on the physiology of emotion in terms of his balance theory. In support he quotes well-established facts; for example, stimulation of the posterior hypothalamus produces rage, whereas lesions lead to somnolence. Or, trophotropic emotion is aroused through stimulation of the touch receptors, the typical picture being a slowing of heart rate, synchronous EEG, pupillary constriction, and a tendency to sleep. He also regards broader aspects of emotion, like mood, as dependent on the ergotropic–trophotropic balance. For example, electroconvulsive therapy, like amphetamines, lifts ergotropic activity and mood, whereas the tranquillizers depress mood and diminish ergotropic hypothalamic activity (Gellhorn and Loufbourrow 1963).

Other aspects of Gellhorn's theory of emotion are very broad. He regards emotional arousal and the modification of the ergotropic–trophotropic balance as coming about through afferent impulses, internal environmental changes which act on visceral receptors or the brain stem, and by direct stimulation of the brain stem, the limbic system, and some subcortical structures. All the relevant physiological mechanisms are in with a fighting chance, including the possibility that similar effects may be brought about by hormonal change. For example, epinephrine acts on the posterior hypothalamus and increases central and peripheral ergotropic discharge. Gellhorn suggests, in fact, that when emotions are aroused, the ergotropic–trophotropic balance must be altered by *both* neurogenic and hormonal processes.

Gellhorn also argues that there is an increasing cognitive involvement in human emotion, implying that a greater part is being played by the neocortex. To this point Gellhorn's theory is reasonably in accord with the facts, but from here onwards it becomes more difficult to accept. He starts by recouching Schachter's results (see Chapter 4) in his own terms. He regards the euphoria and anger produced in Schachter's subjects after they had been injected with epinephrine and experienced the appropriate environmental conditions as reflecting increased sympathetic activity, increased cortical arousal, and, in general, increased ergotropic excitation. Gellhorn extends this by introducing the idea of 'tuning'. He suggests that the hypothalamic ergotropic—trophotropic balance controls the 'group-character' of the emotion, but within this the specific emotion results from cognitive factors and experience. For example, he argues that if we consciously relax then we cannot feel rage. So, we can be ergotropically or trophotropically 'tuned', thereby vastly increasing the likelihood of these types of response. Clearly Gellhorn has moved far into speculative realms; a brief quotation will demonstrate how far:

'. . . facilitation of the activity of sensory projection and association areas of the neocortex as the result of emotion plays a part in man's highest intellectual achievements and in the enrichments of his emotional life'.

(Gellhorn 1968)

However, this type of statement does have relevance to recent ideas on the control of emotion (see Chapters 9 and 10).

Arnold's theory of emotion depends in equal part on physiological speculation and on the cognitive concept of appraisal. Appraisal is discussed in detail in Chapter 4. Here it is mainly the physiological side of her arguments that will be covered. At the outset it should be mentioned that Arnold's theory, although quite complex physiologically, is lacking in empirical support and, like many other physiological theories of emotion, loses power in becoming too speculative.

Arnold's most recent (1970a; 1970b) formulation begins with MacLean's (1970) notion that there are three 'levels' of brain function—reptilian, old mammalian, and new mammalian, and Lindsley's (1970) idea that emotional arousal is reflected in the cortex, diencephalon, and brain stem. Arnold queries how these levels or areas might be related. To answer this, she suggests that we need identification of '. . . the relays that mediate the sequence of psychological activities from perception to emotion and action . . .'.

Although Arnold's theory is physiological, she clearly states that any physiologizing can only occur after a phenomenological analysis. This will allow us to find out what goes on psychologically in emotion, after which possible neural pathways can be traced. She suggests that there are definite activation patterns for particular psychological activities, rather than any sort of action *en masse,* an idea straightforwardly based on a belief in localization of function within the CNS.

Arnold (1960) defines emotion as a 'felt tendency towards something appraised as good (and liked) or away from something bad (or disliked)'. She regards the limbic system as controlling liking and disliking (i.e. cognitive appraisal) and the hippocampus as the spur to recall of memory and impulse to action. In particular, she suggests that affective recall occurs via a neural pathway from the cingulum, hippocampus, postcommisural fornix, and anterior thalamic nuclei, back to the limbic system. Thus the limbic system gives us our experience of liking and disliking both as new appraisals and as remembered affective attitudes. She believes the hippocampus to initiate the emotion in its total form; any pattern associated with a particular emotion (appraisal and affective memory) must be organized before arriving at the motor cortex and being translated to movement. Arnold maintains that action patterns begin at the cerebellum and are relayed to the frontal lobes. When we feel a complete bodily urge to action, then we experience the emotion as an action tendency. Arnold suggests that this experience is mediated by the premotor area in the frontal lobe and that the frontal lobe, in turn, serves motor functions in general. So, any felt urge to action becomes overt action. Arnold proposes that the main function of the cerebellum is that of organization and coordination. Impulses arrive from the hippocampus and are made ready for action—action which includes all the more overt aspects of emotion, namely, movement, facial and bodily expression, and autonomic change.

In distinguishing between emotional and nonemotional behaviour, Arnold argues that there are four main patterns of action. (1) Actions resulting from hormonal change; these lead to an approach towards various 'good' objects and are basically instinctual. (2) Emotional action patterns; these arise from positive or negative evaluations of either perceived or imagined objects and lead both to action and emotion. (3) Action patterns based on feeling, which result from evaluations of something which may be beneficial or harmful 'for our functioning'. (4) Deliberate action.

Arnold's instinctive and deliberate actions are of little relevance here; also, she makes little neurophysiological distinction between emotional and feeling action patterns. In analysing particular action patterns, Arnold focuses exclusively on fear and anger. She simply traces neural circuits which could possibly account for behaviours such as anger, fear, rage, escape, and avoidance. Thus, for example, she suggests that rage is mediated via impulses from the limbic system to the hippocampus, cerebellum, thalamus, hypothalamus, caudate nucleus, and frontal lobe. Similarly, she argues that the desire for flight appears to be mediated by impulses from the hippocampus through the lateral ventral thalamic nucleus to the premotor and motor areas and becomes registered in the prefrontal cortex via the anterior and medial ventral nuclei.

Since Arnold engages in even more intricate physiologizing (it is presented here only in brief outline) than most other theorists, it is worth making some discussion of the empirical evidence which bears on her ideas. Grossman (1967) and Izard (1972) suggest that there is not much supporting evidence, and Arnold (1970) herself realizes that hers is a difficult theory to test experimentally. For example, she regards emotion as not only inclusive of a tendency to behave in a particular way but as also incorporating many physiological and hormonal changes. So, cortical stimulation would not be expected to produce any recognizable emotional expression—although subcortical stimulation sometimes has. Also, for example, although Olds' (1955; 1958) studies show 'reward' and 'punishment' effects from stimulating electrodes placed in the limbic system, as we have seen, the overall evidence from stimulation and ablation studies is ambiguous.

In attempting to account for the confusing results from studies of avoidance learning, CER, and emotional reactivity, Arnold's argument becomes tortuous, subjective, and mentalistic. She speaks of hungry animals 'wanting to find food'—making possible an active avoidance response. If sated, they are without the food drive which means that the fear drive is gone and that there is a deficit in avoidance; and so on.

Experiments bearing on the concept of affective memory are more supportive. Arnold (1970) quotes several studies in which the basic technique involved training rats in successive discrimination tasks in each of the sensory modalities, and also in some passive avoidance. Electrolytic lesions were made either before or after learning in the proposed affective memory circuit to see which lesions in which areas produce what impairments. These studies support the ideas that, for example, the anterior cingulate gyrus mediates the appraisal of head movements, the posterior insula mediates taste appraisal, and so on.

Arnold has produced an odd mixture of good theory and experimentation with seemingly unnecessary subjective aspects to it, especially when it comes to interpretation and evaluation. She makes an honest attempt to combine all of the bodily structures and functions which have been shown to be concerned with emotion. On the other hand, her main contribution on the theoretical side is perhaps her general notion of excitation (1950). She regards the cortex as having excitatory control over emotion. The cortex supposedly focuses on any stimulus, appraising a situation by modifying sensory input to fit in with our expectations. Emotional expression and peripheral changes stem from emotional impulses going from the cortex to the hypothalamus or thalamus. Autonomic changes are then reported back to the cortex, where reappraisals are made.

CONCLUSIONS

The search for the physiological substrates of emotion has produced much research and theory. Inevitably, some of this has been sophisticated, useful, and suggestive and some has been naive, poorly conceived, and on occasion, even obstructive. Unfortunately, however, the better work is inconclusive. The aims of this approach to emotion are straightforward—to further our understanding by studying the relationship between behavioural and physiological responses. For example, it was reasonable to expect that there might be some peripheral response patterning in the different emotions. It is disappointing that such little psychophysiological evidence (except for Ax, Schachter, and Lacey) has been found to support this idea. We can say very little more than that the viscera are necessary to emotion. Whether this is an accurate assessment of reality or whether it is grounded in inadequate conceptualization and/or measurement remains to be seen. However, work on the psychology of emotion has also been important in furthering our understanding of psychosomatic disorder.

The lack of firm, detailed, empirical facts also characterizes the more traditional physiological approach to emotion. We can be certain that the brain stem, the thalamus and hypothalamus, the limbic system, and, to an extent, the neocortex are implicated in emotion. We can also say that endocrine changes are important and that the periphery has a part to play and that there are under-lying neurochemical changes. However, we cannot say how these possible mechanisms interact. We cannot even assign a relative importance to peripheral and central mechanisms, the ANS or the CNS. We cannot be sure that the idea of localization of function on which most of the CNS investigations are based is valid. Nowadays, there are few psychologists who would argue for a mass action concept of brain function. On the other hand, those who work from the localization standpoint use relatively crude techniques; they can rarely be sure of the precise relationship between structure and function.

Given the confusing mass of empirical data which have come from physiological studies of emotion, it is perhaps hardly surprising that the physiologically oriented theories are of little help. Often, they include far too high a ratio of physiological speculation to empirical fact. This enables them to be twisted in any way and, of course, lowers their straightforward predictive power. Or they are sometimes too narrow, attempting to generalize from a consideration of but one aspect of emotion. The best physiological theories of emotion are probably Arnold's and Gellhorn's; they at least aim at an overall unification. However, Arnold's physiological speculations are not well supported by the facts and her cognitive ideas are difficult to test. Gellhorn's theory orders the facts consistently, but eventually becomes speculative in ways which are difficult to test.

It may be that this somewhat depressing picture has emerged because enthusiasm for the efficacy of the physiological approach to the study of emotion has run ahead of calmly thought out research and theory. It is easy to think that physiological investigations could do much to simplify and systematize our understanding of a field of this complexity. However, within psychology in general this reductionist approach has not been especially noteworthy in the quantity and quality of any solutions it has provided. It is instructive that the recent neurochemical work on emotion seems to be following the same course. It is interesting and looks hopeful, but at the moment is not producing obvious solutions to any of the long-standing problems. They may simply have been reduced to yet another level of analysis. It may be that there is more hope for our future understanding of emotion at the behavioural level than may come from any sub-behavioural analysis. Also, in the last few years it has become increasingly apparent that cognitive functions, facial and postural expression, and even subjective analysis must be taken into account to give a reasonable picture of emotion. To end this chapter on a brighter note, there are some very promising current physiological developments. For example, Lacey's work on individual differences in psychophysiological reactivity stands out, as do research techniques such as Delgado's which reduce the artificiality of physiologically based investigations. Finally, the type of careful work in the CIBA symposium (1972) represents the best there is on the detailed role of precise physiological mechanisms in emotion.

Perhaps the most important final point to bear in mind is that whatever frontiers are passed in research into the physiology of emotion, a complete analysis of the subject cannot be made via physiology alone. That there are important physiological concomitants of emotion (as expressed and experienced) is without doubt, but to affirm that emotion is in some way caused by physiological change is as arbitrary as saying that the physiological responses are caused (over evolutionary time) by behavioural change. However, to gain a full understanding of emotion we must analyse the physiological mechanisms involved in it. To do this accurately, there must be more precision on the side of the independent variable (physiological manipulation) and more sophistication and breadth on the side of the dependent variable (behaviour).

4

Cognition and Emotion

There are a number of cognitively based theories of emotion, some of which are supported by interesting research. However, they are not expressed solely in cognitive terms. Instead, they tend to be part cognitive, part physiological. For this reason some of the work and ideas which are elaborated in this chapter are also mentioned elsewhere in the book, but from a different viewpoint.

Those who have stressed cognitive (phenomenological) aspects of emotion have usually taken one of three starting points. (1) They have regarded the fundamental problem as involving a study of whatever cues—either internal or external—allow us to identify and name our emotional states. Theories (for example Schachter's) which have developed on this basis have been less complex and less far-reaching than others within the field. On the other hand, some of the research which they have inspired is of the most fascinating to be found anywhere in the study of emotion. (2) They have assumed that cognitions cause physiological and behavioural change. Therefore we must study the one to gain knowledge of the others. This proposition typifies the 'appraisal' theorists (for example Arnold, Lazarus) whose ideas, although resting on rather shaky empirical foundations, are widely quoted. (3) They have equated emotions with motives and considered both within a cognitive framework (for example Leeper). These are amongst the most speculative theories of emotion and have generated little research.

Finally, there are two recent and very profound theories (those of Izard 1972 and Mandler 1976) which look at emotion in very broad perspective and give an integral place to cognition and subjective experience in their accounts.

INTERNAL AND EXTERNAL CUES IN EMOTION

Schachter (1964; 1965; 1970; 1972) is one of the main exponents of the view that we must study cognitions if we are to gain any understanding of our own emotional states. He drew the impetus for his work from the apparent *lack* of physiological response patterning between the emotions. As was seen in Chapter 3, only Ax (1953) and Schachter (1957) himself had produced any positive support for this idea. And each of these studies merely demonstrated a difference of activation in fear and anger. Also, after several months of testing, even Wolf and Wolff's (1947) man with a gastric fistula had simply shown but two visceral response patterns.

Schachter argues that in any emotion there is a diffuse sympathetic discharge; this becomes named and identified through the situation in which it occurs and through the individual's perceptions of this situation. In other words, the cognition guides the arousal.

In the usual, everyday circumstances, Schachter believes that cognitions and arousal are highly interrelated, one leading to the other, and *vice versa*. Sometimes, however, they are independent. This is exemplified by Maranon (1924—reported by Cantril and Hunt 1932 and Landis and Hunt 1932). He injected 210 patients with epinephrine, which is sympathetic-like in its effects, and recorded their introspections. Seventy-one per cent reported only physical effects and 29 per cent reported in terms of emotion, but the labels which they applied to their feelings were the 'as if' kind. They said they felt 'as if' they were afraid. Maranon could only produce 'genuine' emotional reactions in these people by providing them with appropriate cognitions, by talking of their dead parents for example. Schachter suggests that the 71 per cent who did not show this effect in Maranon's study in fact had a perfectly appropriate cognition to explain their altered state—the injection.

This point led Schachter on to the question which guided much of his subsequent research: what would be the result of a state induced by a *covert* (nonexplicable) injection of epinephrine? Schachter (1959) suggests that such a state would bring about the arousal of evaluative needs, which lead to feelings being labelled from whatever can be perceived of the immediate situation. This argument results in three propositions. (1) If we are in a physiologically aroused state for which there is no obvious explanation, then we will label it according to whatever cognitions are available to us. So the same state could be labelled in many different ways. (2) If we are in a physiologically aroused state for which there is an obvious explanation, we are unlikely to use any alternative possible explanations to label it. (3) With the same cognitive condition we would behave emotionally only to the extent to which we are physiologically aroused. That is, there must be physiological arousal for emotion to occur.

With these three propositions, Schachter states his case for the intricate relationship between cognitive and physiological variables in emotion, both of which he sees as being necessary for the occurrence of appropriately labelled emotional behaviour. Much of his work involves ingenious tests of these ideas.

Schachter's basic studies

The experimental test of the three propositions mentioned above requires: (1) the manipulation of physiological arousal; (2) the manipulation of the extent to which a subject has an appropriate explanation of his state; and (3) the creation of situations which lead to possible explanatory cognitions. The first study produced to these ends, and that which therefore set the procedural conditions for later studies, was that of Schachter and Singer (1962). Subjects were led to believe that the experimenters were interested in the effects of Suproxin (a supposed vitamin compound) on vision. They were persuaded to agree to an injection of this. In fact, they were either injected with epinephrine or a saline placebo. As mentioned above, epinephrine mimics sympathetic discharge in its effects. Systolic blood pressure rises, as do heart rate, respiration, and levels of blood sugar and lactic acid. Cutaneous blood flow is decreased. Subjectively, these effects are experienced as palpitations, tremors, flushing, faster breathing, and so on. In the dosage used, these effects lasted for a maximum of 20 minutes.

Just before the injections were given, subjects also received one of three explanations of the effects, differing in appropriateness. (1) *Epinephrine informed.* The gist of this explanation was that Suproxin sometimes has side effects which may last up to 20 minutes. Subjects were actually given a description of the subjective effects of epinephrine. This was all endorsed by the doctor as he was giving them the injections. (2) *Epinephrine ignorant.* Here, the experimenters said nothing. The doctor, whilst giving the injections, said that they were mild and harmless and would have no side effects. (3) *Epinephrine misinformed.* Both the experimenters and the doctor mentioned possible side effects, but these were described as numb feet, body itches, and headaches. These are impossible as effects of epinephrine. A fourth control group were injected with the placebo and otherwise received the same treatment as the epinephrine ignorant group.

The second independent variable involved the social manipulation of two emotional states. (1) *Euphoria.* Immediately after the injection, the experimenter took the subject into a room which contained an experimental stooge, supposedly another subject. The naive subject was told that he should wait in the room for 20 minutes to allow the Suproxin to become absorbed, then the vision tests would be run. The room was in a mess, for which the experimenter apologized and left. The stooge behaved in a friendly and extroverted way, engaging in a carefully predetermined sequence of activities: playing basketball with waste paper, flying paper aeroplanes, making a slingshot, using a hula hoop. The subject's reactions were observed through a one-way mirror. (2) *Anger.* A similar initial procedure was followed as for the euphoria condition, except that both the subject and the stooge were given questionnaires to complete. These were designed such that the questions gradually became more personal and insulting. The stooge paced his answers with the subject's and at predetermined intervals made standard comments. These progressed from innocence to anger and culminated in the questionnaire being torn up and the stooge walking out. The epinephrine misinformed group was not run in this condition as it was decided that one such control group was enough.

Two measures were taken. The first was simple observation aimed at evaluating the extent to which the subject behaved like the stooge. The second involved a self-report questionnaire; this contained many questions, hidden amongst which were the two crucial ones. How irritated, angry or annoyed would you say you feel at present? How good or happy would you say you feel at present? There was a five-point scale for each question.

Schachter and Singer's results showed that subjects were significantly more euphoric when they had no explanation of their bodily states. Differences between the epinephrine informed and misinformed groups showed this not to be artificial; the epinephrine informed group was distinct from the other two, which were similar to one another. The placebo group was less euphoric than either the epinephrine misinformed or the epinephrine ignorant, but more so than the epinephrine informed; this, however, was not a significant result. Much the same pattern was found with both the observations and questionnaires. In the anger conditions, the epinephrine ignorant subjects were much angrier than the epinephrine informed, and the placebo subjects were midway.

Except for the awkwardness of the placebo groups, the results conformed to the predictions. Schachter and Singer provided an explanation for the placebo group results in terms of the *injection* itself, by arguing that this must have given a reasonable explanatory cognition to the subjects. (Ideally, of course, they would have liked to produce the physiological state without the injection.) Thus, the fact of having the injection would itself be likely to reduce its effects. From their self-reports it seems that some subjects did in fact explain their feelings in this way, so becoming 'self-informed'. With these subjects removed from the analysis, the differences between the placebo groups and the relevant experimental groups became highly significant. Schachter and Singer continued the argument concerning the placebo groups by pointing out that the injection of placebo does not *prevent* sympathetic activity, even though it might not produce it directly. Sympathetic activity might have come about due to the extraordinary experimental conditions. By good chance, Schachter and Singer took a pulse-rate measure for all subjects before and after the experimental manipulations. Those placebo subjects whose pulse rate rose from before to after could be regarded as showing increased activation. *Post hoc* analysis showed these subjects to be more euphoric and more angry than nonaroused placebo subjects.

Schachter and Singer concluded from these results that they had managed to manipulate, via his cognitions, the feelings of someone physiologically aroused but with no explanation for his arousal. Also, they suggested that if such a person had a satisfactory explanation for his feelings, then he would not use any alternative explanations that might be available to him. And, finally, with constant cognitive circumstances an individual will only react if he is aroused. Clearly, these conclusions were somewhat tentative due to the relatively *post hoc* and subjective analyses which were made.

Schachter and Wheeler (1962) took up the point that the differences between the epinephrine and placebo groups had been somewhat obscured. They compared subjects injected with epinephrine with others who were incapable of self-activating their SNS since they had been injected with an autonomic blocking agent. Again, the pretence at a vitamin study was made. Subjects were told that they would receive an injection of Suproxin, a substance high in vitamin C content, after which effects on their vision would be observed by presenting them with black/white stimulation—a film. There were three main groups, injected with: epinephrine, a placebo, or chlorpromazine (a sympathetic depressant, or tranquillizer). It was predicted that when watching a comic film the epinephrine subjects would show more amusement than the placebos, who in turn would be more amused than those injected with chlorpromazine.

Three subjects, one from each group, simultaneously watched the film each time it was shown; they were unable to see one another. Every 10 seconds each subject was observed by two independent observers ignorant of the subject's experimental group. They used five categories to record behaviour: (1) natural, (2) smile, (3) grin (smile with teeth showing), (4) laugh, and (5) big laugh. The amount of amusement shown under the three experimental conditions generally confirmed Schachter and Wheeler's predictions. However, there was no overall statistically significant difference between the epinephrine and placebo groups, although these groups were clearly different when just the stronger reactions were analysed (laugh and big laugh).

Further support for Schachter's original formulations comes from two animal studies. Singer (1961) gave rats injections of epinephrine or of a placebo and observed subsequent behaviour in 'frightening' situations. For example, the rats were put in a box and suddenly and simultaneously subjected to a bright flashing light and to the sound of a doorbell and a buzzer. Usual measures were taken of defecation, urination, etc. Singer showed that the fear state was related to sympathetic activity in that the epinephrine rats were more afraid than the controls. This was supported by Latane and Schachter (1962), who demonstrated that rats injected with epinephrine were better able to learn to avoid noxious stimuli than control (placebo) animals.

Schachter's conclusions

Schachter's (1964; 1965; 1970) first and most important, although tentative, general conclusion from this series of studies is that there may indeed be very little physiological differentiation between emotional states. How we label such states may be largely a cognitive matter. He also suggests that his results would be generalizable to *any* internal states for which there would otherwise be no good explanations. This is partially supported by Nowlis' (1965; 1970) somewhat similar studies of mood, and by Valins' (for example 1970) work on the giving of false information about bodily reactions. However, Schachter also maintains that his results do not support an activation theory of emotion. He suggests that aroused subjects are not necessarily emotional. If the determinants of emotion are cognitive to the extent which Schachter believes, then they should be manipulable by factors similar to those which are known to affect opinions and attitudes. This idea gains some support from Wrightsman (1960), who put 'anxious', 'fearful' or 'calm' subjects together in groups and observed their social interactions. Interaction affected emotion in the direction of conformity; also, subjects who were too anxious were rejected by the remainder of the group. Similar support again comes from Nowlis' studies on mood.

Schachter (1964) devotes some time to a consideration of whether or not his 'cognitive' ideas allow one to deal with the limitations of the visceral theory of emotion. He suggests that three of Cannon's criticisms of James' formulations are overcome by his (Schachter's) ideas. (1) If visceral changes typical of strong emotion are produced artificially then the emotion is not produced. This seems reasonable when Maranon's results are considered. However, Schachter's work shows that if a 'cognitive' approach is adopted then conditions can be specified in which an injection will produce an emotional state. (2) The same visceral changes occur in different emotional states. Although this seems to be the case physiologically speaking, Schachter's ideas bypass it, since they suggest that cognitive and situational factors determine the labels applied to any state of physiological arousal. He argues that it may well be that emotions are characterized by high sympathetic arousal with little physiological differentiation. (3) The viscera are insensitive. This, although a relevant criticism of any purely visceral formulation of emotion, is not relevant to the cognitive ideas.

Schachter views Cannon's final two points as being awkward for the cognitive interpretation of emotion as well as for James. Visceral changes are too slow to provide any emotional feeling, and if the viscera are separated from the CNS then emotional behaviour is not altered. Both James' view and Schachter's need visceral arousal as a necessary condition for emotional arousal. Wenger (1950) and Mandler (1962) argue that any emotional behaviour seen in sympathectomized subjects is very well learned, having been acquired long before. This has two implications: that sympathectomized subjects only *act* emotionally, they do not *feel*. Support for this idea comes from Wynne and Solomon (1955), who showed that sympathectomized dogs learned an avoidance response much more slowly than controls; they also extinguished faster than controls. Two dogs sympathectomized after learning behaved like control animals during extinction. This more recent evidence would suggest that Cannon's criticisms of James' analyses are not so cogent as they first appeared to be.

To support these general ideas, Schachter also draws on a study by Hohmann (1962). He divided 25 paraplegics into five groups depending upon where they fell on a dimension of visceral innervation and sensation; the higher up the spinal cord the lesion, the less the sensation. Schachter would predict decreasing emotional behaviour with higher lesions. The subjects were intensively interviewed in an attempt to make comparisons of their remembered reactions to emotionally arousing events both before and after their injuries. Hohmann's data were somewhat clumsy, nevertheless they were fairly clear in showing that the higher the lesion the greater the decrease in emotionality, at least in fear, anger, and sexuality. Subjects described themselves as acting emotionally, but as 'feeling' nothing. This result adds breadth to Maranon's. His subjects described the visceral correlates of emotion (as produced by the epinephrine), but as they had no relevant cognitions, reported that they 'felt' nothing. Hohmann's subjects described appropriate reactions to emotional situations, but with no visceral arousal did not 'feel' emotional.

From considerations of this kind, Schachter concludes that autonomic arousal facilitates the acquisition of emotional behaviour, but if this behaviour is acquired beforehand, autonomic arousal is not necessary for its maintenance.

Also, without autonomic arousal, behaviour which appears as emotional will not be experienced as such.

As a final point in support of his general position, Schachter draws on some imprecise but interesting observations concerning marihuana. He argues that his central idea, namely, that when an individual is physiologically aroused with no explanation for this he will label his state by recourse to the cognitions open to him, suggests the presence of a drive state. He regards this as similar to Festinger's (1954) evaluative need, which pushes or pulls us to label and understand any new feelings. Marihuana is of interest since its physical effects are quite well defined, but the feelings associated with it are not so easy to describe.

Becker (1953) described a sequence which he believes is typically involved in learning to use marihuana for pleasure. The smoker has to learn to label his physiological symptoms as 'high'. The effects themselves are not enough for this; the smoker has to recognize them and connect them with marihuana before he can have the experience. In other words, the new user must *learn* to notice his feelings and that other people label them in certain ways, i.e. he must notice that he is 'high' and that this is pleasant. In passing, it is worth noting that such an idea gains support from Skinner's (1957) argument that we learn to differentiate emotional states through others labelling them for us by observing the environmental stimuli which brought them about.

Criticisms of Schachter's view

Whilst not wishing to detract from the novelty of Schachter's experimental procedures, his analysis of results can certainly be criticized for its *post hoc* nature. More importantly, several criticisms can be levelled at his general theoretical position and the interpretation he makes of his data. Such criticisms have been most concisely put by Izard (1972), Leventhal (1974), and Plutchik and Ax (1967), and what follows is an amalgam of these.

The first and in many ways the most important point is that Schachter has *not* proved that emotion is dependent on sympathetic arousal and cognition. He *has* demonstrated that it is influenced by both, but this could be so whilst it nevertheless remains independent of them. Schachter argues that a person can induce physiological arousal by his cognitions; it is thus that he accounts for the results of his placebo group in the original study. If this is so, then the subjects in the anger and euphoria groups may also have produced arousal in this way. Also, it is possible to say that the subjects injected with epinephrine could have produced their own physiological tranquillization cognitively.

A similar possibility is that subjects injected with epinephrine may simply become more suggestible and hence more likely to imitate behaviour which is occurring around them. Thus they become more euphoric or more angry depending on their experiences. Also, Schachter shows no good evidence for arousal in *all* of his injected subjects. It is widely known that there are large individual differences in reactions to drugs, pulse rate (used by Schachter) not being the least ambiguous measure of this. This point is made particularly by Plutchik and Ax (1967).

Leventhal (1974) sees the problem as one of showing exactly *how* arousal and cognition combine in emotion. Schachter does not, for example, say when or how arousal contributes to particular states of feeling. Schachter's conceptualization of emotion accords cognitions three possible functions in emotional experience. They allow the interpretation of emotional stimuli, the recognition of arousal, and the labelling of emotion.

Leventhal argues that from Lazarus (see later) onward there is much evidence that a person's expectations are important determinants of his emotional state. The more accurate are these expectations then the more likely he is to become emotional. However, there is no good evidence one way or the other on the recognition of emotional arousal, except some of his own studies which Leventhal quotes to support the idea that expressive behaviour intensifies experience of emotion, but only when reactions are spontaneous and involuntary.

Finally, there is the matter of labelling emotion. Here Leventhal suggests that the important question is: do cognitions label arousal and by so doing create subjective feelings? If this is so, then feelings must be learned. However, Leventhal argues against this viewpoint by questioning how a young child can be capable of feeling anything before he knows the label for the feeling, if it is the label which promotes the feeling. The only way in which this is possible is if the situations are similar in meaning to those for which the child already has labels.

In fact, Leventhal turns this argument round and instead suggests that situations become construed as similar because they generate similar feelings. An innate set of feelings generate meaning. This leads to a final position in which cognitions can be viewed as leading to particular reactions of the CNS and to distinctive bodily reactions, the latter being necessary for feeling. Of course, these bodily reactions mainly take the form of facial expression, thus paving the way for the recent emphasis which there has been on the role of facial expression in emotion.

Be this rather involved discussion of subjective experience as it may, it is evident that there are criticisms which should be borne in mind when considering Schachter's work on emotion. Specifically, his data analysis tends to be rather arbitrarily *post hoc*, and although he may be said to have demonstrated that arousal and cognition can influence emotion, he has not proved that they are necessary to it.

Schachter's applied research

To complete this discussion of Schachter's analysis of internal and external cues in emotion, some of his more recent (1972), applied investigations will be described. Schachter and Latane (1964) began this research with a consideration of the implications of Schachter's previous work for the study of criminal behaviour. Briefly, they suggested that given a criminal impulse and the inhibiting conditions which usually surround it, the probability of the crime being committed should be manipulable by altering sympathetic activation. Thus, it should be possible to either encourage or discourage crime with the judicious use of drugs. They undertook two studies as a test of this hypothesis.

Cheating

Schachter and Latane regard cheating as crime in microcosmic form, and argue that it should vary inversely with the fear of being caught. They describe a study by Schachter and Ono in which the physiological component of fear was manipulated. From the subjects' point of view, this was a study first of perception and then of the evaluation of university courses. In the latter part, subjects were told that they would get extra grade points if they did well on the test that they would be given.

Having heard the usual talk about the effects of vitamins (Suproxin) on vision, subjects took, in pill form, chlorpromazine or a placebo. Schachter was thus attempting to reduce fear physiologically. They were given 55 minutes of fairly trivial tests and a questionnaire and were then asked to help out the experimenters by scoring their own test papers. The main test was of multiple-choice items which they were given too little time to complete. Also, some items on the scoring key from which they had to mark were wrong. Clearly, both of these conditions would encourage cheating. The effects of the drugs were measured by pulse rate and questionnaire.

It was found that more subjects who had had chlorpromazine cheated than did those who had had a placebo. This was not a strong effect. It became more powerful when, in his usual but nonetheless meaningful inquest, Schachter argued that chlorpromazine taken orally has weak effects. He then analysed data from only those subjects whose completed questionnaires and records of pulse rates showed then to have been affected by the drug. The relationship then became statistically significant.

Psychopathy

Schachter and Latane (1964) go on to distinguish two types of crime: (1) where motivation or passion becomes unbearably high, and (2) where fear is weak. They suggest that if the second condition becomes chronic, psychopathy results. Psychiatrists usually describe psychopaths as emotionally flat, and Lykken (1957) found by questionnaire that they were relatively anxiety-free. He also showed that they were almost incapable of learning an avoidance response, which is often thought to be based on fear.

Schachter and Latane had their subjects selected by prison authorities using Lykken's procedures, including his anxiety scale—on which psychopaths should score very low. The selection procedures were rigorous. In the experimental situation, subjects faced an arrangement of lights and switches which represented a 20-choice point mental maze, a correct switch leading to the next choice, and so on. All errors were accumulated on a visible counter; some of these were punished with shock, which, however, could be avoided by the appropriate selection of switches. Epinephrine or placebo was injected just before the experimental run, and pulse, heart rate, and questionnaire measures were taken All subjects were given a variation on the usual pre-experimental talk but were told to expect no side effects from their hormone (Suproxin) injection.

Results comparing normals and psychopaths showed them to learn the positive maze tasks at the same rate. Also, this measure did not distinguish between epinephrine and placebo groups. However, normal subjects steadily learned to avoid shock, psychopaths did not. Avoidance seems to be mediated by fear, which is not present in psychopaths—a replication of Lykken's result. On the other hand, after epinephrine injections psychopaths learned the avoidance task very well, in comparison with normals. There was also a marked relationship between the degree of psychopathy and the post-epinephrine avoidance learning.

The obvious explanation of these results is that psychopaths are less sympathetically responsive, the implication being that they have a different physiological system from nonpsychopaths. But this was not supported by the pulse-rate data. Further analysis showed that the greater the psychopathy the higher the pulse rate. Valins (1963) showed this to be due to *greater* autonomic reactivity in the psychopath, a result supported by Landis (1932) on delinquents and Jones (1950) on adolescents. Schachter and Latane also make the point that the best predictor of avoidance learning in their study was whether or not the subject was sensitive to epinephrine. They also argue that psychopaths are more sensitive to epinephrine and that epinephrine sensitives should tend to behave psychopathically.

In discussing their results, Schachter and Latane conclude that a high autonomic reactivity characterizes both those that are high in anxiety (cf. Duffy 1962) and those that are low. Schachter's other studies show that cognitive and situational factors influence whether a given physiological state will be labelled as an emotion. Hence, the psychopath, although ultra-sensitive autonomically, also reacts to stimuli to which others would not. For him, little stands out from his environment. It may be that he has not learned to apply emotional labels to his states of arousal. On the other hand, the anxiety neurotic *constantly* interprets his world in emotional terms and gives cognitive explanations of what is occurring. Returning to the original idea of two types of crime, the psychopath would be expected to commit the 'cool' unemotional crimes, the 'normal' the passionful ones.

Valins (1970) interprets Schachter and Latane's results somewhat differently. His first suggestion is that the psychopath may simply not perceive his own bodily changes; there is no evidence to support this. Alternatively, he maintains that the psychopath may experience and perceive his bodily changes but nevertheless ignore them; not use them to appraise an emotional situation. In support of this interpretation, Valins quotes one of his own studies (1967a) in which psychopaths were chosen by questionnaire and subjected to his usual false heart rate, nude picture, procedure (see below). They were not much affected. Also, Stern and Kaplan (1967) gave subjects the feedback on their GSR and asked them to produce decreases in their own skin resistance. They found a significant correlation between GSR reactions and scores on Lykken's (1957) psychopathy scale. Psychopath-like subjects could not produce GSR changes, although their usual GSR responding was normal.

Obesity

The most recent extensions of Schachter's work are in a series of studies on obesity. Schachter (1967) found that the labelling of internal cues of hunger seems to be important in determining obesity. He suggests that the eating habits of the obese are relatively independent of bodily changes from hunger. This is supported, for example, by Schachter *et al.* (1968), who set up an experiment that from the subjects' viewpoint was concerned with the interaction between food and taste. Normal and obese subjects were required to miss a meal and were then given either beef sandwiches or no food at all. After this they had to rate many different types of biscuit on various measures of taste. During these ratings they had electrodes attached to their ankles. Some were given low shocks through the electrodes, others were given higher shocks. Before eating the biscuits they completed short anxiety questionnaires. Normal subjects ate more when calm than when frightened and more when they had been deprived of food than when they were sated. Obese subjects ate the same amount under all conditions.

This result gains generality from three further studies. Schachter and Gross (1968) showed the eating of obese subjects to be dependent on the passage of time; if they believed it to be later than it actually was since their last meal, they would eat more. Nisbett (1968) found that underweight subjects were highly responsive to internal, visceral cues of deprivation but not very responsive to external, food-related cues of taste. The picture was reversed for the obese. Finally Goldman *et al.* (1968) carried out three confirmatory field studies. They found that fat Jews were more likely to fast on Yom Kippur than those of normal weight; that fat students were more intolerant of dormitory food than normal weight students; and that fat fliers more easily adjust to time-zone changes than normal weight fliers. Schachter's general point is that the obese are cued far more to the external environment than to internal cues. In this they differ markedly from persons of normal weight. This hyperreactivity to external cues provides most of their reactions, and is not simply restricted to their behaviour at mealtimes or in the presence of food.

Schachter has successfully broadened his analysis of emotion, producing a clear link between the reactions of psychopaths and the obese. However, as Valins (1970) points out, there are still many unanswered questions. For example, is responsiveness to bodily change an important dimension of emotion in its own right? And/or does an individual have many independent responsivities to different internal states? And finally, just *how* are cognition and arousal related to emotion?

Veridicality and bodily change

Breadth is added to the analysis of internal and external cues in emotion by investigations of what is termed veridicality. Valins (e.g. 1970), who gave the impetus to this field, devised a general research strategy based on a very similar proposition to that of Schachter. He suggests that when studying the relationship between bodily change and emotional behaviour, any effects due to the subjects' perception of the changes should be separated from effects based on the changes themselves; they may be reasonably independent. Valins divides work in this field into two broad categories: (1) the general cognitive/physiological approach, and (2) the approach which is concerned with the modification of established emotional behaviour. Within these categories, he subdivides the research into that which deals with (1) veridical bodily perceptions, and (2) nonveridical bodily perceptions. The latter division will form the basis of the discussion which follows.

Veridical perceptions

The 'veridical' approach is best exemplified by Schachter's work. Valins views this as dependent on the idea that we try to understand and label any unusual bodily symptoms that we may experience. If we latch on to certain stimuli in our explanations then emotional behaviour will result. Valins argues that although Schachter and Singer (1962) and Schachter and Wheeler (1962) provide reasonable experimental support for this idea, they leave at least two possible criticisms unanswered: (1) their results may be specific to artificial and extreme autonomic arousal; (2) they make no suggestion as to how a cognition about an external emotional stimulus becomes emotional behaviour. These problems are partially solved by Nisbett and Schachter (1966), who gave their subjects painful electric shocks. One group believed the shock-induced sensations to be the effects of a placebo capsule which they had taken. Another group attributed their sensations to the shock itself, since as far as they were told their placebo capsule had different 'side effects'. Subjects in the first group thought that the shocks were less painful and withstood more of them than those in the second group. Thus, subjective and behavioural reactions to shock were affected by the perception and labelling of artificially induced bodily sensations. This result clearly broadens Schachter's original results and also suggests the possibility that an emotional stimulus becomes reevaluated (Lazarus' reappraisal? see later). It is this reevaluation which perhaps leads the cognition to affect the emotional behaviour.

Other work on the manipulation of veridical bodily perceptions has already been discussed. The best example comes from Schachter and Latane (1964), who were interested in the modification of established emotional behaviour in the psychopath. This was achieved by the external manipulation of bodily perceptions and labelling.

Nonveridical perceptions

Valins' own work has usually involved deceiving subjects about their bodily reactions and observing the effects of this on their subjective responses to emotional stimuli. Subjects have been led to believe that their heart rates are being recorded on somewhat archaic equipment; equipment that is so old and crude as to be audible. They are therefore instructed to ignore the sounds from the equipment and simply to look at some slides that they will be shown. In fact, the subjects hear prerecorded heart beats. The presentation of emotional stimuli is carefully timed so that the experimenter can control the subject's perception (audition) of the apparent size of his reaction to them.

Valins (1966) showed subjects slides of female nudes. One group 'heard' their heart beats increase from 72 to 90 per minute (bpm) when viewing five of the slides, but heard no change when viewing another five. A second group 'heard' their heart beats decrease (from 66 to 48 bpm) to five of the slides but not to the other five. Two control groups experienced the same conditions except that they knew that the sounds were recorded. All subjects rated the attractiveness of each nude, chose copies of five of the slides as a reward, and in a disguised interview one month later again ranked the attractiveness of the nudes. Results showed that nudes to which subjects had heard their heart rate change were liked more than others; this was independent of the direction of the change. No consistent preferences were shown by the control groups.

In general, this again points to our apparent need to account for our own bodily changes in some meaningful way. In Valins' *post hoc* interpretations he points out that other than their apparent change in heart rate, from the subjects viewpoint all other stimuli in the experimental situation were nudes. They could hardly do otherwise than focus their attention on these nudes, and as they (the nudes) were all attractive had little choice but to analyse their apparent sensations in the way they did. The interviews carried out afterwards suggested that to try to explain what their hearts were telling them, subjects looked more closely at those in the presence of which they heard their heart rate change. This was supported by Valins (1967a), who had his subjects rate specific features of the nudes which they were shown. They rated particular features as 'nicer' in those nudes to whom they heard their heart rates react. This perhaps points to some process of selective attention, or perhaps, it should be said, to experimenter bias. It is impossible to be sure which from the study.

These results were extended by Valins (1968) in a study which differed from the previous ones in that it contained a debriefing session. Preferences which the subjects had expressed previously were maintained after debriefing. Their heart beats had made them aware of the positive features of particular nudes; these features had been unnoticed before. From such results, Valins emphasizes the cognitive aspects of the perceptions of bodily changes and suggests that this sort of manipulation does not have important physiological consequences. In passing, it is worth noting that under the usual conditions of Valins' experiments, actual heart rates did not change. This is perhaps an unfortunate finding, since it calls into question the extent to which the slides which Valins used had any 'emotional' effects. However, a recent study (Bloemkolb *et al.* 1971), although somewhat naively presented, does add generality to Valins' work. The same basic method of study was followed but slides of positive stimuli other than nudes (attractive food, scenery, etc.) were presented to subjects, as also were slides of negative stimuli (for example wounded people). General results were similar to Valins' and clearly pointed to the possibility that cognitive events can be used to evoke or reduce emotional experience.

As before, the other aspect of nonveridical bodily perceptions comes from studies involving emotional behaviour which is already established. Valins (1970) suggests that Wolpe's (1958) techniques of systematic desensitization for the treatment of anxiety can be construed in these terms. (See Chapter 9 for a discussion of this, and Davison 1968 for a review). The technique is based on the assumption that anxiety depends on ANS response patterns. If these are inhibited by some antagonistic response pattern, then the anxiety will disappear. The patient is generally taught to relax whilst thinking of stimuli at some point within a hierarchy of anxiety-provoking stimuli. Valins makes a cognitive rather than physiological interpretation of this technique, he suggest that the individual may be anxious because he thinks: 'that stimulus has made me react'. Desensitization leads him to think: 'that stimulus no longer makes me react'. It is this which Valins thinks reduces anxiety—a subjective idea which it would seem difficult to test.

In an attempt at an empirical investigation of systematic desensitization, Valins and Ray (1967) instructed subjects so that they thought they were having their heart rates measured in response to (1) slides of snakes and (2) a slide of the word 'shock', followed seven seconds later by a shock to the fingertips. They heard what they believed to be their heart rates increasing to shocks and to shock slides but not to snake slides. Valins and Ray argued that these subjects should approach live snakes more than would control subjects, since they presumably were not affected internally by snakes. Control subjects were put through the same procedure but as usual knew that the heart beats were recordings.

Each subject was then put into a room with a small caged boa constrictor and had to: (a) enter the room and look at the snake, (b) take the cover off the cage and look down, (c) reach his hand in so the wrist was below the cage top, (d) touch the snake once, (e) pick up the snake a few inches, (f) take the snake out for as long as possible. Experimental subjects approached significantly nearer to the snake and significantly more of them completed each of the six stages. This result was repeated with subjects who were selected because they were generally more frightened of snakes. Valins suggests that this result supports a cognitive analysis of emotion by implying that there is no evidence for any physiological substrate to systematic desensitization. However, there would have to be more information concerning actual physiological changes during this study before such a conclusion could be drawn with any confidence.

In a very useful review, Harris and Katkin (1975) both criticize and extend Valins' ideas. They argue that two research approaches are important in this area. (1) The significance of cognitive evaluations of ANS feedback in labelling emotional experience, and (2) the role of *actual* ANS activity and its feedback, ignoring cognition. They point out that the necessary, and rather confused, background to the work is to be found in Schachter and Singer (1962). They see Schachter as bracketing both the Cannon–Bard theory and the James–Lange theory in that he does not view individual emotions as being linked to precise ANS patterns and yet does view ANS arousal as necessary to emotion. Of course, Valins simply argues that all that is necessary is that a person *believes* he perceives his own ANS arousal.

In developing their argument, Harris and Katkin seek to integrate with Valins' work the results of three subsequent social-psychophysiological studies. Goldstein *et al.* (1972) showed that if external stimuli were not strongly emotional then *actual* heart rate was affected by false feedback. However, with strong emotional stimuli, the ANS system seems to be independent of false feedback and subjects' reports of emotionality were related to actual rather than false heart rates.

In a similar vein, Stern *et al.* (1972) demonstrated a significant effect of false feedback on both heart rate and heart-rate change and argued that Valins' effects may have been produced by *actual* physiological changes. Finally, Hirschman (1975) presented *subjects* with very negative emotional stimuli (slides of mutilated bodies) and found that false feedback of increasing heart rate affected the rate of electrodermal responses and tonic electrodermal levels. He also found a relationship between false feedback and the subjective experience of discomfort which was elicited by stimuli associated with the feedback.

Harris and Katkin suggest that these experiments give ambiguous results leading to two different views of the role of the ANS in emotion. First there is that which stems from the James–Lange theory, namely, that ANS arousal is necessary to emotion. Second is the view promulgated by Valins, namely, that the cognitive perception of ANS arousal (rather than the arousal itself) is necessary to emotion. Research has been concerned with actual and with false ANS arousal.

The various studies on true or false feedback of heart rate appear to show that emotion can be indexed either by the attribution of affect (observable behavioural consequences thought to follow emotional experience) or by the self-report of emotional experience. Harris and Katkin point out that false feedback does not allow subjective experience to be analysed and may *not* be concerned with emotion at all.

Harris and Katkin go on to integrate these various findings and two views of emotion by recourse to a classification into primary and secondary emotion, terms they use somewhat differently from the way in which they have been used by others. They describe primary emotion as a state which includes ANS arousal as well as the subjective perception of it. Secondary emotion they see as a state which does not necessarily involve ANS arousal but which may include non-veridical perception of that arousal. This may be produced by situational contexts or, of course, by false laboratory feedback.

So, in secondary emotion there is no visual excitation. It is merely indexed by self-report and observation and is akin to Cannon's 'sham' emotion. It is also possible that arousal is independent of emotion; it is necessary but not sufficient for primary emotion.

Finally, Harris and Katkin argue that the elicitation of secondary emotion depends on a prior association with a primary (or visual) emotional experience. This idea leads to a clarification in the way in which Valins' original studies should be interpreted. In these studies the actual emotion (primary) is confused with the 'as if' emotions (secondary) since, although Valins developed an interesting experimental procedure and some significant results concerning false feedback, it is debatable as to how much they were concerned with emotion at all.

Mood

A final line of research which is related to internal and external cues in emotion involves the study of mood. Since 1953, Nowlis and Nowlis have been making a conceptual and empirical analysis of mood, their results partially endorsing Schachter's view of emotion. Nowlis (1953; 1959; 1963; 1965; 1970) regards mood as a 'multidimensional set of temporary reversible dispositions'. It refers to some constancies in behaviour and experience which endure over some time. Nowlis believes the 'entire' individual to be involved in mood. He also suggests that the determinants of mood are often obscure or inaccessible although its main function is to monitor or control behaviour. Hence, in its breadth, the concept of mood is more or less equal to that of emotion. However, it is discussed here since it also overlaps with emotion. In Nowlis' terms, some moods may be emotional, while others are not. In general, though, he regards emotion as more temporary than mood. When both are involved in some behaviour and experience, he views emotion as the onset and mood as the continuing steady state. In this sense, emotion is seen as more intense and explosive, whereas mood is less intense but more available for inspection. Clearly, Nowlis has a somewhat restricted view of emotion. Further, although he suggests that the determinants of mood are obscure, he also maintains that it can follow from three types of experimental manipulation. (1) Those that bring threat, pain, frustration, reward, etc., which he regards as eliciting emotional responses, and therefore, indirectly, mood. (2) Those that cause persistent intraorganic changes such as illness, shock, fatigue, and brain injury. (3) Persistent environmental stimulation or deprivation.

Basic studies

Nowlis and Nowlis have used one basic procedure throughout most of their analyses of mood. This involves the giving of drugs such as dramamine, benzedrine, and seconal to groups of four men interacting in various laboratory settings. Regularly, over a five-year period, such groups would meet for lunch in the laboratory, where their interactions were observed and recorded and they were given questionnaires and tests. This was repeated three hours later following the administration of drugs (or placebo). During each session, subjects had piles of envelopes labelled by time and containing instructions for tasks, check lists to complete, and capsules to take. There was further study or recreation during the evening and further observations during the following morning.

There are a number of significant points about this general design. (1) Students were used as subjects, because of the apparent reliability with which they would arrive for experimental sessions. (2) Only a few subjects were studied over many occasions in order that they should be maximally relaxed in the experimental situation. (3) Records were made of a wide range of behaviour. (4) Only moderate oral doses of drugs were administered. (5) Double-blind procedures were used throughout.

Of the various measures which they took, Nowlis and Nowlis emphasize the adjective check list (ACL) for self-report of mood. They state that there are 'good' and 'fair' agreements between this and their observational ratings. Also, they suggest that verbal report is the best index of mood since we learn to assign verbal labels to the self-regulatory responses of mood. (This verbal behaviour may then influence more behaviour.) A description of how the mood ACL was devised is given in Nowlis (1970).

The general results showed that dramamine increased the amount that adjectives such as tired, detached, lazy, and sluggish were checked, and decreased the use of businesslike, genial, cheerful, etc. Benzedrine produced approximately the reverse of this. Benzedrine plus seconal led to increases in generous, cheerful, and expansive for example; whereas in larger doses they produced adjectives such as assertive, confident, decisive, and fearless. However, these results were all dependent on how many of the four interactants received a drug, and, of course, on whether or not they all received the same or different drugs. For example, Nowlis reports one study in which there was systematic variation of which man in the group was given dramamine whilst different numbers and combinations of the remainder of the group received either dramamine or seconal. ACL data showed that dramamine had its usual effect of increasing scores in the cluster of adjectives concerning inactivity whilst decreasing those concerning activity. Also, seconal had the general effect of increasing the checking of words describing control and elation (for example mischievous, wilful) and, like dramamine, decreased responses to the active/industrious words. However, although they were dependent on task and individual differences, the results also demonstrated subjects on seconal to be far more influenced by the mood swings of their partners than those on dramamine.

Conclusions and recent developments

Nowlis (1970) rightly argues that it is difficult to develop the concept of mood because it is basically a nontechnical word. It is therefore correspondingly difficult to say whether or not his analyses of behaviour in terms of mood are helpful. Although the experimental techniques used are similar to Schachter's and sometimes the behaviours studied fall under the head of emotion, their precise relevance is difficult to determine. Studies by Kamiya and his colleagues are important in this context (Kamiya 1969; Stoyva and Kamiya 1968; Tart 1969). These put together reports of subjective states and EEG alpha rhythms. The techniques used are based on feedback systems and allow a simultaneous concentration on private events, verbal reports, and neurophysiological processes. Nowlis suggests that Kamiya's work provides two solutions to the problem of how to observe states of mind. (1) Training subjects in awareness, discrimination, and verbal reports of subjective states. (2) Focusing on inter-relationships between subjective variables, physiological responses, and verbal report. The eventual outcome of this approach could be the autoregulation of mood rather than its manipulation by drugs.

Be this as it may, it is important to evaluate the extent to which Nowlis' work is relevant to our understanding of internal and external cues in emotion. Given his broad definition of mood, it is fair to say that he demonstrates that it depends on an interaction between internal factors (manipulated by drugs) and external factors (the tasks being performed and the behaviour of the other people in the situation). To the extent that some of the behaviour displayed by Nowlis' subjects must be emotional, although not specifically described as such, his results and general propositions add breadth to Schachter's. The techniques of are similar but the behaviours involved differ; that in Schachter's studies is clearly emotional (aggression, euphoria) whereas that in Nowlis' is more concerned with the complexities of social interaction.

EMOTION AS APPRAISAL

The second major 'cognitive' approach to the study of emotion has the concept of appraisal at its core. For theorists with this orientation, appraisals are the cognitions which intervene between environmental stimulation and physiological and behavioural responses. Essentially, appraisals are evaluations of the personal worth of any incoming stimulus. We appraise any stimulus as to whether it is 'good' or 'bad' for us, i.e. whether it is worth our while to approach or avoid it. An appraisal is a hypothetical construct which allows us to give some 'meaning' to our environmental situation. Both Arnold and Lazarus believe appraisals to be essential to the generation of emotion.

Arnold

Arnold's (for example 1960; 1970a) theory of emotion is a mixture of the cognitive and physiological approaches to the subject. As was seen in Chapters 2 and 3, her theory depends very much on the concept of appraisal as a determinant of emotion, itself a felt tendency to action. It will be remembered that Arnold regards correct appraisals and consequent actions as requiring: (1) memories of sensory and motor events; (2) memories of previous positive and negative attitudes; and (3) the rehearsal in imagination of the appropriate actions. She also spends much time in neurophysiological speculation as to the substrates of these hypothetical processes. Enough space has been given to a description of Arnold's theory, so at this point a few words of evaluation will suffice.

Arnold's (1970a) latest starting point is that we know little about brain function, particularly in emotion. To obtain this knowledge, she suggests that we need to identify the physiological mediation of the process which runs from perception to emotion and action. She argues that this is best achieved at first by a cognitive analysis. Before pursuing this argument, it is worth pointing out that it is to some extent debatable whether or not we *need* to search for the physiological substrates of emotion. Assuming for the moment that it would be helpful to do this, then one may also question why Arnold should regard perception as important. Again, it may be perfectly possible to study emotional processes without once considering perception.

In support of her plea for a cognitive analysis of emotion, Arnold maintains that if we can find out what is going on psychologically between perception, emotion, and action, then we are in a better position to hypothesize about possible physiological substrates. This may well be so. However, if we find out in enough detail what is going on psychologically in emotion, then this might be enough to make the necessary predictions. Arnold would argue, though, that knowledge of the physiology would provide a useful check on the psychology. This cannot be denied, as long as it is clear what is meant by psychology in this context. Arnold seems to use the word in the somewhat old-fashioned sense of being synonymous with 'cognitive'. If this is so (and there are many that would argue that it is not), then it is difficult to see how a knowledge of possible physiological mechanisms would allow us to check it. It would seem that cognitive notions such as appraisal can basically never be more than subjective. It is unlikely that physiology will enable us to say how an appraisal occurs or where an affective memory is stored and in what way our imaginations allow us to rehearse appropriate emotional actions.

It is perhaps on the cognitive side that Arnold's theory is found most wanting. Although her physiologizing has led to a number of testable predictions and in that way has furthered the study of emotion, it is difficult to see what predictions can be made from her concept of cognitive appraisal, especially as it is a process which she regards as occurring almost instantaneously. Her theory is well integrated but very speculative, and at the end of the day there are serious questions left unanswered. For example, Arnold characterizes some appraisals as being immediate, intuitive, and innate and at the same time gives a very important role to general cognition in emotion. If cognition is so heavily involved, the implication is that man can control his emotions. How can this be so, if appraisals are immediate, intuitive, and innate? Finally, and perhaps even more fundamentally, why should it be assumed that appraisals exist at all? This may involve accounts of emotion in an unnecessary, unparsimonious extra step; a criticism which can also be made of the theories of emotion to follow which have been suggested by Lazarus and his coworkers.

Lazarus

Other than Arnold, the main proponent of the appraisal view of emotion has been Lazarus (see, for example, Lazarus 1968; Lazarus et al. 1970; Lazarus and Opton 1966). His theoretical contribution consists partly of an attack on motivational theories of emotion; this will be discussed later when reviewing Leeper's recent ideas. Lazarus regards emotion as a response, but suggests that this does not deny emotion as an intervening variable. It simply places a different emphasis on it. Like Arnold, his basic viewpoint is that cognitive processes are causes which arouse coping processes to deal with an appraised situation; a cognitive/adaptive argument. Before discussing the details of Lazarus' theoretical approach to emotion, his research strategies will be briefly described.

The four research strategies which Lazarus has followed have been mainly concerned with an analysis of the possible determinants of appraisal.

1. *Direct manipulation.* The work for which Lazarus and his coworkers are best known is that involving stressful films. The basic technique is to show subjects stressful films with various soundtracks added to them, or to compare the effects of these films with those of more benign films. (See Lazarus *et al.* 1965 and Spiesman *et al.* 1964 for reviews of this work.) The main film to be used has been on subincision—'a ritual performed by men of an Australian stone-age culture in which the penis and scrotum of male adolescents are cut deeply with a sharpened piece of stone'. In comparison with benign films, the subincision film typically generated far more emotional disturbance. This disturbance was enhanced or reduced as a function of the type of soundtrack added to the film. Lazarus interprets these results as demonstrating that emotional appraisal can be directly manipulated, the different degrees of emotional reaction being regarded as dependent on appraisal. These results were reflected in both autonomic and subjective measures.

2. *Indirect manipulation.* This strategy has involved the manipulation of those variables on which Lazarus believes cognition to depend rather than 'direct' manipulation of the cognition itself. The main emphasis has been on anticipation. Generally, stress (emotional) reactions increase as confrontation time approaches, although this effect is modified by factors such as the duration of the anticipation, prior experiences, and so on. For example, Folkins (1970) made subjects wait either 5 sec, 30 sec, 1 min, 5 min or 20 min for an electric

shock. Control subjects waited during similar lengths of time for a light to come on. There was a large, obtrusive clock on which time could be counted off. Folkins found a complex relationship between physiological measures, stress, and time of anticipation. For instance, physiological reactions were at their height in the 1 min group, they fell in the 3 and 5 min groups, and rose again in the 20 min group. Lazarus argues that these physiological reactions result from *cognitive* attempts at coping, an idea, of course, which leads to unlimited speculation about the nature of such appraisals.

3. *Self-report.* There are obvious disadvantages to a methodology which depends on the self-report of thoughts after some stressful experience. However, it may be indicative of other hypotheses which could be tested, or act as support for results gained from other strategies. Folkins (1970), for example, found data from affect-rating scales, word association, and interviews to run parallel to his physiological data. Lazarus *et al.* (1962) in a film study showed there to be three response patterns observed in self-reports: (1) an emotional flooding, (2) an intellectualized detachment, and (3) a denial (I'm not bothered). However, there were no concomitant autonomic differences in subjects who typically gave one of these types of report. Clearly, this result is not in line with those from the direct manipulation studies. Lazarus suggests that this discrepancy is due to subjects only developing appropriate responses when they have time to prepare them or when they are provided with a ready-made way of coping.

4. *Dispositional variables.* The final strategy involves the selection of subjects with different emotional dispositions. For example, Spiesman *et al.* (1964) in their film study chose deniers and intellectualizers. Stress reactions were more reduced when deniers heard a film-track expressing denial and when intellectualizers heard an intellectualizing track superimposed on the same film.

Appraisals

As a cautionary note before discussing Lazarus' theoretical analysis of emotion, it should be borne in mind that a common theme to his research is stress. Many of his studies have been based on comparisons of the effects of stressful and nonstressful stimuli. It is not appropriate in this context to spend time attempting to define stress. It is enough to say that it is probably more inter-related with the extreme types of emotional reaction than with the mild. Strictly speaking, Lazarus' views should be regarded as applying only to the 'strong' emotions. Empirically, he does not much concern himself with the 'weak' or 'mild' emotions.

Lazarus suggests that there are two broad types of appraisal: benign and threatening. Benign appraisals have three possible adaptive consequences.

1. Adaptive, *automatic* coping may occur without the emotion. This is in fact some sort of automatic self-protection, the type of response we may make when crossing the road. The evidence for this is shaky; Berkowitz (1962) and Buss (1961) both cite many examples of the inhibition of aggression, but it is impossible to tell whether it is aggressive behaviour or the emotion of anger which is being inhibited. Lazarus seems to be saying that appraisal is involved. It

is only if we appraise something as dangerous, for example, that we will experience a negative emotion. But he is also saying that under some conditions we can adaptively and automatically avoid things without making such appraisals; we simply do not consider harm as a likely outcome. From this analysis, however, it is difficult to say when any particular stimulus will lead to an appraisal and when it will not.

2. A benign stimulus may provide us with more information such that it requires reappraisal. A simple example might be the sight of his favourite dish to a hungry man being reappraised when he discovers that it has been burnt. In fact, a benign stimulus may be reappraised as benign or threatening and a threatening stimulus may be reappraised as benign or threatening. This is pointing to a continuous interplay between emotional reactions and appraisals.

3. Positive emotional states may follow from benign appraisals, although Lazarus can cite no evidence for this. He suggests that such states follow from three nonthreatening conditions, each of which involves the absence of serious threat (when it has been overcome). If this occurs by itself, there is elation. If it occurs with an unusual sense of security, there is euphoria. And if it occurs with a sense of identity, belonging and warmth with another, there is love. Lazarus describes a complex interaction between these possibilities, which can be summarized by people apparently seeking danger to experience the pleasure of overcoming it. At best, these notions are extremely subjective and lean heavily on undefined concepts. Lazarus makes little attempt to operationalize concepts such as belongingness or love and can offer no empirical support for these ideas. They are highly speculative.

Lazarus suggests further that threatening appraisals involve two possible processes. The primary process deals with an evaluation of threat or nonthreat and the secondary deals with how to cope with the threat. This has two consequences, each representing a way of coping with the threat. (1) Direct action; impulses or tendencies to remove the threat. This is essential to emotion since its success or failure or any feedback from it changes the cognition and hence the emotion. Lazarus regards these tendencies to direct action as leading to the usual classifications which are made of emotional behaviour. (2) Benign reappraisal; this is entirely cognitive, might or might not be realistic, and occurs when the stimuli suggest that no direct action is possible. Again, fluctuations in emotion are seen as reflections of this continuous cognitive appraisal and reappraisal. The basic problems then are those of describing the cognitive factors in particular emotions and of attempting to describe the empirical conditions which lead to them. Without such a description, any theoretical system of the sort proposed by Lazarus is circular in that cognitive factors can only be inferred from behaviour, both verbal and nonverbal.

Emotional response patterning

Difficulties which Lazarus sees both for his theory and for any other are those of defining emotion and of establishing satisfactory criteria for distinguishing between different emotions. He believes, however, that ultimately emotional states will be distinguished from one another by the identification of specific physiological, cognitive, and behavioural patterns, and eliciting events. On the other hand, he realizes that at present this is not possible.

More particularly, Lazarus does not think that Schachter's approach to these problems is justified by his research. He rightly summarizes Schachter's viewpoint as regarding all emotion as characterized by sympathetic arousal—a common, one-dimensional state. Thereafter, labels resulting from cognitions give emotions their particular qualities. Lazarus agrees with Schachter on the importance of cognitive processes in emotion but argues against emotions being a single state of physiological arousal to which a cognitive label has been applied. He suggests that in reality emotions do not depend on epinephrine injections, but on appraisals of situations; arousal follows. Schachter, though, would surely not disagree with this. Lazarus also criticizes Schachter for over-emphasizing the labelling of emotion whilst placing little importance on the possible steering functions of cognitive activity. However, his alternative is not very different. He suggests that physiological patterns might be associated with the various adaptive tasks which follow directly from cognitive appraisals. He also argues that what he regards as each emotional response system—the cognitive, behavioural, physiological—has its own adaptive function. This implies that there are special transactions between a person and his environment on each of these levels. He suggests from this that we may learn most about emotion where we find apparent discrepancies between the various response systems. It should be pointed out, however, that these may not be different response systems. It could be argued, for example, that physiological responses in emotion are simply an underlying substrate to behavioural responses and that the cognitive aspects of emotion do not lead to any predictions which cannot be made at the more overt level.

Be this as it may, it is important to describe what Lazarus regards as causing any lack of agreement between response indices or measures of emotion. He suggests two possibilities. Such discrepancies might be due either to methodological inadequacies in experimentation and/or they might simply reflect an individual's various attempts to cope with the situation. The second possibility is again based on the idea that each dimension of response has its own adaptive functions. Ekman and Friesen (1969, see Chapter 8) provide good examples of this in an analysis of 'nonverbal leakage', in which they stress the importance in emotion and social interaction of bodily and facial movements of which we are often unaware. Everyday examples of discrepancies between the dimensions of emotion are easy to imagine: no, I'm not angry—with clenched teeth, fists, and legs. Lazarus maintains that these apparent contradictions should be expected and that they give us much extra information about emotion.

In a paper concerned with cross-cultural studies of emotion, Averill *et al.* (1969) put Lazarus' theory in a slightly different light. They state that each emotion is a complex response system within which are three subsystems. (1) Stimulus properties. They point out that a stimulus may be influenced by responses which are made to it, since an emotional response may also be a stimulus and add to the quality of the emotion. (2) Appraisal subsystem. The brain evaluates incoming stimuli, the primary appraisal reducing the stimuli to a unitary concept such as threat, and the secondary appraisal being a mechanism for coping. (3) Responses. Here Averill *et al.* suggest that emotional responses can be divided into cognitive, expressive, and instrumental, with poor correlations existing between them. The cognitive responses are defence mechanisms, the expressive responses occur mainly in the face, and the instrumental responses are merely symbols which signal the presence of affect.

So, Averill *et al.* describe an emotional response system which can interrupt and modify ongoing behaviour, whilst being selfcontained. They also argue that any attempt to distinguish between emotions should not be through possible differences in structure but should dwell on eliciting conditions, response patterns, and developmental changes.

EMOTION AS MOTIVATION/PERCEPTION

Leeper

The third major cognitive approach to emotion is provided by Leeper, who although analysing emotion in motivational terms, regards motivation itself as a perceptual or cognitive process.

Leeper's (1948) original formulations were as much a critical attack on previous theories as they were positive suggestions. He argued that experimental psychologists usually stressed disorganization when discussing emotion. At that time the concept therefore had little application to other, more applied, fields. Depending on the basic standpoint, emotion was seen either as disorganized behaviour or as having a disorganizing effect on behaviour. Leeper suggested that the idea of emotions as disorganizing sprang from an everyday and psychoanalytic and technological background which placed (and probably still does) value on intellectual processes and denigrated anything that detracts from them. Emotion was regarded as something that did detract; it simply impeded the higher activities of man—a slightly more modern conception of the rationalist doctrine.

Leeper extended his critical argument in two ways. First, he quoted from writers such as Munn (1946) to demonstrate that the concept of disorganization had been ill-defined. For example, he asked, is the disorganization the emotion, or does it produce the emotion, or both? Second, he set out to look more closely at the concept of disorganization and then to demonstrate that the facts of emotion did not fit it. He maintained that disorganization must depend on whether functional changes in the organism can be random and chaotic or whether they tend to mesh with any ongoing function. He tested this idea in three ways: according to the 'facts' known about visceral processes, behaviour, and conscious experiences.

Leeper argued that viscerally, during fear for example, a person is in an overall state of organization (for flight perhaps). However, he may seem disorganized because, amongst other things, his heart rate is speeded up and his digestion is slowed down. Leeper believed that changes in behaviour and in conscious experience are consistent with the organizing visceral changes. So the behaviour involved in fear tends to include running away; and associated with this is a persistent series of thoughts. He also argued that it is not appropriate to say that emotion disorganizes whatever behaviour precedes it since any sort of stimulus may do this. Unless emotions are seen just as 'foolish and inappropriate responses', then, he urged, it is not meaningful to suggest that the change is a disorganization because it involves a switch from constructive activities to useless ones. However, in cases of extreme emotion he did believe that disorganization can occur. A man may become so angry that he cannot retain any skill whatsoever.

As mentioned above, Leeper was not just critical of earlier ideas. He first made out a reasonable case against emotions as disorganizing and suggested instead that they are organizing. In fact, he viewed emotional processes as motives which both arouse activity and also give it direction and persistence. For example, if we arouse love in someone, this makes it more likely that certain behaviour will be energized and maintained in particular directions. And, except in extreme cases, the more it is aroused the more likely the behaviour will be.

More recently, Leeper (1963a; 1963b; 1965; 1970) has updated his motivational/organizational theory of emotion. He first puts forward a case against separating emotions and motives, the traditional division of which he thought to be dependent on preferences to think in terms of categories rather than hierarchies. He suggests that emotions should be seen as part of a continuum of motivational processes ranging from physiological motives through to clearly emotional motives. He also considers that dichotomy which puts emotions and physiological motives together and distinguishes them from perceptual/cognitive processes. The former tend to be viewed as lower processes, evolutionarily, phylogenetically, and ontogenetically. Recently, exponents of such theories have seen the role of motives as arousing and energizing, not directing (for example Bindra 1959; Brown 1961; Duffy 1962; Hebb 1955).

Leeper suggests four reasons for this viewpoint: (1) motivation is relatively old, phylogenetically; (2) the influence of the arousal theories of motivation; (3) traditional studies have shown perceptual processes to be transient, brief, end products which are tapped via verbal report; (4) the assumption that the brain only operates rapidly, its short-term consequences being the domain of perception; motivations/emotions are long-sustained.

Against these points, Leeper argues that (1) is simply not so. Many so-called older parts of the brain also serve 'higher' functions, and the responsibility for emotion/motivation is cortical as well as subcortical. Second, he maintains that arousal theorists do in fact emphasize that behaviour has directional properties but that these can only be predicted when we know an organism's motivation. They circumvent this difficulty by focusing on 'drive stimuli' as directors of behaviour, but Leeper states that these are simply some sort of intervening variable whose workings we do not know. He suggests that this view is little different from the older one that motives both arouse and direct behaviour. Third, Leeper believes that the more traditional ways of studying perception are changing. For example, there is less reliance on introspective report and more emphasis on material such as speech which is extended in time. He therefore suggests that it may be appropriate to subsume motives under the general heading of cognitive processes. Finally, he maintains that the idea of the brain as a transmission device and brain processes as only short-term is being gainsaid by modern work.

Leeper's alternative viewpoint is that it is reasonable to look on motives/emotion as perceptual processes. He puts forward three propositions. (1) There was evolutionary advantage in animals responding perceptually to situations in which crucial features stood out. Also, behaviour would be guided by perceiving such situations in terms of anticipations of other perceptual effects which might occur if particular actions were followed. (2) There would be biological advantage in such perceptions being fast. (3) For maximal advantage such perceptions should have some effects on activity. For example, rapid perceptual processes might sometimes make the organism forego present satisfaction to escape impending danger—it is far more adaptive to have the *fast* perceptual mechanism also as a mechanism of motivation.

Leeper is not saying that all perceptual processes are also motivational, but that the perceptual domain is large, complex, and contains many dimensions. Clearly, motives/emotion have much in the way of autonomic and 'older' brain involvement. But even the simplest perceptual processes are dependent on cortical arousal, from the lower brain stem. Leeper argues that subcortical processes and the viscera influence thought through the contributions they make to cortical processes. He regards such *representational* processes as motivational. Thus, perceptions range from motivationally/emotionally neutral to motivationally/emotionally very powerful processes.

Finally, Leeper proposes that his organizational/motivational/perceptual theory of emotion has three important implications. (1) Our emotional life should become very diverse as time goes on. (2) We must often create our own objective realities, since our perceptions allow us to recognize these and our emotions involve perceptions of life situations. (3) Leeper suggests that man has been through two great ages, tool-using and technology/scientific or endeavour/education, and that these have each deemphasized the emotional aspects of life. He believes that his theory might occasionally edge us towards dwelling on emotional experiences—perhaps leading to the third great age of man. Such speculation, which hints at the control of emotion, will be taken up again in Chapter 9.

At face value, Leeper's analysis of emotions as motives and of emotions and motives as perceptual or representational processes would seem to be parsimonious. However, this apparent parsimony is perhaps little more than the replacing of one nebulous concept with another. As Bolles (1967) points out, motivation has not proved to be a particularly helpful explanatory or predictive concept. It is merely taking a further step in the same direction to then speak of emotion/motivation as aspects of the even broader concept of perception.

In evaluating Leeper's theory, it is worth bearing in mind some of Lazarus' (1968) criticisms of emotion as motivation. He suggests that this idea has five disadvantages. (1) It takes emphasis away from emotions as substantive states in their own right. (2) It takes attention away from the causes and antecedents of emotion. (3) It leads to a theory of behaviour in which one emotion (anxiety/fear) does most of the work. (4) It artificially separates some components of emotional states. (5) It is not predictive of adaptive responses, although given the terms in which he speaks, Leeper would presumably debate this last point.

Finally, Leeper's theory can be criticized on the grounds that it has led to little experimental work; it does not have very much general empirical support. Indeed, it is difficult to derive any testable predictions from it. Having read Leeper, one is left with two ideas. (1) Mild emotions have organizing characteristics. (2) Anomalously, emotion does not really exist.

EMOTION IN A BROAD COGNITIVE CONTEXT

The ideas on emotion to be discussed in this final section have two major points in common. First, they are very grand, ranging across many of the traditional divisions within psychology. Second, and it is for this reason that they are included within this chapter, they assign a central role to cognition in explaining emotion.

Mandler

In his erudite book, Mandler's (1976) aim is to develop a psychological (by which he means mental) theory of emotion within a framework provided by cognitive psychology. Although his theory was described in Chapter 2, it will be summarized briefly here as will some of the considerations he took into account in developing it. Mention of some of these background points is made since it may be useful to apply them to any context in which a theory of emotion is being developed.

Mandler begins by endorsing the frequently made point that the study of emotion is bedevilled by a lack of precision in some of the words which it virtually has to use; words such as happy or angry are simply not denotative enough to be used with freedom. As an alternative and also because psychologists are not yet in a position to deal adequately with the mind–body problem, Mandler argues that it is important to deal with the mental requirements needed to account for emotion. He suggests that at a minimum there are four such requirements. (1) Inputs from the environment. (2) A structure system which interprets such input events. (3) Two output systems, one reflected in action and the other in physiological arousal. (4) Feedback, for the perception of arousal and the monitoring of action.

In a way which is simultaneously old-fashioned and yet very modern, Mandler argues that the notion of *mind* best summarizes all the inferences that can be made in emotion concerning the structures of input and output, the relationships between them, and their history, be this dependent on genetic or environmental factors. Thus, for Mandler, the beginnings of a theory of emotion must involve a consideration of mind and its mechanisms and structures and a discussion of consciousness. Also, because emotion covers a large admixture of mechanisms and processes, any theory of emotion must not make it independent of more general processes.

Parameter of emotion

Mandler presents a view of emotion which at one level is a discussion of the parameters involved, and at another level is a summary of a system of emotion. The three parameters which he emphasizes are arousal, cognitive interpretation, and consciousness, with special stress being laid on the interaction between arousal and cognitive interpretation, and the analysis of meaning in emotion.

Briefly, Mandler argues that the perception of ANS activity leads to undifferentiated arousal the conditions for which lean heavily on cognitive interpretations, especially where these involve any interruption or blocking. Such arousal has two adaptive functions, either homeostasis or activity involving the seeking of information. Although somewhat akin to appraisal, Mandler's ideas on cognitive interpretation go further. He suggests that such interpretation is made up of mental structures, innate reactions to events, and an evaluation of self-perceptions. The expressive movements in emotion generate automatic cognitive reactions which are themselves modified by re-interpretation. Emotional experience and emotional behaviour result from a complex interaction between automatic arousal and cognitive interpretation. Arousal gives emotion its visceral quality and intensity, and interpretation not only adds to quality but also allows the categorization of the experience. Finally, Mandler argues that emotional experience itself takes place in consciousness, output from which is coded into language, thus making possible communication about the experience.

This summary is sufficient to give the gist of Mandler's view of emotion, although some of his ideas on anxiety will be explored in Chapter 9. He has made an important attempt to come to grips with consciousness and mental activity in his view of emotion, a consideration which most other students of emotion have left well alone. Yet, in the expression of his ideas he is not very far removed from the other appraisal theorists, particularly those like Schachter who also stress sympathetic arousal. Whether or not Mandler's attempt to put consciousness and the mind in a framework of an empirically based and scientifically acceptable theory is successful remains to be seen. Clearly, however, it is a worthy and ambitious endeavour, the like of which could have far-reaching influences on future theory and research in psychology.

Izard and Tomkins

Separately and together over a period of some years, Izard and Tomkins have put forward a very complete theory of emotion. Given that their various viewpoints cut across most aspects of emotion, they could have been described in a number of different places in the present book. However, since like Mandler they afford a central role to cognitive factors in emotion, their ideas are included in this chapter.

Tomkins

The earliest of their views was expressed by Tomkins (1962; 1963), who began by equating emotion with affect, describing the affective system as primary and the drive system as secondary and arguing that the two systems continue to give drive its urgency. He characterized affect as unrestrained; thus it can be at any intensity, insatiable, and very changeable.

Tomkins suggested that affects are mainly reflected in facial responses, an idea which was clearly influential in Izard's (1972) more recent and potentially more important theory. If feedback from this facial expression is self-conscious then it can be rewarding or punishing, the organized facial patterns themselves being innately determined and triggered subcortically. Tomkins lists the primary affects as: interest/excitement, enjoyment/joy, surprise/startle, distress/anguish, disgust/contempt, anger/rage, shame/humiliation, and fear/terror and hypothesizes about ways in which they might be instigated.

Izard and Tomkins

In developing these imaginative but largely untested ideas, Izard and Tomkins (1966) rely on four main notions. (1) Affect is motivation (Tomkins 1962; 1963). (2) Positive affect provides the background motivation to effective functioning and to creativity (Izard 1960; Izard et al. 1965b). (3) Positive affect is important to learning, perception, and personality (Izard 1965; Izard et al. 1965a; 1965b). (4) Negative affect is disruptive and suppressive (Izard 1964; Izard et al. 1965a; 1965b).

Their general theory starts with the suggestion that personality is made up of five interrelated *and* autonomous subsystems: homeostatic, drive, affect, cognitive, and motor. By this they presumably mean that these subsystems sometimes function together and sometimes independently. The first two subsystems mainly concern biological maintenance and the remaining three provide the foundation for more complex human behaviour. Affect is the primary motivational system, cognitive is the primary communication system, and motor is the primary action system. Under different conditions any one of these subsystems can dominate and then become the main determinant of behaviour. If affect becomes dominant, they suggest that behaviour will probably be maladaptive. Affect itself can only be fully understood by looking at personality as a *process* of communication both with and within a social and physical environment.

The aspect of this theory which is of interest here dwells on affect as the inherent primary motivational system. Izard and Tomkins suggest that it has three components: (1) neurological—concerning density of neural firing; (2) behavioural—facial, bodily, and visceral responses; (3) phenomenological—affect as a motive. The affect system is seen as relatively independent of the others and as laying down cognition, decision, and action.

Izard and Tomkins postulate three neurological activators of affect: (1) an increase in stimulation, leading to surprise, fear, and interest; (2) a stable level of stimulation, leading to distress and anger; (3) a decrease in stimulation, leading to enjoyment. Hence, there is emotional sensitivity to novel stimulation, enduring stimulation or waning stimulation. By intensifying neural messages, affect is regarded as slowing all the motivational systems.

Behaviourally, Izard and Tomkins place more emphasis on facial than bodily or visceral responses, although they view feedback from any of them as making us aware of our response patterns and therefore of our affects. They define the same eight innate affects as mentioned by Tomkins which are expressed facially.

Phenomenologically, the picture is even more complicated. Izard and Tomkins state that an individual's purpose is an image (of an end state), often of doing or achieving something. The affects involved and what is being done may be quite independent. For example, in any habitual action affect definitely has no place. Also, they suggest that on occasion affects do not join with cognitions to form purposes. We sometimes may not act on our preferences for positive and against negative affects. On other occasions we may be unaware of the affect that is driving us. When affects compete, that with the greatest density of neural firing becomes conscious and there is a complex relationship between intensity of stimulation, novelty, and the likelihood of the consciousness of affect. The affect system with its learned and unlearned aspects is the main provider of the blueprints for cognition, decision, and action. This phenomenological analysis must be seen to be lacking in that it provides for any contingency in a highly speculative way. It is impossible to unravel any firm predictions from it.

Izard and Tomkins use fear/anxiety to exemplify their position. They regard cognitive processes as the most general and pervasive instigators of fear. We have purposes, achieved through feedback. These are mainly conscious images of possible end states made up of the memories and perceptions that must govern behaviour. Feedback from the cognitive constructions that make up the image activates affect; this in turn initiates and maintains any behaviour that will close the gap between the achieved state and the image. Specific fears may occur through cognitive constructions (which may often be wrong). Or the memory of anticipation of fear itself instigate fear.

Fear also strongly determines what we perceive, think, and do, and thus has a very constrictive influence. From this point of view, anxiety is often considered to be the most important and basic pathological emotion (see Chapter 9). However, there has been little experimental work on the phenomenology of anxiety. An exception to this is Bull (1951), who induced 'fear' hypnotically in her subjects. Afterwards, but while still in a trance, they described their experiences. The same pattern was mentioned by her seven subjects. This was a conflict between tensing-up or freezing of the body and a desire to get away. Finally, Izard and Tomkins suggest that in the face of a fear-producing object, adaptive behaviour requires a cognitive appraisal, cognition also being needed for a plan of action. Basically, they are proposing the sequence: fear (emotion), cognition, action, and in so doing are not far away from Arnold, Lazarus, and Leeper, although the terms they use in getting there are far looser. The criticisms which were levelled at Leeper can also be levelled at Izard and Tomkins' theory. The main point against it is that it covers too much ground at too many levels of analysis. It is impossible to anchor it to concrete empirical possibilities.

Izard

Reference to Chapter 2, in which Izard's (1972) theory is summarized, will show that he has developed it considerably from its earlier origins, although the same basic idea of complex interrelated systems is retained. In this more recent formulation, Izard still argues that there are three components in the emotion process, but now labels these as neural activity, facial–postural activity, and subjective experience. He also sees these as three levels of emotion.

In particular, in this statement of the theory, Izard goes further than previously in delineating the various person–environment and intraindividual processes which can activate emotion. He also lays great stress on the role of facial expression (see Chapter 8), discusses the development of emotional expression (see Chapter 7), and especially makes an interesting case for the control of emotional reactions via therapy.

Overall, Izard and Tomkins have made a considerable contribution to the conceptual analysis of emotion, particularly in its more cognitive and phenomenological aspects. They are especially helpful in attempting to place emotion in an interrelated context of other important systems. Also, in recent years Izard has contributed important work on the determinants of facial expression in emotion. However, as a final caveat it should be borne in mind that Izard and Tomkin's theories are often quite speculative and therefore a little difficult to ground in empirical fact.

CONCLUSIONS

From the incisive ideas discussed in this chapter it is clear that there have been sufficient conceptualizations of emotion which give an important, if not crucial, role to cognition to ensure that these types of analysis are firmly entrenched. Until recently, Schachter's views were probably the most important in this field, namely, that there is scant physiological differentiation between emotional states; rather, distinctions are made on the basis of cognitive labelling. This notion gains support from the work of Valins and others on the perception of bodily change as distinct from the bodily change itself. Breadth is also added by Nowlis' work on mood. In general, these three types of investigation point to an interaction between internal and external cues in emotion.

An important result of Schachter's type of approach to the study of emotion is to have given greater credence to James' ideas. Schachter deals convincingly with a number of Cannon's criticisms of James, and although his own work is not above criticism it does point forcefully to the significance of visceral arousal to emotion.

The second major influence on cognitive analyses of emotion has come from the idea of appraisal, although this has less to be said in its favour. As used by Arnold and Lazarus, the appraisal tends to be an elusive concept empirically. At best, appraisals can only be inferred from behaviour, although of course it may be that they have a neurophysiological substrate.

Finally, there are the recent large-scale conceptualizations made by Mandler and Izard. These are ambitious and far-reaching, and sometimes deal very credibly with concepts such as consciousness which psychologists have been too ready to leave out of their consideration. It is likely that these views will become very influential in the next few years, and in the context of this chapter it is significant that they give a central role to cognition in emotion. Such potential influence is made more probable since they lay great stress on expressive behaviour. This is leading to some important empirical developments in the social psychology of emotion and interesting theoretical developments in the control of emotion.

Overall, it is a hard matter to determine whether or not the cognitive approach to emotion is worthwhile. It leads to hypotheses which are sometimes difficult to test directly. On the other hand, it has inspired some ingenious and interesting research, which is meaningful and worthwhile in its own right: specifically, Schachter's drugs, Valins' nudes, and Lazarus' stressful films. The main problem is that with a cognitive or phenomenological emphasis (see Chapter 5) we are not simply dealing with one level of discourse, as is the case, for example, with the physiology of emotion. Instead, we are faced with hypothetical processes, intervening between stimuli and responses. These are believed to be produced by the former and to affect the latter. Such ideas will further our knowledge only to the extent that they lead to testable predictions which do not emerge from noncognitive theories. At the moment the problem cannot be resolved. It may well be that a purely behavioural (or physiological) analysis of emotion is possible. If so, parsimony would suggest that we accept it.

Assuming that cognitions are important determinants of emotion, then it should be pointed out that even then they may only apply to certain types or classes of emotion. The usual emotions discussed by the cognitive theorists are the milder ones. Although Lazarus, for example, speaks of investigating stress, this is very much stress in the laboratory and as generated by films. Stress in real life may be quite differently determined. In fact, it would seem likely that if cognitive factors do have significance, then this will be for the milder forms of emotion. More extreme emotion may be better analysed in some more direct way.

Finally, though, it does seem likely that the next few years will see a proliferation of research into emotion with very much of a cognitive bias. Much is being done in the area of expressive behaviour, and information-processing models of emotion such as Leventhal's (1974) may well begin to appear.

5

The Phenomenology of Emotion

PHENOMENOLOGICAL PSYCHOLOGY

... phenomenology is that empiricistic philosophy which asserts that the givens of experience are configurational entities having a unique integrity of their own and are, therefore, not reducible to sense or to any other elemental structure.'

(Turner 1967, p. 60)

In order to describe some of the many phenomenological conceptualizations of emotion, it is necessary to set the scene with a brief description of phenomenological psychology. Turner's definition is of the philosophical foundations of phenomenology as conceptualized in the early part of this century by European philosophers such as Husserl (1913). Husserl argued that our thoughts and feelings have a purpose and that this purpose must come from the 'essential' person. Also, a thought or feeling is always about something, it reaches out, and is therefore *intentional*. Husserl believed that our senses give us a direct knowledge of the world, a view of the world as it really is, but suggested that the intent in our perceptions might distort this reality. In other words, what a person puts into perception may distort the information he is gaining from his senses. Such a distortion could take many forms, from racial prejudice to the effects produced by simple visual illusions. Husserl argued that our perceptions or experiences are usually distorted simply because our minds are a confused mass of ideas, hypotheses, and expectations. To overcome this, we must concentrate exclusively on what we experience as we experience it. In Husserl's view, if we do this time and time again we will gradually come nearer a true understanding of what an object is *really* like.

Husserl's type of reasoning provided a foundation from which modern phenomenological psychology developed. The latter is not phenomenological philosphy as it was originally conceived, nor as it has since been refined, but probably arose in an attempt to answer psychological questions which were exposed by men such as Husserl. Philosophical phenomenology would be virtually impossible for a psychologist, who is by implication a scientist, or at least a research worker, to accept. It would be too extreme an approach to human behaviour, stressing as it does only the unique experiencing individual, at the expense of all else. All possibility for generalization is lost, and the psychologist almost always wishes to generalize. Of course, by a similar token, radical behaviourism is too extreme to be accepted by most psychologists, assigning as it does no status at all to individual experience.

Phenomenological psychology then is a compromise, but one which is much nearer the experiential end of the scale than the behavioural. It is the study of consciousness and experience. Such an aim carries with it a number of assumptions, some of which will be discussed below. From the viewpoint of the phenomenological psychologist it is an individual's perception of the world which is the crucial aspect of psychological investigation. The implication is that each of us perceives the world, or some situation or object within it, in a unique fashion, although there might, of course, be common elements in the perceptions experienced by different people. *And it is these perceptions or experiences that determine the way in which we react or the way in which we behave.*

Clearly, phenomenological psychology is working from a model of man which is very different from that of the behaviourist, or even that of the middle-of-the-road conventional scientific psychologist. However, as Severin (1973) points out, phenomenological psychology is not phenomenological philosophy. Ultimately, it is concerned with an empirical study of man rather than with sheer speculation. As might be expected, though, it is an empiricism which is different in kind from that followed by the experimental psychologist. Severin (1973) suggests that some phenomenological psychologists regard their approach as little more than an attitude of mind of which the overriding principle is a reaction against trying to characterize man by operational definitions alone. A second approach is to use a phenomenological analysis to take a novel look at a research problem in its early stages. And a third approach is that which gives pride of place to phenomenological analysis in the future of psychology.

Although the present aim is to explore the relationship between phenomenology and emotion, it is worthwhile now to point out some of the characteristic of the general phenomenological approach. The main concern is with what a person is experiencing here and now, at this moment, in this place, in his present state. What a person experiences can be manipulated by controlling his prior experiences in precisely the same way that the experimental psychologist manipulates his subject's behaviour. Naturally, similar controls can be employed as well. But the data of experience are necessarily subjective; they are personal reports of a person's conscious process, of his experiences. So for the most part the phenomenological psychologist is dealing with what the behaviourist would call verbal report, and it is often his own rather than that of somebody else. But he is interested in the content of the report, not its form. Unlike the behaviourist, he sees no reason to doubt the report, under many circumstances anyway; he gives it credibility and uses it as a building block for his theories. And to emphasize a point already made, he assigns to a person's experience or conscious processes a *causal* role in determining his behaviour.

Apologists who stress the importance of phenomenology in psychology (e.g.

Giorgi 1970) argue that phenomenology gives the psychologist the one really special approach he can get for his set of specialized problems. The basis of their argument is that psychology is very different from the natural or biological sciences since its object of study is man, and man has consciousness; it is this which sets him apart from all else. In Giorgi's view then, it is consciousness which should be the proper and foremost concern of psychologists. Such a concern will require special techniques of study, somewhat different from those of conventional science, though the latter are more than adequate for the study of behaviour *per se*. These techniques are those of phenomenological psychology.

An alternative way of describing the substance of this chapter is to say that it is aimed at exploring the possible roles of some aspects of third-force psychology in the study of emotion. Third-force psychology is difficult to define. It is third because it follows two other great forces, psychoanalysis and behaviourism; and its basic concern is with putting the whole man back into psychology; its approach is holistic or synthetic rather than analytic. Other than this it is difficult to be precise, since third-force psychology is an umbrella term for a number of different approaches to the study of man, for example phenomenology, existentialism, Gestalt psychology, self-theory, and so on.

Bugental (1966) gathers together these various approaches and abstracts from them a number of common elements. The following points are a summary of these. Psychologists should be concerned with the functioning of the whole person and not just break him down into isolated processes such as learning and memory. Within limits, man has choice, free will to choose what he will do next. Consciousness is man's basic process and its study is inseperable from the study of man himself. Psychologists should be concerned with the real-life needs, problems, and motivation of fully functioning people, not just with laboratory studies of things like schedules of reinforcement. Psychologists should devise methodologies appropriate to their subject matter rather than simply continue to apply the techniques of conventional science. Because of the psychologist's unique subject matter, he should not shirk the making of value judgments. Finally, psychologists should be concerned with aiding people to understand themselves rather than with concentrating solely on the prediction and control of behaviour.

In the context of these prescriptions, the general aim of this chapter is to try to give answers to three main sets of questions. First, is it possible to produce a phenomenological theory of emotion which has the characteristics of a good theory, i.e. is anchored to the real world, makes an adequate summary of any data, is internally consistent, and leads to predictions? Second, how much common ground is there between phenomenological theories? Do they form a reasonably consistent picture when they are put together? Can they be subsumed under one type of theory, and if so, what is it? Third, are the phenomenological approaches to emotion testable with any sort of empirical research, be it within the methodological framework of conventional science or not?

SOME PHILOSOPHICAL ACCOUNTS OF EMOTION

One way into phenomenological descriptions of emotion is via the ideas put forward by philosophers. In the present context it is important to consider some of these, since phenomenological psychology has firm philosophical roots. Also, the type of analysis of emotion made by philosophers suggests some important cautionary notes for psychologists. To these ends, the ideas on emotion of three contemporary philosophers will be briefly discussed.

R. S. Peters

The work of Peters (e.g. 1969; 1970) provides a good starting point since, to put it straightforwardly, he seems to fall midway between the psychologists and the philosphers in his approach to emotion, and yet to hold a viewpoint which is heavily larded with commonsense. He begins by asking a very basic question: can we derive any useful information by listing what we 'naturally' might call emotions? He suggests that if someone sets out to make such a list of emotions, then his main criterion for selecting a term for inclusion is that it show a link between emotion and cognitive appraisal. He holds that emotions as appraisals are brought about either by external conditions or by things which people have themselves generated or suffered.

Peters states that this aspect of emotion has been given very little emphasis in psychology, although there has been a recent upsurge. He suggests that the reason that cognitions have been left out of psychological conceptualizations of emotion is that psychologists have been continually involved in a search for scientific respectability, and it is hard to maintain respectability when speculating about cognition. He argues that psychology has long been restricted by behaviourism's obsession with what is palpable. When a concept such as consciousness has been brought into the consideration of emotion then it has usually been restricted to an awareness of physiological state. But, Peters argues, an emotion cannot even be identified without some knowledge of a person's appraisal.

Peters' way out of this problem is to insist on what he terms a commonsense approach. He takes it as virtually axiomatic that there is a strong link between emotion and appraisal and states that consideration *must* be given to a broad range of emotions, not just fear and anger, which are those that most experimental psychologists have dwelt on. If we do this, and then make a list of all the emotion words we can think of, then Peters argues that we will find that most of these words also characterize motive. Thus, in Peter's view, at this commonsense level there is considerable overlap between emotion and motive.

However, Peters goes on to draw an important distinction between emotion and motivation. In everyday language we speak of motives in situations in which we are searching for explanations of behaviour—'he criticized what you said *because* he feels a need to be dominant', 'he ate *because* he was hungry'. Peters instead suggests that we speak of emotions in situations where people are passive, where they are being overcome by emotion—'he was blinded by anger', 'he could do nothing to stop himself trembling with anxiety', 'he was overcome by love'. In particular, Peters holds that we tend to view emotions in this way if we judge their antecedents to be dangerous or frustrating. Peters is therefore arguing in support of an everyday conceptual connection between motivation and action, and between emotion and passivity or inaction. Although motivation and emotion are connected in that they each involve appraisals, they are distinct in that emotion is not connected to action. Peters maintains that even when there seems to be a relationship between emotion and activity within the autonomic nervous system, the activity involved is still passive—we go white with fear or blush with embarrassment, responses it is very difficult to control. Such responses tend to occur in spite of our better judgment.

Peters suggests further that there are other linkages between emotion and motivation and emotion and action, but these are rather more indirect. He affirms that emotion can suppress or enhance motor performance. For example, if we are angry then we might well act more vigorously than if we were not angry. Looked at in this light, a phenomenon such as anger can function simultaneously as a motive and an emotion. We feel the emotion and at the same time are propelled to action. Similarly, Peters argues that actions such as blindly lashing out in extreme frustration or anger have an intermediate status. They are not like an automatic reaction to a stimulus such as electric shock, nor are they fully-fledged, carefully judged actions. They fall somewhere between these two and in Peters' view are based on intuitive appraisals.

Peters extends this view to suggest that there is a *de facto* relationship between emotion and higher mental processes such as memory and perception. Any appraisal which is connected with an emotion must alter the general assessment which is being made at the time. For example, if we appraise something as unpleasant or bad for us, then under some conditions this will obscure what might be relevant for adaptive behaviour in the situation, and under other conditions will highlight it. Either way, however, there is distortion. It would seem that with views such as this, Peters is rejecting Arnold's analysis of emotion, even though he is using similar concepts to characterize it. Arnold (see Chapter 2) links emotion and action, believing that an emotion involves us in a feeling tendency towards or away from something. Peters, on the other hand, believes that an emotion simply comes over us, again as a result of an appraisal, and that there is very little that we can do about it.

As a final stage in his analysis, Peters argues that there is a conceptual connection between emotion and wishing. Motivation is concerned with 'wanting', which leads to action; emotion is concerned with the much vaguer 'wishing', which does not lead to action. Peters cites the example of grief. If a woman is mourning her dead husband, she is in fact wishing he were still alive. However, there is obviously no action she can take which will bring him back to life, so the emotion wells up. Although this is an obvious and extreme example, Peters holds that all emotion is like this—we wish for things and can do little or nothing to gratify our wishes and the emotion overcomes us.

A further distinction can be drawn here between the views of Peters and those of Arnold. Arnold emphasizes the immediate quality of emotion and contrasts it with slower, more deliberate, rational understanding. Peters suggests that it is just the appraisal which is immediate and intuitive, and any actions which follow are uncoordinated and certainly cannot be regarded as means to an end. Essentially, then, Peters is suggesting that although emotion involves appraisal, it is a passive, nonmotivational phenomenon about which we can do very little, but which can impede or enhance our motor (or perhaps rational) behaviour.

A. R. Louch

Louch (1966) takes an entirely different tack from Peters. He puts forward, via an analysis of the difficulties which beset any conceptualization of emotion and which attend the traditional rational/emotional distinction, a strong argument that emotion is firmly linked to action, and indeed can be used to explain it.

Louch's starting point is that pleasure and pain can be regarded as different ways of evaluating objects or qualities. If this is so, then emotion must be viewed in the same way. Secondly, he believes that emotions are both caused by stimuli and are themselves causes of behaviour. As a background, he also points to various difficulties which confront any theory of emotion, be it philosophical or psychological. For example, there is the problem that the labels of emotion tend to be used in a number of ways, as distinguishing between attitudes which are for something and those which are against something (e.g. love or hate) or to distinguish between different intensities (e.g. dislike and hate, like and love). Also, in different contexts we regard people either as acting emotionally or as feeling emotion. This of course implies a very basic point about the study of emotion, that is, we can *never* be sure of what another person is feeling—is that child *really* sad? Is that man *really* angry? and so on.

Louch develops his viewpoint by contrasting it with that of Austin (1961). Austin argues that if actions are regarded as simply expressive of emotions, then there are occasions on which we could observe a man's behaviour and be quite sure of what he must be feeling. However, against this, it might be that the man is falsifying his behaviour, is creating a purposeful discrepancy between his emotion and his action in order to conceal what he is really feeling. He could have many reasons for doing this. Secondly, we do not need to look at our own behaviour to decide what emotion we are ourselves experiencing. Austin would disagree with this. He suggests that to say 'I am angry', or 'I am afraid' is itself a performance of behaviour; it is part of the anger or fear, not just a description of it. Also, when we decide that someone is truly angry or truly afraid we do so on the basis of an evaluation of his situation as well as his behaviour, which of course is a point which has been well explored by social psychologists of emotion (e.g. Frijda 1969). Thus Austin is making emotion a truly *rational* and clear response.

Louch sees a number of difficulties with this view. First, he argues that emotions are frequently regarded as passions or forces (much as Peters views them) rather than as expressions of behaviour. These are forces which we cannot control. Also, contrasts have frequently been drawn between emotional and nonemotional (rational) behaviour. Even if this distinction is disregarded and both emotional and nonemotional actions are viewed as justifiable responses to particular situations, the term emotion is still often applied to behaviour which is generally disapproved and the term rational to behaviour which is approved.

Second, Louch affirms that the labels of emotion classify feelings which come about as a result of situations which lead to emotional behaviour. But very different emotional states are described in terms of similar feelings. For example, the statement 'I feel tense' could apply to all manner of emotional states. This means that we cannot easily, or with any certainty, identify an emotion by making reference to a feeling.

Third, Louch argues that there is a very wide variation in emotional behaviour, with enormous idiosyncracies involved. It is therefore difficult to think of emotion as a conventional expression of standard situations. And at present it is still not known the extent to which learning is implicated in emotion. Of course, we often tend to use the situation to account for the emotion, as Austin suggests. But a situation which makes one man angry might leave another man unmoved, and what one man appraises as frightening might go unnoticed by another.

Consequently, Louch suggests that it is more appropriate to ascribe emotions to behaviours occurring in particular contexts which have been appraised in particular ways by people. Naturally, there may well be some similarities between people's appraisals which will lead to the emergence of various patterns. The problem comes when we can see no sensible connection between the context and the emotion which is being expressed in it. This will frequently be the case with what has been termed abnormal emotion, in schizophrenia for example. At this point we need some technique to find the individual's unique perception of the world—a very difficult exercise to pursue but one which clearly suggests phenomenological investigation.

By these and similar arguments, Louch arrives at a general statement of his views. 'Desires and emotions, pleasures and pains, are identified in ourselves and others, in the light of what we regard or infer or see as desirable, appropriate or entailed by the situation in which we find ourselves.' (1966, p. 93) Louch uses terms such as these to explain actions, the main purpose of his book, by regarding the situation as in some way entitling the action, in the case discussed above via emotion. In this, Louch's ideas are in obvious contradistinction to those of Peters.

G. Ryle

It is Ryle (1948) in his influential book *The Concept of Mind* who takes the hardest look at emotions from the viewpoint of modern philosophy. In so doing, he brings together the sort of ideas put forward by Peters and Louch, whilst going further than this and making a considerable analysis of the concept of feeling. His starting point is the affirmation that emotions are made up of, or suggest, inclinations (motives), moods, agitations (or commotions), and feelings. Of these, the first three are simply propensities; they are not occurrences in the way that feelings are. He develops his argument by drawing a series of contrasts between these different aspects of emotion as he sees it.

Ryle begins with what is perhaps the most important comparison, that between feelings and inclinations. He states that feelings are what people describe by phrases such as 'a thrill of anticipation', and they are also names for specific bodily sensations, for example qualms of apprehension or sickness. Thus we tend to give to some feelings specific locations whilst others are assigned a general coverage of the whole body (a flash of anger or a glow of pride). It is clear then that Ryle is suggesting that feelings can be emotions. But people also tend to characterize emotions as *motives*. For example, the behaviour of a clever leader is explained by saying that he carries with him certain dispositions, to be dominant and resourceful, and so on, and that on occasion these will be manifest in his behaviour. However, as well as being expected to behave in certain ways, a man seen as a leader is also expected to feel certain things, although these feelings do not indicate his leadership as well as does his behaviour. Ryle argues that it is wrong to say that because a man takes over some situation and tells another what to do then he must be a leader. Leadership is a disposition, not an event. Ryle believes that the impulse to behave in a particular way, to tell someone else what to do or to set an example, comes from a feeling.

Ryle would argue that a leader would never actually feel full of leadership; there is no specific feeling for this. The leader will instead have specific feelings which are associated with particular activities which might be involved in leadership. Ryle is rejecting the idea that words which are descriptive of motives are names of feelings or even of tendencies to have feelings. Via a very explicit example, Ryle goes on to clarify the two ways in which we commonly explain anything. The first is causal: 'the glass broke *because* the stone hit it'. Here, 'because' refers to an event. The second way of explanation is propositional: 'the glass broke *because* it was brittle'. Here, 'because' means, if the glass were struck sharply then it would just shatter. In this sense the breakage is explained when the first and the second events (striking and shattering) satisfy the proposition.

These two senses of explanation can be just as simply applied to accounts of human action. When we speak of someone we commonly ask: 'why did he behave in that way?' With this question we could either be asking to be given a cause or a character analysis. If we are given an answer in terms of motive then this is character analysis; it is a propositional explanation. But due to the form in which the answer is given, it *sounds* as if it is a causal account when it is not. For example, if we say that a man ate because he was hungry, then we are making a propositional statement of the kind: if food were to be put into the man's mouth, then he would chew and swallow it.

Ryle puts forward a number of suggestions in support of this general argument. First, he suggests that we can never be sure, we can never 'know', that the cause of something is a feeling; there is no direct test which can be made of this. However, it is possible to speculate about the existence of motives, although such speculations may only end with the status of hypothetical propositions. There is no way in which a proposed motive such as the need to be dominant, for example, could be studied or seen directly.

Second, Ryle argues that it is possible for us to be quite wrong in 'explaining' an action with a motive. The behaviour in question may simply have occurred through force of habit. In such a case the action would be explained by a very specific disposition, not a general hypothetical one. And third, Ryle points out that we can never know how many motives are at work at any time, all underlying some act. It is difficult to uncover such possibilities by questioning people as to their feelings, since as Ryle suggests, their answers are notoriously unreliable.

To summarize so far, if we say that someone did something because of a particular motive, we are merely saying that, in our judgment, he *would* behave in a particular way if .... One aspect of this argument is that a person will *feel* something when he is engaged in these acts. So, in Ryle's terms, both the motive and the feeling are part of an emotion, but the former is a disposition and the latter an occurrence, albeit a difficult one to pin down for study.

A second comparison which Ryle makes is between inclinations (motives) and agitations. He uses the concept of agitation to describe any degree of commotion which apparently interferes with coherent thought. Defined in this way, an agitation is quite different from a disposition. A person would not be so bursting with leadership that he was incapable of leading. Ryle argues that agitations imply that there exist inclinations against which the agitations work. For example, grief might be regarded as an inclination to affection which has been thwarted by the death of the person to whom we wish to direct the affection.

Ryle holds that in everyday discourse, emotion is often used to refer to agitations. If this is a correct way of conceptualizing emotion, and Ryle is clearly saying that it is not, then motives and inclinations cannot be emotions. Some emotion words, such as 'worried' or 'anxious' or 'embarrassed', are used to refer either to *moods* or to proneness to moods. If such a proneness becomes continual or chronic, then we have a character trait. In Ryle's terms, this concept of mood does not imply action; rather, it stands for liabilities. To say that someone is in a certain mood (for example gloomy) is to describe his present behaviour whilst simultaneously predicting his future behaviour. Ryle also regards agitations as liability conditions, but such as not to involve intention, as moods might. If we are agitated, then we give no thought to what we should do or what we should think; our normal behaviour and thought processes are interfered with. This, then, is yet another aspect of emotion in Ryle's view.

In his analysis of *mood,* Ryle suggests that if we say that someone is in a certain mood, we have judged him to be in a frame of mind to say or to do many things between which there is some kind of loose connection. In other words, if a person is in a mood, it is monopolizing his behaviour. Looked at in this way, the words which we use to describe moods refer to short-term tendencies which are characterizing the complete 'set' of the person at the time.

Ryle believes that people often use mood words also as feeling words, but suggests that this is wrong usage. Feelings come and go rapidly, whereas moods are lasting and presumably have a slow onset and offset. Ryle states that this mistake is made because, very naturally, people say, for example, 'I feel depressed' or 'I feel better', but depressed and better are not feelings, at least not in the sense of emotion. However, to be in a particular mood is to be ready or set to have certain types of feeling in certain types of situation. If, for example, we are in a gloomy pessimistic mood, then we will be set to greet any suggestion made to us with feelings of dullness and heaviness.

Putting together two of Ryle's ideas on emotion produces yet another problem. There are many words which are used to refer to feelings and also to bodily sensations. For example, 'I feel sick' can be used quite literally to designate a feeling in my stomach, or metaphorically as a comment on the life I am leading. Obviously, we have to learn to designate bodily sensations in communicating to one another. We experience such sensations in particular situations, and because they are important to us we try to describe them. Other people correct and refine our descriptions and reinforce them when they are correct in terms of their own experience and learning in similar situations. It makes good sense to ask from what motives bodily sensations spring, and Ryle suggests emotional feelings belong causally to agitations; they are signs of them.

Ryle makes a final distinction, between feeling and pleasure (or pain presumably). He argues that pleasure suggests certain kinds of moods and certain kinds of feeling. Ryle illustrates this by pointing out that the word pleasure can be replaced by verbs such as 'enjoy' or 'like', or by words such as 'delight' or 'rapture'. The latter are mood words which imply agitation. However, states or descriptions of states such as delight or enjoyment are not feelings in Ryle's estimation. Most sensations or feelings are neither enjoyed nor disliked.

In conclusion, Ryle suggests that there are three major ways in which the idea of emotion is commonly used. In the first two it is employed in an attempt to explain behaviour by referring to emotions. Hence we use emotion in the sense of motives or inclinations on the basis of which more or less intelligent actions are made, or we use it to refer to moods, including agitations or perturbations. The third sense in which Ryle believes emotion to be commonly used is in reference to pangs and twinges. These are feelings and emotions, although this usage clearly does not allow any explanation of behaviour to be made.

Finally, Ryle argues that we gain an understanding of a person's inclinations and moods by what he says, how he says it, and the gestures he makes whilst he says it. We also use the same information to discover our own motives and moods, although this is arguably more difficult. Ryle believes that we cannot get at moods and inclinations in any direct way by consciousness and introspection; and he holds that they are no more special experiences than are habits or illnesses.

Here, then, are three related but differing views of emotion. They provoke at least two questions: what, if any, is the common ground between these viewpoints? and what can psychologists learn from them about the study of emotion? The common ground comes mainly from the manner in which the analyses have been made. Each of them starts from the viewpoint of everyday usage of the word emotion, and of the various terms which are associated with it. They then make thorough attempts to understand the fine distinctions that we make, perhaps to our surprise, in our everyday discourse. Frequently, this type of approach is glossed over very rapidly by the psychologist.

To answer the second question, perhaps what can be gained from these ideas is a fairly severe cautionary note. After reading Ryle, for example, there can be no doubt that emotion is not an easy concept which can be dismissed lightly, or defined and studied and understood simply. First, there needs to be made a conceptual analysis. Of course, given that there is rough agreement as to the subject matter of emotion, it is perfectly reasonable and quite valid for the experimental psychologist to undertake his empirical research. However, it is also necessary that some thought be put in at the conceptual level to gain a proper understanding, particularly if concern is with a phenomenological analysis of the cognitive aspects of emotion. This of course is the other common ground of the three philosophers; they each state or imply that a crucial facet of emotion is the experiential.

THE PHENOMENOLOGICAL APPROACH TO EMOTION

Buytedijk (1950) makes a systematic attempt to state what is involved in a phenomenological approach to emotion. A basic assumption is that behaviour is a series or system of *intentional* acts, an idea which is utterly opposed to the assumptions of radical behaviourism or any of its milder derivations. The most appropriate way to understand intentions is through an analysis of consciousness. The assumption here (although Buytedijk would call it a fact) is that consciousness is necessarily of something which has a meaning because the consciousness is directed towards it intentionally. Viewed in this way, consciousness is not imaginary, nor is it merely hypothesis; it is real.

Quite rightly, Buytedijk points out that science is concerned with facts, but he goes on to question what a fact is, and more especially, whether or not feelings are facts. If I say, 'I feel angry whenever I am in the presence of my colleague X', is this factual? Buytedijk's definition of a feeling is that it is an *act* which is intentionally present. The meaning of feelings then comes from what they signify. If we feel happy or we feel angry, then this implies that we know the meaning that certain situations will have for us.

The general phenomenological approach begins with the idea that consciousness is always consciousness of something else, and that we are also conscious of existing. This means that we are aware of being in situations in which we must respond, that is, we must have attitudes and feelings and make intentional acts. Feeling and emotion function to assure us of our attitudes in various situations.

Each situation has its own special feeling for us. It is a spontaneous response to a situation which transforms the situation into a new world. Some sort of choice must be involved here. Our emotional attitude to a situation is confirmed by a feeling, although we choose (in some nonreflective way) to become happy in some situation in order to alter our feeling towards it.

Within this sort of context, Buytedijk suggests that emotion is *not* intentional, it is akin to sensation or excitation. I am only conscious of myself. If I loathe someone, then I project myself as loathing and make further projections about the person. This is brought about by feeling. Such projection rebounds and has the character of emotion. Thus we cannot experience emotion without feeling, but emotion is not intentional, it is the quality of our existence which occurs through feeling. Although feeling and emotion, viewed in this light, are spontaneous and unintentional, we can alter our feelings by the situations which we can create with the words we use. So, we use language intentionally to modify, enhance or suppress our feelings.

Buytedijk argues that there are two extreme ways in which our existence meets its limitations; these are resistance and no-resistance, as intentional acts. This purportedly leads to four ways in which we can feel pleased or pleasant and four in which we can feel displeased or unpleasant. We feel pleased if we: (1) are with something or someone, (2) have a flowing-in or a flowing-out existence, (3) expand our accentuated self, or (4) assimilate. We feel unpleasant if we: (1) are thrown back, (2) are subdued, (3) are injured, or (4) lose part of ourselves.

Buytedijk argues that this phenomenological analysis of the essence of various situations can be used to understand the meaning of emotional expressions. One of his examples is the smile. What is characteristic (phenomenologically) of situations which cause a smile? He suggests that a smile anticipates something in the future. We are moderately excited and know that this excitement will remain moderate in our intentional act. A smile is an easy physical act which springs from a general attitude of active inactivity. There is an implicit paradox in this. Smiling is an activity which points to a relaxation, a threshold of something such as joy or elation. So, with a smile we are making a transformation of the situation which faces us, and at the same time are confronting ourselves with this transformed world, that is, we are aware of it.

Clearly, a truly phenomenological analysis of emotion is not an easy matter. What then is its value? Is it worth pursuing? Buytedijk takes a definite stand on these questions. He points out that the phenomenological approach is not introspection; that is, it is not an inspection of subjective experiences. Rather, it is directed at experienced phenomena and towards different acts such as perception, thinking, feeling, and so on, even though these might not be viewed analytically. It is worth noting that this is a very different use of the word 'act' than is found amongst the behaviourally oriented psychologists.

It is irrelevant whether or not the phenomenon being considered is real. The emphasis is on what is termed its *essential structure*. Hence, asking the question 'What is guilt, or anger?' is asking no more than 'What is a chair, or a table?' It is not causal relationships which are sought, but an exploration of the inner essential structure, in this case the structure of emotion. A phenomenological approach, then, needs more and more complete description in these same terms. The aim is to make these analyses of the experience of feelings in various situations, in order to discover patterns and invariances in our usual, normal modes of existence.

Hillman's theory of emotion

Hillman (1960) provides the most complete phenomenological account of emotion. Having drawn a picture of emotion as an exceedingly complex set of phenomena (and this is largely ignoring the large amounts of empirical research which have been carried out), and having summarized previous attempts at phenomenological accounts of emotion, Hillman argues that it is not enough merely to provide a complex theory which takes into account all these complexities. Instead, Hillman wishes to *explain* emotion, and to do this bases his analysis on Aristotle's four causes. He believes that such an analysis gives explanation and also provides answers to why? questions. By way of comparison, Ryle's (1948) analysis of emotion, or indeed any behaviourist analysis, limits the cause in emotion to efficient cause, which Hillman avows to be insufficient.

Efficient cause. Hillman argues that emotion is more than a cause and effect relationship. There exist some events that cannot easily be separated in time and space in the way that cause and effect can be. Hillman suggests that efficient cause in emotion (that is, stimuli which have been suggested as causing emotion) falls into two groups. First, there are representations, conflicts, and situations. Second, there are those supposed causes which have a physiological basis, such as arousal, instinct, constitution, and physical energy. There are also theories which construe emotion as without efficient cause, for example those which hold that emotion is spontaneous or continuous.

Hillman integrates these various viewpoints with the concept of the *symbol* as an efficient cause. He conceives of the symbol as a mixture of inner and outer, conscious and unconscious representations. In these terms a situation will arouse emotion if it is perceived symbolically. 'Emotion is thus the symbolic apprehension of the subjective psyche . . .' (1960, p. 253). Here, Hillman is not simply referring to inner subjective reality; he argues that emotion is also concerned with symbolic aspects of objective reality.

One implication of Hillman's idea that emotion proceeds through symbolic perceptions of the world is that emotion must be partially learned, since one aspect of the symbol which brings it about is also learned: that is the social context. However, emotion must also be partially innate, since the relevant symbols also have their unconscious aspects. As we grow and mature and increase in our general capacities, this must mean that as part of this growth there is a change in the symbolic representations which cause emotion. There will also in Hillman's view be changes of this sort as the various stages of life are passed through.

Hillman also argues that the symbols of emotion, which he regards as being irrational, autonomous, and therefore creative, must have their corresponding bodily and physiological representation. But by the same token, he also maintains that the effectiveness of any physiological change will depend on what he terms its psychic realization. Finally, to let Hillman summarize for himself his view of the efficient cause in emotion: 'There is emotion because the world is being apprehended and lived through a symbol' (1960, p. 258).

Material cause. The concept of material cause as applied to emotion asks the question: what is the stuff of emotion? In discussing this, Hillman follows Aristotle in regarding matter as synonymous with form. Typically, there are six criteria which are used to establish evidence for the existence of material cause. Hillman discusses these as they may be applied to emotion.

(1) Matter is an abstract principle which is universible and unknowable; in this light, emotion is energy. (2) Matter is chaos; this suggests that emotion is an unconscious weakness, a disorder on which everything else is founded. (3) Matter is an extension of the body; this means that matter and the body may be regarded as one and the same, and implies that we know and experience emotion through our bodies. (4) Matter is building materials; emotions are representations. (5) Matter is inertia; we know our emotions through muscular tension. (6) Matter is a field of force; emotion is an interplay between invisible forces both within us and outside ourselves.

Hillman argues that, as applied to emotion, these six criteria of material cause can be integrated by viewing emotion as energy. He describes the basic emotional experiences of positive and negative energy as being love and anxiety. To be able to say that emotion is present, there have to be gross bodily changes plus representations of these in consciousness. At the same time, however, emotion *is* the body as we experience it here and now. Thus the body becomes the material cause of emotion and the order of its energy is a person's homeostatic balance.

The implication of this view of the material cause of emotion is that emotion is the psychological aspect of general energy, and as such must be occurring all the time. Emotion is bridging the gap between ourselves and the world, putting us into an inseparable interaction with the world.

Formal cause. Although Aristotle puts form before matter, Hillman simply regards them both as necessary but not in any particular order. As in anything else, the formal cause of emotion must be its essence, its essential defining qualities, that which distinguishes it from all else.

The two types of theory which are possible here are firstly that emotion can be defined through its expression, and secondly that it can be defined through a qualitative analysis of inner states. Hillman regards the concept which unites these two possibilities as being the soul, but prefers to refer to it as the psyche. The psyche then, in Hillman's view, is the formal cause of emotion; emotion is the total pattern of the psyche, a sort of generalized and very complex whole. Looked at in this way, Hillman believes that emotion can be distinguished from more limited psychical events such as sensation and will.

The implications of this analysis of the formal cause of emotion are that both the conscious and unconscious systems in emotion must be at work simultaneously. Also, it is implied that inwardness in emotion occurs when a person identifies himself with the central quality of his emotion. As will be seen later, this is a clear statement of the existential view of the here-and-now quality of emotion, a person's being-in-the-world.

The energy of material cause is not sufficient to explain emotion as Hillman sees it. The psyche gives emotion its form and allows both experience and behaviour to follow. This links easily with Hillman's conceptualization of efficient cause in that the symbolic realizations which are an essential part of emotion change the whole personality. Symbol and form are seen as corresponding to each other, and to occur at all they both need energy.

Hillman believes that this view of the formal cause of emotion makes sense of the idea of total emotional (that is, psychic) problems and also allows us to see why emotion is often thought to be a disorder. The individual (or his ego) must be able to withstand a possible massive and total psychic response. If he cannot do this then he may become overwhelmed, an idea which has shades of the view of emotion proposed by Peters.

Final cause. There are two ways of looking at Aristotle's concept of final cause. It can be seen as the purpose or the goal of something, or, more simply, it can be seen as the end of some operation. Hillman reconciles these two possibilities by suggesting that the finish of any emotional process is an achievement; this is its purpose. Such an achievement is not necessarily something which is final in time. Emotion, in Hillman's view, *can* be an event in which the final cause is contemporaneous with the efficient, material, and formal causes. Thus the final cause of emotion is its value.

From the various theoretical standpoints which have been taken towards emotion Hillman picks out three which seem to speak of it in terms of value: emotion can achieve survival, or signification, or improvement. He links these three with the very broad concept of change. Hillman believes therefore that emotion occurs in order to change things, and also that emotion is itself change, within the terms of the four causes. Of course, it must be asked how the change purportedly involved in emotion can be distinguished from any other sort of change. Hillman argues that it is possible to make this distinction by using the idea of transformation. Hence, emotion becomes a transformation of conscious representations in terms of symbolic reality; it is a transformation of energy, of the whole psyche.

This still does not state what the possible value of emotion might be. When is emotion good? Here, Hillman's argument becomes rather more tenuous. He suggests that *true* emotion (that is, not just deep feelings, or concentrated willing, or abortive emotion) always achieves its purpose; it is always 'good'. Its results, however, may be good or bad, though emotion itself is always an improvement of some sort.

There are at least two reasons why this argument is a little difficult to accept. First, it seems to be not much more than a firm statement, an avowal with no good backing. And second, it is not easy to see how it is possible to distinguish between true emotion and deep feelings or abortive emotions. It would be hopelessly circular to attempt this distinction simply in the terms that true emotion is always good. However, if Hillman's avowals are accepted, then this way of conceptualizing the formal causes of emotion brings with it immediate implications for therapy, which is one of Hillman's main concerns. Such implications would be based on the general idea that true emotion should always be more highly valued than the conscious system alone.

Finally, to let Hillman speak for himself:

'Each emotion has: its own pattern of behaviour and quality of experience, which is always a total attitude of the whole psyche; its own distribution and intensity of energy in the field of the human body situation; its own symbolic stimulation which is partly conscious and partly not presented to consciousness; its own achieved transformation which has some survival value and is some improvement compared with nonemotional states'.

(1960, p. 287)

Sartre's theory of emotion

In conjunction with the philosophical conceptualizations of emotion described earlier, this summary of Buytedjik's and Hillman's ideas gives the flavour of a tradition of work very different from that which comes from psychology's usual background of conventional science. Such ideas are also reflected in theories of emotion propounded by various existential psychologists. Sartre (1948) provides the best example of this approach, although the interested reader should also look at the work of Goldstein (1951) and Strasser (1970). Unfortunately, Sartre's starting point for a theory of emotion is somewhat of an overgeneralization, namely, that psychologists tend to think of consciousness of emotion as reflective, a state of mind. Even in 1948 there were many psychologists to whom this summary statement would not apply, and in fact some who would not even see the usefulness of any analysis of the consciousness of emotion. Just to give one example, Harlow and Stagner's (1933 theory of emotion was couched almost completely in behavioural terms and made no mention of consciousness. However, assuming that Sartre did not set up a straw man, he argues that an emotion such as fear does not begin as the consciousness of being afraid. Instead he maintains that emotional consciousness is *non-reflective*, at least to begin with. Sartre believes that emotional consciousness is a general consciousness of the world.

Fear, to continue with this example for a moment, is characterized by Sartre as always *of* something, of some object or situation. Hence, emotion begins from a perception and then continually returns to the object which is perceived. An emotion such as fear cannot then be in any way free-floating; it is always attached to the environment through perception. In talking of perception in this way, Sartre is perhaps implying some process of appraisal and reappraisal, much as Arnold does. To Sartre, the emotional subject and the object of the emotion are inextricably bound up. *Emotion, then, is a manner of apprehending the world.* For example, if we are faced with a problem which it is imperative that we solve, then we see the world through whatever actions we may take in trying to solve the problem. If our solution fails, then we see the world through the irritation which this causes. For example, if we believe that our wife or husband is losing interest in us, then we see our every action in terms of what to do about this. If we fail in our attempts, then again our perceptions are thoroughly coloured.

According to Sartre, reflection, a state of mind, comes into the picture in another way. We *can* reflect on our activity, our behaviour, but we can also do things without reflecting. For example, at present I am (hopefully) conscious of what I am writing, but I am not conscious of being conscious of it. In other words, I am not conscious that these words are being written by me, at least I wasn't until I thought of using it as an example. In short, to act, or to behave, we can be conscious of *what* we are doing without being conscious that *we* are doing it.

A second important point in Sartre's theory is that he believes emotion to be a *transformation of the world.* With this idea, Sartre is envisaging situations in which we are being pushed and pulled by needs and desires, but the possible paths for realizing these are blocked, or they are too difficult to follow, or they are in conflict. So, in attempting to cope with this we try to change the world, the reasoning being that we cannot deal with the world as it is, whereas we might be able to cope with a changed world. Sartre does not see this as an effort which is conscious of itself, rather it is a different way of getting something. The normal way is closed, so we try to change the world with our emotions so that new ways exist. Sartre holds that the impetus for making this new emotional approach comes directly from the impossibility of solving the problem with what is already available to us. Intervening between the insoluble problem and the emotional transformation is consciousness or reflection. For example, if some-one has said something critical to me in an important social context, I am in the situation of wanting to be thought well of but having been criticized. I cannot just sit quietly and accept this, nor is there anything which I can say calmly in return—normal channels of social intercourse are blocked. So I become righteously angry, which at least allows me a way of responding to the situation.

Sartre sees emotional behaviour as different from other sorts of behaviour, even though they each might be coping with some problem. For example, he distinguishes emotional behaviour from the sort of behaviour we engage in if our problem is hunger and we solve it by seeking and eating food. Sartre argues that emotional behaviour is not effectual in this way. Emotion is an attempt to make a *qualitative* change in an object, to give it an altogether new quality without changing it substantively. Directed by our consciousness, the body changes its relationship with the world—we are suddenly seeing a world with changed qualities. It should be understood that Sartre is *not* saying that our emotions change the world in reality; the real world, outside us, is still the same as ever. Rather our emotions create a *magical* transformation.

An example will help to make this point clear. Sartre states that if we are afraid and run away from the source of our fear, then we are usually reckoned to be behaving in a rational way. He argues that this is not rational behaviour though. In his terms, we are not running to gain shelter, or security, or protection, but because we cannot 'annihilate ourselves in unconsciousness'. Our fear and running away brings about a magical change in the world so that the dangerous object, with which we can deal in no other way, is negated. It is as if, by running away in fear, we are pretending that we are in a world in which the dangerous object does not exist. So, as Sartre views it, fear is consciousness magically negating or denying something which substantively and dangerously exists in the external world.

In his book, Sartre gives many examples of emotions which can be analysed according to the schema he suggests. Simply to make clear the descriptions given so far, one such example will be discussed.

According to Sartre, passive sadness is neither a state of dejection nor a motionless turning away. Rather, it is what we experience when something important to us has been taken away or removed, a friend has suddenly died for example, or we have been sacked without warning. In these circumstances we have to search for new ways of doing things which do not involve our friend or our job. Sartre argues that if we are not up to solving such a problem directly, then we might react with the melancholy of passive sadness, which has the effect of suppressing the necessity to look for new ways of doing things. Our sadness transforms the world, magically, into something which has an undifferentiated structure. It puts us into a world in which we can behave as though there were nothing else expected of us; we no longer need to try and live as before, to make other friends or to get another job. Our sadness has made everything bleak, so we withdraw from this bleakness into shelter. This view of passive sadness characterizes it similarly to a Freudian defence mechanism; it is working to protect us from the harsher and more practical realities.

In developing his ideas, Sartre makes the point that simple behaviour is *not*, and can never be, emotion. In Sartre's view, emotion always involves a qualitative transformation of the world. However, he argues that there are some behaviours which at first sight seem to be emotion. For example, it is commonplace to see people pretending to anger or pretending to joy. Sartre describes these as spurious or false emotions (although he does not make clear how it is possible observationally to distinguish between real and false emotions. On occasions, this will presumably be difficult, if not impossible). Sartre's main point here is that real emotion is always accompanied by a belief. We use our will to give new qualities to objects in the environment and then believe these qualities to be real. This means that to be identified as real, an emotion must be experienced; it is not something which we can simply stop when we wish to, or merely cast off because it is unpleasant. Sartre argues that to be genuine an emotion must fill us and overflow. Subjectively, the force of this argument is easy to see in distinguishing between something like false anger which we can turn on or off at will, and real anger which simply overtakes us and which we can do little about. Of course, it may be that if we engage vigorously enough in false anger it is possible to turn this into real anger, but Sartre makes no special provision for this possibility.

Sartre regards the physiological concomitants of emotion as the phenomena of the type of belief described above. It is they which show us the genuineness of the emotion. He also views the physiological responses as not being translatable into behaviour—we can stop running but we cannot stop trembling, at least not easily. Although behaviour is the form of the emotion, Satre holds that it occurs in a somewhat independently disordered body, physiologically speaking. This may very well be so, but the argument made above also applies in this case, and perhaps has even more force. First, it is possible to engender physiological responses which are very similar to, if not indentical with, those involved in emotion in other ways, by vigorous exercise for example. Hence it is not possible to say that because a certain set of physiological responses are present then this is a sufficient condition for emotion. And second, there is a great deal of recent evidence that it is possible to exercise an impressive control over physiological functioning, certainly to the extent that we could stop trembling (e.g. Miller 1969).

Returning to Sartre's thesis, he supports his general position by arguing that the body is two things simultaneously. It is an object which exists in the world, and it is also something which is actively *lived* by our consciousness. In this light, emotion is then picked out as a phenomenon of belief. Our consciousness *lives* the new magical world which it has created, it puts us right into an emotional world. This is the new world which has a completely new quality. Sartre points out that bodily, the physiological aspects of emotion are commonplace and might indeed be experienced in a fever. Bodily emotion is a local disorder, whereas in Sartre's view it is the consciousness which lives the emotion and realizes it.

Sartre next turns his attentions to the *origins* of emotion. These he regards as coming from a spontaneous debasement which is lived by the consciousness in the face of the world. It is an alternative way of enduring something which would otherwise be difficult to endure. The bodily changes which occur as part of the emotion are just the biological belief as lived by the consciousness, but as it is seen from the outside.

However, the explanation is not as simple as this. Sartre makes the point that the consciousness is not conscious of itself in emotion. If it were, then the emotion would be false. If I am aware of myself being angry, then this is no longer true anger. The consciousness itself believes and so it is caught up, it is entirely absorbed in living the belief. In emotion, Sartre holds that the consciousness knows *only* itself. As soon as the consciousness becomes aware of itself, then the emotion no longer exists as true emotion. The consciousness is in its turn moved by its emotion and heightens it. We run faster and in so doing become more afraid than we were to begin with. In Sartre's view, emotions all give a transcending quality to an object or situation. These are always magical qualities and they seem infinite. It is this which transcends and maintains our emotions, according to Sartre.

Sartre also has it that not all emotions are fully-fledged. Subtle emotions simply give us momentary glimpses of the unpleasant or the excellent. These are dim intuitions which are full of potential. They give us a vague sense of disaster or of something very good. Sartre views the social world as full of such potentialities; it is always magical. Sartre sees two possibilities here. Either we constitute the magic of the world or the world suddenly reveals itself as magical. He also believes that these two ways of apprehending a new world can interact, and that they are not just confined to the human level, but may also occur in animals.

The modification of the world which Sartre assumes take place in emotion are not just a matter of accident. *Everything* is modified to give a new quality to the world; to give it a horrific or a beautiful quality, or sometimes even a combination of the two. Emotion has to be like this, Sartre maintains, since the view of the world we have when we are in an emotional state cannot be achieved in the ordinary everyday deterministic world. When we are in an emotional state, it is as if we were dreaming in Sartre's view, or as if we were in a fever. The *whole* world is transformed and perceived in a different way.

Overall then, in Sartre's view, there are two possible interactions between consciousness and the world. On the one hand, our consciousness in the world can be a rational, deterministic, practically utilizable sense. On the other hand, our consciosness may, through emotion, make us see the world as a huge non-utilizable whole. In this second sense, the world appears to be absolutely coherent—it all hangs together, magically. Finally, Sartre holds that emotion comes from the inside rather than from the outside. It is a sudden drop of consciousness into the magical. It is a different mode of existence, a way of existentially being-in-the-world.

MEASUREMENT

Can phenomenological accounts of emotion be put to empirical test? Can the ideas expressed in this chapter be placed within the domain of more conventional psychology? An answer to these basic questions will be attempted by discussing possible empirical investigations of emotional experience within the context of a conceivable scientific basis for phenomenological psychology.

Although Mandler's (1976) analysis of the role of consciousness in emotion is broadly relevant here, the most appropriate background comes from Tart's (1972) consideration of measurement possibilities in the study of altered states of consciousness (ASC). The general point is that it might be reasonable to add emotion to Tart's list of ASCs which are capable of scientific investigation. When experiencing emotion, the individual is in a particular state, although often only partially, which is different from his normal state of consciousness. Phenomenological psychologists would argue that he is experiencing a new perception of the world, a new series of insights, perhaps even a magical transformation of the world as Sartre (1948) might suggest.

The general possibility of the semiscientific investigation of the phenomenology of emotion can be explored further within the framework of

Tart's four major principles of science: observation, public techniques, theory, and verifiable prediction. There are a number of ways in which a particular emotional experience can be observed. The investigator can record his own emotional experiences, either whilst they are ongoing or afterwards. Or he can ask other people to make records of their own emotional experiences either during them or afterwards. These would provide his basic data. Of course, there are standard methodological objections which can be made to any technique such as these. For example, the recording of emotional experiences while the person is in an emotional state might interfere with the experience of the emotion, or if records are made once the experiences are finished then some essential points might be forgotten or otherwise lost. However, such objections could perhaps be overcome in the way that Tart suggests, by obtaining a general knowledge of the person so that his various biases could be taken into account, and also by insisting on consensual verification.

Could personal observation of emotion be made public? In Tart's terms, to belay this problem there must be consensual validation. This could come in many ways. Comparisons could be made of a person's reports during an emotional experience and afterwards and these could be compared with those of other people who are experiencing or have experienced emotions following similar sets of precipitating circumstances. Naturally, this sort of consideration of the private observation of emotion, and the making public and hence repeatable of such observations, presupposes either trained observers or some techniques which the investigator can use to make up for any lack of training in those he studies.

The next major principle of scientific endeavour according to Tart is theory; theory which is both consistent and useful. This theory exists, mainly because it has been based on the personal observations of a number of phenomenologists who in their own way are as well trained as the more conventional scientists. Such theories are reasonably consistent internally, and appear to make good sense of experimental data, even though they are often couched in terms very different from theories espoused by experimental psychologists.

Finally, there is the question of verifiable prediction. Again, there is little problem here. If data are gained about the experience of emotional states in various situations, then there is no reason why these should not be used to make predictions about other *experiences* in similar situations. As Tart suggests, prediction here is from experience to experience rather than being empirical in the usual way of science, but it is nevertheless verifiable. This is simply another level or another means of verification.

Having established a possible case in support of investigations of, rather than speculations about, the experience of emotion, three specific research possibilities will be considered as examples.

In studies of self-actualization, Maslow's (e.g. 1972) basic ploy was to select for detailed study some two dozen people whom *he* liked or admired very much. These were either Maslow's contemporaries or were eminent individuals from history. They were all older people and all from Western culture. His basic data came from a close study of these people's lives and values, which he gained either from asking questions or from reading. He drew the data together with the concept of self-actualization. One of the central characteristics of the self-actualized person is that he has peak-experiences. Maslow studied peak-experiences in the same way, simply by asking questions of people whom he knew to have had them. In this way he produced a composite picture of peak experiences.

Without going into the details of Maslow's findings, it is perhaps worth saying that they have since been supported by *similar* research conducted by other investigators (e.g. Rogers 1961). Of course, with this sort of research it is impossible to determine the extent to which Maslow's original formulations influenced other investigators to find what they expected to find, or to unwittingly design their studies in such a way that their results would support Maslow's ideas. However, by now, there is a reasonable array of survey-type evidence to support Maslow's original findings. It may be that emotional experience could be studied in similar ways.

A second way of carrying out research into the phenomenology of emotion was suggested and begun by Block (1954), although it has scarcely been followed up since that time. Block used the semantic differential method developed by Osgood (1952). This technique involves the evaluation of an object, or person, or in this case an emotion, on a number of bipolar dimensions separated by seven-point scales: dimensions such as high–low, cold–hot, good–bad, and so on. Fifteen emotions were evaulated by many subjects on twenty such scales.

Block put forward two arguments to support the idea that individual emotional experience could be fairly indexed by the semantic differential. First, he pointed out that there are no conventions to describe emotions. The only way of doing this is by searching private emotional experience, to which of course the characterization of emotion by semantic differential directs he who does it. Second, Block argued that language habits as they have developed, and as exemplified by semantic differentials, when applied to emotion reflect its experiential or phenomenological qualities.

Block carried out two simple descriptive studies, the precise results of which are of little matter here. It is enough to say that he demonstrated convincingly that the semantic differential could be used to make two quite different comparisons of the phenomenology of emotion, and showed that such results could be analysed by the standard statistics used in semantic differential studies. In general, his results showed that male and female Americans describe emotional experiences in very similar ways, and that these were predictably different from descriptions coming from a different culture. As was mentioned above, this work has not been extended, other than by Davitz, whose techniques are similar; it perhaps should be.

A third possible series of methods for studying the experience of emotion can be derived from Kelly's (1955) theory of personal constructs and the repertory grid measurement techniques which he devised to explore the theory (see Bannister and Fransella 1971 and Bannister and Mair 1968 for review).

The repertory grid technique could be straightforwardly applied to investigate experiential aspects of emotion. For example, a person could be asked to list his significant emotional experiences and the underlying constructs elicited in the usual way. Or this could be done for either positive or negative experiences, or for a single emotion. Comparisons could be made between the emotional constructs of people at different developmental stages, in different social circumstances, between normal and abnormal emotion, and so on. Alternatively, a person could be asked to list the major emotions which he believed to have influenced the course of his life, and the usual questions put. This would enable a set of constructs to be drawn out which would represent the person's view of emotion in general There are very many possiblities for study here.

CONCLUSIONS

The aim of this chapter has been to give some idea of what might be considered as views of emotion which are alternatives to those deriving from the traditions of experimental psychology. Of course, these are very much concerned with the experience of emotion rather than its behavioural and physiological aspects. Nevertheless it would seem that such ideas are open to empirical observation, of a sort. Naturally, the possible techniques of study within this general framework can all be criticized on a number of grounds. However, it may be that such criticism leads to their eventual improvement.

Whether or not a causal role is assigned to emotional experience, it cannot be denied that it exists. Perhaps, then, a more complete understanding of emotion would come from the techniques and interests of both conventional and phenomenological psychology. It would seem to be both meaningful and appropriate to attempt to carry out scientifically based investigations of the experiential phenomena of emotion, rather than to leave such things solely to theoreticians and speculators. Whether this type of investigation supports the types of ideas which have been summarized in this chapter remains to be seen. The important point is that such ideas be tested.

6

Emotional Behaviour

For the most part, research and theory in emotional behaviour has focused on what is directly observable and directly measureable. Those interested in emotional behaviour usually see emotion as a response, or a large class of responses, which is basic to life and survival, rather than as a state of the organism. They also sometimes tend to bracket emotion with motivation. They make no attempt to say that emotional states or feelings do not exist, but simply take the emphasis from them and put it instead on what is (at the moment) more open to investigation within the framework of conventional science. Viewed in this way, emotion can be easily defined in terms of the operations necessary to bring it about, an approach which has traditionally been of importance to science, but which may seem too restricted to apply to as broad an aspect of behaviour as emotion.

There are three main lines of research into emotional behaviour; although often conceptually related, these have progressed fairly independently of one another. (1) The first is based on the straightforward observation and measurement of 'emotionality'. Investigators of emotionality have tended to centre their interest either on behaviour in the 'open-field' situation or on the perseverative effects of noxious stimuli. Such an approach has its roots in Hullian theory, which in fact provides an important background to the study of emotional behaviour in general. (2) The second line of research has grown out of the central theoretical emphasis laid on the general role of emotion in conditioning and learning by such as Miller and Mowrer, and recently culminating in Amsel's frustration theory. (3) The final approach could just as well be called 'behaviouristic' as behavioural, stemming as it does from Watson and, later, Skinner. It owes much to an ingenious experimental technique developed in the early 1940s by Estes and Skinner. In the last decade, this technique, for studying the conditioned emotional response (CER), has produced a proliferation of research.

As implied above, much of this chapter is concerned with recent work which depends on developments of Hullian theory made by N. E. Miller and Mowrer; their ideas will be briefly discussed now. Drive theorists such as Miller have tended to view fear (or anxiety) as the salient emotion; they regard it as a necessary part of theoretical accounts of avoidance learning. In such a context, fear is an acquired drive. To Miller (1951), fear (or emotion in general) is: (1) an unconditioned reflex, mainly an ANS reaction which can be brought under stimulus control; (2) a discriminative stimulus; and (3) a drive—new responses can be learnt by the reduction of fear. This formulation leads to two basic hypotheses: (1) that learnable drives such as fear follow the same laws as overt responses; and (2) that they have the same drive and cue properties as strong external stimuli. This in turn suggests a two-factor theory of avoidance learning. For example, a painful shock produces fear (an unconditioned response as an interoceptive stimulus). Fear then acts as a drive which motivates behaviour. In avoidance learning, a neutral stimulus is paired with shock; by classical conditioning this will come to elicit fear, which will bring about avoidance via drive reduction.

Although having the same type of Hullian background, Mowrer's (1960) theory differs from Miller's. Mowrer regards emotion as being of central importance in learning, viewing emotions as drives which have particular eliciting conditions. He suggests that there are four fundamental emotions; fear, hope, relief, and disappointment. Fear occurs with the onset of some environmental stimulus which signifies that danger will follow. When this same stimulus ends, there is relief. With the onset of some stimulus which indicates that a period of safety (from noxious stimuli) will follow, then hope is experienced. When the safety signal ends, there is disappointment. A more detailed discussion of Mowrer's ideas appears later, but for the present it should be noted that although there is a reasonable amount of evidence which supports his operational definitions of fear and hope, there is less to support relief and disappointment. In general, Mowrer believes that sensations from an organism's own behaviour may signify these four states. This enables emotion to come under instrumental control.

As must be implied by this brief introduction to the more behavioural study of emotion, much of the work it has led to has been with infrahuman subjects (mainly rats, pigeons, and monkeys). Arguments for and against 'animal' studies of emotion were mentioned in Chapter 1. From these arguments, it is clear that many techniques of study *must* be developed with animal subjects and thereafter applied to humans. We still do not know whether or not the determinants of emotion are similar in man and animals; of course, from the behavioural view-point it is usually regarded as more parsimonious to work as if they were. But it is of obvious importance that any techniques developed with animals should as far as possible be refined for human study. Fortunately, investigators in the field of emotional behaviour have realized this necessity, and where they have produced relevant work it will be discussed. Also, many non-behaviourally oriented investigators of emotion would vigorously deny the assumption of continuity between man and the animals. Man is, after all, a cognitive being and many psychologists believe cognitive functions to lie at the heart of emotion.

EMOTIONALITY

Open field

The study of emotionality in the open-field situation began with Hall (1934a). (The basic procedure consists of placing an animal, usually a rat, in a large open space which it has not previously encountered. To begin with, this produces in the animal what, at the everyday level, would be called fear—urination, defecation, crouching, freezing in one position, squeaking, etc. The floor of the field is usually marked off in squares, and observational tallies are made of the animal's movements and various other behaviours which might be considered relevant.)

Hall (1934a) defined defecation and urination as *the* measures of emotionality (fear, anxiety) in the open field, presumably because they have the physiological respectability of dependence on the ANS, and also of course because they make good sense anthropomorphically. The main questions to have arisen from this are: whether or not eliminative behaviour is a valid index of emotionality, and how does it compare with other possible measures? As Gray (1971) points out, it is important to show that the various measures of emotionality co-vary, do not correlate with other behaviours, and that a particular measure correlates highly with others. Hall (1934a; 1934b) found that eliminative signs habituated with repeated testing and suggested that they did seem to give a reasonable measure of emotionality. However, there are a number of objections to this. For example, Hunt and Otis (1953) found no correlations between the number of boli produced in the open-field situation and in the emergence-from-cage test. Using a classical conditioning procedure with rats, they paired a neutral stimulus with electric shock. During the study, they compared changes in the rate of defecation with other possible behavioural indices of fear conditioning (for example crouching). They found a rise in the number of fecal boli produced during acquisition when the conditioned stimulus (CS) was presented, and a fall during extinction. But crouching appeared earlier in the sequences than defecatory changes and disappeared later. Also, Broadhurst (1957a; 1957b) found no increase in the amount that an animal would walk about with repeated experience of the open field, whereas elimination habituates. Ambulation may, of course, be dependent on many factors other than those concerned with emotionality.

It has also been established that emotionality, as indexed by elimination, can be inherited (Broadhurst 1960; Hall 1941). Although Tryon *et at.* (1941) originally found support for Hall's results, this did not hold good for male rats, and they also found that their criteria of emotionality (defecation, hiding, vocalization) did not generalize across situations. Billingsea (1942) in a factor analytic study of many 'emotional' responses found three factors, emotionality, timidity, and freezing, and also suggested that the responses shown by his animals were situation-dependent. This was endorsed by O'Kelly (1940) and Tobach and Schnierla (1962), who concluded that defecation is situation-specific rather than a characteristic general reaction of an animal.

One measure which does appear to stand out from the rest is that of latency of the approach to food and its consumption in the open field. The argument is that if emotionality is high then this should be reflected in a failure to eat food which is easily available. Hall (1934) found a high negative correlation between approach to food and defecation and urination scores. Animals which scored highly on eliminative measures were slow to approach food, and *vice versa*.

Weiskrantz (1968) suggests that the open-field situation has two main effects: (1) it leads to specific respondents such as defecation; (2) it interferes with behaviour such as eating. These effects are correlated and show habituation with repeated exposure to the situation. This conclusion, however, ignores the apparent situation-specificity of defecation.

If the open-field situation can be regarded as a reasonable testing ground for emotionality, then a further problem is evident—do differences in emotionality as measured in the open field have anything to do with behaviour in general and, more particularly, with drive strength? (Emotionality was, at first, thought to be indicative of drive strength.) Broadhurst's results (1957a; 1957b) have most bearing on this. He found (1957a) that animals bred for emotionality (measured by elimination) are more responsive to situational stimuli than are animals bred for nonemotionality. Motivation being 'bred in' may simply add to energy rather than to emotionality in certain situations. Broadhurst (1957b) forced emotional and nonemotional rats to swim and make brightness discriminations to escape from an underwater alley. They were held under water for varying lengths of time before being allowed to swim. The response was the correct solution of one of three brightness discriminations which varied in difficulty. This study supported the Yerkes–Dodson (1908) law, i.e. as the discrimination was made more difficult, so the optimum deprivation of air for the best performance decreased. More relevant to the present discussion, Broadhurst also found that the supposedly emotional and nonemotional rats failed to differ as they should have. Thus, genetically determined emotionality does not add to total drive in the same way that air deprivation does. There has been no convincing demonstration that the extra 'motivation' in animals bred for emotionality in any way energizes behaviour.

At this point is it worth summarizing the conclusions drawn by Gray (1971) on rats selectively bred for high or low defecation in the open field. He suggests that: (1) changes that occur in open-field defecation due to selective breeding are general, rather than situation-specific; (2) the genetic factors are promoting a general change in the level of fearfulness; (3) defecation under stressful conditions is a valid measure of fear; (4) changes in behaviour in the area of emotionality through selective breeding are dependent on genetic factors; and (5) fearfulness (emotionality) is to some extent under genetic control.

It is difficult to assess whether or not the idea of emotionality is a useful one in accounting for the behaviour of animals placed in open-field and similar situations. It is probably fair to say that the two main criteria of emotionality which have emerged are reasonably good. In that one is a respondent (elimination) and the other an operant (approach-to-food), at least there is breadth. However, Broadhurst's work has demonstrated that emotionality cannot be explained by using the Hullian concept of drive. Open-field emotionality does not energize behaviour, as was at first believed. Thus we are left with a concept which is more descriptive than explicative. In certain novel situations, there are alterations in behaviour which habituate with time, i.e. as the situations becomes less novel. Such changes can best be described as dependent on emotionality.

Also of relevance in this context are studies of the effects of early experience on later emotionality (see Chapter 7 for a discussion of these). They have usually involved giving young animals electric shock or systematic handling by the experimenter, and testing them as adults in open-field situations. The most general finding (for example Levin 1962) has been that increased stimulation of any sort during infancy produces more robust, less emotional adults. Or, to put this another way, that an exposure to stress early in life increases a later resistance to it. This is perhaps working against inherited predispositions.

Walsh and Cummins

This section will be concluded with a summary of some of the implications drawn and pointers for future research made by Walsh and Cummins (1976) in their thorough critical review of the open-field test. They argue that the usual way of deciding *what* is measured in the open-field test has been intuitive or anthropomorphic, and that this has led to the general use of the concept of emotionality. They describe emotionality as '... an entity underlying the nonspecific affective components of behaviour'. From attempts to validate this concept more precisely it can only be concluded that defecation and latency are reasonable indexes—a point which was made above. Walsh and Cummins also indicate that in the context of open-field research fear has often been used as an explanatory construct. But they can find no good way of distinguishing between fear and emotionality.

Walsh and Cummins make a number of pertinent prescriptions for future research using open-field techniques. First, they urge a precise description of subjects used, apparatus, measurement techniques, and so on. It would not of course be only open-field research which would benefit from this endeavour. Second, they argue that multifactor experiments should replace those in which only one independent variable is manipulated. The reasons for this suggestion are that such studies are more economical and also that they make no assumptions about the additivity of behaviours—assumptions that have often been made unwarrantedly in previous open-field research.

On the side of the dependent variable, Walsh and Cummins highlight the need for the testing of reliability and validity for broad bands of conditions and subjects. Also, they urge that the attempt be made at construct validation via factor analysis and ecological data. This would perhaps also help to guard against the making of unjustified generalizations.

It is certain that research into emotionality using the open-field test would benefit from the specifications made by Walsh and Cummins. However, whether or not this would provide a better understanding of what is an essentially hypothetical construct remains to be seen.

Perseverative effects of noxious stimuli

There have been various studies concerned with the effects of prior or contemporaneous but noncontingent aversive stimuli on ongoing behaviour, either consummatory or instrumental. (See Myer 1971 for a review of this work within the context of noncontingent aversive stimulation in general.) This area sprang up in an attempt to provide supportive evidence for the hypothesis that fear is a drive which will facilitate behaviour which is based on other drives (Hull's idea of the summation of relevant and irrelevant drives). Thus, if fear could be produced independently of other behaviour then it should lead to facilitation. When considering the studies which have devolved from this original idea, there are two problems which sometimes make evaluation difficult. (1) Slightly different experimental procedures have been followed in different studies; the use of shocks of differing intensity and/or duration for example. (2) There has been some doubt as to how to describe and explain the effects obtained. For example, the perseverative effects of shock have sometimes been labelled simply as the perseverative effects of shock, or as 'anxiety', or as 'emotionality'. Basically, however, most of the studies have been concerned with the unconditioned effects of aversive stimuli measured indirectly on a behavioural baseline; they seem to be dealing with 'emotionality' in some form.

Consummatory behaviour

Siegel and Siegel (1949) deprived rats of food and water on a regular regime and measured their water intake. On the test day, just before their normal time of access to food and water, the experimental group were shocked at a 'fairly intense' level. The rationale for this procedure was that shock inhibits salivation which should promote drinking. A control group remained unshocked. There was a tendency for the experimental group to drink more than the controls. However, this effect was provided mainly by one animal.

At the time of the Siegels' study, the facilitatory effect of prior shock on consummatory behaviour was explained within the Hullian framework of an irrelevant drive (produced by shock) summating with a relevant drive (produced by food or water deprivation). Conversely, the effects could have been due to some immediate and perseverative emotional effects from noxious stimuli. Studies by Amsel and others added complexity to this picture. Amsel (1950) measured the running speeds of rats in a straight alley. They had to leave the start-box in order to escape shock. They were also either 0 hours or 22 hours food-deprived, although they were not fed in the runway. By the third day, the irrelevant hunger group were running significantly faster than the controls. Amsel explained this as the summation of the hunger drive with the residual effects of shock. Amsel and Maltzman (1950) allowed rats 10 minutes' access to water every 12 hours. Having established this regime for 14 days, they then shocked the rats in a different situation immediately before they were due to drink. All animals were shocked in this way for three days. Then followed two further days in which half the animals were shocked on the first and half on the second. Although water intake rose significantly during the first three days, at this point there were no unshocked control animals. Also, when shocked and unshocked animals were compared on the last two days, there were no differences. Amsel and Cole (1953) extended this result by showing that the degree to which shock interferes with consummatory behaviour depends on the similarity between the shock and the test situations. There was no facilitation observed in this study, nor in that of Levine (1958) delivering shock in a different situation to the drinking cage. At this point, it was difficult to assess the status of the emotionality-drive sort of hypothesis. Amsel and Maltzman (1950) had made the only definitive statement when they distinguished between pain: a reaction to noxious stimuli; anxiety (fear): a conditioned pain reaction; and emotionality: a continuing reaction following pain. However, the mainly suppressive results at this time could be explained as a generalization of the usual suppressive effects of shock on ongoing behaviour.

More recently, it has been clearly shown that 'emotionality' does facilitate drinking. Moyer and Benninger (1963) demonstrated that intense pre-shock facilitated drinking in rats whose water intake had previously been depressed for some time by handling. Moyer (1965) suggested that novelty effects of emotionality might overcome any facilitatory effects. Hence, only animals that had previously experienced emotionality in the drinking situation would be likely to drink more. He confirmed this in a very full study involving the production of emotionality by handling, shock or placement in a shock-box. His results were significant and showed facilitation of drinking to occur in those animals who had had some prior experience with emotionality; the novelty of emotionality must have habituated.

Levine (1965) also showed clear evidence for a facilitation of drinking in a pre-shock group (0.8 mamp for 20 sec) and in a group simply placed in the shock-box before drinking. Suppression was shown in groups either shocked for four 20-sec durations separated by 10-minute intervals or simply placed in the shock-box for these durations. Although these results add to Moyer's, it is not at all clear what determines the contrasting effects that they show.

The generality of these findings on pre-shock and water intake has been extended in a number of ways. Siegel and Brantley (1951) placed rats on a 22-hour food-deprivation schedule. On the sixth day of this regime, the experimental group were taken to a different situation and shocked just prior to eating. They ate more than an unshocked control group. Strongman (1965) provided evidence of a similar facilitation of eating. He placed rats on a 23-hour food-deprivation schedule until intake had stabilized. On the test day, in a shock-box completely different from the home cages, they were given one of three durations (3, 30 or 300 sec) of shock (2.65 mamp). This occurred immediately before their usual time of access to food which, on the test day, was for some subjects adulterated with quinine. With normal food the 3-sec shock group showed significant increases in intake in comparison with unshocked controls, while the 30-sec and 300-sec groups showed decreases. When the food was adulterated with quinine, there was a monotonic decrease in intake with increasing shock durations. The results were interpreted as reflecting an interaction between 'anxiety'—the perseverative effects of shock (emotionality)—and the incentive value of the food. It was also argued that the shock effects were temporally biphasic at the higher levels: immediate suppression of eating occurred, followed by a gradual recovery for the groups receiving normal food. With the quinine groups there was an initial suppression which as it dissipated would allow the quinine to exert its effects and keep intake down. The time course of the effects supported this interpretation.

Myer (1971) suggests an alternative interpretation of Strongman's results which is in accord with Moyer's discussion of the novelty of emotionality. Thus, it is possible that the food intake of the quinine groups was depressed after low shock because of the novelty of the quinine. Any change in the test situation should therefore magnify possible *suppressive* effects of prior shock. As Myer points out, this should even be so if the food is sweetened rather than embittered. Further light is thrown on this by Strongman et al. (1970) in a parametric study which also confirmed the facilitatory effect of pre-shock on eating. The intake of food-deprived rats was measured until it had stabilized. They were then subjected to 3 or 30 sec of shock at intensities of 0, 0.5, 1.5, 2.5 or 3.5 mamp immediately before their time of access to food. On the test day the food was adulterated with 0 per cent, 10 per cent or 25 per cent sucrose. Shock intensity was found to be insignificant, there being a general enhancement of intake after 3 sec and a general suppression after 30 sec. There was no interaction between sucrose adulteration and shock, a result at variance with the earlier quinine findings, but also not quite in line with the novelty hypothesis.

Instrumental behaviour

A second line of research into the generality of the effects of prior aversive stimulation has dwelt on instrumental rather than consummatory behaviour. However, there is little evidence for facilitatory effects. Baron (1963) and Baron and Antonitis (1961) found respectively that pre-shock in one situation suppressed subsequent exploratory behaviour and unconditioned responding in other situations. Similarly, Ellis (1957) and Anderson et al. (1968) found that pre-shock either has no effect on, or interferes with, the subsequent running of alleys to food. And studies by Bevan et al. (1967) and Strongman (1967) each demonstrated pre-shock to suppress subsequent lever-pressing for water or food. The only study which goes against the general finding that pre-shock suppresses instrumental behaviour is that of Ducharme and Belanger (1961). However, the information available from this study concerning response rates before shock was introduced does not permit the conclusion that other factors were not involved.

Also relevant in this context are those studies in which aversive stimulation has been administered *during* ongoing behaviour. The most dramatic results in this field come from Webb and Goodman (1958) and Siegel and Sparks (1961), who showed that flooding a Skinner box with half an inch of water increased the response rate of rats previously working at a stable rate. This again brought attention to the idea that emotionality somehow energizes behaviour. These studies are at one extreme of a fairly large literature on the effects of unconditioned aversive stimulation on behaviour such as aggression (for example Azrin *et al.* 1966) or eating (for example Pare 1965; Sterritt 1962). (See Myer 1971 for a review.) The general finding has often been of enhancement of whatever behaviour is occurring at the time of or immediately after the aversive stimulation. It may be that moderate shock (the usual aversive stimulus to be used) simply facilitates whatever behaviour is predominant at the time, or there could be some special (and unknown) relationship between shock and consummatory behaviour.

Finally, it is worth describing in some detail the work of Deaux and Kakolewski (1970), since they suggest further factors which should be taken into account in any research into the basic facilitatory effects of 'emotionality' on consummatory behaviour. They investigated the effects of handling rather than shock, initially to ascertain whether or not rats that had only been rarely handled would differentially increase one or other consummatory response (eating or drinking) after stress-inducing activity. To test this they handled previously unhandled rats for $1\frac{1}{2}$ min and at the same time seven days later rotated the same rats on scales for $1\frac{1}{2}$ min each. On each occasion and at the same time after a further seven days they observed the rats for a subsequent two-hour period. There was a significant increase in drinking but not in eating after both handling and rotation. If the stressful experiences had simply had a general energizing effect, then an increase in both eating and drinking would have been expected.

In their second study, Deaux and Kakolewski deprived rats of water, allowing them 4 ml per day. 0.5 min after this each rat was removed from its cage; half were returned immediately, the other half were handled for $1\frac{1}{2}$ min. Handling eliminated the *eating,* which in the control group began within the first minute after they were returned to the cages. (On schedules such as this, eating habitually occurs *after* drinking.) This was confirmed in a further study with rats that were less used to water deprivation. Deaux and Kakolewski's basic hypothesis was thus supported, i.e. that handling raises body-fluid osmolality by raising 'emotionality'; an hypothesis based on supportive biochemical analysis. Their argument is that: (1) in food-deprived rats an increase in body-fluid osmolality leads to the emergence of thirst during food intake; and (2) in water-deprived rats a decrease in body-fluid osmolality induces hunger during water intake. Their studies show that anxiety or emotional excitement (i.e. emotionality) increases body-fluid osmolality, which induces thirst, which in turn leads to drinking and delay or elimination of eating. This clearly points to the necessity for considering both types of consummatory behaviour in any future study, even though deprivation may have occurred in only one of them; food and water intake interact at a basic level, any emotion-induced changes in one possibly being due to changes in the other.

Conclusions

It is difficult to draw a definite conclusion from the studies reviewed in this section. Aversive noxious stimuli affect subsequent behaviour. When any effects are suppressive, as is often the case, they can be easily explained in terms of 'fear' conditioned in one situation generalizing to another. However, studies which have demonstrated facilitatory effects are now too numerous to be ignored, and are not in any way accounted for simply by recourse to the emotionality-drive idea. It would seem improbable that experience with noxious stimuli leads to some sort of autonomous 'emotionality'. Explanations for both the facilitatory and the suppressive effects of prior aversive stimulation are far more likely to be found by a more detailed consideration of the general testing situations. Such variables as amount of deprivation, type of reward, the relative novelty of the shock-box (if shock is used) or experience with emotion-producing stimuli need careful investigation before anything further can be said. It may well be that exploration of these variables would undermine the usefulness of any explanation in terms of general emotionality. Which, of course, is not to say that they would deny that some form of emotional responses follow aversive stimulation or indeed that animals vary with respect to general emotionality, a condition which to some extent is genetically determined.

FRUSTRATION—A NEO-HULLIAN APPROACH TO EMOTION

The most recent line of Hullian inspired research into emotional behaviour comes from Amsel (for example 1958; 1962). It is based on a technique which Amsel developed for investigating frustration and also on the theoretical ramifications of the so-called frustration effect (FE). However, frustration was a broad topic before Amsel's contribution. Thus, before discussing the FE and the theories of frustrative nonreward to which it has led, brief mention will be made of earlier research into frustration.

Early theory and research on frustration

Excellent summaries and discussions of the earlier work on frustration can be found in Yates (1962) and Lawson (1965). As the present purpose is merely to provide a background against which to view Amsel's contribution to the field, the surface of the earlier work will only be skimmed. In the 1930s and 1940s four major theories of frustration appeared. They each depended on Freud, but also saw frustration as a unique topic, attempted to define it operationally, and produced definite hypotheses about behaviour. In regarding frustration as unique they differed considerably from the more recent theories.

Rosenzweig (1934; 1938; 1944) viewed frustration as an obstacle which prevents the satisfaction of a need; in other words, it somehow blocks motivation. This definition and its various riders generated little research and was significant only in its position as a progenitor of those which followed.

The frustration–aggression theory of Dollard et al. (1939) contained two basic propositions. (1) Frustration increases the tendency towards aggression. (2) Aggressive behaviour is sufficient evidence to conclude that frustration must previously have occurred. Again, frustration was seen as an interference with any behaviour which would normally lead to a goal or reinforcement. This theory was tied to both Freudian and commonsense notions of frustration. It has led to a reasonable amount of empirical work and ideas (for example Berkowitz 1962; Miller 1948; Sears 1950). However, Yates (1962) summarizes the criticisms that may be made of it. (1) Aggression is not unitary. (2) Frustration situations are not all alike. (3) Aggression could occur for reasons other than frustration.

A similar theory was proposed by Barker *et al.* (1941). On the basis of rating children's 'constructiveness' with toys, they suggested that frustration results in regression, i.e. produces behaviour which is characteristic of an earlier level of development. However, they also thought that frustration could have effects other than regression and their theory generated very little research. Also, two fundamental objections can be made to their original investigations. (1) The intelligence range of the children they studied was very limited. (2) Data were gathered by experimenters who were aware of the experimental conditions and who might therefore have shown bias.

Maier (1949; 1956) was the final theorist to view frustration as a unique concept. He suggested that any behaviour which follows frustration becomes fixated, an effect which he believed to have nothing to do with normal processes of learning or motivation. He based this idea on results obtained from training rats to make discriminations from a jumping-stand for a food reward. When they could do this satisfactorily, Maier presented them with a series of insoluble problems, reward positions being at random. At first, the rats refused to jump; they were encouraged further by blasts of air from the rear or raps on the tail. They began to jump, but always to one side or to one stimulus, irrespective of whether or not this led to a reward or a bump on the nose. Their behaviour remained fixated even when the problems were made soluble. Since it has possible implications for neurosis, this is an attractive theory. However, again, there are two objections to the data on which it was based. (1) Given the air-blasts and tail-raps, it is likely that the rats in Maier's studies were jumping to escape punishment rather than in any positive sense. (2) As their jumping gained them access to reward on roughly 50 per cent of occasions, they were in fact on a partial reinforcement schedule, which of course tends to strengthen behaviour.

Lawson (1965) describes the next stage in the development of frustration theory and research as being characterized by: (1) far more experimental work; (2) closer connections with general concepts of behaviour; (3) a recognition that many independent variables are involved in studies of frustration; (4) a belief that there is no unique behaviour which is characteristic of frustrating situations. This more general approach is of clear importance to the broader study of emotional behaviour, and these developments have been mainly productive through Amsel's theory of frustrative nonreward. However, there are two other theories which should be mentioned, since they are each important to Amsel's ideas.

Child and Waterhouse (1952; 1953) extended the theory of frustration–regression. They suggested that a frustrating situation, or its emotional consequences, arouses responses which (1) interfere with ongoing behaviour, and (2) bring about changes in motivation. This idea of frustration denied the concept any unique qualities. In situations which could be defined in a general way as frustrating, goal-directed behaviour is interfered with, motivation changes, and other responses become more likely. Thus, in Child and Waterhouse's view, there is no one reaction which is typical of frustration.

Brown and Farber (1951) regarded frustration as a higher-order hypothetical construct—a construct integrating several interrelationships between antecedent and subsequent events. This is a very Hullian formulation. A response tendency is interfered with and other response tendencies are therefore aroused. This results in conflict between the original tendency and the alternative. Frustration is the relationship between these two tendencies. Brown and Farber argue that the effects of this frustration are mainly to increase drive; and responses which are already strong (more probable of occurrence) are strengthened further. Also, internal 'emotional' stimuli are aroused. Other than this they mention no specific outcomes of frustration. Besides helping to set the scene for Amsel, the importance of this theory is that it strengthened frustration as a technical rather than an everyday term.

Amsel: the frustration effect (FE)

It has been known for some time that an animal will often respond with momentarily increased vigour when extinction conditions are first instituted, i.e. when reinforcement is withheld (for example Marzocco 1951; Miller and Stevenson 1936). This is the basic FE and has frequently been taken as evidence for an increase in drive. However, there is not much hard evidence that frustration has the functional properties of a drive, although Eysenck (1976) does argue that frustration can be viewed as functionally equivalent to pain (see Chapter 9). As Bolles (1967) points out, an increased response rate is by no means an increased vigour of response; the initial increase in response rate during extinction may be due to an elimination of eating. Also, Marx (1956) and Lawson and Marx (1958) doubt many of the supposedly demonstrated FEs, and where they do exist attribute them to associative relationships. They suggest that blocking of behaviour produces a frustration state. This state will elicit either innate and/or learned responses, one of which may be reflected in an increase in vigour. This word of interpretative caution should perhaps be borne in mind throughout the discussions below.

Amsel's first and most important contribution to this field was to define frustration operationally. He suggested that it is what occurs when an organism experiences nonreward after previous experience with reward. This definition was based on a study by Amsel and Roussel (1952) which has proved prototypical for much of the recent work on frustration. Their apparatus consisted of a two-unit runway with a goal-box at the end of each alley. Rats were trained to run the first alley (A1) to the first goal-box (GB1) where food was available, and then run A2 to GB2 where there was further food. Each trial ended after food had been eaten in GB2. This procedure was followed until running speeds had stabilized. On 50 per cent of the trials during the subsequent period, food was no longer available in GB1. Measures were taken of the start time from GB1 and the running time in A2. Rats showed significantly faster start and run times during those trials when food was withheld in GB1 than during those trials when it was not. This is the FE.

Two refinements were soon made to this basic procedure. (1) Amsel and Ward (1954) and Amsel and Prouty (1959) replaced A2 with a choice situation. To obtain food in GB2, the animals had to make one response on frustrated trials and another on rewarded trials. Such a discrimination was rapidly learned and seemed to be dependent on the immediate effects of nonreward. (2) Seward et al. (1957) suggested that the FE might be due to response suppression—a comparative depression in A2 running speed on rewarded trials due to relative satiation with food. Wagner (1959) overcame this objection by running three groups of animals. The first was never fed in GB1, the second was fed during test on a 50/50 basis in GB1, the third was always fed in GB1. Wagner found that on nonrewarded trials the second group ran faster in A2 than animals in either of the other groups. Similar controls for possible response suppression have usually been incorporated in more recent runway studies of the FE.

Frustrative nonreward

One interpretation of the effects of reward and punishment has been based on the Hullian notion of fractional, anticipatory goal responses (for example Miller 1959; Mowrer 1960a, 1960b; Spence 1956). For example, in a food-deprived animal, the stimuli in a stimulus–response sequence which ends with food elicit fractional components ($r_g- - - s_g$, hope) of the primary emotional responses to food. The elevating effects of a food reward on behaviour are then attributed to the energizing influences of these fractional (hope-elicited) responses, which can either be regarded as hypothetical constructs or more concretely as actual responses such as salivation. Similarly, the depressing effects of punishment on behaviour can be attributed to fractional fear-elicited responses which are incompatible with the criterial response. Amsel (1958; 1962) suggested that nonreward could also be viewed in this way. After reward, nonreward will elicit a primary aversive emotional reaction—frustration—which is related to the magnitude of anticipatory reward. (For discussion of the relationship of extinction to magnitude of reward see Wilton and Strongman 1967.) Amsel regards the components of such frustration as becoming conditioned to antedating stimuli, resulting in anticipatory frustration. If this is so, then the decrement in instrumental behaviour which results from the withholding of reward may be due to: (1) suppression effects of incompatible responses, which are learned via anticipatory frustration; (2) the acquisition of avoidance responses reinforced by a reduction in frustration-associated cues.

With the development of the double-runway technique and the theory of frustrative nonreward, Amsel has made two important contributions to the study of frustration. (1) Frustration is defined using one basic operation: nonreward after experience with reward. (2) The idea of anticipatory frustration has been used extensively as an explanation for other problems in learning and motivation: extinction, the partial reinforcement effects and discrimination for example (Amsel 1958; 1962; 1967). The theory contains three fundamental generalizations. (1) Frustration is defined solely by nonrewarded trials in conjunction with rewarded. (2) Anticipatory frustration is seen as being conditioned to specific stimuli within the environment. (3) Anticipatory frustration affects response strength by increasing overall drive strength (motivating immediate behaviour), by acting as a drive stimulus the reduction of which is reinforcing and to which other responses become conditioned, and finally by inhibiting overt behaviour (cf. Brown and Farber 1951; Miller 1959). To date, this is the most rigorous analysis to have been made of frustration. It has generated a great deal of research and thought, some of the more interesting aspects of which will be discussed below.

The aversiveness of frustrative nonreward

Wagner (1966; 1969) offers an alternative theory of nonreward in terms of aversive events—events that an organism will terminate or avoid. He argues that the transition from nonreward to reward is reinforcing, and that this is due either to the initiation of reward or to the termination of nonreward. The same is true of avoidance; it can be seen as the avoidance of nonreward or as the prolonging of reward. This is doubtless a logical possibility, but there is some question as to its usefulness. Leitenberg (1965), for instance, finds the concept of aversiveness unnecessary when accounting for the effects of time-out (TO) from positive reinforcement (see below).

Wagner's view implies that nonreward is frustrating and aversive in proportion to the degree to which reward has been anticipated. The usual double-runway studies support this idea by showing increased running speed in A2; nonreward is more aversive and better motivating of escape behaviour in GB1 (for example Amsel and Roussel 1952; Wagner 1959). Anticipatory reward extinguishes as a function of experience with nonreward. McHose (1963) demonstrated that in turn this leads to a reduction in the aversiveness of nonreward. Of course, many studies (for example Amsel 1958; Amsel and Ward 1965; Peckham and Amsel 1967) show that the active properties of nonreward are dependent on the previous history of reward. But Wagner (1969) argues that it is impossible to deduce from such studies whether or not the *escape* from GB1 is reinforcing in that it may increase the probability of some new contingent response. Frustrative nonreward theory simply points to a nonspecific energizing effect of frustration, just assuming by exclusion that escape is unimportant.

There are few studies which are directly relevant to Wagner's basic view of frustration, and even these can be criticized on methodological grounds (for example Adelman and Maatsch 1956; Church 1969). However, they support the idea that nonreward has active properties as a result of previous history of reward, and that these properties are aversive in that their reduction or avoidance is reinforcing. The best of the studies is Wagner's (1966), in which frustrative nonreward was associated with distinctive cues. These cues motivated new learning (hurdle-crossing) far better than in control groups.

Wagner extends his argument with a parallel between fear and anticipatory frustration. He suggests that if fear and frustration are capable of similar 'anticipatory' explanations, then the effects of punishers (with fear presumably responsible) will not be very different if frustrative nonreward is the aversive event. In support of this, Barry et al. (1962), for example, showed a disinhibition of the FE in rats with alcohol and sodium amytal, both of which are known to disinhibit responding which had been inhibited by punishment (fear).

Further, Wagner maintains that if there is some similarity between the anticipatory stimuli produced by fear and those stemming from anticipatory frustration, then behaviour learned in the presence of one emotional response should generalize to occasions when the other is aroused. Rescorla and Solomon (1967) support this idea by showing that any stimulus which would elicit anticipatory frustration would enhance avoidance responding based on fear, whether the cue came from Pavlovian or instrumental conditioning. Also, Amsel (1958; 1962) argues that, during partial reinforcement, frustrative nonreward is less decremental in its effects when the animal has been trained such that anticipatory frustration will elicit responses compatible with the ongoing instrumental response. Fear would seem to be similar. Miller (1960) showed that rats receiving gradually increasing shocks at a rewarded goal are more resistant to the decremental effects of intense shock than are rats without such experience. This is supported by Brown and Wagner (1964).

Wagner, then, puts forward a convincing argument that frustrative nonreward may have properties which make it, like punishment, a response-contingent aversive event, and also that fear and anticipatory frustration appear to have much in common.

Frustrative nonreward in humans

At the human level, Amsel's idea of frustrative nonreward has usually been applied to children—it has implications for learning, the building of frustration tolerance, and so on. This work has been thoroughly reviewed by Ryan and Watson (1968). They bring together the literature concerned with the FE and the partial reinforcement effect in children, consider the relationship between nonreward and failure, and mention subject variables such as age, sex, and personality. Some of their conclusions will be briefly discussed.

From studies on children, it is clear that nonreward leads to increased vigour of performance at some tasks, and also that frustration may become conditioned to previously neutral stimuli. In forming discriminations, nonreward may have a greater effect on learning than reward. All of which is in line with work on infrahumans. The reaction of a child to nonreward appears to depend quite heavily on individual variables. For example, reward expectancy is related to both chronological and mental age, but not necessarily directly. Thus it is possible that older children and brighter children react to nonreward by devising various strategies for 'solving the problem', rather than by simply showing increased vigour of responding. Also, nonattainment of social reward has similar effects on performance to those of the nonattainment of more concrete rewards.

Such conclusions are important to any behavioural study of emotion, since they suggest that in the end there may be implications for behaviour outside the laboratory. With the FE, however, this is not surprising since it probably originated in commonsense notions; one's own reactions are instructive when, having put money into a cigarette or chocolate machine and pulled the drawer, nothing happens.

The FE in the Skinner box

There have been two developments which add some generality to Hullian derived analyses of emotional behaviour. The first extends the idea of frustrative nonreward in the double runway by demonstrating similar effects in the Skinner box. The second analyses another 'emotion' using similar techniques.

Staddon and Innis (1966) trained pigeons to respond on cyclic presentations of two identical fixed-interval (FI) schedules separated by a brief TO period (delay in GB1 of a double runway). During test trials, omission of rewards after the first FI component led to FEs in the second component—a higher than baseline rate of responding. These results were extended by Staddon and Innis (1969), using blackout rather than reinforcement at the end of 25 per cent of the first components of two linked FI schedules. For both rats and pigeons they reported FEs in the second component, which were largely attributable to a decreased latency of the first response. Blackout duration was inversely related to start latency.

These results are clearly similar to those from double-runway studies of the FE. However, a third operant study obtained somewhat discrepant findings. Wilton et al. (1969) showed that, if the reward which normally followed responding in the second component of a two-part chain was sometimes omitted, then immediately subsequent responding was sometimes elevated and sometimes depressed. This result is difficult to account for other than in the broad terms that rate of bar-pressing may be a measure of behaviour which is more sensitive to emotional disruption than that of running an alley. Be this as it may, the important feature of this study is that responding was measured *immediately* following nonreward. This is not so in the double runway, where a delay in GB1 on nonrewarded trials is usually instituted to control for the time taken by eating on rewarded trials; nor in the Staddon and Innis experiments, where TO responding was largely suppressed. Amsel, however, clearly points to the FE being an increase in response vigour immediately following nonreward (1958, p. 103).

The most recent study of frustration in the Skinner box again provides support for the runway studies. Wookey and Strongman (1971) showed that responding during the 10-sec TO between two linked fixed-ratio (FR) schedules increased following nonreward on the first FR. This was the case during the test period for a group of rats previously rewarded at this time but now only receiving reward on a 50/50 basis, and also throughout training for another group never rewarded at the end of the first FR, but, again, experiencing 50/50 reward/nonreward in test. Little effect was seen on subsequent instrumental responding. Wookey and Strongman argue that the results from the increased reward group were due to 'comparative frustration', a notion first put forward by Karabenick (1969, see below). Thus the effect of an introduction of reward after the first FR on 50 per cent of the trials was to reduce intercomponent TO response rate following reward below that of the baseline rate of the other group rewarded after the first FR from the start of training.

As well as adding generality to the double-runway effects, operant studies of frustration also emphasize the importance of looking in detail at the behaviour which immediately follows nonreward (or reward—see below) in the first goal-box.

'Elation' in the double runway

The other 'emotion' which has been studied within this empirical framework is elation. Work on this has developed in an attempt to outline the effects of a reward increase rather than decrease in GB1. Intuitively, this might be expected to have an 'elation' effect in A2, which, like the FE, is reflected by an increased running speed. However, with one exception, results from the relevant studies do not point in this direction.

The first study to contain a reward-increase group was that of Bower (1962) using a triple runway and rewards of eight, eight, and one pellets in the three goal-boxes during a long period of training. During test an increase in BG1 up to 12 or 16 pellets on a 50/50 basis led to a *suppression* of running speed in A2 in comparison with normal trials. However, there was no unshifted control group in this study, i.e. no group to receive larger reward throughout. Meyer and McHose (1968) used a standard double runway, their experimental groups receiving either one or four food pellets in GB1 throughout 48 training trials. For each of these groups, reward in GB1 was raised to seven pellets during testing. This was, surprisingly, on a one in six basis. Meyer and McHose found that A2 running speed and starting speed were *lower* after seven pellets than during the training, but *greater* than those of a control group always receiving seven pellets in GB1. They refer to these results as demonstrating an 'apparent elation effect', although the within-subject analysis showed a suppression.

Strongman and Wookey (1969) gave the relevant group in their study 80 training trials with one pellet in GB1. During testing this was increased to two pellets on a 50/50 basis. A2 running speed was faster after one pellet than after two. Also, there were no differences between running speeds on trials with increased reward and those of controls always receiving the larger number of pellets. On the other hand, test trials where the reward was as in training produced faster A2 speeds than in any of the control or experimental groups during training. The authors interpreted this as a rapidly developing frustration effect.

Karabenick (1969) gave rats 30 trials with either 15 pellets or one pellet in GB1 and GB2. Then, for a further 30 trials, half of the subjects in each group were shifted to the other reward magnitude in GB1. Increased reward led to decreased A2 running speed, although this was still faster than that of unshifted control animals—'apparent elation'. Within subjects there was frustration following decreased reward, but this was not upheld with the control animals. Karabenick developed the concept of 'comparative frustration' to account for his results, an FE building up during acquisition due to the different reward in the two goal-boxes. This would also tend to obscure any effects in studies involving reward increase which used different levels GB1 and GB2. As mentioned above, this result was borne out in a Skinner box study by Wookey and Strongman (1971) and also by Prytula and Braud (1970) in a double runway.

Taking a somewhat different look at this problem, Wookey and Strongman (1972) increased GB1 reward qualitatively rather than quantitatively. After training rats with two standard pellets in both goal-boxes, on 50 per cent of the test trials the reward in GB1 was changed to two sucrose pellets for the experimental group. This produced no change in A2 run times, but start times tended to be greater than those following normal food pellets. So subjects remained longer in GB1 after a preferred food than a normal, but this was a transitory effect and one which did not extend to performance in A2.

In spite of the very different parameters used in these studies of reward increase in GB1, it is possible to draw two conclusions. (1) An increase in reward in GB1 of a double runway after training at a lower level of reward to within-subject performance decrement in A2. (2) Under some conditions A2 performance does not fall as low as that of unshifted control animals always receiving the larger reward. Such experimental procedures, measurement techniques, and results are so far removed from everyday conceptions of elation that for the moment no attempt will be made to extrapolate from one to the other.

CONDITIONED EMOTIONAL RESPONSE (CER)

The other behavioural approach to emotion developed from two important advances made by Watson (1929). (1) He asked questions about the *external* causes of emotional behaviour rather than speaking in the necessarily more speculative terms of emotional states. (2) His study with Rayner (Watson and Rayner 1920) laid the groundwork for the present large and increasing literature on CER. Watson and Rayner demonstrated that a young child who had previously shown only approach responses to a white rat could be conditioned to 'fear' it. They associated the rat with a sudden loud noise—a stimulus which leads to crying, moving away, etc., in a young child. This 'fear' of the rat was long-lasting and generalized to similar animals and objects. (It is worth noting that although this study formed the background to the Estes and Skinner (1941)

CER technique, the two procedures differ in one important respect. Watson and Rayner measured 'emotional' behaviour directly, whereas the CER procedure measures it as indirectly expressed in changes in ongoing operant behaviour. See below.) However, before developing the discussion of CER it should be pointed out that the early classical conditioning of emotional responses does not appear to be as simple as would be thought from Watson and Rayner. For example, Valentine (1930) repeated Watson and Rayner's study on his own daughter. His findings led him to suggest that there are some stimuli which elicit a background fear *innately*. A large reaction can be obtained more easily with such stimuli than with others. It is not therefore a simple matter of classical conditioning. This point will be returned to later in a consideration of Gray's (1971) ideas.

Through a long chain of empirical research and theoretical discussion, Watson and Rayner's finding has led to the general behaviouristic viewpoint that emotions are names that we can give to the disruptions and enhancements of behaviour which occur as immediate consequences of presenting organisms with positive or negative stimuli (S+ and S—). It is argued (for example Millenson 1967) that there are two operations that bring about such alterations in behaviour. (1) The presentation or termination of primary reinforcers. (2) The presentation of previously neutral stimuli which have been associated with primary reinforcers by a process of Pavlovian conditioning. Emotion is regarded as changing the reinforcing value both of primary reinforcers and of general activity. In this it is like motivation, but Millenson (1967) argues that its antecedents are different; for motivation they are deprivation and satiation, for emotion they are abrupt stimulus change.

After Watson, the next major (technological) step was taken by Estes and Skinner (1941) and Hunt and Brady (1951; 1955). It mainly involved the development of a technique for studying conditioned emotion in a methodologically 'tight' manner. The basic procedure consists, for example, of having thirsty rats in a Skinner box bar-pressing for water on a variable-interval (VI) schedule of reinforcement. When their response rate is steady, an occasional conditioning stimulus (CS), a clicker for example, is presented for five minutes, at the end of which the rat receives a brief shock (unconditioned stimulus—US). Initially, the CS has no effect, but the US results in a lowered response rate. After a few pairings of CS and US, the response to the US becomes adapted and response rate is lower only during the CS. 'Fear' responses originally made to the US have become conditioned to the CS. When these effects were first observed, they were termed conditioned anxiety reactions.

The basic CER paradigm

The basic experimental paradigm for studying CERs can be expressed by the notation: CS --- US, where CS is neutral at first, US is an unavoidable, inescapable, aversive stimulus, and --- is a short time interval. This procedure is superimposed on an ongoing operant baseline. Since, typically, there is a suppression of operant behaviour during CS, this basic procedure has recently become known as conditioned suppression (Lyon 1968). However, the CS - - - US paradigm *may* lead to acceleration during the CS. Sidman (1960), for example, superimposed a CS linked to unavoidable shock on a baseline which was maintained by negative reinforcement. He found an increase in response rate during the CS.

From this it may be seen that the basic CER paradigm leads to a number of logical possibilities for the study of conditioned emotion (see Strongman 1969 and Weiss 1969 for a fuller exposition).

	CS - - - S—	CS - - - S+	CS - - - $—	CS - - - $+
Positive baseline	Anxiety	Elation	—	—
Negative baseline	Anxiety	Elation	Relief	Anger and aggression

In this analysis, positive baseline refers to a steady ongoing operant response maintained by positive reinforcement (for example food), and negative baseline refers to a steady ongoing operant response maintained by negative re-inforcement (for example shock avoidance). Superimposed on these can be CSs which precede four types of emotion-producing event: S— (for example shock), S+ (for example food), $— (for example TO from shock), and $+ (for example TO from food). This leads immediately to the six possibilities which are shown; such a breakdown brings about the four 'human' emotional possibilities of anxiety, elation, relief, and anger, although Millenson (1967) collapses elation and relief into one. (Of course, no great claim can be made for the validity of these particular 'emotion' names in this somewhat rarified context. However, intuitively, they seem to be reasonably appropriate and they can at least function as shorthand descriptions of the basic procedural operations.) The two remaining sections have been left blank, since at first sight they appear difficult to establish empirically. However, as will be discussed at the end of this section on CER, they can perhaps be regarded as other aspects of relief and anger. A discussion of how this scheme can incorporate the more complex human emotions will be reserved for later. First, the research which can be fitted under each of the four headings will be briefly reviewed.

Anxiety—conditioned suppression

There has been a great deal of work on conditioned suppression. It has already been well reviewed and analysed by Davis (1968), Hearst (1969), Hoffman (1969), Kamin (1965), and Lyon (1968), for example. By comparison, what follows will inevitably be brief.

Conditioned suppression is defined as a decrement in response rate during a pre-shock stimulus which has been superimposed on, and is independent of, ongoing operant behaviour. This superimposition is achieved by a classical conditioning procedure. This distinguishes it from 'punishment' procedures where the noxious stimulus is response-contingent (Azrin and Holz 1966). Also, the US in conditioned suppression is believed to have its effects on respondents, heart rate for example (De Toledo and Black 1966). Changes in responses such as these are incompatible with the continuation of normal operant performance. Usually, an appetitive baseline has been used, with shock as the US; its effects are reasonably reliable. When they are used in CER studies, other aversive stimuli, TO for example, sometimes produce an acceleration of responding (for example Leitenberg 1966).

An alternative procedure which has sometimes been followed (for example Hunt and Brady 1951) to overcome possibly post-US disruptions of the baseline is to give the animal CS - - - shock pairings in a 'grill-box' which has no bar and from which there is no escape. Then the CS alone is superimposed on the operant baseline in the Skinner box. Here, of course, the disadvantage is that acquisition is not measurable.

The species used to study conditioned suppression have varied considerably. They have mainly been rats and pigeons, but also include fish, mice, guinea pigs, cats, dogs, and monkeys. Results obtained from these species have shown marked variations (for example Valenstein 1959). Conditioned suppression has rarely been investigated in human subjects, perhaps largely for ethical reasons. Recently, however, other CER procedures have been studied at this level (see below). A final general point is that once it has been established, conditioned suppression seems to be very stable over time. The most extreme demonstration of this stability is Hoffman et al. (1966), who showed pigeons to retain suppression after a five-year period.

The major variables which affect conditioned suppression are those which stem directly from operant conditioning. For example, the type of reinforcement is important. Gellar (1960) showed that the acquisition of conditioned suppression was slower and its extinction faster with a reinforcer of higher incentive value. Also, Brady and Conrad (1960) demonstrated complete suppression in monkeys working for sugar pellets but no effect in those working for intercranial stimulation (ICS). Rats, on the other hand, showed similar effects with water reinforcement and ICS. (In fact, the work involving ICS and conditioned suppression is far from clear, perhaps because the ICS is usually sited in the limbic system, which is imprecisely implicated in the substrates of emotion—see Lyon 1968 for a good résumé of this work.)

Schedule and frequency of reinforcement are the other operant variables which affect conditioned suppression. Brady (1955), for example, demonstrated that conditioned suppression could be established in eight pairings on a VI schedule and that it would extinguish faster when superimposed on ratio schedules than interval schedules. Also, Stein et al. (1958) showed that response rate within the CS increased as the length of the stimulus increased in relation to the interstimulus interval; but this was so only to the extent that the suppression did not much reduce the overall number of reinforcements received during the experimental session (the 'reinforcements lost' hypothesis—see below). However, this idea was refuted by Carlton and Didamo (1960), who achieved the same result with the overall number of reinforcements held constant. Conversely, Lyon (1963) and Blackman (1966; 1967) show local reinforcement rates to be important. The higher the frequency of reinforcement the greater the resistance to suppression, although higher rates of responding lead to greater suppression.

Lyon (1964) suggests that conditioned suppression on VI or variable-ratio (VR) schedules is determined largely by reinforcement frequency, while suppression on FI or fixed-ratio (FR) schedules is determined more by the interval between the onset of the CS and the scheduled reinforcement. There is some support for this notion (Lyon and Felton 1966a; 1966b).

Apart from obviously relevant variables such as CS duration and US intensity, deprivation is the only other significant variable to affect the course of conditioned suppression. Estes and Skinner (1941) showed that suppression is reduced as deprivation increases, a result supported by Hoffman and Fleshler (1961).

At this point, mention must be made of the main study of conditioned suppression on a negative baseline. Sidman (1960) gave rats and monkeys signalled unavoidable shock on a baseline response which was maintained by a Sidman avoidance schedule. The rate of bar-pressing increased during the CS. This is perhaps another line of evidence to support the idea that 'emotionality' may have bidirectional effects. Comparisons can be made with Amsel and Maltzman (1950), Levine (1968), Moyer (1965), Strongman (1965), Strongman et al. (1970), and Weiss (1968), who each showed shock to enhance behaviour.

There have been four main interpetations of conditioned suppression. The first and most obvious is the interference hypothesis. For a long time there was a general consensus of opinion that supression was caused by the interference of conditioned respondents with ongoing instrumental behaviour. Any conditioned suppression study can be interpreted in this way. However, the important question, to which little attention has been paid, then becomes: what are the respondents? The only good study to attempt an answer to this is De Toledo and Black's (1966). They measured changes in heart rate and showed them to occur independently of the course of conditioned suppression. The study of overt behavioural measures such as defecation and urination have been no help in this context.

The punishment hypothesis suggests that the results of conditioned suppression can be explained by an adventitious contingency between the behaviour and the aversive stimulus; early in the procedure, there is a high probability that shock will be delivered while the animal is operantly responding. Hunt and Brady (1951) found no differences in suppression in rats with response-contingent and conditioned-suppression procedures. But in their contingent group it seemed that only terminal bar-pressing was punished. With pigeons, the results of this comparison are equivocal. Azrin (1956) found punishment superior in suppressing behaviour, Hoffman and Fleshler (1965) found conditioned suppression superior, and Leitenberg (1966) found no differences. Cohen (1967) resolved these apparent contradictions by using a procedure which involved discrete trials, a retractable bar so the subjects could not be responding while being shocked, and a response–shock delay interval. With increasing shock intensity he found the complete range of effects from no suppression to severe suppression. When the response–shock delay interval was increased, to achieve the same degree of suppression the shock intensity also had to be increased. The explanation is more complex than a simple reliance on shock intensity. Although the punishment hypothesis has a certain amount of face validity, it cannot easily account for: (1) the rapid acquisition of conditioned suppression observed by some investigators (for example Annau and Kamin 1961); (2) results from studies using the 'grill-box' procedure (for example Hunt and Brady 1951); (3) Cohen's (1967) findings.

An 'invariant reinforcement rate' or 'reinforcement lost' hypothesis was proposed by Stein *et al.* (1958). The gist of this is that suppression is constrained to the extent that only up to 10 per cent of baseline reinforcement density would be given up. This would not seem to have enough generality to account for all conditioned suppression effects. Finally, Millenson and de Villiers (1971) regard conditioned suppression as a negative drive which might be expected to detract from other, positive drives, particularly that which is maintaining baseline performance. This is similar to an idea proposed by Estes (1969). This hypothesis brings together many apparent discrepancies in the CER literature but has at least one basic difficulty. It would lead to the prediction that a *positive* US would produce CS facilitation for all *positive* baselines. This is not necessarily so (see discussion below of Pliskoff 1963 and Azrin and Hake 1969).

This brief summary of some of the research and theory in the field of conditioned suppression permits a number of conclusions. (1) Conditioned suppression is not a straightforward effect; it is influenced by many variables, including those from the underlying baseline. (2) The theories which have been put forward to account for it all suffer from some deficiency. (3) However, it is a useful procedure for the study of 'negative' emotion in that it allows the definition of stimulus conditions which suppress many forms of behaviour at once. (4) It offers a useful way of systematizing the other approachs which have been made to emotional behaviour.

Elation

Referring back to the basic CER paradigm, it will be recollected that the term elation was used to describe the superimposition of a signalled positive stimulus (free reward) on either a positive or negative operant baseline. For the most part, the empirical research within this area of conditioned emotion has only accrued relatively recently. It began with Herrnstein and Morse (1957). They established pigeons on a DRL five-minute schedule of reinforcement. (Such a schedule differentially reinforces a very low rate of responding by requiring one response to be separated from the next by five minutes.) Then, independently of the animals' behaviour, key light changes for one minute signalled access to food for five seconds. This led to an overall increase in response rate which gradually became restricted to the CS. However, Herrnstein and Morse's procedure did not control for the possibility (albeit an unlikely one) that this effect could have been maintained by adventitious reinforcement of superstitious behaviour. Brady (1961) established a positive VI baseline in rats and superimposed on this a CS leading to ICS in the septal region—where it is generally believed to have positively reinforcing effects. There was an acceleration in response rate during the CS. The final report to give impetus to the behavioural investigation of elation was that of Longo *et al.* (1964). They took baseline measures of activity in pigeons and demonstrated increased activity during a CS which signalled free food.

The early 1970s produced a small crop of animal investigations of elation within the CER paradigm. Unfortunately, comparisons between them are made difficult since they differ on background variables such as species, baseline, and CS length. Azrin and Hake (1969) established rats on a VI one-minute schedule. They added to this a 10-sec CS which led to a US of free food, free water or ICS. For each animal the reinforcer used in the operant baseline was qualitatively or quantitatively different from the US used in the classical conditioning pairings. They found CS *suppression* in almost all subjects under all conditions; they termed this *positive* conditioned suppression. Henton and Brady (1970) established monkeys on a DRL 30-sec baseline schedule. With an 80-sec CS leading to free food they found an acceleration during the CS, but no effect with shorter CSs. Meltzer and Brahlek (1970) showed suppression in rats during a 12-sec CS on a VI baseline, no effect with a 40-sec CS, and an acceleration in rate with a 120-sec CS. This was partially confirmed by Miczek and Grossman (1971). They found suppression in monkeys with a short CS but no acceleration with a longer CS. Finally, Remington and Strongman (1972b) showed CS facilitation, but with pigeons classically conditioned off the baseline in a separate box and only when they were tested during extinction. Similar effects were seen following both VI and DRL schedules.

In spite of the apparent discrepancies between these results, Azrin and Hake (1969) do show positive conditioned suppression to be the general case when short CSs are used to signal free reward. A more general suppression effect was found by Pliskoff (1961). He established pigeons on multiple VI VI schedules which alternated every 15 min, the alteration being signalled within the last 3 min of each component of the schedule. For one group, the baseline condition was mult VI 1 VI 1, for the other it was mult VI 10 VI 10. All animals were tested on mult VI 10 VI·1. These conditions, although complex, do consist of a non-contingent signalled change in reward. All subjects showed a downwards shift in response rate during the CS which signalled the more favourable schedule and an acceleration during the CS which signalled the less favourable schedule. This result, together with those from other parts of the study, led Pliskoff to conclude that transition in reinforcement schedules from high to low produces effects which are like those of signalled TO–acceleration (see below), whereas a shift from low to high reinforcement density has suppressive effects. Pliskoff (1963) added generality to this result with a study in which signalled changes to higher or lower reinforcement schedules were superimposed randomly over a VI baseline. Results were essentially the same as in the earlier study.

Azrin and Hake (1969) argue that, like the conditioned-suppression procedure, the elation paradigm produces 'emotionality' and that this depresses response rate. Pliskoff's data support this. But it is also apparent that signalled low-payoff VI reinforcement schedules or extinction tend to produce rate increases. Further, all studies which have complete classical conditioning out of the experimental situation have shown facilitatory effects during the CS (Bower and Grusec 1964; Estes 1948; Hyde *et al*. 1968; Morse and Skinner 1958).

From this work it is clear that at least four variables are important in the conditioned elation paradigm: (1) whether the CS - - - US pairing takes place before or during responding on the instrumental baseline schedule; (2) whether the CS is presented against an ongoing operant or during extinction; (3) the nature of the operant reinforcement schedule; (4) CS duration.

Breadth is added to these results by some recent studies on standard conditioned suppression. Blackman (1968b) showed that extinction of conditioned suppression is a function of schedule-dependent response rates (with reinforcement held constant) and reinforcement density (with response rate held constant). Also, Blackman (1968a) showed that on DRL schedules with low levels of shock as the US, rate of bar-pressing increased during the CS and decreased for higher shock levels. The Azrin and Hake and Herrnstein and Morse studies differ on both schedule and rate. Blackman also observed disruption of timing responses, leading to increases or decreases in response rate; such an interpretation could be made of Herrnstein and Morse's results.

Up to the present, there has been only one study where a CS leading to free reward has been set against a negative baseline. Coulson and Walsh (1968) superimposed a one-minute CS leading to 10 sucrose pellets on a VI Sidman avoidance baseline with rats. They used a Rescorla (1967) control condition (discussed at the end of this section) and incorporated a delay in the procedure to prevent adventitious reinforcement. With rats at 70 per cent of *ad lib* weight (they are usually run at 80 per cent or 85 per cent) they found response facilitation during the CS. However, as their subjects had *not* to respond for 10 sec in order to get the US (the normal control procedure for the effects of adventitious reinforcement), this may have led them to be shocked on their baseline schedule, so bringing about a superstitiously maintained increase in response rate.

From these studies on animal subjects it can be concluded that a CS which signals free reward almost invariably produces a change in response during that CS; this may facilitate or suppress criterial responding. As yet there is no one explanation of these effects.

Finally, there is one study which demonstrates the application of conditioned elation techniques to human subjects. Remington and Strongman (1972a) established students on a lever-pulling response. They were working for points linked to a monetary reward. Reinforcement schedules were either VI 30 sec or DRL 15 sec. Superimposed on these were half-minute CS presentations leading to either one or 10 free points. Each of these experimental conditions was also followed in other groups but with the CSs and USs presented randomly and independently (Rescorla 1967). There was a response facilitation during the CS, mainly within the experimental groups. This was independent of magnitude of free reward, and primarily within the group working on the VI baseline. DRL experimental subjects showed no effects. Other studies, with infrahuman subjects, have tended to show an acceleration on DRL schedules, and a suppression on VI schedules. Kaufman *et al.* (1966) showed instructional control to outweigh any schedule effects with human subjects, a result supported by Remington and Strongman (1970). In Remington and Strongman (1972a), subjects working on the DRL schedule obtained almost maximal reinforcements. Accurate responding in DRL produces positive feedback, the controlling effects of which may overshadow those of a small monetary reward.

(A note on the Rescorla (1967) control procedure. In some of the earlier CER studies, the CS alone was presented to subjects during pre-test baseline measurements. If the subject has not had previous experience with both the US and the CS, then any effects during testing may be simply due to the introduction of the US rather than to its continuity with the CS. This, and other considerations, have led to the Rescorla control conditions in which the CS and US are both presented randomly and independently. With rats and pigeons this is clearly a useful procedure. But Remington and Strongman (1972a) show that it may be less straightforward with human subjects, with whom, to avoid boredom, experimental sessions must be short. The Rescorla control procedure requires *many* random independent CS and US presentations to avoid any possible effects of trace conditioning (Kamin 1961). Human subjects may well form some associations between the CS and US in short control sessions, thereby negating the control.)

Anger and aggression

Anger and aggression are used to describe the procedure in which, following a signal, positive reinforcers are withdrawn from or are no longer available to a subject working on a positive baseline. This is generally known as TO. With the exception of one or two more recent studies, what little work there is under this heading is reviewed and discussed by Leitenberg (1965). The general finding is that during the presence of a stimulus which signals TO from positive reinforcement there is an increase in response rate. This has been demonstrated by Ferster (1958) with chimpanzees, and Herrnstein (1955) and Leitenberg (1966) with pigeons. There is some confusion in Ferster's and Herrnstein's studies between punishment and TO, but Leitenberg's is quite clear-cut in showing the facilitatory effect with either response-free or response-contingent TO. However, using the same procedure, Leitenberg *et al.* (1968) show a pre-TO stimulus to produce a suppression in response rate in rats. At present, the reason for this discrepancy between species is unknown.

Before discussing two recent human studies on the effects of signalled TO, it is worth mentioning an investigation in which Azrin *et al.* (1966) showed the aversiveness of TO, rather than conditioned TO, and also demonstrated what might reasonably be termed 'anger'. They established pigeons on a key-pecking response where continuous reinforcement alternated with extinction. Meanwhile, strapped in one corner of the conditioning chamber, was another pigeon. Rapidly, with the onset of extinction conditions, the experimental bird began to attack the 'target' bird. (The everyday parallels to this are too numerous and too near home to need mention.)

Trenholme *et al.* (1969) demonstrated that signalled TO leads to CS facilitation in human subjects working for a monetary reward. Their procedure began with a long period of baseline (CS only) training, followed by a DRL 20-sec schedule and then a VI 1.33-min schedule with a concurrent DRL 5 sec. They ran their subjects for 12, 50-min sessions, but the effect of the first DRL schedule on response rates caused the observed response facilitation to be associated with greater reinforcement frequency. This obscured their results.

Remington and Strongman (1970) used a VI 30-sec schedule and a Rescorla control procedure to obtain a comparative baseline. Subjects worked for points linked to a monetary reward. Also, instructions varied, either verbally establishing the TO discrimination, or not. Facilitation of response rate during the CS was found to be mainly a function of instructions, being much greater following those which did not specify the significance of TO. This study showed a clear facilitatory effect on response rate during a pre-TO stimulus which was independent of any increase in reinforcement density.

Relief

This refers to that procedure which would involve allowing subjects signalled TO from a negative baseline. Any disruption of the ongoing operant could be termed relief and would probably be predicted to take the form of an increase in response rate. At present there is no work on this within the CER framework, but see later for a discussion on Hammond's (1970) ideas with reference to Mowrer's concept of relief.

Relief and anger—other aspects

There are two sections of the schema for the logically possible studies of CER which have not yet been discussed: (1) signalling TO from a negative stimulus on a positive baseline; (2) signalling TO from a positive stimulus on a negative baseline. With appropriate controls, studies involving these procedures could take the form of:

1. Establishing subjects on a VI baseline for food reinforcement until they had reached a stable response rate and then superimposing on this a continuous aversive stimulus (for example loud white noise) which would lead to an overall reduction in response rate. A CS would be used to signal TO from the aversive stimulus.

2. Establishing food-deprived subjects on a Sidman avoidance schedule independently of which they occasionally and unpredictably receive free food.

Once a stable response rate had been established, then an occasional CS would be superimposed signalling a period of TO from the possibility of free reward.

Such procedures could be regarded as aspects of relief and anger.

To summarize, within the CER framework, there has been a great deal of work on conditioned suppression (anxiety) but as yet its determinants are far from clear. The basic technique has been extended to the study of conditioned elation and conditioned aggression and has led to some straightforward human investigations. Conditioned relief is an unkown quantity. Clearly, there is much scope in this field, particularly for parametric studies systematically manipulating variables such as CS length, US intensity, and baseline schedule. However, the CER procedure has been used extensively in other fields of research and provides a good structure for the study of emotional behaviour.

THEORETICAL CONSIDERATIONS

There are no completely behavioural theories of emotion. This is perhaps not surprising, since many thoroughgoing behaviourists would adopt an anti-theoretical attitude to psychology in general. There are, however, a few primarily behavioural theoretical syntheses of some aspects of emotion.

Millenson

Millenson's (1967) theory or, more properly, model of emotion is one of the most recent and perhaps most extreme formulations of the behaviouristic approach to emotion. It owes a great deal to Watson and is directly dependent on the CER technique. Basically, he takes Watson's X, Y, and Z factors and puts them within a CER context. He suggests that CS leading to an S— produces some degree of anxiety which suppresses positively maintained operant behaviour whilst sometimes facilitating that which is negatively maintained. A CS leading to an S+ or to the removal of an S— invokes some form of elation which enhances some operants. And a CS leading to the removal of an S+ produces anger which can increase both the strength of some operants and the frequency of aggressive behaviour.

Millenson recognizes that anxiety, elation, and anger do not provide an exhaustive list of human emotions. He extends his ideas by making two fundamental assumptions. (1) Some emotions differ from one another only in intensity, for example joy and ecstasy. (2) Some emotions are basic, others are compounds of these. Millenson regards the three basic patterns of emotion as those described above. Again, his reasons are twofold. (1) He believes that in their unconditioned form, fear, elation, and anger cover all the logical possibilities for the presentation and withdrawal of positive and negative reinforcers. (2) In their conditioned form, they cover all the conceivable simple classical conditioning paradigms.

This reasoning leads Millenson to a three-dimensional 'emotional coordinate' system, as shown in Figure 9. It can be seen from this figure that Millenson's three primary emotions are represented as vectors and the various emotions are portrayed as dependent on different intensities of the reinforcer which forms their basis (this model is only representative—many more terms could be fitted to it). The emotions at the extremes represent extremity in every way. The convergence of the three vectors on one point is meant to indicate that as the emotions become less intense they become more difficult to distinguish behaviourally.

A point of awkwardness in this model is that it is based on only three primary emotions, but there are four possibilities for the basic manipulation of reinforcers. Millenson overcomes this difficulty by suggesting an equivalence between the withdrawal of a negative reinforcer and the presentation of a positive reinforcer—he terms both of these elation. In the schema presented earlier, the withdrawal of a negative reinforcer was termed relief. Whether or not this collapsing of the likely effects of the two procedures is justified remains to be seen. As the procedures themselves are easily distinguishable, the answer is likely to be an empirical matter.

Millenson is aware that his three-dimensional system does not include all the 'human' emotions. However, he argues that those which it excludes are simply mixtures of the primary emotions. A neutral stimulus can become paired with two or more primary emotions or with a US that contains more than one primary reinforcer. Millenson cites the example of a child stealing a cookie. The cookie is a CS for the S+ of eating it, *plus* a CS for the S— of punishment. He suggests that this combination is usually called guilt. Where a CS is paired with a US that has both positive and negative characteristics there is conflict, of the

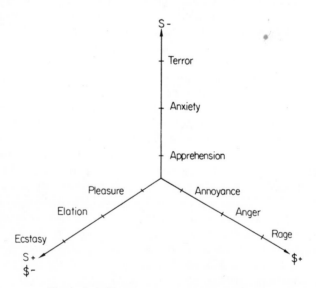

Figure 9. Millenson's three-dimensional model of emotional intensity.

kind seen in experimental neurosis. Also, Millenson suggests that what we usually term sorrow or despair or depression is the result of removing a generalized reinforcer, such as would be involved in the death of a close friend. (See Chapter 9.)

Finally, Millenson extends his ideas on emotion by commenting on emotional control and pathological emotion. He proposes, from the behavioural viewpoint, that we use three methods of controlling our emotions. (1) Adaptation to the continual presentations of emotion-producing stimuli; this leads to the building of a tolerance to frustration and also to 'good' things losing their effect. (2) Masking respondents with opposed operants, for example keeping a 'poker face' or a 'stiff upper lip'. (3) The avoidance of emotion-producing situations. Similar ideas have recently been explored in great detail by other non-behavioural researchers and will be discussed in Chapter 9. Millenson's view of pathological emotion is straightforward but oversimplified. He simply regards prolonged 'anxiety'-producing situations as leading to neurosis, and psychosis as due to the more extreme, normal positive reinforcers being either drastically disrupted or absent altogether.

Weiskrantz

Weiskrantz (1968) ranges idiosyncratically across many of the behavioural approaches to emotion, drawing together a somewhat selective set of evidence. His basic view is that if reinforcers can be defined as stimuli which are consequent to responses, then emotion can be defined as responses which are consequent to reinforcers. He indicates that reinforcing stimuli can be positive or negative; also that the onset of one is often difficult to distinguish from the offset of the other in its effects. For these reasons, he defines responses very widely and speaks of emotion as a *state* which includes many responses. He also follows Skinner's (1938) distinction between operants and respondents and points to the latter as being the subject matter of the study of emotion. That they may be difficult to distinguish (for example Miller 1969; Rescorla and Solomon 1967) he views of little account.

Weiskrantz discusses the problem of stimulus stability and then, more importantly, gives his view of specific respondents. He suggests three reasons for not accepting autonomic activity and EEG as straightforward indicants of emotion. (1) Sympathetic activity or EEG activation are not sufficient conditions to infer the existence of emotional states—cognition may be necessary, as Schachter argues. (2) There are many problems and opposed view-points on the relevance of autonomic responding; the questions these have raised have so far only produced theoretical answers. (3) Autonomic and EEG changes cannot yet be differentiated to discriminate different emotional states. As an alternative view, Weiskrantz regards it as necessary to study respondents in general. He places these on a 'practical' dimension depending on the extent to which instrumentation has been used in their study. Within this framework, he reviews some of the literature on respondents.

Finally, before a brief discussion of fixation and conflict, Weiskrantz makes a number of useful points about emotion in general, taking illustrations from the CER literature. He suggests that in an everyday sense emotion often refers to alterations in characteristic *patterns* of behaviour, for example not smiling, shoulders drooping, not eating. This implies that the effects of emotion-producing stimuli are to make ongoing behaviour either more or less vigorous. He regards this as supporting the idea of emotion as a state, or perhaps a collection of responses.

Studies on conditioned emotion lend some weight to this view. In particular, Weiskrantz raises the interesting notion that if conditioned suppression, for example, can be seen as similar to a conditioned respondent such as heart rate, then it should be able to be used to monitor emotional states. However, it should be borne in mind that De Toledo and Black (1966) found this not to be so. On the other hand, Kamin *et al.* (1963) provide evidence which is more positive. They trained rats in a shuttle-box either by giving them pairings of tone and shock which they could neither avoid nor escape, or by giving them conditioned avoidance trials. They had all been trained previously to bar-press in a Skinner box. They were later returned to the Skinner box and presented with the CS which had been used in the shuttle-box. For the CER group, suppression in response rate was found to be a monotonic function of the number of CS - - - US pairings they had received, but for the avoidance group it was a U-shaped function relating suppression to the number of consecutive successful avoidance trials. Also, when the avoidance response had extinguished, the CS still produced strong suppression. This result suggests that if suppression is a (conditioned) respondent, then the operant and respondent aspects of conditioned aversive stimuli are somewhat independent.

In summary, Weiskrantz regards emotion as respondent behaviour, and suggests that emotional states are reflected by alterations in large classes of behaviour. He argues that to speak of emotional states has an heuristic value, as long as the 'situational context' is not forgotten. There is much to be said for this view of emotional behaviour. It is clear, based on few assumptions, and gains reasonable empirical support. However, there are some areas of study which it does not easily encompass. Amsel's FE for example; Weiskrantz makes no mention of this. Also, it is surprising to find a behaviourally oriented theorist speaking of emotional states. This might have a convenient, shorthand value, but also carries confusing implications. Perhaps Weiskrantz's main contribution is to emphasize the respondent aspect of emotional behaviour and to remind us that, at best, changes in operant behaviour can only be an indirect index of this.

Gray and Brady

Following Millenson and Weiskrantz it is worth including a brief description of the behavioural models of emotion put forward by Gray (1971) and Brady (1975). These models are clearly expressed and, although differing in some details from those of Millenson and Weiskrantz, and Hammond (1970) below, do not suggest anything especially new.

As already mentioned in Chapter 2, Gray (1971) argues that it is possible to define three distinct emotional systems by analysing the relationships between reinforcing stimuli and response systems. He describes: (1) an approach system in which the reinforcing stimulus is a CS for reinforcement or nonpunishment; (2) a behavioural inhibition system in which the reinforcing stimulus is a CS for punishment or nonreinforcement; and (3) a fight–flight system in which the reinforcing stimulus is unconditioned punishment or nonreinforcement.

Brady (1975) regards appetitive and aversive behaviours as approximately congruent with respondent and operant behaviours. Then, in what seems to be becoming a strong tradition in the behavioural analysis of emotion, he makes the point that there are four possible ways in which classical conditioning procedures can be superimposed on ongoing instrumental behaviour. This leads him to define four general categories of emotional behaviour which he argues can be operationally defined and which have their commonsense parallels in subjective feelings.

Hence, in Brady's terms, when (1) the operants and respondents are both appetitive, joy results, (2) the operants are appetitive and the respondents aversive, there is fear or anxiety (CER), (3) the operants and respondents are both aversive, there is anger, and (4) the operants are aversive and the respondents are appetitive, there is relief.

Conditioned emotional states

Hammond (1970) provides the best recent synthesis of behavioural work on emotion. This will be described in detail since it brings together some of the Hullian based research with some of the Skinnerian. Hammond regards emotion as a central state (CES) of the organism, which is elicited by both learned and unlearned stimuli. The unlearned stimuli may be rewards and punishments (or their absence); the learned are those which signal the unlearned and which, through classical conditioning, acquire similar properties. Broadly, this is emotion within a motivational framework.

Hammond begins his argument by reviewing Mowrer's (1960) contribution to the CES concept. Mowrer's main idea was that rewarding events lead to decremental processes (drive reduction) and punishing events lead to incremental processes (drive induction). These are correlated with pleasure and pain and represent unlearned emotional states which motivate the organism. If a neutral stimulus occurs just before an incremental event it is a 'danger' signal; if it precedes a decremental event it is a 'safety' signal. Also, the nature of the emotional state which is produced depends on whether the signal is turned on or off:

Danger signal: on - - - fear, off - - - relief
Safety signal: on - - - hope, off - - - disappointment

The CESs are learned through classical conditioning, with the signals as predictive of reward or punishment.

Such a schema provides a straightforward way of specifying the development of the signals, with behaviour being simply measured as approach or withdrawal. Motivational behaviour within a test situation gives a measure of whether or not the CES has been produced; hope and relief should elicit approach and fear and disappointment should elicit avoidance. Parallels with Brady's (1975) views are clear.

Fear and hope are easily dealt with. The conditioned suppression paradigm has provided a mass of supportive evidence for fear. Wike (1966) reviews studies of hope, more traditionally called secondary reinforcement. Stimuli preceding reward increase the probability of new responses being made when such responses are followed by the onset of that stimulus. Also, the onset of such safety signals can have facilitatory effects on ongoing behaviour. Relief and disappointment are less clear; they depend on the idea that stimulus offset produces a qualitatively different state from stimulus onset. As mentioned earlier, because of the difficulty in distinguishing between these in many studies, Bolles (1967) believes relief and disappointment may be redundant concepts. However, Hammond goes on to suggest that Rescorla and Solomon's (1967) argument has revitalized these concepts.

Rescorla and Solomon reemphasize Pavlovian inhibition and excitation. Pavlov distinguished two types of conditioned reflex. (1) Excitatory; signals followed by reinforcement. (2) Inhibitory; signals not followed by reinforcement. Most Pavlovian studies have been on excitation, but Rescorla (1967; 1968) makes the idea of inhibition more plausible. He suggests that the important relationship between a CS and a US is *predictive*. The *value* of the CS in predicting the US leads to conditioning. If the likelihood of shock, for example, is independent of the CS then no conditioned fear will develop, whereas if the likelihood of the shock increases after the CS, then conditioned fear will develop. So, if the probability of shock (or some other noxious stimulus) *decreases* after the CS, then this is inhibitory Pavlovian conditioning. This points to the possible importance of the absence of reinforcement where reinforcement existed before. A CS which predicts a decrease in the occurrence of shock is similar to Mowrer's relief condition.

If these excitatory/inhibitory ideas are applied to Mowrer's original formulations, they change the defining operations for his conditions:

1. Stimuli predicting an increase in the occurrence of an aversive event lead to fear—excitatory.
2. Stimuli predicting a decrease in the occurrence of an aversive event lead to relief—inhibitory.
3. Stimuli predicting increase in the occurrence of a rewarding event lead to hope—excitatory.
4. Stimuli predicting a decrease in the occurrence of a rewarding event lead to disappointment—inhibitory.

Given this general framework , there are many studies which become relevant to relief and disappointment. For example, Rescorla and Lolordo (1965) trained dogs on an (unsignalled) Sidman avoidance schedule until they had established a high rate of jumping from side to side of a shuttle-box. They were then penned in one side of this and given pairings of a CS and unavoidable shock. One tone signalled shock, another its absence. They were tested in the avoidance situation. The excitatory stimulus led to an increase in the jumping rate but the inhibitory stimulus to decreased jumping. This inhibition of behaviour is 'relief'. Similar results are reported by Hammond (1966) with rats in a CER procedure. Also, Hammond (1967) combined fear and relief signals during testing. There was less conditioned suppression than was seen with the fear stimulus alone. And Hammond (1968) showed the acquisition of fear to be comparatively retarded when a relief stimulus was changed so that it signalled shock. Both the latter results are supported by Rescorla (1969). So, there are many studies which show that stimuli which predict the absence of punishing events acquire conditioned properties akin to relief.

Given Hammond's (1970) reconceptualization, Mowrer's disappointment is supported by the many studies on the FE—this fits the paradigm as described; it is operationally similar. The properties of the stimuli which produce conditioned, anticipatory frustration are seen as based on Pavlovian inhibition.

Finally, Hammond engages in some interesting physiological speculation. He maintains that CES theory is useful for the physiological investigation of emotion. He believes this to be supported by the emotional interpretation which can be given to the limbic system (see Chapter 3). For example, septal lesions facilitate shuttle-box avoidance learning (for example King 1958) but bring about deficits in passive avoidance learning (for example McCleary 1961). Therefore the suggestion is that limbic lesions produce response perseveration in such situations (for example Douglas 1967; McCleary 1966), leading to the prediction that animals with septal lesions will be temporarily unable to learn to withhold high-probability responses. Also, Beatty and Schwartzbaum (1967; 1968) and Schwartzbaum et al. (1967) showed that rats with septal lesions overreact to the incentive value of reinforcement. For example, when water was adulterated with quinine, rats with septal lesions drank less of it than controls; when it was adulterated with saccharine, they drank more.

Hammond suggests that it is possible that lesioned animals perseverate due to an enhanced emotionality. However, the studies which support the idea of response perseveration can also be interpreted in terms of enhanced frustration. For example, passive avoidance animals with lesions show a deficit in performance since they are more persistent; it may be that primary frustration from the shock is enhanced, so they continue to approach rather than to avoid. But Hammond argues further that septal lesions do not enhance all emotional responses; frustration is differentially affected. He suggests that, it this were not so, then in passive avoidance an increase in fear would cancel the increase in frustration.

Hammond provides an illuminating setting of more recent work on emotional behaviour within a framework of Pavlov and Mowrer, particularly as he is also able to accord this an interesting although speculative physiological basis.

Elation—broad aspects

A similar although not so far-reaching attempt at synthesis within the field of emotional behaviour has been made by Strongman *et al.* (1971). They concentrate on elation, which they define as a noninstrumental change in the vigour of responding which is brought about by upward shifts in the conditions of reward. They argue that any change in reward has both instrumental and Pavlovian components, the latter being immediate, unconditioned effects which can be conditioned associatively, usually with a baseline of ongoing instrumental behaviour as a reference point.

As mentioned previously, there have been other behavioural conceptions of elation. For example, Millenson (1967) suggests that it is the change in responding brought about by a signalled or unsignalled noncontingent reinforcer; and Meyer and McHose (1968) see elation as an increase in response vigour (in comparison with control groups) brought about by an increase in contingent reward. However, given the definition proposed by Strongman *et al.*, then the various forms of elation depend on parameters of reward change. Reward change can be: (1) contingent or noncontingent; (2) signalled or unsignalled; (3) the same or different in quantity or quality from that which went before. In combination, these three possibilities lead to eight methods of changing reward.

Strongman *et al.* examine studies which appear under each of these eight conditions, and which have used ongoing instrumental baselines against which to assess any emotional effects. These include investigations of the CER using the 'elational' paradigms and those within an Amselian framework but involving the upward shifts rather than downward shifts in GBI reward. Also discussed are CER studies of anger and behaviour contrast (for example Reynolds 1961).

On the basis of their analyses the authors can draw only putative conclusions. An upward shift in reward does have immediate emotional effects on ongoing behaviour, but sometimes this takes the form of an enhancement or facilitation (for example Herrnstein and Morse 1957) and sometimes impairment or suppression (for example Bower 1962; Wookey and Strongman 1971). However, they also argue that the depressive effects sometimes produced by these procedures may be in accord with everyday notions of elation, since excitement and euphoria can be facilitatory *or* disruptive. They suggest that the term elation should be restricted to procedures and not to effects; then the effects produced by the individual procedures should be studied—a view which points to the need for parametric studies in this field and indeed in the area of emotional behaviour in general. As has been constantly evident in this chapter, many of the existing studies are difficult to compare, since they have varied in so many experimental or procedural details.

CONCLUSIONS

Finally, it should be apparent that the topic of emotion studied from a behavioural viewpoint is a relatively new area which at present is producing a great deal of empirical research. It is progressing on three fronts, which can be broadly conceived as emphasizing: (1) emotionality and perseverative effects of various (usually aversive) stimuli; (2) further research within a Hullian framework which has recently become narrowed to an analysis of effects found in the double runway and its analogues (although with ideas such as Hammond's this narrowing tendency may reverse); (3) Skinnerian based studies on conditioned emotional responding. However, it is equally apparent that behavioural analyses of emotion have added little in the way of theory. Any theories which have appeared do not apply to the whole field and are deficient in one or more respects. Other than Millenson's model, there is no general theory of emotion which places emphasis on behaviour. There is clearly scope for one.

It may well be that these are models rather than theories of emotion from the behavioural viewpoint, because most behavioural analyses have been *post hoc* and hence descriptive rather than explanatory. What is certain is that behavioural conceptualizations of emotion, for all their neatness and apparent precision, do not go far enough. They are far removed from the subjective experience of emotion and, perhaps more importantly, they do not take account of any cognitive influences. Not only does this detract from the qualitative richness of emotion, but it also seems less than justified in terms of current thought and research. Of course, a behavioural analysis of emotion is by no means incompatible with a cognitive analysis, even though their roots and aims may be different. It may be that any future analysis of emotional behaviour finds a place for cognition as well. It would then cease to be a pure behavioural conceptualization but would perhaps be better for it in this particular field of psychology.

7

Emotional Development

Research into emotional development is a mixture of very well conceived and very poorly conceived studies. Broadly, the division is between investigations and ideas involving animal subjects and those involving humans. For the most part, the recent animal studies are well controlled, methodologically reliable, and provide interesting ideas. Equally, with some exceptions, the human studies are of questionable methodology and illuminate very little, often being not much more than slight extensions of commonplace ideas.

Generally, human-based studies of emotional development are characterized by a lack of definition and precision. Terms such as anxiety, fear, love, aggression, and emotionality are bandied about with few attempts to operationalize them. They are used mentalistically and come to connote a great deal—denotatively they are lacking. Even with the better quality animal research, one question always intrudes—how relevant for the important issue of human emotional development is an analysis of infrahuman emotional development? Few would deny the inherent importance of research with animals, but on theoretical or practical grounds an understanding of the emotional development of children would seem to take priority.

There is far more animal than human research into emotional development. This has created a double-edged situation. Were the work with children better, it would be useful to have more of it; as things are, its proliferation would be of small benefit. One reason for the paucity of work at the human level, presuming it is not simply due to a lack of interest, may be concerned with the difficulty of study. It can be argued that emotion is simply one aspect of all behaviour; at the level of everyday observation, this would seem likely. Emotional development then becomes difficult to study in any way distinct from the remainder of development. Investigations with children have often been from the viewpoint that changes in emotional behaviour may account for other developmental phenomena. Rather than dealing satisfactorily with the problem, this may just be pushing it one stage further back. Also discussions of emotional development frequently degenerate into a consideration of the relative importance of genetic and environmental influences. Whilst not wishing to deny that this is an important consideration, it does seem to be one which often stultifies research and theory rather than promoting them.

Overall, the field of emotional development is confused. It is unsystematized and, indeed, it is difficult to impose any system on it. Unfortunately, an attempt

t integration is not a matter (as was once thought) of considering in turn each
f the 'emotions' and what we know of its development. It is a question of
utting together some widely differing approaches involving a broad range of
pecies and including research strategies ranging from abysmal to, if not exactly
deal, then quite good. One way of achieving this is to retain the human/animal
listinction and to discuss representative samples of the work and ideas within
ach category.

CHILDREN

Apart from Watson's (1930) observations of fear, rage, and love in children,
Bridges (1932) set the scene for the study of emotional development. Her
analysis is summarized in Figure 10. She considered that a child is born capable
of showing only undifferentiated excitement, which by the age of three months
or so has become differentiated into positive and negative aspects—delight and
distress. Following this, she suggested that there is increasing differentiation
until about two years of age, when the child displays most of the complex adult
emotions. Although this seems to be a very neat schema, Bridges' data were
based on observations rather than experimentation, her definitions were
inadequate, and she paid scant attention to neonate behaviour. This last point is
well made by Schneirla (1959), with whom it is worth comparing Bridges (see
below).

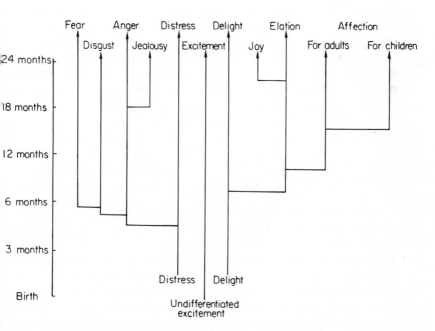

Figure 10. Bridges' scheme of emotional development (adapted from Bridges 1932)

In spite of these objections to Bridges' work, it provoked a series of similar investigations. Some good examples of these are summarized in Singer and Singer (1969), who build their discussion of emotional development on the reasonable if subjective foundation that a child experiences pleasure and displeasure which are caused either by internal processes or by external stimuli. However, it is in considering the relevant empirical evidence that confusion is met. Nevertheless, such ideas have been partially endorsed by Izard's (1972) work, which shows that the recognition of emotion is closely related to age, although the development of the ability to recognize emotion far outstrips the development of the ability to label it appropriately.

Smiling and crying

The two emotional responses most studied in young children are smiling and crying. These are presumed to be representative of pleasure and displeasure. Research into smiling has mainly been concerned with the degree to which it is learned or innate. If a very young infant is handled he will usually smile; this is thought to point to some innate component. On the other hand, at a fairly early age he will smile when he sees a human face, which seems unlikely to be an innate response. Salzen's (1963) work provides a good example of research into the smiling response. In observing one child he found that it first smiled to an external stimulus at seven weeks of age '('smiles' which appear earlier than this are usually regarded as facial grimaces caused by internal discomfort). By eight weeks, Salzen's subject was smiling quite distinctly and to a human face; this may, of course, have been due to a maturational process. However, the child was then shown three, 13-inch cardboard ovals, one white, one black, and one white with a black rim. The child smiled at them all, particularly if they were moved about, a response which was maintained over many presentations, independently of the order in which the child was shown the stimuli. After the eleventh week, he was more likely to smile in response to speech or to noisy moving stimuli than to anything else. Salzen concluded that smiling in infants can be produced by any type of change in contrast or brightness. (In passing, it is interesting to speculate whether or not this response is in any way akin to the following response which forms the basis of imprinting—see below.)

Both Ambrose (1961) and Brackbill (1958), for example, suggested that the smiling response is largely learnt. Ambrose showed that smiling tends to appear earlier in children raised at home than those raised in institutions. Brackbill extinguished smiling in three-and-a-half to four-and-a-half year olds by simple nonreinforcement—although this, of course, does not *necessarily* mean that it was learnt to begin with. On the other hand, Spitz and Wolf (1946) argued that the smiling response is innate, since an infant will smile at face-like configurations from a very early age. There is a good deal of this sort of research and conjecture—it has only been sampled here—but it allows little in the way of definitive statements. However, as with all heredity/environment questions, the conclusion is that they interact.

Research into infant crying has followed much the same course as that for smiling, with the general conclusion that there is a large component to it, but one which is capable of easy modification by experience. At one time it was thought that crying in the very young would only occur to noxious (pain-producing) stimuli. However, a number of studies have shown that from quite an early age various nonpainful stimuli which are presumed to bring about anxiety and fear may also instigate crying. West and Farber (1960) provide a good example. They investigated a girl who was congenitally analgesic. Her disability was such that at the age of two she was breaking limbs with equanimity and by the age of seven she was almost blind from rubbing her eyes whilst they were open. No sources of what would normally be regarded as extreme stimulation made her cry. However, she did show negative emotional reactions to a tongue depressor, which had often made her gag; and she would cry when spanked by her mother. Presumably she was not physically hurt by the spanking, although it may have represented a discriminative stimulus for the withdrawal of positive reinforcement.

Thus, the negative, displeasure side of infantile emotion also allows no definitive statements to be made. Like the positive aspects, it has necessarily been bedevilled by the nature/nurture question. Indeed, in the case of crying it would seem likely that two distinct responses are involved. The first to appear is respondent crying—a reflexive type of response to stimuli of pain or discomfort (for example hunger). Operant crying would seem to appear a little later in the course of development—here the response is clearly dependent on its consequences (for example receiving adult attention). Many parents believe that they can easily distinguish between the sounds of these two types of crying. It is reasonable to suppose that respondent crying is innately determined. Also, although it never entirely disappears, it would seem to lead to the development of operant crying which is then under environmental control.

Deprivation

Throughout the last 25 years many comparisons have been made of the development of children raised in institutions and that of children raised under the usual family conditions (for example Bowlby 1951; 1953; 1960; Spitz and Wolf 1946; Yarrow 1964). This work is clearly related to that of Harlow on chimpanzees (see below). It has generally been claimed that in comparison with their more fortunate peers, institutionalized children are often intellectually impaired and emotionally flat, even to the extent of showing 'anaclitic depression'. However, these claims are often not justified by the research on which they are based, and the studies themselves are frequently of dubious methodology. Be this as it may, there have been various proposals to account for the possible effects of early deprivation. Some of these ideas and investigations are relevant to an understanding of emotional development.

The most frequently suggested aetiological argument in this field stresses the significance of breaking the social/emotional tie which exists between a parent (particularly the mother) and a child. This tie is regarded as rooted in the initial feeding situation, although Harlow's (e.g. 1970) work with animals extends the limits of this idea where ethically it would not be possible with human subjects. Schaffer (1958), for example, demonstrated what he termed overdependency in infants who by chance had been removed from their homes and then returned after varying periods of time. If removal occurred before they were seven months old then they were simply depressed, staring 'anxiously' at everything. Similarly, Yarrow (1964) suggested that by six months of age, 86 per cent of the infants he studied were showing serious emotional disturbance following permanent separation from their mothers. Bowlby (1960) went further and suggested that an emotional reaction may occur within a few hours if separation is experienced within the latter half of the first year of life. He argued that this is expressed by frequent crying and depression, and even happens to a limited extent if the parents go out for a few hours and the child remains with baby-sitters. Bowlby maintains that the child in this situation has been emotionally hurt by his parents and may therefore be hostile to them when they return.

A permanent separation quite commonly experienced by young children results from adoption. Scott (1968) suggests that any adverse effects of adoption depend more on breaking the old relationship than beginning the new. He believes, basing this largely on evidence from animal studies (see later), that once the primary social relationship has developed—by about seven months in children—then there is a fear reaction to strangers. This in turn increases the likelihood of a more severe reaction to adoption. Thus, adoption is best pursued before this age, since, according to Scott, if it is not maladaptive 'emotional damage' may occur.

There is then support for the idea that emotional disturbance may result from the breaking, even temporarily, of attachments to familiar individuals and places. It is likely that temporal factors are important in this, but it is as yet unclear in exactly what way. Any effects must also depend on such variables as the type of relationship which existed beforehand. At the animal level, the significance of early experience for later emotional development has led to the emotionality hypothesis (Levine 1956; Denenberg 1964—see later).

Aggression

In recent years, there has been much speculation about childhood aggression. The viewpoint of the ethologists has been frequently taken over: that within us there are reservoirs of aggression which build up due to certain environmental circumstances. If this is not given expression, then it may well overflow in an apparently pointless direction. This is speculation which is difficult to anchor empirically and as such is perhaps best ignored. On the other hand, aggression is one aspect of emotion and its development must be of significance. As an example of the type of investigation which has been made into the development of aggression, the relevant parts of Sears' et al. (1957) famous study on child-rearing will be discussed. (For a good general analysis of the concept of agreession, see Singer 1971.)

Sears *et al.* define aggression in mammals as behaviour intended to hurt or injure someone, and suggest that this may take the form of fighting or the expression of rage. Their definition emphasizes *intent*, which places it outside the realms of objectivity. However, given this definition, it is clear that aggression will be modified and attenuated by the process of socialization.

At this point it is perhaps useful to digress in order to say a little about the extreme difficulty which psychologists have had in defining aggression. Sears' definition is but one of many, and another has already been discussed in Chapter 6. Buss (1966) provides what is still probably the best classification of human aggression.

	Direct	Active indirect	Passive direct	Indirect
Physical	Hitting	Practical joke	Sit-ins	Refusing to do something
Verbal	Insulting	Malicious gossip	Refusals to speak	Refusing permission

Comprehensive though this categorization is, it nevertheless leaves out any consideration of intent and any distinction between intent and accident. Also it makes no mention of anger, which at first sight would seem integral to aggression. However, aggression can occur without anger, and anger can have outcomes other than aggression—anxiety or depression for example.

To return to Sears *et al.*, they stress the place of anxiety in the development of aggression in children. They suggest that a common parental response to a child's aggression is to meet it with more aggression. in fact, from their surveys they gained the impression that children are punished more for aggression than for any other behaviour. Sears *et al.* suggest that one of the consequences of punishment is anxiety, and that throughout childhood anxiety *may* therefore become attached to aggression. This, in turn, will become modified to a 'mental sensation' of unease whenever an aggressive impulse is felt. Hence, by adulthood, we willingly tolerate neither our own aggression nor that of others—which, of course, is highly appropriate to the smooth running of society. In parallel to this, the child develops techniques for dealing with punishment. Thus, punishment does not stop the impulse to aggression, it simply makes it more selective. Finally, Sears *et al.* suggest that extreme punishment *increases* aggression, since it is thought to induce more frustration in the child.

As an adjunct to this analysis, Sears *et al.* studied the effect of maternal permissiveness towards aggression, and found, not surprisingly, high permissiveness to be associated with high aggression. However, although these ideas are interesting and fit well with intuitive ideas of childhood aggression, as Sears *et al.* admit, they are based entirely on ratings of punishment, aggression, etc., made by mothers; such ratings might be open to any kind of bias. Also, in their theoretical analysis, Sears *et al.* make use of many concepts such as anxiety and frustration which, if anything, are more difficult to define than aggression itself. However, in spite of this, the general approach to the development and socialization of aggression is well worth pursuing.

Internalization and emotional development

The concept of internalization embodies an even more mentalistic approach to human emotional development than those considered so far, and also extends Sears' work on aggression. It rests on the idea that anxiety becomes associated with punished behaviour. On future occasions, this anxiety may suppress the behaviour (thereby reducing the anxiety). If a child learns to suppress some aspects of his behaviour without any obvious external intervention, then he is said to have internalized the behaviour of stopping himself from doing something. Hence, emotional changes mediated by cognitive evaluations are believed to form the basis of self-regulatory behaviour through internalization.

Internalization refers to a child's learning of what we normally term self-control through the cognitive aspects of emotional changes (cf. Skinner 1953). From the subjective point of view, this means that either pleasure or fear and anxiety become attached to everyday acts, which of course lead to reward and punishment. It is thought that these positive or negative emotions can then become associated with a child's understanding, i.e. cognition, of a situation. In putting forward this argument, Aronfreed (1968) concludes that the child may become happy or afraid when he *thinks* of doing something, before he actually does it.

Some aspects of the results of a well-conducted experiment by Parke and Walters (1967) are regarded as bearing on Aronfreed's ideas. They divided six to seven year old children into four main groups depending on the time and manner in which they were to be punished. Punishment consisted of verbal castigation and unpleasant noise for choosing a toy which they were led to believe was actually meant for another child. Punishment either occurred early (when they started to reach for the toy) or late (after they had picked it up). After training, the toys which had been associated with punishment were placed on a table and covered with a cloth; the child was left alone with them for 15 minutes. Those children who had been punished early picked up the toys from the table less often, waited longer before they did so, and if they handled them at all did so for less time. This can be interpreted as supporting the hypothesis that early punishment leads to greater internalized suppression of behaviour. However, all that can be firmly concluded is that suppression of behaviour occurred. It is a result similar to that obtained from conditioned suppression studies in animals.

Aronfreed (1968) extends his theory by emphasizing that for internalization to come about all a child need do is experience some emotional change in connection with some behaviour; this may happen simply through observation. In stressing the importance of imitation, he suggests that a child imitates as a result of the pleasure he has gained from observing the model. Hence, feeling good becomes associated with his perceptions and cognitions of the model. Aronfreed considers cognitions to be crucial, since they allow the self-control which the child exerts over his own emotions to expand. He can remember his social experiences and those memories will have emotional components. So he comes to be able to represent to himself, and hence anticipate, reward and punishment. In the end, he is acting to produce 'good' feelings and to avoid producing 'bad' feelings. This general thesis is very similar to Arnold's (for example 1970a; 1970b) ideas of appraisal and effective memory.

Another aspect of Aronfreed's (1968) concept of internalization accords well with the possible significance for emotional development of initial social attachments. Internalization is thought to presuppose an initial attachment to some person (although, in passing, it might be noted that such was not the case in Parke and Walters' study). This implies that the threat of withdrawal of love or nurturance from the child is important to emotional change and development. Self-criticism is the internalization of this; the child is taking away 'love' from himself. A study by Grusec (1966) exemplifies the empirical approach to self-criticism. Five and six year old children were divided into three groups. Initially, an experimenter either: (1) played with them and was friendly and approving (i.e. showed a high degree of warmth); or (2) mainly ignored them (i.e. showed a low degree of warmth); or (3) showed a high degree of warmth and then withdrew it. A game was rigged to go wrong. Each child was led to believe that it was his fault, after which he was then questioned to determine the extent to which he was self-critical. In general, the children were judged to be more self-critical if the experimenter had been warm towards them, but this self-criticism only generalized to a new situation if the experimenter had also shown withdrawal of affection.

In a final extension of his argument, Aronfreed suggests that a child learns to reduce the cognitive force of unpleasant emotions by being self-critical. Thus, the rejected or neglected child will have no love to lose, will not become self-critical, and may therefore end as a delinquent. In Aronfreed's terms, a child behaves so as to maintain his emotional bonds, an idea which is similar to those on attachment expressed earlier.

To summarize, Aronfreed suggests that emotional development is dependent on the process of internalization. Thus, the child learns to control his own behaviour by paying attention to the cognitive aspects of his emotion. Emotional change may come about through direct experience or by the child's imitations of rewarding models. So, internalization is more likely to occur if the young child has formed a good social bond with some adult. This way of analysing emotional development is an odd mixture of a concentrated cognitive approach and a somewhat dilute behavioural theory. The cognitive elements are often untestable and the behavioural aspects are often undeveloped. It would be more useful if the cognitive arguments gave way to a clearer behavioural exposition, or the cognitive aspects were developed further and in ways more open to empirical test.

Play and emotion

A view couched in terms rather similar to Aronfreed's is put forward by Izard (1972) concerning the relationship between children's play and emotion. His basic assumption is that children use repetitive play to help them to cope with situations which would otherwise be overwhelming; to control possible anxiety for example. He further assumes that play has a significant role in integrating the various components of emotion and hence in the development of a more mature personality. Thus emotions both instigate and sustain play, which in its turn has influences on emotion.

Izard develops these views by putting forward a number of propositions. Although he generated these on the basis of his theory of emotion and his work on the development of emotional recognition and labelling, they may still be regarded as hypotheses yet to be tested.

1. Emotion is a primary motivational system which promotes play, although high drive does not bring it about.

2. Interactions between cognition and emotion enliven play and hence stimulate intellectual development.

3. Interactions between emotion and states of high drive act to make more likely the disruption and distortion of play.

4. Play is primarily enhanced by the fundamental emotions of interest and enjoyment.

5. If play which is motivated by interest is thwarted, negative emotion results, the form this takes being determined by the personality of the child plus the nature of the block. For example, sometimes anger may result or sometimes anxiety.

6. An interaction between interest and anger leads to aggressive play.

7. The extent to which a child withdraws socially and/or indulges in make-believe will depend on the relative balance between shame and shyness, and interest and enjoyment in what he is doing.

8. If a low degree of fear oscillates with interest, excitement is raised, whereas a high degree of fear will suppress interest and therefore reduce play.

9. Disgust will lead to avoidance of the activity.

Although these propositions are reasonable, particularly within the context of Izard's theory, the extent to which they will be borne out by research remains to be seen. They certainly provide a useful framework in which to study play, a difficult area of research, and may even provide guidelines for studying activities such as sport which pass for play in adults.

The biology of emotional development

This consideration of the emotional development of children will be completed with a brief analysis of the biological or physiological approach to the subject, since in many ways it is representative of the most interesting ideas and best-conducted research in the field. Again, the tendency has been, and still is, to build on somewhat shaky foundations. To take two examples from a modern and avowedly psychobiological psychologist:

'... early childhood is a time of feeling rather than knowing'.

'Emotion is, indeed, the driving force that enables the organism to overcome or circumvent a block to dissatisfaction'.

(Nash 1970, pp. 327 and 307)

In fact, the biological approach to emotional development rests on the idea that to begin with emotion is only associated with physiological need—the infant cries when it is hungry or cold. In other words, emotion (or at least negative emotion) is said to be experienced when a drive state is blocked.

Bousfield and Orbison (1952) appear to have initiated two quite profitable lines of speculation concerning the ontogenesis of emotional behaviour. These rest on two assumptions. (1) Neonates are functionally decorticate, cortical control becoming increasingly apparent throughout development. (2) Infants are partially lacking in hormones which are important to stress reactions.

The cortex and its interrelationships with the thalamus have often been implicated in emotion (see Chapter 3). There is little 'downwards' inhibitory influence in the brain at birth. This should mean that the emotional responses of children are similar to those of animals, since as adults the latter are comparatively lacking in cortex. In turn, this suggests that emotions in children, although quickly aroused, should not stay aroused for long. They should dissipate rather than persist or reverberate. This certainly is in accord with everyday observations. Bronson (1965) even goes to the lengths of seeing infantile emotions as mediated mainly in the brain-stem reticular activating system, thus resulting in a generalized arousal which is not oriented towards any particular goal, a view which is reminiscent of Bridges (1932) and also of Schneirla (1959). (It should be noted here that there are 'downward' CNS influences in animals, and there is little evidence that their emotions are easily aroused.)

Emotional states are thought to increase in vigour with age (cf. Hebb 1949), and this vigour is thought to be largely due to the influence of the adrenal glands. The development of the adrenal glands themselves seems to follow an odd course. By the time the child is two they have decreased to half their weight at birth, following which they rapidly increase in weight up to about five years, increase more slowly until 11, and then accelerate until 20. It is not until the age of about 16 that they are back to their birth weight. Presumably, output is associated with weight. Although it is mainly the adrenal medulla which is growing throughout this time, the adrenal cortex is known to be essential to life and important for controlling prolonged reactions to stress. Also, there are differences in the secretions of the adrenal cortex between childhood and adulthood, although what exactly these differences are is unclear. Overall, this relationship can only be tentatively suggested.

Funkenstein et al. (1957) provide the most detailed hormone-based ideas on the development of emotion. From the fact that the adrenal medulla secretes both epinephrine and norepinephrine, they suggest that the former is related to passive, nonaggressive reactions to stress (and predominates in the rabbit for example) and the latter to solitary, aggressive reactions (and predominates in the lion for example). On the basis of their studies, Funkenstein *et al.* also argue that amongst humans there are two sorts of anger. There is that of the anger-inners (who bottle up everything and blame themselves—a predominance of epinephrine), and that of the anger-outers (who show anger and blame others—a predominance of norepinephrine). They also claim that in childhood there is always a preponderance of norepinephrine, which by adulthood has either balanced out with epinephrine or still carries greater weight. It should be pointed out that, although of considerable interest, these ideas are highly speculative.

Clearly, Funkenstein *et al.* seem to be stressing physiological maturation and individual differences in their account of emotional development. They are tracing much the same line as Aronfreed, although in a different manner and with different emphases. However, they also argue that anger-inners and anger-outers tend to experience different upbringings, which of course puts us more squarely into the learning camp. They regard anger-outers as having parents with whom they identify. Their mother provides them with affection and their father is an angry authoritarian. The anger-inners have good relationships with both parents; there is little difference in parental authority, but the mother is again the more affectionate. These ideas are all based on retrospective, questionnaire studies, the results of which have led Funkenstein even further into speculative realms. An acceptable way of testing them is not immediately apparent.

Conclusions

From this sample of the literature on emotional development in children, one can say that there is more discussion than hard data and that any empirical information has often been gathered in ways which are open to criticism. Although there are some common threads, systematization is difficult. However, it is possible to draw a few tentative conclusions. (1) Emotional development in children depends on a combination of genetic and environmental factors. The genetic factors seem to be reflected in the maturation of the cortex and endocrine system. A central environmental influence would appear to be the child's first relationships with significant adults and places in its life. (2) Throughout childhood, there may be increasing differentiation of the emotions. This might simply involve the continuous refinement of the labels which a child is taught to use in describing his emotional states. Alternatively, it could result from increasing differentiation of the CNS and endocrine system, or reflect an increasing range of social experiences, reactions to which the child has internalized in various ways. (3) Like any other aspect of the subject, emotional development can be viewed from a cognitive and/or a physiological and/or a behavioural viewpoint, although the tendency is increasingly to point to the possible role of cognition in general and cognitive evaluations in particular.

ANIMALS

Research into the emotional development of infrahuman species is more abundant than human research and more capable of systematic discussion. The approaches which have gelled over the years range from investigations of genetic factors and heritability, through ethological and physiological analyses of the nature/nurture problem, to theories, research, and applications of the concepts of early emotionality and infantile affection.

Heritability and emotionality

Research into heritability and emotion rests on two assumptions. (1) There are differences in emotionality or emotional reactivity between individuals. (2) Some variations in behaviour are due to genetic variation. Here, the term emotion is in a context of biological adaptivity, referring to processes concerned with both self- and species-preservation, these being the usual fighting, escaping or avoiding, eating, reproducing, and caring for the young. The emphasis is on 'instinctual' species-typical behaviour. Bruell (1970) distinguishes between the genetic determination of a behavioural trait and its heritability. Some inter-species differences in behaviour are genetically determined. But whether or not behavioural differences within a species are due to genetic variation, namely, heritability, is a question which must be answered empirically.

This argument has led to the development of two procedures designed to investigate the effects of heritability on emotionality. Each of these will be exemplified by one study. First, there is that strategy which involves breeding animals selectively so as to minimize or maximize particular behavioural characteristics. Hall (1951) placed each of 145 rats in a bright circular enclosure for two minutes per day. Any urination or defecation in this enclosure led to a score of +1 for that day. After 12 days, high-scoring animals were mated with one another, as also were those with low scores. Similar separations were made in succeeding generations. In the original sample, the mean defecation score was 3.86. After 12 generations, the mean score for the group of 'emotional' rats was 10.4 and that for the 'non-emotional' group was 1.65. Clearly, if defecation in a strange environment is accepted as an index of emotionality, as it sometimes has been (see Chapter 6), then emotionality must have been heritable in Hall's original rat population.

The other main research strategy in the study of heritability involves comparisons between inbred strains of animals. Bruell (1965), for example, investigated 'timidity' in 1500 mice by using a tunnel-emergence test. The mice would be placed singly into a narrow, eight-inch long tunnel which opened into a rectangular, lighted, open box. Bruell found significant differences in the times which it took different strains of mice to emerge from the tunnel to the box. He interpreted this as indicating that one strain was more timid, or emotional, than the other, and that in consequence it is possible to infer that timidity must have been heritable in the original parent population. Although Bruell (1970) supports this with closely reasoned genetic/mathematical arguments, his data are open to other possible interpretations. His mice may have been fortuitously bred with different visual capacities for example, which might lead them to show behavioural variations such as those described.

The use of these two fundamental techniques has produced research into the heritability of many types of behaviour. For the present three of these will be mentioned to illustrate the point. In their analysis of aggressive behaviour, Scott and Fuller (1965) maintain that there are huge differences between the aggressiveness of various breeds of dog, which for centuries have been bred more or less selectively. Also Guhl *et al.* (1960) found differences by the second generation when selectively breeding aggressive and nonaggressive chickens. Secondly, with respect to what might loosely be termed affection, Hess (1959) managed to selectively breed in one generation high and low imprinters. (See below.) Finally, Hale and Schein (1962) found a sevenfold difference in the frequency with which turkeys mated after nine generations of selective breeding. As Bruell (1970) points out, this last is an odd result (although it does not stand alone), since sexual behaviour might be expected not to be heritable. Natural selection must work in favour of the better reproducer, and time should therefore have dispensed with any inappropriate sexual behaviour generations ago; any variation should by now be of environmental origin. On the other hand, such a result is less surprising if it can be assumed that one mating every so often is enough to produce all the eggs that a female turkey can lay.

There has been much research demonstrating the heritability of many different forms of emotional behaviour; those mentioned here have simply been examples. However, one overall point is that all the studies have shown quantitative differences. The same emotional behaviour has been observed within a species but at different thresholds. Emotional reactions appear to be species-typical; within any species any differences are never qualitative—although Man is perhaps an exception to this rule.

Innate fear

The problem of innate fear is given special mention for two reasons. (1) Because there is always much conjecture (although little useful research) about built-in fears in children. (2) It highlights the broader controversy over the nature/nurture question which existed for many years between ethologists and psychologists. Recently, however, there has been something of a rapprochment in that heredity and environment are seen as interacting, one being clearly unable to exist without the other, their effects being interdependent.

The discussion of innate fear began with reports from a number of ethologists (see Thorpe 1956) that many birds that are nest-reared show fear if a cardboard shape representative of a flying bird of prey (usually regarded as a hawk) is passed over them. When its direction of 'flight' is reversed, that is it becomes long of neck and short of tail, no fear is shown. The usual argument has been that this apparent fear remains intense over some time during the birds' early life, in the absence of any obvious reinforcement. Traditionally, stress has most commonly been put on an 'innate' explanation (i.e. there exists a 'blueprint' for a hawk) but with little information on the precise conditions of the early environment.

In order to clear the ground a little, Melzack *et al.* (1959) carried out a more exact study of this phenomenon. They raised a group of mallard ducks in a very restricted environment for 25 days after hatching. They were housed in individual cages with the only visual outlet being upwards. Throughout this time they were presented with 'hawk' or 'goose' models. In a series of tests conducted after day 25, it was found that ducks which had had such experiences were *less* fearful than those which had not. (Fear was defined as either high-level excitement, short jerky movements, wing-flapping and shrill sounds, or avoidance, running as far as the cage space permitted, flapping and vocalizing as they went.) When the object was moving fast, there was more fear of the 'hawk', otherwise there was not. The exception to this was that ducks raised in restricted conditions initially showed more fear of the 'hawk'. However, under all conditions, any fear tended to dissipate (habituate) rapidly.

It is worth noting that Schneirla (1959) suggests that these effects are due to differences in the intensity of the stimulation generated by the two directions of travel. However, Melzack *et al.* interpret their results as generally supporting the idea of some innate component to the fear. But they also suggest that *any novel* stimulus produces fear. They regard the 'hawk' fear as emerging from what is initially a great variety of fears of new objects, with inherited mechanisms favouring the continuation of this fear whilst others habituate more rapidly. Their results, however, definitely point to the importance of environmental factors.

Gray (1971) gives the most searching recent discussion of the degree to which fears might be innate or acquired. From a consideration of the evidence and his own conceptual analysis, Gray suggests that the stimuli which promote fear can be classified under four general headings: those which are intense, those which are novel, some which stem from social interaction, and those which indicate special evolutionary dangers.

Reviewing the hawk/goose type of evidence, Gray argues that although there are some pointers in the direction of innate factors, the likelihood is that under conditions of natural rearing young birds will see more goose-like than hawk-like shapes. It is therefore, possible that they show a fear reaction to a hawk because of its novelty.

The question of stimulus intensity is obvious and so will not be dealt with further. However, on the question of social interaction, Gray maintains that an important source of stimuli which elicit fear is the recognition of threat by observation of the behaviour of conspecifics—a point which does not necessarily bear on the innate/acquired question. Finally, Gray argues that fear *may* be caused by stimuli which have previously been responsible for the deaths of large numbers of the species. Thus, for example, fear of the dark or of heights may well be inherited through its evolutionary usefulness.

On the course of the effects of these fear-eliciting stimuli, Gray suggests that fears which stem from intense and/or novel stimuli diminish with age. On the other hand, socially derived fears increase with age, and those which arise for evolutionary reasons do not change.

With the foregoing as a background, Gray criticizes the notion that early classical conditioning is at the basis of learned fears. He quotes the example of Valentine (1930), who applied the Watson and Rayner (1920) procedure to his own daughter. From his observations, Valentine concluded that fears are not acquired simply through classical conditioning. He suggested that some stimuli innately elicit a background fear and that a major reaction can be obtained more easily when these stimuli are used in a conditioning procedure than when more neutral stimuli are used.

This type of analysis leads Gray to conclude that the idea of innate fears, plus the proven effects of classical conditioning, make it possible to impose a reasonably coherent classification on stimuli which evoke fear. However, he also argues that to determine the *extent* to which a specific fear is innate or learned, a number of questions must be asked. For example, does the species have a discernible class of behaviour relevant to the fear? does this result from a particular neuroendocrine state? is the proposed index a reliable and valid measure of the state? (see Chapter 6).

Critical periods

By now, there is an extensive literature on critical periods in development, imprinting, and early experience in general, although not all of it is relevant to emotional development. Moreover, these three topics are intertwined; for example, it is impossible to consider the evidence concerning critical periods without going on to the broader question of early experience. However, for the sake of convenience, they are separated in this discussion.

Scott (for example 1967; 1968) has done much to further the importance of the concept of the critical period in development. The evidence from his work with dogs revolves around the notion of there being, early in life, a critical period for socialization, during which the animal is maximally sensitive to social stimuli. Scott maintains that a young puppy shows 'distress vocalizations' when it is removed from the objects and/or situations which it has experienced during its critical period. This emotional distress can only be relieved by the presence of other puppies or familiar surroundings. Scott regards this as a simple innate response. More important, he views it as a response which *maintains* an attachment to another member of the species. This thesis leads to the prediction that if other negative emotions are produced an intensification of the attachment should result.

Scott takes his argument one stage further by suggesting that many animals form emotional attachments to certain familiar physical surroundings—a phenomenon he terms *primary localization*. For example, he suggests that young puppies form these attachments very soon after their eyes open. Support for this is derived from marked changes in their 'yelp' rate if they are put into a strange environment. Scott believes this also to be the case with human infants, although any evidence for human critical periods is sketchy to say the very least, even though the idea has some appeal.

Scott is more tentative when discussing the possible effects of these early emotional experiences on later behaviour. He supposes that safety and security might be felt when a return is made to a familiar area or individual. If a young human infant is put into a strange locality for a time, then he may (1) always associate this locality with unpleasantness (which could, of course, be straight-forwardly seen as classical conditioning), and (2) become even more positively attached to his more familiar environment.

The concept of critical periods will be evaluated later, when exploring the general effects of early experience.

Imprinting

Imprinting refers to the formation of specific attachments by young precocial birds. It is generally regarded as developing from approach and following responses and not to be simply explicable by recourse to the principles of conditioning. (Although it should be noted that the capacity to be reinforced is greatly enhanced by proximity to the source of reinforcement.) The usual example of imprinting involves a young chick which follows the first moving object which it encounters—normally the mother. However, in numerous studies the young of various species have been induced to follow virtually anything, from wooden blocks to rows of lights that become illuminated in rapid succession. In the limiting case, even approach and following do not seem to be crucial for imprinting to take place; it is merely necessary for the young animal to see an apparently moving object. However, the basic conditions are as have been outlined, immediately suggesting the (biological adaptivity) conclusion that under 'natural' conditions imprinting is a highly appropriate way for the young of a species to become attached to older members, on whom they are anyway dependent.

Imprinting is regarded as occurring during a critical period. Much of the creative endeavour which has been put into the study of imprinting has been directed towards providing theories to account for the *end* of this sensitive period. These theories can be reduced to four main possibilities. (For a fuller analysis of these theories and a description and analysis of imprinting in general see Sluckin 1964.) (1) Sensitivity ends with maturation. (2) Sensitivity is inhibited through socialization. (3) Sensitivity ends with the growth of timidity. (4) Sensitivity ends because a state of low anxiety also ends. The first theory simply suggests that the ending of the critical period depends on innate, internal factors. This is difficult to refute entirely, although some studies have shown that critical periods can be extended (see Sluckin 1964). The second theory is perhaps more self-evident. It implies that the sensitive period for imprinting ends when imprinting has occurred. This has some support. However, the last two theories are of more relevance to emotion and will therefore be considered in more detail.

Timidity/fear

Within the context of imprinting, fear is variously viewed as immobility or flight, or as a response to sudden, intense stimuli or to particular species-specific stimuli. There is evidence from studies on young birds that some objects (for example food) sometimes produce approach responses, others (for example humans) sometimes produce fear responses, and others (for example other members of the species) sometimes produce both (see for example Hinde *et al.* 1956). Often the birds have been observed to be apparently in the throes of an approach/avoidance conflict.

This sort of fear is not seen in a newly hatched bird but only appears after a day or two, gradually developing thereafter. It is this which led to the view expressed by both Hinde (1955) and Hess (1959; 1962a; 1962b) that this fear gradually inhibits any approaching and following, since the overwhelming responses to new objects become freezing or flight. However, it is not as simple as this.

Sluckin (1960) suggests that an animal may develop a fear of fluctuating stimulus patterns and a fear of a static environment. Together, these lead him to conclude that strangeness is the main determinant of fear (cf. Salzen 1962; Schaller and Emlen 1962). Thus, new objects or new grounds are accepted to the extent that an animal is familiar with them. Also, the longer spent in any environment, the stranger will be any new environment. If the environment is strange and one part of it (the figure) is familiar, then Sluckin (1964) regards the environment as 'pushing' the animal to the figure. If the figure is unfamiliar, following is inhibited, while fear of the ground promotes following. Fear of the environment can either occur through strangeness or can be conditioned. Either way, the animal fearing the environment will move towards the figure. In support of this, Moltz *et al.* (1959) showed that shock-conditioned fear of a runway increased the strength of an already imprinted following response. Fear may also arise from too intense or insufficient stimulation—loud noises, bright lights or darkness, solitude—otherwise early fears are of novel or strange stimuli (for example Melzack 1952; Salzen 1962).

Sluckin (1964) suggests that the recognition of strangeness depends on experience rather than simple maturation; to run from something strange there must have developed enough 'knowledge' to perceive it as strange. There are many reports in the imprinting literature that initially there is no fear in very young birds, for example for the first 24 hours in chicks. Hence, imprinting can take place before objects are strange enough to be feared. Also, there are many observations that a bird will later follow an object which was originally feared, although Hess (1959) does not believe that animals become imprinted to such objects. In fact, fear seems to develop with imprinting and then, after imprinting is complete, to lead to the development of withdrawal from strange stimuli.

Anxiety

In this context, to distinguish it from fear, anxiety tends to be defined as a general fearfulness in the absence of any obvious stimuli. Not surprisingly, the proposed indicants of anxiety are difficult to distinguish from the proposed indicants of fear—perhaps the concepts themselves are not easily or usefully separated.

Moltz (1960) is the main exponent of the anxiety view. He suggests that the young imprinting bird is in a state of low anxiety, but at the same time is very receptive to the sight of moving objects. In Moltz's terms, this may lead to the object in question inducing a drive state. (This follows from Mowrer's (1939) view of anxiety being acquired in an avoidance-learning situation and then its subsequent reduction motivating new learning.) Moltz argues that a newly-hatched chick comes to associate a (rewarding) state of low anxiety with a moving object. In turn, the object comes to act as a reinforcer which can mediate new learning. Following and imprinting occur because they bring the chick nearer to this reinforcer. So Moltz maintains that the critical period for imprinting ends when the state of low anxiety ends.

Salzen and Tomlin (1963) take a slightly different view; they suggest that the sight of the moving object *produces* the state of low anxiety—there is an initial fearlessness simply because imprinting has not yet occurred. This question is not yet resolved, nor is it known whether or not imprinting is explicable in emotional/learning theory terms or is a quite independent process. However, as can be seen above, some facts and ideas about some aspects of emotional development have emerged from its study.

Early experience and emotionality

The typical procedure in studies of the effects of early experience on later emotionality involves subjecting animals as young as possible to conditions such as handling by the experimenter or electric shock. After this, they are reared individually under standard laboratory conditions. As adults they are tested in situations believed to allow a measure of emotionality, the 'open-field' test for example (see Chapter 6). The degree to which they behave emotionally is compared with that of untreated control animals. The degree to which control subjects are untreated is a determinant of how firmly any conclusions can be drawn.

An important theorist in this field is Denenberg (see particularly 1964). His thesis begins with an attack on Scott's (1962; 1968) ideas concerning critical periods. Scott implies that there are *limited* periods during development when certain stimulation has profound effects. Before and after this period the effects are more restricted. However, studies designed to test this idea (mainly involving mice, rats, and dogs) have not often shown positive results. Denenberg maintains that the only hard evidence in support of the critical period concept comes from studies which used physiological measures (for example Levine and Lewis 1959). His argument is based on an analysis of many studies, including his own. He suggests that any purported critical period is an artifactual result of stimulus intensity, both within the early experience and during the adult tests. Consequently, by chance or by a conscious manipulation of stimulus intensity as an independent variable, an investigator could easily find evidence for what looks like a critical period but which is, in fact, not. Experiments involving shock in infancy and later avoidance learning (in mice) and handling and gentling and later emotionality (in rats) do *not* support the critical period hypothesis. Denenberg suggests the advisability of concentrating on the relationship between various classes of independent and dependent variables between birth and weaning, rather than trying to isolate critical periods—a view reminiscent of Yarrow's (1961) on maternal deprivation and Anastasi's (1958) on the nature/nurture problem.

Denenberg then considers the problem of finding a common factor in studies of the effects of early stimulation. He suggests that any stimulation between birth and weaning reduces 'emotional reactivity'. The greater the infantile stimulation, the less the emotionality in adulthood. Thus Denenberg's main hypothesis:

> '... *emotional reactivity is reduced as a monotonic function of amount of stimulus input in infancy*'
>
> (1964, p. 338, italics his).

There are a number of lines of evidence which support this general proposition, although they are usually concerned with either handling or shock. For example, rats that are handled more in infancy, as adults are more active and defecate less than control rats in open-field tests (for example Denenberg and Smith 1963). Rats handled and shocked in infancy and later deprived of water (such deprivation being a novel situation) drink less than controls (Levine 1957; 1958; 1959). (Of course, an increase in water intake would also have supported the 'emotionality' argument.) Or rats stimulated in infancy are bolder than unstimulated controls as adults in emergence-from-cage tests, and handled rats are less emotional than non-handled on measures of avoidance learning. Also, in general, rats given early shock are less emotional than controls in open-field tests (Denenberg and Smith 1963). This evidence suggests that stimulation in infancy reduces adult emotional reactivity. Further, various studies imply a monotonic relationship between amount of early stimulation and later reduction in emotionality (for example Denenberg and Smith 1963; Lindholm 1962).

Denenberg (1964) takes the argument a stage further by equating emotionality with motivation, that is, the more emotional animal · is more highly motivated. He also suggests that there should be an optimal level of emotionality for efficient performance. This puts us squarely in the inverted U country, which Denenberg represents as in Figure 11. This suggestion is supported by evidence from Karas and Denenberg (1961), Denenberg and Morton (1962), and Denenberg and Kline (1964). Set against this should be the lack of more general support for this hypothetical relationship between motivation (arousal) and performance, and the inappropriateness of motivational accounts of motivation.

Finally, Denenberg admits that his data have been usually restricted to rodents that have been stimulated before weaning; weaning has been the cutoff

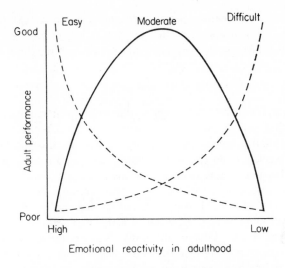

Figure 11. The proposed relationship between
adult performance and emotionality for tasks of
varying difficulty (taken from Denenberg 1964).

point, since all a rodent's senses are functioning by then. This would naturally
make the effects of handling and shock quite a different (an idea which suggests
a critical period).

It is clear that Denenberg (and others such as Levine) has shown that early
experience affects late behaviour. Also, emotionality appears to be a reasonably
useful hypothetical construct to account for the mediation of these effects.
However, the generality of early experience effects, particularly at the human
level, is an open question. Few species have been studied and few sources of
stimulation used. Intensity of early stimulation is likely to be an important
variable, but it has appeared in few investigations and then has provided scant
support for Denenberg's hypothesis suggesting a monotonic relationship
between stimulus input and emotional reactivity. Finally, Denenberg argues
that intensity of infantile stimulation is a major parameter affecting later
differences in 'chronic' (i.e. general) level of arousal. Again, however, this is
simply trying to explain one rather unwieldy concept (emotionality) by another,
and in the absence of more precise definition and firm evidence should be treated
with caution.

Affection, fear, and aggression—Harlow

Harlow (for example Harlow and Harlow 1962; 1970) is accorded a section to
himself in this discussion of emotional development, since: (1) his approach is
unique; (2) he normally studies rhesus monkeys, results from which can perhaps
be more meaningfully extrapolated to the human level. Harlow regards social
and emotional development as being intimately connected. He suggests that

there are three fundamental patterns of social response, which make their developmental appearance in the sequence: affection, fear, aggression. Anything which distorts this sequence may distort social–sexual development.

Affection

Harlow and Harlow (1962) suggest that the initial reciprocal attachment between mother and infant lays the groundwork for later social development both in subhuman primates and to a large extent in humans. At birth, rhesus monkeys reflexively cling to their mother's body, and move up to the nipple. Harlow and Harlow believe emotional attachment to develop in the first month or two of life due to the satisfaction of hunger, and comfort, warmth, and support from the mother. They suggest that the grooming and caressing of their young by adult females is a reflection of reciprocal emotional satisfaction.

By the second month of life, infant monkeys evince interest in their peers. The contacts between them lengthen, turn into play, and lead to the development of emotional attachments. Harlow regards this new type of attachment as growing with the decline of mother–infant attachment; it is not simply generalization. Alexander (1966, quoted by Harlow and Harlow 1970) showed that infant monkeys that have been deprived of peers are very wary when first exposed to them and never develop any strong ties with them. Harlow and Harlow (1970) then argue, but with only discursive, observational support, for the ubiquitous nature of peer affection in primates, including humans. Early on, sexual differentiation is unimportant, but after three or four months, male monkeys become progressively more dominant and females more passive. In the juvenile period (one to two years in monkeys), friendship pairs are usually like-sexed—the human parallels are clear. Harlow and Harlow suggest that culture merely emphasizes and moulds sex differences which already exist. They view peer affection as a main factor in learning effective adult social and sexual adjustment—learning the appropriate place in the group.

Fear

Harlow and Zimmerman (1959) affirm that fear in rhesus monkeys only begins after the first two months of life. They scream, cling to or run to their mothers if shown unfamiliar places, objects or humans, objects moving towards them, or unusual and loud noises. If they are separated from their mothers they cry and clasp themselves. Harlow and Harlow regard the development of fear as partially dependent on experience, since it involves perception of potential danger.

Aggression

Harlow and Harlow state that playful *attacks* are obvious from the start of social play. Free aggression towards peers does not appear until about ten to twelve months in monkeys raised in a group, but earlier in those raised in isolation. The latter also inflict worse injuries on one another. Once the dominance hierarchies have been established in socially raised monkeys, there is relative peace. Monkeys raised in isolation often show uncontrolled or undiscriminated aggression, or sometimes incapacitating fear. Harlow and Harlow conclude that affectional relationships are necessary precursors to normal social aggression, which keeps physical injury at a minimum.

Much of Harlow's research has involved social isolation. Monkeys are raised from birth in stainless-steel chambers with diffused light temperature and air control and food, water, and cleaning accomplished remotely. Typically, the monkeys see *nothing* living for either three, six or twelve months, after which they are placed in individual cages and a few days later they have their first social experiences. Often, they are put together in a playroom with another isolate plus two cage-reared monkeys for half and hour per day, five days per week, for six months.

The main response to removal from isolation seems to be fear. This fits well with work on imprinting. The three-month isolates recovered (became normal) in a few days or weeks. In the six- and twelve-month animals the fear remained predominant. They did not defend themselves against attack and they did not form social attachments. In the six-month group, minimal play was observed, in the twelve-month group none. When six- and twelve-month animals of the same age were put together, the twelves were attacked by the sixes with very accentuated aggression. After these tests the monkeys spent two years in standard laboratory cages and were then tested with strangers, either large, powerful adult monkeys, normal peers, or normal one year olds. All the experimental monkeys were terrified, but this was punctuated by isolated, extreme, violent, suicidal, aggressive attacks. It seems that the fear and aggression had intensified with time. These results perhaps point to the three-to-six-month period being critical in a monkey's development.

Further support comes from Harlow's observations that even monkeys reared with their mothers but whose peer experiences were somewhat delayed showed a measure of this fear and aggression. Also, very immature, long-lasting clinging was seen in monkeys raised with no mothers but continually in contact with peers. If four monkeys are reared together with no mother, they spend most of the time sitting clinging in a line, like carriages in a train, to use Harlow's analogy.

The emotional inadequacies in monkeys reared in isolation also extend to their sexual behaviour. The separate behaviours involved in copulation are evident, but they never become integrated into a whole unless the monkeys are taught by an 'experienced' adult. The sex drive seems to be as strong as in normal monkeys, but the behaviour is typically autistic and onanistic with short bursts of aggression.

On the basis of this and similar work, Harlow and Harlow (1970) draw a number of conclusions. They believe the absence of mothering to be partially surmounted by peer associations. Also, given a mother's presence, peer deprivation can occur without much harm for quite long periods. Hence, they suggest that there are two independent by interchangeable affectional systems—that which is based on peer socialization and that which is based on mother–infant socialization. Finally, they maintain that for fear and aggression to develop 'normally', then the positive affectional system must develop *first*.

SCHNEIRLA'S THEORY OF EMOTIONAL DEVELOPMENT

Before drawing any conclusions, it is appropriate at this point to include a theory; a theory which is of emotion in general but which is clearly relevant to emotional development in particular, and which even depends on the concept of development for its structure.

Somewhat similarly to Leeper (1970), Schneirla (1959) regards perception, motivation, and emotion as intricately bound together, but in ontological development. He defines emotions as:

'(1) episodes or sequences of overt and incipient somatic adjustment, (2) often loosely patterned and variable, (3) usually with concurrent exciting sensory effects, perhaps also perceptual attitudes characterisable as desirable or undesirable, pleasant or unpleasant, (4) related to the intensity effects or perceptual meaning of a stimulus, (5) synergic with organic changes of A- or W-types.'

(1959, p. 26)

Schneirla's A- and W-types are fundamental to his view of emotion. They refer to *biphasic* mechanisms of receptors, central and auxiliary nervous systems and effectors which Schneirla regards as basic to *all* ontogeny. A-type arousal is caused by weak-intensity stimuli and leads to local or general approach to the source of stimulation. W-type arousal is caused by strong-intensity stimuli and leads to local or general withdrawal.

Schneirla argues that a James–Lange type of theory may be useful for studying the early ontogeny of animals when these A- and W-type patterns overwhelm behaviour, depending on stimulus magnitude. Equally, he suggests that a Cannon–Bard approach is more germane to the later stages of emotional development, which are far more perceptual and motivational in nature.

Quite differently from Bridges (1932), Schneirla weighs the evidence concerning very early emotion and believes that it warrants the conclusion that the reactions of neonates are essentially biphasic, although the evidence which Schneirla draws on at this point is very early and quite obscure (for example Peiper, 1926). Schneirla also argues that emotion and motivation are fundamentally related. He suggests that there are physiologically prescribed biphasic states, which in maturing lead to the advancement of emotion and motivation. He supports these contentions by detailed analyses of smiling and reaching. It is sufficient to describe his analysis of smiling.

Schneirla maintains that in mammals there are two antagonistic systems of facial muscles, one pulling the lips downwards, the other pulling them up. He cites Koehler (1954) as representing the view that the smiling pattern is innate in man, but argues that any very early smile is in fact a grimace, physiologically determined by low-intensity stimulation (see Dennis 1935; Spitz and Wolf 1946). Also, the studies cited do not suggest any unconditioned stimuli which may bring this response about. Schneirla opines that it is elicited by a *class* of stimuli, their common characteristic being low intensity. Thereafter, he believes that smiling develops through a gradual conditioning process. As noted previously, Spitz and Wolf (1946) report that the smiling response occurs to visual stimuli after three months, in particular to faces and face-like objects. Initially, smiling is general and diffuse, but gradually becomes more refined. By six months there is more definite expression which is under stimulus control, after which it indexes a discrimination between familiar and unfamiliar faces. Hence, in Schneirla's terms, there is an initial biphasic substrate which makes possible an 'approach' response to many types of low-intensity stimuli. This gradually becomes conditioned and refined to specific social situations, thereby suggesting the increasing importance of motivation and perception to emotional development.

CONCLUSIONS

The wide range of research strategies which have been used to study emotional development make it difficult to draw any firm conclusions. There has been too little research with human infants and much of what has been done is too subjective to permit concise evaluation. The biological approach perhaps provides an exception to this. On the other hand, conclusions drawn from infra-human investigations are more justified by the less criticizable research techniques on which they are based. However, the relevance and extrapability of this work to human emotional development can only be tentatively pursued.

In general, work on animal species has been concerned with the effects of early experience, either appreciated or depreciated, on later (adult) behaviour. Often any effects have been accounted for by the idea of emotionality. It is argued that the effects of early experience ranging from handling to electric shock cause the animals involved to be less emotional (fearful) later on. Such work has pointed to the possible inportance of critical periods (of maximal sensitivity to certain stimuli) to these effects. And also to the significance for emotional development of early attachments or bonds between an animal and other members of its species (usually adults). It may be that human emotional development is equally dependent on initial familial attachments. Perhaps there are critical periods which are also important at the human level, and of course a form of imprinting may even take place. There is no direct evidence for these ideas, but it is clear that those who postulate internalization as a necessary part of human emotional development rely on the quality of the early mother–child interaction in their explanations. Also, Harlow's work has done much to bridge the gap between human and animal studies based on these ideas. In addition, the idea of early attachment both to people and places is crucial to the influential views of psychologists such as Bowlby.

At both levels of investigation, emotional development is seen to depend on an interaction between genetic and environmental influences. This is implied by studies of smiling and crying in children, and of critical periods in animals. Of course, this is little different from the position found with almost any aspect of development; there is a nature–nurture interaction. Indeed, it is often difficult to distinguish emotional development from development more broadly conceived, social development for example. It would seem likely that we are born with the capacity to respond to certain stimuli with increased general activity. From this, more specific emotional responses become refined by experience (learning). However, this may involve little more than learning to use and name (culturally) appropriate expressions in particular situations. Such learning could well be dependent on our initial social attachments and on periods of increased sensitivity in our development.

These rather speculative conclusions have some resemblance to Bridge's original ideas of emotional differentiation. It is important to bear in mind that as yet there has only been direct support for them at the observational level. However, Schachter's work, with its emphasis on situational cues allowing us to label physiologically undifferentiated states, has obvious relevance. Finally, it is clear that a first priority in the general field of emotional development must be for a rapprochment of the observational techniques used with children and the more experimental strategies used with animals. And also it is important to make a conceptual and empirical analysis of the significance and course of early emotional experience, attachment, and the role of play.

8

Emotional Expression and Recognition

Since a social psychologist's main concern is with social interaction, his interest in emotion tends to be limited to its communication within a social context. He spends little time in broad considerations of emotion, but instead focuses either on emotional expression or on the recognition of emotion. Apart from the study of emotional expression and recognition being interesting in its own right, the problems which beset it and the attempts which have been made to solve them are instructive for more general analyses of emotion. In recent years they have even led to some of the comparatively full theories of emotion (e.g. Izard 1972).

Whenever we interact with another person, whether face-to-face or otherwise, we are continually expressing emotion. Simultaneously, we are monitoring and interpreting the other person's emotional expressions He (or she) is doing the same. It is fair to say that it is this complex and possibly often unconscious process which gives social interaction much of its subtlety and depth. Our emotional expressions are providing stimuli to anyone with whom we might be interacting. He in turn responds to these stimuli. He observes, judges, and classifies, and then perhaps engages in some 'answering' expression. It is with how we express ourselves emotionally and with how accurately we identify such expressions in others that the social psychologist has been concerned. It is worth noting here that the identifying response is not made to the emotional expression itself, but to the *meaning* behind it. For example, a frown can be an expression of emotion. However, it is the state which is underlying the frown which we try to interpret. A thought about the complexities of this will show that in this chapter we are dealing with a particularly awkward and difficult area of research.

Frijda, who has produced excellent reviews and analyses of this field (for example 1960; 1970), suggests that the recognition of emotion may be broken down into three aspects. He means that when we express emotion we refer to three events, and when we recognize emotion we use three systems of identifying response (1) We recognize emotions by the *situations* in which they occur. If we are asked to describe fear, for example, we refer to some recent situation in which we 'felt' afraid. (2) Emotional expression *anticipates action*. We observe an emotional expression in another person and ask what behaviour is likely to follow it. (3) We *experience* emotion. The meaning of any expressive behaviour may be bound up in our subjective emotional experiences or attitudes. The observer may represent this experience to himself in some empathetic way, or even make fractional empathetic expressive movements himself.

The first part of this chapter will survey the major work in this area, drawing attention to some of the difficulties which have beset it and highlighting some of the better research and theory. Following this, some recent promising approaches will be mentioned. There are two points which should be borne in mind when appraising this field; in a sense they are both methodological. (1) Although we are directly within the sphere of the social psychologist, emotional expression and recognition is only one aspect of communication, and communication is also of concern to others, notably the clinician and the ethologist. Often, the research methods of such people differ from those of the social psychologist. This sometimes makes evaluation and comparison difficult. (2) The problem which any social psychologist has to face somewhat more squarely than does the 'individual' psychologist is that of artificiality. Do results gleaned from laboratory studies of social behaviour tell us very much about social behaviour in real-life settings? This problem is intensified for the investigator of emotional expression. How does he produce 'real' emotion in the laboratory? How does he measure the way in which it is judged? Is the identification process the same as that which we use from day to day? How does the investigator even decide what to study? And finally, how does he decide whether or not some observed facial behaviour is pertinent to emotion?

Finally, attention is drawn to several interesting reviews of emotional expression and recognition; each has its own emphasis. Davitz (1964)—social psychological; Ekman *et al.* (1972)—social psychological; Frijda (1969; 1970)—social psychological; Izard (1972)—social psychological; Knapp (1963)—clinical; parts of Vine (1970)—human ethological; also the thorough reader should begin with Darwin's (1872) *The Expression of Emotions in Man and Animals.*

FACIAL AND VOCAL EXPRESSION OF EMOTION

Basic research and problems

The facial expression of emotion has been studied in many ways, the main problem being the choice of stimulus material. The solution to this has varied from posed photographs (more typical of the early studies, for example Frois-Wittman 1930) or schematic drawings (for example Frijda 1956) through fully acted live expressions (for example Osgood 1966; Thompson and Meltzer 1964) to spontaneous expressions (for example Coleman 1949; Frijda 1953). Typically, during recognition, subjects have been asked to provide verbal labels for the emotions expressed, or they have been given rating scales to complete, or have had to match the photographs of emotional expressions to stories. Laboratory studies using animals report even more ingenious measures (for example Miller *et al.* 1959a; 1959b, see below). Another difficulty concerns the number of responses which have been required of a subject. In describing the emotion he has seen, he may have two adjectives to choose from, or a hundred. He may have a check list or be asked for a free description. He may be asked to respond strictly in terms of the emotional expression or be allowed to concentrate on the situation as well.

Similarly, various strategies have emerged for the study of the vocal expression of emotion. Here, the main problem has been to devise a method for cutting out the verbal content of speech while leaving nonverbal aspects. There are three solutions to this. (1) Subjects have been asked to express various emotions while reciting the alphabet (for example Davitz and Davitz 1959a), which on the face of it seems an awkward task. (2) Or they have been asked to express the same few neutral sentences in different ways (for example Polack *et al.* 1960). (3) Or, finally, electronic filtering techniques have been used on recorded speech (for example Soskin and Kaufman 1961). Again, as with studies of facially expressed emotion, the task set to the subject and the number or type of responses required of him have varied enormously.

Any evaluation of investigations into emotional expression and the degree to which its recognition is accurate is made difficult by this multiplicity of factors. Studies vary according to the task the subjects are given, the selection of response which they are allowed, and the type and number of stimuli with which they are presented. This means that no definitive statements can be made about the accuracy of emotional recognition. Also, it is instructive to consult Brown's (1965) discussion of accuracy in this context. He 'explains away' the concept by suggesting that it may simply be the result of fortuitously appropriate projection, knowledge of the group to which the other person belongs, and/or a fortunate response bias. However, some general statements can be made. For example, most studies based on spontaneous emotional expression in adult subjects lead to the conclusion that the performance of judges of the emotion is better than chance (for example Coleman 1949; Dittman 1962; Ekman 1965a; 1965b; Frijda 1953). Also, most studies of the vocal expression of emotion agree that emotional meanings can be communicated by vocal expression. For example, Davitz and Davitz (1959a) instructed eight speakers to express 10 different feelings by reciting parts of the alphabet. These were tape-recorded and played back to 30 subjects, who were each given a list of 10 feelings and asked to use them to identify what they heard. Results were significant but showed marked variation within listeners, speakers, and feelings—a lack of coherence which, incidentally, accords well with other work on vocally-expressed emotion (see Davitz 1964 for review).

On the general question of accuracy, Ekman *et al.* (1972) suggest that to make a good judgment of accuracy of expression it is necessary to develop criteria based on at least four related sources of information: (1) antecedent events; (2) concomitant responses (physiological and bodily); (3) consequent events (such as self-reports and the behaviour of other people); (4) consensus of opinion by trained judges. As might be expected, there are few studies which have taken into account all such measures.

Ekman *et al.* (1972) also suggest that four major questions should be asked concerning the generality of any results which come from studies of the facial expression of emotion, be these based on posed or spontaneous emotions expressed in artificial or natural conditions. (1) Is the finding germane to other settings? If so, which? (2) Is the finding relevant to the facial behaviour of people in general? If not, what are its limitations? (3) Is the finding general across time, or is it transient or occasional? (4) Is the finding specific to the judges used (particularly if they are trained observers), or would anyone make similar judgments? Clearly, these are excellent questions to ask, but very few investigators have asked them. To ask them on their behalf demonstrates the somewhat limited nature of much of the research in this area.

Examples of earlier research and interpretation

Coleman (1949) provides an exhaustive study of facially expressed emotion. His two basic procedures involved the elicitation and recording on film of facial expressions of emotion and the subsequent identification of these from the eye or mouth regions or from full face. He filmed 12 subjects while they were either responding 'naturally' or acting out the 'appropriate' response to squeezing a dynamometer, hearing a horn blast, receiving an electrical shock, being threatened with an electric shock, treading on a snail, being told a joke, and being 'natural'. From the overt responses and introspections of his 12 filmed subjects, Coleman concluded that emotional feelings had been elicited but with marked individual differences. Films of two subjects (one male, one female) were chosen and shown to 379 students, with either the mouth region, the eye region or the full face in evidence. These judges were provided with a list of the situations used and in each case were asked to identify the situation which led to the expression. Although identifications were no better from the mouth region or the eye region, some expressions were identified better from one than the other. Identifiability depended on the subject, the facial region viewed, and whether the expression was acted or natural. From subjective report, Coleman concluded that the method used for identification could best be described as empathy, a point which will be picked up later in a consideration of Sotland's (1969) work.

Frijda (1953) provides further examples of similar work. He took 68 short film sequences of two women, each sequence showing some emotional movement. He showed these sequences and photographs taken from them to 40 subjects and asked them for free descriptions. These descriptions were then scored or a five-point scale according to their judged correspondence to the 'true' emotion. This true emotion was based on Frijda's evaluation plus the introspections of the person filmed. This was a weakness in methodology, but no other method seems obviously better. Frijda's results showed that recognition of emotion had occurred, but not at a high level.

This would seem to be the right point to introduce the important work of Woodworth and its development by Schlosberg. Woodworth (1938) reanalysed data from earlier studies, and proposed a six-point scale of emotional recognition. (1) Love, mirth, happiness, (2) Surprise. (3) Fear, suffering.

(4) Anger, determination. (5) Disgust. (6) Contempt. Woodworth and Schlosberg (1955) turned this into a circular rather than linear scale, with contempt alongside love, mirth, and happiness. Finally, Schlosberg (1952; 1954) proposed a dimensional representation of emotional expression and recognition. This implied that all emotional expression could be represented according to the three dimensions of: (1) pleasantness/unpleasantness; (2) attention/rejection; (3) activation level (sleep/tension). These analyses all seem quite reliable and have led to considerable developments in the study of emotional recognition. They will be discussed in detail later.

By the 1960's the investigations described above, and many similar studies, although providing useful information, had raised more questions than they had answered. Then, with a series of basic studies, Davitz (1964) broke much new ground. Further, R. E. Miller and his coworkers produced a series of investigations which, with an interesting technology and animal subjects, lent support to the human studies.

Davitz—earlier work

Having reviewed previous work on facial and vocal expression of emotion, Davitz (1964) devotes the remainder of his book to a description of the research undertaken by his group. He suggests that the field of vocally expressed emotion is an open one, research having shown little more than its probable occurrence. He poses two basic questions concerning facially expressed emotion. (1) To what extent is it innate or to what extent acquired? (2) To what extent does it depend on individual differences? Two earlier research strategies had been directed at the nature/nurture question in emotional expression. There had been a few studies based on the proposition that if learning is important to expression, then cross-cultural recognition of emotion should be poor. May's (1938) study, although methodologically weak, did demonstrate some similarities between the recognition of emotion from photographs by Chinese and American subjects. Cross-cultural similarities were supported by Triandis and Lambert (1958) with Greek college students. The other type of study had concentrated on subjects blind from birth. Both Goodenough (1932) and Thompson (1941), for example, had found strong similarities between the emotional expressions of the blind and the sighted (innate influences), although the range and extent of the expressions of the blind were not as great (acquired influences). Also relevant were studies by Jeness (for example 1932b; 1932c) which showed that brief periods of training increased the accuracy of recognition of emotion.

Previous work on individual factors had been more or less restricted to sex differences (for example Coleman 1949; Jeness 1932a), with no general effects being found. Also, other than a few studies (for example Weisberger 1956) which had shown low positive correlations between intelligence and the ability to identify facial expression, there had been very little work on personality variables.

In describing the contribution of Davitz's group to this area, Beldoch's (1964) work will be mentioned in detail, as it provided the basis of many of the other studies. He constructed tapes of male and female speakers reciting an emotionally neutral passage in ways expressive of various emotional states. He presented these tapes twice to 58 subjects. From their responses he produced a final tape containing those items most often correctly identified and representative of 10 emotional meanings. He followed the same procedure with musical tapes created by musicians in the same way—i.e. aimed at the expression of 10 emotions—and also with abstract art created for this purpose. All this stimulus material was then presented to 89 subjects with an adjective check list (ACL), a questionnaire concerning their general background in these three media, a self-report scale of sensitivity to the emotional expressions of others, and a simple test of verbal intelligence.

Beldoch found significant correlations between the ability to make correct judgments in all three media, and also with vocabulary scores. Background training and interest contributed nothing and the ACL did not distinguish between high and low scorers. However, scores of sensitivity to emotional expression on the self-rating scale were positively related to those on the speech and graphic art material.

Levy (1964), using 'content-standard' material derived from Beldoch, studied the ability to express feelings vocally, the ability to identify such expressions, and also the ability to identify one's own vocal expressions of feeling. Subjects had to judge vocally expressed emotion, to record similar items which were then judged by others, and finally to try to recognize their own tapes (i.e. feelings) one–two weeks later. Levy found significant correlations between each of these measures, which still held when controlling for intelligence (although she only used graduates as subjects). There were no sex differences. Since self-perception, other-perception, and expression each contributed significantly to the variance on Levy's results, she considers them as implying a general 'communication factor' which underlies at least three specific abilities.

Davitz himself takes up this idea of a general communication factor. In his first study, again using Beldoch's tapes and 33 personality variables derived from a number of tests, he found no reliable correlations between personality and the ability to identify vocal expressions of emotion. But in a further study, he found that this ability did correlate with general auditory ability, abstract symbolic activity, verbal intelligence, and knowledge of the vocal characteristics of emotional expression. Putting these together, he found a multiple correlation of 0.60 with emotional sensitivity and tentatively suggested that general emotional communication is perhaps some sort of symbolic process. He is, however, well aware of the dangers of reading too much into purely correlational results.

The other studies reported in Davitz (1964) each make a cogent contribution, but there is little point in itemizing them in detail here, since the interested reader will find Davitz's book rewarding in its own right. However, two particularly relevant findings will be mentioned. Levitt (1964) studied the relationship between the ability to express emotional meanings vocally and facially. He made films of 50 subjects portraying six emotions through both voice and facial expression. The judges of these films were presented with sound alone, film alone, or both. Levitt found significant correlations between facial and vocal expressive abilities. However, full (vocal/facial) presentations were no better than facial communications alone. It may be that the vocal cues in the full presentations contributed little information. These results again provoke conjecture as to whether emotional communication is a matter of a general factor and/or a number of specific factors.

In what is probably the most interesting paper presented in the book, Blau (1964) devised a test of various commonly held hypotheses about the ability of the blind to communicate. For example, that the blind differ from the sighted in their ability to identify feelings from nonverbal cues, that blind females are better at this than blind males, that the blind pay more attention to 'affect' than the sighted, and that they can make much fuller descriptions of sounds and are more confident in their judgments of feelings and sounds. He studied 57 blind adolescents and 66 sighted adolescents, both groups being comparable in other ways. The blind were significantly better than the sighted at judging sounds, but controlling for this ability, the sighted groups were found to be better at judging fellings. In fact, where members of the blind group sometimes scored better than the sighted, this was later shown to be dependent on differences in mental age. There were no sex differences, but the blind paid significantly more attention to affect and were the more specific reporters of sounds. However, they were not more confident than the sighted in their judgments of sounds and feelings. Blau concludes that sensory compensation exists to an extent, but not sufficiently to make the blind any better at judging emotion.

Although the research techniques reported by Davitz have resulted in such interesting exploratory findings, he is aware that they are not above criticism. The main question is whether or not they lead to results which are at all representative of real life. Most of the studies he describes rely on experimental instructions rather than actual emotional states; nevertheless, the overall findings are reasonably consistent. Also, he sets a fairly stringent operational definition of what he means by communication, and sticks to it. It requires 'many' listeners to agree with the intent of the speakers and within this agreement the number of 'correct' responses being beyond the 0.01 level of significance. But Davitz does not make too strong a claim; he simply regards this work as a start and not necessarily representative of fine-grained, sensitive, everyday nuances of the communication of emotion.

Davitz is also aware of the need for theory. At the basis of his approach was an association between words like anger or joy and their expressive, behavioural referents. From the consensus of opinion obtained from judges, there is clear evidence of communication in Davitz's investigations, but words such as anger and joy also refer to 'felt' rather than expressed emotions. Some theory is needed to bring the two together. Although Davitz has recently proposed his own theory (see later), in 1964 he suggested that Schachter's physiological/cognitive ideas could best account for his results. He argued that the verbal aspects of speech might affect the cognitive determinants of emotion and that the vocal aspects might be a function of activation. This is a crude analysis, but it does lead to definite predictions for any work involving the use of the semantic differential, where one of the three main factors is activation.

Davitz (1964) also engaged in somewhat vague speculation as to the relationship between emotional sensitivity and intelligence. He suggested that emotional sensitivity involves both perceptual and cognitive variables. Also, that there may be some general factor which influences the many behaviours involved in nonverbal emotional communication, although overlaying this there may be special factors. Finally, he argued that emotional sensitivity may be a sort of intellectual ability which is made up of a type of 'g' factor (intellectual), plus various nonintellectual variables. However, other than saying that it is not necessarily related to intelligence, he did not specify the nature of this intellectual factor. Although Davitz's early research was stimulating, his theoretical speculations were confused and added little to our understanding of emotion.

R. E. Miller

Miller has produced a very different, but equally interesting, series of studies to those of Davitz. These began in 1955, when Murphy *et al.* conditioned rhesus monkeys to make instrumental shock-avoidance responses using other monkeys as conditioned stimuli. This was followed by Mirsky *et al.* (1958), who first conditioned and then extinguished an instrumental shock-avoidance response in monkeys. After extinction was complete, they exposed the experimental monkeys to a stimulus monkey who was behaving apprehensively. Even though they received no further shock, the monkeys immediately began to make the instrumental response. This was described as the perception of affect and empathy, and was confirmed by Miller *et al.* (1959a; 1959b) using coloured photographs of calm or apprehensive monkeys as their stimulus material.

As part of a more complex series of studies, Miller *et al.* (1962), for example, trained three rhesus monkeys to bar-press to avoid shock within 6 sec of the presentation of a light. After acquisition training, any two of the monkeys were placed opposite one another, one with a bar but no light, the other with a light but no bar. As each had incomplete information, Miller argued that the only way in which they could avoid shock was by the communication of affect. As a control condition the monkeys exchanged roles, and also, except for their faces, were often hidden from one another by a screen. Results showed significant evidence for cooperative avoidance; the monkeys must have been giving and receiving visual auditory emotional cues. In a further extension of this procedure, Miller *et al.* (1963) trained six monkeys in the usual instrumental avoidance response and tested them in pairs as in the previous study; the stimulus animal had only the conditioned stimulus, the response animal had only the bar. The responder could observe the face of the stimulus monkey via a television screen. Under these conditions, what Miller describes as the emotional expressions of the stimulus monkey elicited avoidance responses from the observer monkey. This suggests that different, specific expressions of affect may be learnt in this way. As a final example of this procedure, Miller *et al.* (1966) studied positive affect and took physiological measures. They trained monkeys to press a bar for food and then presented the conditioned stimulus to one of a pair. The other, with the bar, could see the face of the first on a television screen. In six of the 12 pairings responses showed the communication of what might be positive affect, accompanied by changes in heart rate. They suggested that their six failures were of recognition rather than expression.

Clearly, this is a most promising line of research, using highly controlled but to some extent 'natural' situations, and one which might provide useful suggestions about emotional expression. However, it should be borne in mind that at best these studies can only be said to deal with the first two of Frijda's (1969) aspects of emotional recognition—the situation and the anticipation of action. It would be going too far in the direction of anthropomorphism to speak of animals having emotional attitudes and inner empathetic representations.

CONCEPTUALIZATION OF EMOTIONAL EXPRESSION AND RECOGNITION

In this and the next few sections some of the more recent work and theoretical views of emotional expression will be discussed. This research has usually been based on one of two approaches. These can be called *component* studies, in which facial behaviour as a response is put in a context of its relationship to the measurement of emotion, and *judgment* studies, in which facial behaviour provides the stimuli to be judged.

Again it is Ekman *et al.* (1972) who have some very cogent points to make about these research strategies. They suggest that any failures in accuracy or agreement by judges of emotional expression do not necessarily mean that the components of facial behaviours are unrelated to the eliciting stimuli, although they could be meaningless. However, failures in judgment observed in such studies might be due to defects in the task, in the sampling of observers, in the sampling of facial expression, in the recording, or in the sampling of persons.

Ekman *et al.* argue that the best research strategy is to combine both component and judgment procedures and then to determine how much information an observer can interpret, what facial behaviours relate to his inferences, and what facial behaviours vary with emotion but are not recognized as such by observers. In essence, they are recommending consistency and purity at all stages of this difficult type of research. Such qualities have not been overly abundant; however, it is worth bearing them in mind in considering the work now to be described.

There are three main ways in which emotional expression and recognition have been conceptualized. (1) Categories: emotions as expressed could be classed into any number of distinct, unrelated events. Tomkins and McCarter (1964), for example, assume that there are eight primary 'affects': interest, enjoyment, surprise distress, fear, shame, contempt, anger. They also assume that each of these is primarily a facial response which is under the control of some innate subcortical programme. The main point about any categorization system is that the classes are unrelated and unordered. (2) Dimensions: from the dimensionality viewpoint, expressed emotions can be regarded as mixtures of pleasantness, activation, etc. (Statistical techniques based on factor analysis lead to the enumeration of distinct factors underlying behaviour. These may be conceived as occupying hypothetical n-dimensional space, each dimension being orthogonal to the remainder. Although this is easily understood with three dimensions, we need mathematical or philosophical analysis to conceive of more. Emotional expressions can be conceptualized in terms of such underlying dimensions.) This type of analysis can account for some of the more surprising similarities between emotional expressions (for example between contempt and mirth). Equally well, it can account for differences and the various nuances of emotional expression in general. However, it quickly becomes unwieldly if too many dimensions are proposed. (3) Hierarchy: this refers to a combination of categories and dimensions. In a particular region of n-dimensional emotional space there may be differentiation between emotion in terms of the dimensions especially pertinent to that region. Emotions may be comparable as regards dimensions both within and between categories, although each category may have its own distinguishable qualities.

Are these ideas sufficient to define emotional expression? The answer must be no. Ideas of categories, dimensions or a hierarchy are abstract. And emotions as they are distinguished in the language cannot be distinguished in the same way from their expression. They are confused by observers. Frijda's (1969) analyses show that subjects use many different labels for any one expression (this is also implicit in Davitz 1969), all of the labels frequently being quite wrong. Also, different emotions can produce the same expression. This strongly suggests that there is something more or perhaps finer than is given by possible dimensions of emotion. The necessary richness could come from cognitive factors, as is suggested by Schachter. However, if cognition is important, then emotion could not be fully recognizable from expressive behaviour.

Frijda (1969) explains the facial expression of emotion by the concept of 'positionality'. He defines this as: (1) tendencies to approach, withdraw, and attend; and (2) the degree of control of activity. He regards these as usually but not necessarily being combined with possible cognitive determinants of emotion and argues that the naming of emotion follows from the recognition of positionality. Finally, Frijda suggests that there may be a sort of balance between cognitive and behavioural factors in emotion; when one is high the other will be low, and *vice versa*. However, why the behavioural components are sometimes well differentiated and sometimes not is unclear. Also, for any one emotion, there are numerous behaviours and expressions which are considered to be appropriate. The problem really is that many different states may share one expressive pattern, and that many different expressions may characterize one emotion. Analysis and conceptualization become difficult.

DIMENSIONALITY

The idea of dimensionality in emotional communication, relatively quiescent since Schlosberg (1954), has recently begun to assume more importance. The basic hypothesis is that errors in the recognition of emotion run parallel to similarities between expressed emotions, and these similarities are in fact proximities in multidimensional space. Thus, emotional recognition becomes a matter of placing emotions in this multidimensional space. This is extended by the similar idea that *named* emotions are also reducible to combinations of fewer dimensions than are immediately apparent; a notion which is important to Davitz's (1969) more recent work (see below). The concept of dimensionality has led to a search for the number of dimensions which will describe hypothetical emotional space more simply. Although Schlosberg set the scene, the three dimensions he proposed appear arbitrary and unsatisfactory. Other studies have found evidence for the pleasantness/unpleasantness (P/U) dimension and the sleep/tension (S/T) dimension, but often the attention/rejection (A/R) dimension has been missing (for example Abelson and Sermat 1962; Shepard 1963).

There have been two approaches to the study of dimensionality. (1) Judgment of the meaning of emotional expression through the use of ACLs or rating scales. (2) Judgment of similarity using paired comparison techniques or their extensions into triads or groupings.

Osgood (1955) provides a good example of the former. Subjects had to select one from 40 emotional-state labels which, in their estimation, best characterized a live, motionless expression portrayed by an actor. From an analysis of the frequency of usage of each label for each expression, Osgood plotted his results on three dimensions. There was a P/U dimension, an 'intensity' dimension (corresponding to S/T), and a 'control' dimension. Control can be regarded as a dimension peculiar to Osgood's experimental technique, since it distinguished expressions started by the 'actor' from those simply coming from the environment.

Frijda's (1969) methodology was a little different. He reanalysed his own earlier work (Frijda and Philipszoon 1963) using factor analytic techniques. Originally, he had gathered 27 sevenpoint scales which were representative of 400 terms used by 30 subjects in a free-labelling of expression study. The scales were then used by 12 judges for rating photographs of an actress portraying various emotional expressions. Frijda found six main factors which were accounting for 92 per cent of the variance: (1) P/U; (2) activation—but Frijda described this as corresponding to intensity rather than S/T, since the low end was a lack of expression rather than sleep; (3) similar to Schlosberg's A/R, but more like what might be called interest, since the low end was disinterest rather than rejection; (4) Frijda found this dimension difficult to label, but suggested social evaluation or something akin to Osgood's control; (5) and (6) smaller factors, the first being described as surprise, the second as simple/complicated. Frijda draws particular attention to factors (2) and (3), since they are both to do with activity. He regards (2) as emotional intensity or activation as Duffy (1962) might use the term; it refers to the mobilization of energy. (4) concerns the arousal of attention; it is akin to the orienting reflex. It is worth noting that these results are supported by a similar study which used Schlosberg's original photographs as stimulus material (Karsten 1965, quoted in Frijda 1969).

If emotional expressions can be reduced to dimensions, two questions require answering. (1) Do the dimensions delineate the 'meaning' or 'real' emotion which underlies expression, or, more mundanely, do they simply reflect the words used to describe emotional expressions? Frijda maintains that at least his first four dimensions correspond to expressive meaning; to support this he quotes a study by Elshout (1967) correlating expressive meaning and facial features. (2) How many dimensions are there? The only study to point to as large a number as Frijda's six factors is Osgood's (1966), which involved semantic differential-scale responses of judges. He found that his usual three dimensions could be divided further into nine interpretable clusters or factors, a number almost large enough to bring us back to a list of primary emotions: anger, amazement, boredom, quiet pleasure, disgust, sorrow, interest (expectancy), joy, and fear.

Typically, studies using matching techniques for the judgment of similarities between photographs of emotional expression have found far fewer factors (for example Abelson and Sermat 1962 who found two, or Gladstones 1962 who found three). However, such studies have normally used only a few posed expressions. An exception to this is Stringer (1967), who used the same 30 photographs as in Frijda's original study. His subjects were allowed to group them freely and then label each one. A great deal of data manipulation only yielded three factors.

From the standpoints of their experimental requirements, the major difference between these two sorts of study is that when endeavouring to label an emotional meaning a subject has to make a discrimination, whereas when he is estimating similarities between emotions he must overlook any differences. From this point of view, Frijda (1969) maintains that pleasantness and interest are more important to the estimation of similarity than are intensity or artificiality.

It can be concluded that the search for dimensions of emotion has proved to be an important influence in the study of emotional expression. However, this is due more to the research which it has generated than to any fundamental theoretical contributions. Clearly, the parsimony implicit in the idea of dimensions could be significant in any analysis of emotion, but any economy is lost when, as has often been the case, too many dimensions are proposed. Also, it is sometimes difficult to compare dimensions between studies. Various research strategies and techniques of data analysis have been used, and difficulty is often met with in describing and naming the dimensions when they have been found. Of course, naming is perhaps not important, since dimensions are anyway mathematical/philosophical abstractions.

Finally, it should be remembered that, given the research techniques most often used in this area of study, any dimensions of 'emotion' may simply be reflecing verbal behaviour. Also, none of the studies carried out to date make it clear exactly what subjects are responding to; they may well be responding to dimensions, or conversely to the actual categories of emotion. At present it is impossible to say whether the category, dimension, or category and dimension approach will be the most fruitful.

OTHER ASPECTS OF EXPRESSION

So far, only studies involving the facial expression of emotion have been discussed. However, behaviour may reflect emotion in many ways; before considering other factors which might influence emotional expression in general, some of these will be mentioned.

When reviewing studies each of which has used still photographs, it is easy to forget that in real life emotional expression extends in time. Again, it is Frijda (1953) who has shown the importance of the temporal extension of expressive behaviour. He found an increase in accuracy of almost 50 per cent when comparing judgments of emotion from 10-sec films with judgments made from stills of the culminating points of the same films. He also showed that the effects of single expressive movements are mainly due to their onset and offset. He found that: (1) a rapid onset of an expressive movement was usually interpreted as being caused by a sudden change in stimulus leading to a voluntary change in the direction of behaviour, or simply as a spontaneous impulse which disrupts control; (2) a gradual onset of response suggested a spontaneous, integrated emotional response; (3) a very slow onset indicated a lack of energy or inhibition; (4) a rapid offset of the response implied a disruption of continuity; (5) a gradual offset indicated that the emotion had followed its natural course. Frijda regarded this as a dimension of voluntariness versus spontaneity. This is perhaps going too far from data that are anyway oversubjective. Clearly, more research is necessary in this field.

Recently, some interesting investigations have been made of body movements in emotional communication. Ekman (1965a; 1965b), Ekman and Friesen (1967a) and Dittman et al. (1965) have all shown that bodily posture and movement contribute to the recognition of emotion, particularly its intensity. Body cues do not seem to be especially important for the P/U dimension. In extending this idea, Ekman and Friesen (1969) provide a novel slant on emotional communication. They suggest that nonverbal behaviour escapes the efforts that we make at deception and in fact allows our 'real' feelings to leak out. They propose that there are two types of deception, each of which contains much simulation. (1) We attempt to deceive others about our feelings. Even if we are discovered in our deception we may carry it through, with subtle changes, since open verbalization might prove embarrassing. (2) We may deceive ourselves. This is a somewhat 'clinically' viewed blocking from self-awareness of feelings that might arouse anxiety if they were given free expression.

Ekman and Friesen regard these deceptions (which we all make) as having three dimensions. (1) Saliency—the degree to which the deception is of obvious importance to the interactants; clearly a function both of the situation and the personality of those involved. (2) The roles adopted by the interactants—i.e. whether they are both deceiving and/or detecting, or one adopting each role, etc. (3) Collaboration or antagonism—an implicit or explicit pact (or lack of it) about the discovery and/or the continuation of the deception (psychotherapy is a collaboration to discover deception). They also suggest that each of us has a certain sending capacity for nonverbal signals; we can send them quickly or slowly, we can send many or few, and we can make them easily visible or not. Ekman and Friesen maintain that according to each of these measures, the face is the best sender of nonverbal information, the feet and the legs are the worst, and the hands and arms fall somewhere in between. Further, they stress the importance of external feedback. Nonverbal behaviour from B is perceived by A as in response to his own nonverbal behaviour. Even so, it may be inappropriate to openly comment on this. For example, although we may comment if someone frowns in our presence, we shall probably not mention his squeezing his legs together. Finally, there is internal feedback—conscious awareness of what we are doing. Again, there is the progression face, hands, feet, this time in terms of the amount of nervous system feedback we obtain from these areas.

Ekman and Friesen's concluding suggestion is that the legs and feet are the worst senders of messages, they are the least responded to, they are the least in self-awareness, and *therefore* they provide the best source of information about leakage or clues to the deception that it is being practised on us. From this point of view, the face is the worst source of information and the hands and arms are again in between. Ekman and Friesen provide some support for these ideas with studies involving ratings of filmed interactions; the raters see only the head or the hands and arms or the feet and legs.

There is self-evidently an unfavourable ratio between speculation and hard data in Ekman and Friesen's work. Their ideas, however, certainly appear to have face validity and point to the possibility of an interesting field of research.

The final more 'living' aspect of emotional expression to be briefly described is eye-gaze, a topic which has engendered a great deal of research recently (for example Argyle 1967; Argyle 1969; Argyle and Kendon 1967; Strongman 1970; Strongman and Champness 1968). With eye-gaze we are back to facial expression, but often with procedures based on the systematic observation of ongoing social situations by trained observers or on the study of filmed interactions. The fundamental concern has been with the patterns of looking towards and away from another's eyes during a conversation. For obvious reasons, emphasis has fallen on mutual gaze. Typically, this is expressing social sentiments and social attitudes. Clearly, the length of time we spend looking into another's eyes, how often we do so and who breaks eye contact first have importance for the communication of emotion, although as yet few definitive statements can be made. (For reviews of such work see particularly Argyle 1969 and Vine 1970.)

Related to the last two areas of research discussed is the question of the relationship between facial expression and psychotherapy. Apart from Ekman and Friesen's work, which shows that useful inferences about adjustment can be made from nonverbal expressive behaviour, there has been some interesting work by Haggard and Isaacs (1966) on micromomentary facial expressions. From an analysis of filmed psychotherapeutic interviews they observed a number of fleeting ($\frac{1}{8}$th–$\frac{1}{5}$th sec) facial expressions, which cannot be observed under ordinary conditions, i.e. when the film is played at normal speed. They speculate with some force that such movements may well relate to the psychodynamics of the relationship between the patient and the person he was discussing at the time.

In recent years there has been increasing discussion in the clinical literature of the importance of nonverbal behaviour in emotional communication. Although such discussions are speculative and concern data which come from rather dubious research techniques, they are nevertheless suggestive. They are well exemplified by Jorgensen and Howell (1969), who analysed head and shoulders audio-visual tapes of four experimentally naive females during the stress and relief phases of structured interviews. Two of the four described themselves as outgoing (expressive) and two as unemotional (suppressive). 162 judges and the subjects themselves were shown the films and had to rate the emotions they saw expressed as 20 semantic differentials.

Jorgensen and Howell draw four main conclusions from their results. (1) Males and females made equally good judgments. (2) Suppressive individuals were judged more accurately than were expressive, although this result may have been due to the narrower range of emotions they expressed being in accord with generally conservative judgments. (3) Pleasant emotions were better judged than unpleasant. (4) The best judgments of the pleasant emotions were made with the face and no soundtrack, and the best of the unpleasant emotions came from the written transcripts alone (no face and no sound). Finally, it should be stressed that although results such as these are interesting and suggestive, they are based on relatively crude research techniques.

CONTEXT AND CULTURE

During normal, everyday life expressive behaviour is perceived in context; this would seem to be an important aid to judgments of emotion. Evaluations are made on the basis of information about body type, facial characteristics, purposive actions, the situation, behavioural constants, personality, age, sex, cultural group, and so on. Much of the standard research involving such variables is to be found in social psychology texts and is not pertinent here. However, before going on to a discussion of the *general* role of context in the judgment of emotional expression, brief mention should be made of some of the recent and thorough research involving cross-cultural comparisons in such judgments.

Izard (1972) reports a number of fine studies which demonstrate agreement in the recognition of emotion across a series of American, European, Oriental, and

African cultures. However, he also reports that the members of these various cultures respond differentially to fundamental emotions in the free-response labelling of expressions. There were even greater cross-cultural differences in attitudes towards the various emotions. In reviewing and evaluating such research, Ekman *et al.* (1972) conclude that there is definite evidence for a cross-cultural element in facial behaviour and emotion. From this they argue that there must be an association between the movements of particular facial muscles and emotional concepts. At present, it is impossible to say whether this is dependent on innate neural programmes or common developmental learning experiences.

To return to the general matter of context, there would seem to be a two-stage process at work: (1) an evaluation of (Frijda's) general positional activity pattern; this is made from the actual emotional expression; (2) the more precise specification of this pattern from contextual cues. Cline (1956), for example, demonstrated the possible importance of context in judging emotional expression. He manipulated the context by making schematic drawings, unarguably a very artificial technique but nevertheless one from which putative conclusions can be drawn. He found, for instance, that the drawing of a face was perceived as angry, jealous, and unhappy when paired with a smiling face, but aloof, independent, domineering, and unafraid when paired with a frowning face. Out of context it was judged to be glum.

It was once thought that the context was the only way in which we can recognize emotion and at best the expression itself was secondary (for example Landis 1929). However, it is now clear that expression does give important cues, although perhaps when there is an obvious context available such expressive cues may become less important. This point implies that contextual cues may possibly conflict with expressive cues.

If contextual and expressive cues are dissonant, which is dominant? Flores d'Arcais (1961) gave the first answer to this by using films with either correct or incorrect soundtracks. Expressive cues were dominant. This finding has been confirmed in a series of studies by Frijda. His basic experiment involved the use of photographs with either concordant or discordant descriptions. The design called for free ratings of the photographs and also ratings including the information given by one or other of the descriptions. Ratings shifted in the direction of the expression rather than the situation. Interestingly, the discordant description seemed quite acceptable to the subjects, a point made by Luchins (1958) in a different context. It may be that in real life such apparent paradoxes are not uncommon. Frijda (1969) quotes two further studies (Jaanus 1966; Warries 1963) which support the dominance of expression over context. They showed, for example, that if a person behaves happily or sadly when from the context we expect something different, then we believe his behaviour. However, both studies also showed the situation to be important to the recognition of emotion.

It is simple to suggest factors that might influence the dominance of expressive over contextual cues when the two conflict, for example, ambiguity in the cues, the nature of the expressive cues, the nature of the contextual cues, and so on. It is more difficult to specify the process of judgment when there is such conflict. The obvious answer is a sort of compromise. But, as usual, it is Frijda (1969) who provides the more subtle and more interesting explanation. He suggests that the person making the judgment forms various hypotheses until he has an aggregate of them. He believes that 'gap-filling' hypotheses are often produced, i.e. possible additional factors are hypothesized to have their effects between a particular situation and a facial expression which may be gibing with it. If the discordance persists, then Frijda posits four possible ways of reducing it. (1) Divorce the emotion from the situation. (2) Divorce the emotion from the situation and accept the situation. (3) Divorce the expression from the emotion. (4) Deny the situation. There are obvious resemblances between these ideas and those proposed by Festinger (for example 1957) for the reduction of cognitive dissonance.

Ekman *et al.* (1972) reach a conclusion rather different from Frijda's, namely, that no definite statement can be made about the relative influence of facial expression and context on the judgment of emotion. They feel that on different occasions either can be dominant. They suggest that investigators in this area need to address themselves to three research questions. What are the parameters of facial expression and context that determine their relative influence? What cognitive mechanisms resolve any discrepancies between face and context? What is the nature of the occasions when either the face or the context gives more information than the other?

OTHER LINES OF RESEARCH

Movement

There has been little follow-up of Michotte's (1950) work on the emotional significance of movement. This is surprising, since the research technique looks as though it has reduced the communication of emotion to an elemental level. Michotte's experiments are based on one simple paradigm. There are two small coloured rectangles which can be moved along a horizontal slot. They can be stopped or started at any moment; they can have their direction, extent, and speed of movement altered. The observer of these moving rectangles tends to invest them with emotional significance; certain conditions produce compelling impressions. For example, A 'runs away from' B, A 'goes to find' B 'and take it away', A 'pushes' B, and so on.

Michotte argued that these impressions are very primitive phenomena rather than emotional 'meanings'. The observers often drew analogies with human action when they were describing the 'behaviour' of the rectangles, the descriptions often implying emotional states, attitudes, and tendencies. Michotte accounted for this by suggesting that fundamentally any human inter-action involves these same elements: two people move in relation to one another.

More theoretically, Mishotte divides emotions into two groups, according to whether the 'interactants' imply an integrative or segregative relationship to one another. In more usual terms, this is simply 'positive' or 'negative'. Motor reactions include either approach and contact or escape, withdrawal, and avoidance. Michotte extends this idea to suggest that the physical expressions of emotions produce similar impressions of movement to those of the rectangles. He also believes that, in different situations, integration and segregation take on different characteristics. Speed seems to be particularly important. For example, rapid movement often implies violence, whereas slow movement implies gentleness. On this basis, Michotte lists a whole range of impressions.

Via similar speculations to these, Michotte eventually comes to the view that motor reactions *per se* are fundamental to expressive behaviour. However, it is difficult to pin down the emotion in Michotte's arguments. His studies, although related to emotional expression, are vague and subjective. And his theoretical analysis goes far beyond his data.

Empathy

Stotland (1969) puts together social and physiological aspects of emotion in a similar way to that in R. E. Miller *et al.*'s recent (for example 1966) studies. Stotland's work rests on the intuitively reasonable assumption that we share other people's feelings. This sharing of feeling does not necessarily imply any sympathetic *behaviour* on the part of the observer. Stotland defines empathy as '. . . an observer's reacting emotionally because he perceives that another is experiencing or is about to experience an emotion'. He regards emotion as a state of physiological arousal, with strong subjective concomitants. He is not unaware of the problems which such a notion carries with it, but relies on Lacey (1950) to support the idea that psychophysiologically people show arousal in different ways. However, the subjective aspects of emotion as Stotland sees them are unreliable for the usual reasons; physiological arousal is broader than emotional arousal—the latter only exists when there is also some affective component. Stotland realizes that the foregoing might imply that the observer and the observed are experiencing different emotions. But he suggests that even if emotional response patterning has not been convincingly demonstrated physiologically, it exists subjectively. Thus, he goes no further than to dichotomize emotions into positive and negative and then make any further differentiations via subjective report. It is then a little difficult to see why he brought physiology into the picture at all.

Stotland distinguishes empathy from those situations in which a person's experiences may carry implications for the welfare of one who might observe them. For example, when his father frowns a child might expect unpleasantness to follow. This is not empathy; the other's perceived emotions are acting as discriminative stimuli (sources of information) about the observer's possible or probable fate. Stotland also distinguishes empathy from predictive empathy. In the latter he suggests that the observer does not have to *experience* the emotion he is perceiving to predict what it may be. However, he also argues that predictive empathy and nonpredictive empathy must share any factors which influence the perception of another's emotional state. Also, they may interact.

Stotland distinguishes between his own work and that of Schachter (for example 1964); his distinction relies on the hypothesized direction of influence. Schachter proposes that we use the behaviour of others to interpret our own, perhaps amorphous, feelings. Empathy is the reverse of this; we perceive another's emotion and then change our own emotional state—both physiologically and subjectively. Rather than contradicting each other, these directions of influence may happen in sequences or in different conditions.

Stotland's (1969) experimental procedure typically involves five or six subjects observing another, pseudo-subject, undergoing some positive or negative experience. The observers' reactions are measured by palm sweating and vasoconstriction; and also by self-ratings of their feelings immediately after the emotion-producing stimulus has ceased (a limited but inevitable measure in such studies).

In the first study, subjects observed another, with instructions to either (1) imagine how they would feel in his position, or (2) imagine how he felt, or (3) watch his physical reactions closely. The pseudo-subject was treated to one of three possible experiences in a 'diathermy' machine—pain or neutral or pleasant heat to the arm. There were various baseline controls taken of the physiological measures. The confederate subject acted his part. Stotland's general findings were of differences in physiological measures between pain, neutral, and pleasure conditions for the two 'imagining' sets of instructions, but not for the 'watch him' one. He concludes from this that 'set' is important to empathy and that an interpersonal process which leads us to *imagine* ourselves in the position of another leads us to empathize.

Finally, Stotland describes a series of experiments in which the main independent variable was the relationship between the observer and the observed. Such relationships presumably alter empathetic responses by altering perception. The most important variable Stotland mentions seems to be birth order. For example, later-born people empathize more with someone similar to themselves than with someone different; the empathy of first-borns remains unaffected by similarity. This is extended to later-borns empathizing more with those with whom they have interacted, although first-borns do not.

Such results are interesting and the general research strategy is promising. However, the findings often show a lack of consistency between the physiological measures and the self-ratings. And, as often seems to be the case with investigators of emotional expression and recognition, Stotland goes further than is justified by his data.

The language of emotion

Davitz (1969; 1970) makes one of the more fruitful recent approaches to the social psychology of emotion. He deals with a problem which sprang from the final stages of Davitz (1964)—'What does a person mean when he says someone is happy or angry or sad?'. Davitz believes that this should be answered descriptively—a belief which characterizes the social psychology of emotion in general. His answer leads him, by a completely different route, to a concept of dimensionality reminiscent of Frijda's.

Davitz (1969) suggests that the meaning of the various emotions depends on our experience. He argues for a study based on language. A problem which all psychologists must face is having to use everyday terms in a more rigorous, restricted context; the everyday connotations of words simply cause confusion, 'anxiety' perhaps being the best example. Davitz therefore aimed to produce a dictionary of emotional terms, drawn from what he calls 'commonalities of meaning'—verbal descriptions of emotional states. Clearly, such an aim is likely to result in enormous subjective confusions. Davitz is aware of this but hypothesizes that any common ground may appear in mathematical abstractions from the basic data.

Davitz asked 30 people to imagine a time when they experienced a given emotion and then to describe it. From this and from judgments about information relevant to the emotional experiences, he ended with 556 statements which referred to (in decreasing order of frequency) physical sensations (for example 'I feel soft and firm'), relations to the external world (for example 'Everything seems unimportant and trivial'), cognitive events (for example 'My thinking is rapid'), relations to others (for example 'I feel outgoing'), self-reference (for example 'I feel aimless'), impulses to behave or to control behaviour (for example 'I want to be tender and gentle with another person'), and formal aspects of the experience (for example 'It's a steady, ongoing feeling').

Terms for labelling the emotions were taken from *Roget's Thesaurus*. The 400 words obtained in this way were read to 40 subjects who were asked to say which of them they would use to label an emotion; 137 of these were well agreed on, of which 50 were chosen on the basis of their coverage of the vocabulary of emotion. Each subject was asked to think of a critical experience for each of these emotions, describe it, and then use the check list to find each statement which agreed with the experience. Next, 50 subjects used this large check list, each describing a range of emotional situations. Although these subjects were taken from both sexes and from negroes and whites, they were all highly verbal graduates; this is a clear limitation to the generality of Davitz's findings. Arbitrarily, Davitz included in his final definition of a term any statement which had been checked by at least one-third of the subjects in their descriptions. Finally, each of these definitions was given to 20 judges with instructions to rate (on a four-point scale) their adequacy in describing both the emotion and their own experience of it. Davitz then presents his reader with the actual list of phrases and his resultant dictionary of emotional meaning.

One obvious advantage of Davitz's dictionary is that it gives a vocabulary which can be simply used for phenomena which are normally very difficult to describe. On the other hand, as Davitz shows himself to be well aware, it must represent an oversimplification. He oversimplified further by carrying out an analysis of 215 items that each appeared in the definitions of at least three emotions. He found 12 clusters to which, with caution, he assigned labels: (1) activation, (2) hypoactivation, (3) hyperactivation, (4) moving toward, (5) moving away, (6) moving against, (7) comfort, (8) discomfort, (9) tension, (10) enhancement, (11) incompetence/dissatisfaction, and (12) inadequacy. These clusters were then factor analysed, and the results led Davitz to suggest four dimensions of emotional meaning. Working from the clusters, (1), (2), and (3) concern levels of *activation*, (4), (5), and (6) concern *relatedness* to the environment, (7), (8), and (9) concern the *hedonic tone* of an emotional state, and (10), (11), and (12) refer to a sense of *competence* in relating to the environment.

Davitz gathers some background support for his four dimensions of emotional meaning. Activation and hedonic tone have often appeared in the literature on emotion. Many writers have discussed both (activation: for example Block 1957; Duffy 1962; Schlosberg 1954; hedonic tone: for example Block 1957; Harlow and Stagner 1933; Schlosberg 1954). However, support for the other two factors comes more from Davitz's interpretation of what others have said than from their actual words. For example, he changes Duffy's (1941) 'direction' to his own 'relatedness'. And stretches Sartre's (1948) existential theory and Plutchik's (1962; 1970) notions of adaptive emotional behaviour to fit his concept of competence. Although similar terminology provides broad support for Davitz, it can in no sense be considered validation.

Davitz's (1969) tentative theory of emotion can be reduced to six main propositions. (1) Emotion is partly concerned with private (experienced) events—a clear, phenomenological, subjective viewpoint. (2) Emotion embraces specific states which are labelled, and each label refers to experiences about which there is reasonable common ground within a culture. This proposition comes more directly from Davitz's dictionary. (3) The language of emotion reflects experiences but is also directly influenced by linguistic considerations; people make mistakes in their descriptions of emotion, and, in fact, learn to label the emotion from the situation (see 5 below). (4) Definitions of emotional states fall into 12 clusters, which can fit into four dimensions of emotional experience: activation, relatedness, hedonic tone, and competence. (5) Labelling emotion depends on experience. Any change in experience will change the label and the state. (6) Emotional states come about from stimuli which are psychologically relevant to the four dimensions of emotional meaning.

Davitz is aware that these propositions fit neither phenomenology, a psychoanalytic approach, nor behaviourally oriented ideas. In fact, as a theory, it leaves much to be desired, since it is both lacking in formal properties and is not well anchored to empirical fact. However, he believes that his proposals do lead to productive research. For example, he quotes Farmer (1967), who with interview techniques studied the development of the language of emotion in 64 children from the ages of seven to 14. He found that as children grow older their reports of emotional experiences become more like those of adults. Also, that those clusters of emotion most emphasized by adults appear earlier in the children's reports. These results are hardly surprising. Also, Allerand (1967), for example, argued that as there is a physiological basis to emotion, those who are genetically similar should also be more similar in their verbal reports of emotion than those who are genetically dissimilar. He carried out a study involving 24 pairs each of monozygotic twins, dizygotic twins, and siblings aged 13 to 18. He recorded their descriptions of some emotions and found a significant difference between the monozygotes and others in the similarity of their emotional reports. These are just two examples from a number which Davitz quotes in support of his approach to emotional language.

In making an evaluation of this work, one must conclude that the experiments are weak and the implications of the theory on which they are based are not expanded sufficiently to be useful. Davitz's (1969) main contribution is clearly the dictionary of emotional meanings. It is a fresh approach to the social psychology of emotion and may provide the impetus for some fundamental descriptive research.

Ethology

Recent advances in the ethological approach to emotional expression bring us back full circle to the Darwinian starting point. Interestingly, modern ethology has been extended to man as well as animals. However, the study of animals is instructive since it perhaps points to the origin of emotional expression. Tail-wagging in dogs and purring in cats are obvious examples of this. Ethologists believe such responses to have a communicative function; to act as releasers for the coordination of social behaviour.

Eibl-Eibesfeldt (1970) argues that, evolutionarily, expressive behaviour is often derived from other behaviour that had been accompanied by frequent arousal or activity. For example, in many species social grooming always indicates that social contact may proceed. Sometimes it has become ritualized into expressive movements. The lemur, for instance, greets other lemurs with the movements it uses to comb its fur. Similarly, Eibl-Eibesfeldt maintains that behaviour which once led to attack has evolved into gestures of threat. It may, for example, be reduced to preparing to jump, or to jumping and falling short. One unfortunate aspect of such evolutionary arguments is that they tend to lead to useless speculations about similar mechanisms in man. To take the last example, a man stamping his feet in anger can be said to be showing incipient, but ritualized, attack movements; a point which can be neither proven nor disproven and which is of limited although sensationalistic value.

The ethological suggestion is that ritualization—the modification of behaviour to make it communicative—is the main process underlying the evolution of expressive movements. The changes that it produces in behaviour are regarded as all-important to signalling. Eibl-Eibesfeldt (1970) describes eight changes in behaviour which accompany ritualization. (1) Behaviour changes in its function. (2) Ritualized movements change their *apparent* motivation. (3) Movements become simpler but exaggerated both in frequency and amplitude. (4) Movements 'freeze' into postures. (5) The actual behaviour occurs to a greater range of stimuli. (6) Orientation changes. (7) The behaviour becomes stereotyped and occurs with a constant intensity. (8) The variability of behaviour is suppressed. He also suggests that these changes are often accompanied by the development of conspicuous bodily structures. Although these ideas may appear good sense from the viewpoint of biological adaptivity, it is difficult to see how they may be substantiated. They are speculative in the extreme. However, at the descriptive level, there are many possible examples of the process (see Eibl-Eibesfeldt 1970 for review). For instance, many carnivores feed their young by pushing food into their mouths, and also often greet one another by pushing together their muzzles and rubbing them. (In this case, the ethologist would maintain that the latter has evolved from the former by a ritualization process). Also, both apes and man sometimes feed their young with a mouth-to-mouth method and greet one another by kissing. More interestingly, Eibl-Eibesfeldt suggests that ritualization may begin to occur within ontogenesis as well as phylogenesis. He supports this by the exaggerated, rhythmic, and stereotyped behaviours seen in zoo animals; these often seem to be directed towards 'begging' food for example. The alternative explanation for this is that it is just superstitiously maintained operant behaviour usually seen when animals are interacting with man; dogs 'shaking hands'.

Modern ethologists also provide classifications of expressive behaviour. Again, to take Eibl-Eibesfeldt's (1970) work as an example, he classifies expressive movements according to their function. His major division is between intraspecific and interspecific releasers. The intraspecific group are: (1) signals that promote group cohesion; these are precise signals which regulate interaction and attraction, for example courtship behaviour, submissive gestures, and behaviour which establishes and maintains contact; (2) communication about the external environment; for example, warning and distress is signalled in squirrels and birds, and chemically in some fish; also there is the famous bee language (for example von Frisch 1950; 1968; Johnson 1967; Wenner 1967), in which the direction and distance of a food source from the hive is communicated; (3) intraspecific threat signals; for example certain bird songs, a gorilla's chest-beating, various ritualized attack behaviour. Eibl-Eibesfeldt subdivides intraspecific expressive releasers into two: (1) contact readiness, in which many members of different species live near to one another to mutual advantage; (2) threat postures, for example back-arching in cats.

An important (although implicit) thesis in recent ethology is that an obvious way to overcome the difficulty of laboratory studies of emotional expression in man is to study them using more 'naturalistic' techniques. Brannigan and Humphries (1971) exemplify this approach. They criticize the more traditional photograph-based studies of emotional expression by pointing out that their validity depends on the correctness of the basic definitions of the emotion on which they are based. Also, of course, the expressions are not occurring within their usual dynamic context. They suggest further that the actual expressions which have been studied have not received enough ethological analysis. Such analysis is complex, but they argue that a sound ethological description of an emotion should be the starting point.

Brannigan and Humphries discuss the descriptive breakdown of behaviour into units and describe in detail changes in facial expression. For example, 'Smiles are characterized by an upward and outward movement of the mouth corners, and may be clarified into various categories according to the degree and form of mouth opening and tooth exposure'. Each smile occurs in a characteristic situation.

A further problem that Brannigan and Humphries consider is that of 'what do the signals signal?'. Subjective projection makes it easy for man to judge man, but by the same token it is difficult to be objective. Of course, the broad answer to the question is that the signals are expressions of emotion. But Brannigan and Humphries feel that this is too vague and too difficult to separate from the 'behaviour patters themselves'. Instead, they argue that as well as expressing emotions, communicative signals give information about likely behaviour and also give feedback on the receipt of one's own behaviour. They consider that it may be wrong to try to give each signal some specific emotional context; a frown may occur in several different situations although it looks the same in each. In general, they are saying that the traditional approach to the study of emotional expression is oversimplified.

CONCLUSIONS

There is only one conclusion which can be drawn from the many different approaches to the social psychology of emotion: there exists some immediate and, to use an everyday term, intuitive perception of expressive meaning. But this by no means accounts for all the findings in this field. Although the recognition process occurs very quickly, much knowledge and experience must intervene. Clearly, the recognition of emotion is determined by a very complex process. This process depends on the integration of many cues, from facial expression through body movement to the situation and the more static features of the interactants; whilst at another level, the process depends on any hypotheses which we may hold about life. Frijda (1969) offers the most complete formulation. (1) The understanding of a situation and its implications. (2) A store containing factual and emotional implications; many possible emotions connected with varying probabilities assigned to each situation. (3) We are 'set' for a person in a situation to experience a particular emotion. (4) A store of emotional knowledge; emotions and their scale values—from which we also get our own emotional expression. (5) The system must be able to register expressive behaviour and code it. (6) A working out of expressive meaning. (7) A comparison of expressive meaning and situational suggestions. (8) A combination of (4) and (6). (9) An emotion is selected from the store in (4). (10) An adjustment is made if the selected emotion does not conform to expectations. (11) A mechanism to resolve any continuing discordance. (12) The selected mechanism then defines a new emotion. (13) Finally, there is the construction of situational components to fit with the selected emotion.

Frijda (1970) simplifies this formulation to three main points. (1) Categorizing an observed behaviour pattern in terms of a set of general dimensions of emotion. (2) Further differentiation. (3) The specification of probable emotion from situational cues or suppositions. Theoretically, Frijda (1970) suggests that his view of emotional expression is also applicable to emotion in general. But the relationship between expressive behaviour and emotion is too complicated for this sort of direct inference to be made. It is clear that every emotion can occur in many different expressions, sometimes with very little in common, and often with little hope of its recognition out of context. On the other hand, all the complex combinations of expression make sense in their situational context.

It should be said that in spite of the various attempts to define dimensions of emotional meaning, the process is much more complicated than simply inferring the dimensions of emotion directly from the dimensions of the recognition of emotional expression. And in real-life situations with all their other cues, our recognitions and even the recognition process itself *may* be quite different from those suggested by laboratory studies.

In spite of the above conclusions, recent research (Izard 1972; Ekman *et al.* 1972) has demonstrated the importance of the facial expression of emotion. Its most significant aspects concern the relationship between facial behaviour which is associated with emotion and that which is not, the social interactional consequences of emotional expression, and the degree to which facial expression should play a necessary part in any theory of emotion for its therapy (see Chapter 9). The general implication of Izard's and Ekman's research is that facial expression may fill an informational gap which is left in any primarily visceral and cognitive theories of emotion. It allows emotions to be distinguished, allows emotions to change quickly, and also gives more possibility for subjective feedback than is given by the viscera alone. Thus it is reasonable to argue that any theory of emotion should, like Izard's (1972) or Mandler's (1976), not only include visceral physiological arousal and cognition, but also facial expression.

Following these general considerations, it is important to conclude with some of the more cogent theoretical analyses of the role of facial expression in emotion. These are taken from the ideas of Tomkins (1962) and more particularly Izard (1972).

Tomkins argues that innately determined subcortical programmes generate organized patterns of emotional facial expression, such patterning also occurring in the viscera, the endocrine system, and indeed in physiological responses generally. He also suggests that when we become aware (via feedback) of facial responses, then we become aware of the emotion. However, emotion can also occur with such awareness, which then becomes a sufficient but not necessary condition for emotion.

Izard rests his analysis of facial expression on two assumptions. (1) Emotion is a complex of the physiological, muscular, and phenomenological, and has a biological and psychological function for the individual and a social function in interaction. Also, the three levels of emotion are both independent and interdependent. It is feedback which permits an integration of these components into a process and which also allows differentiation between the emotions. (2) The relative importance of facial and bodily activity in emotion has changed during the course of evolution, such developments being parallelled in ontogeny. The general point here is that the importance of the face in emotional differentiation and communication increases with phylogenetic and ontogenetic development, this being in accord with a similar development of the facial muscles.

Of particular importance in this context is ontological development. On this matter Izard argues, on the basis of observations made by Goodenough (1932) and others, that in early infancy emotional expression is underlaid by undifferentiated excitement in the striate muscle. However, by the end of the first year the facial muscles are developed fully enough to allow the expression of any emotion. Thereafter the role of the face in emotion changes, whereas posture for example remains constant. Also, the suppression of facial patterning hinges on cognitive development. Here Izard suggests that there are learned proprioceptive patterns of particular facial configurations, with memory perhaps substituting for the actual pattern on occasion. Furthermore, in Western culture at least, the expression of strong emotion is increasingly discouraged by parents and peers throughout a child's development. Such suppressed expression might well show up in micromomentary movements. Izard even goes so far as to argue that if parents severely punish a young child's facial expressions, this causes a significant repression and leads to constricted emotions and a considerably attenuated emotional development characterized mainly by primitive undifferentiated disturbance in other areas (e.g. the viscera).

Izard assumes that feedback from facial expression generates increased hypothalmic activity and a correspondingly more intense emotional experience than would be given from a memory image alone. The experienced emotion would be more precise and complete.

Finally, Izard points to the importance of facial expression in communication, especially between parents and young children, even suggesting that the very first means of communication are the smile and frown. So facial expression is significant in both brain–body communication and interpersonal communication.

Some of the points made above concerning suppressed and hence potentially abnormal emotion will be returned to in Chapters 9 and 10. For now, it is enough to say that Tomkins and, more recently, Izard have produced the most throughgoing analyses of the role of facial expression in emotion.

9

Abnormal Emotion

To some extent abnormalities of emotion characterize most of the psycho-pathologies of man. For example, emotion is implicated in all of the affective disorders, schizophrenia often involves emotional change, the neuroses are largely characterized by problems of anxiety, the emotional difficulties of old age can become pathological, and so on. Any abnormal behaviour can be viewed as an emotional disturbance, or at least as involving unusual or in-appropriate links between stimuli and emotional responses. The abnormality lies not in the emotion itself but in the interaction between the individual and his circumstances.

In spite of the central role played by emotions in abnormal behaviour or mental disorder, the tendency has been to denigrate emotion by concentrating on man as a rational, intelligent being whose primitive affective impulses should be ignored or suppressed. However, in recent years, a number of writers have pointed out the shortsightedness of this approach, arguing instead that without emotions man would not have evolved, and that due attention should be paid to their abnormalities and techniques for their control (e.g. Leeper 1970; Peters 1970; Izard 1972). In fact, it is even reasonable to say that an individual with emotions so suppressed as to be regarded as nonexistent is extremely dangerous. It is therefore important to attempt to gain an understanding of abnormalities in emotion and of what can be done about them therapeutically.

Izard's (1972) is probably the best worked out general view. He puts the work of investigators such as Plutchik (1954) on the significance of muscular tension in maladjustment together with his own work on the importance of the striate muscle (mediating facial expression) in emotion and argues that emotion must therefore be central in individual dysfunction. He suggests that if emotion follows its natural course then it will lead to function or action, which in turn are regulated by cognition or verbal expression. Unwanted muscular tension might well stop this action and lead to maladaptive behaviour. Izard even goes so far as to suggest that man's understanding and control of his emotions will determine whether or not civilization advances, urging that neurosis, psychosis, and perhaps even societal violence result from overintellectualism and an ignoring of emotions.

Although it is appropriate in a book such as this to consider abnormal emotion, there is little profit in attempting to cover the whole sphere of mental illness in one chapter. Any understanding that this might bring would be severely limited by its lack of depth. However, there are two topics in which the role of emotion in abnormal behaviour is more obvious than any others—anxiety and depression—so these will be covered in some detail. They will be followed by descriptions of some theories and models of relevance to abnormal emotion and finally by a discussion of various types of therapy in which emotion is a key consideration.

ANXIETY

In the extended discussion of anxiety which follows, there are certain problems which occur frequently and are characteristic of this difficult field of study. The most obvious of these problems is that of definition. These are many definitions of anxiety, all of which leave unanswered questions. For example, is anxiety a convenient shorthand for certain behaviours which typify particular circumstances? Or is it an internal state which causes, and can therefore be used to account for, some abnormal behaviour? What is the distinction between normal and abnormal anxiety? In reading what follows it will be helpful to bear in mind questions such as these.

Clinical descriptions of anxiety

Mayer-Gross *et al.* (1969) give a complete description of anxiety from the clinical viewpoint. In this context, anxiety reactions are regarded as normal adaptive responses which carry unpleasant emotional overtones. They are described as involving a strong expectation of danger, threat, and distress for which an extra effort will be needed, but about which nothing can be done at the time. Physically, there is increased ANS activity, a rise in the output of adrenalin, and a rise in blood pressure and heart rate. The skin becomes sweaty and pale and the mouth dry. Respiration is deep and frequent and the muscles lose tone. Rate of defecation and urination increases. If this state continues for some time, then fidgety movements begin to appear and digestion and sleep are affected.

From such a description it is difficult to decide whether we are dealing with a bodily state, a complex of feelings, or a set of behavioural and physiological responses. However, anxiety is recognized not only as the most common neurosis but also as basic to the other neuroses. It is often believed to occur as a secondary reaction to depression and it is implicated in specific phobias which tend to develop after stress in someone already suffering from an anxiety neurosis. Prolonged anxiety inevitably leads to physical debilitation, which in turn will often lead to hypochondriasis; an hysterical reaction may then result. Sometimes 'depersonalization' is seen in those anxiety states which are also symptomatized by agarophobia.

Anxiety is regarded as coming about through organic conditions or as an accompaniment to involutional melancholia and the depressive psychoses. Genetic and constitutional factors become implicated when it is seen as associated both with immaturity and advanced age. For example, tendencies to anxiety are usually described as lessening markedly when the normal individual moves from adolescence to adulthood. Also, in any anxiety neurosis there is usually some precipitating factor. This may vary from organic stress to psychological stress. It is thought to be more likely to occur in those who are unsure of themselves; they are doubtful of their own ability to achieve and to cope; they magnify their own failures, worries, tensions, and apprehensions. At best, they are people who need a great deal of support from others; they are immature, dependent, and sexually cool. After the precipitating event, there is fearful anticipation, tension, and restlessness. Relaxation is replaced by fidgety, stereotyped movements. The emotional state is unpleasant, often with depression. Sleep and concentration are each broken and poor, and the person becomes irritable, short-tempered, frustrated, and impatient.

The measurement of anxiety

If it is assumed that anxiety is a state of the organism, then at present it cannot be measured directly. However, it is usually regarded as being reflected both behaviourally and physiologically, and measures have been developed accordingly. It is these measures that will be described below. Also, many scales have been constructed which aim to measure subjects' self-reports of reactions to specific situations, which, of course, must be the aim if anxiety is viewed as a cognitive variable (e.g. Mandler 1976).

Anxiety and behaviour

Anxiety has frequently been analysed within the terms of learning theory. It is viewed as a secondary drive and a source of secondary reinforcement, the primary drive being pain. Neutral stimuli associated with pain come to elicit fear, which has drive properties, such conditioned fear being defined as anxiety. The reduction of such anxiety is reinforcing and therefore brings about learning (e.g. Miller 1948; 1951).

At the human level, Eysenck (e.g. 1969) is the major advocate of the usefulness of this view of anxiety. He argues that if anxiety is a drive, then it should be governed by laws which apply to drives in general. These are seen most easily via the Yerkes–Dodson law (cf. Broadhurst 1959), which proposes a curvilinear relationship between drive and performance. Intermediate drives lead to optimal performance, optimal drive level depending on the difficulty of the task being performed. Although there are many examples of this relationship in the literature (e.g. Easterbrook 1959 or Eysenck 1964), they lack clarity and there is no single study which demonstrates the inverted U relationship to exist within one subject.

Such propositions imply that anxiety may be produced by particular situations and have its effect on virtually anyone who experiences it. However, anxiety-producing stimuli do not have similar effects on everybody; some seem to be habitually more anxious than others, reacting more strongly to situations which would not be productive of anxiety in others. Eysenck believes that studies of anxiety as a personality variable are best conducted via his own two-dimensional model, with neuroticism (stability/unstability) and extraversion/introversion as the two orthogonal dimensions. He suggests (1967; 1969), as does Gray (1970), a strong hereditary basis for these dimensions and argues that they accord well with psychiatric classifications. For example, dysthymic neurotics are introverted and unstable, whereas psychopaths are extraverted and unstable. He believes that these dimensions have a firm physiological basis.

A problem with the studies from which Eysenck's views on anxiety derive is that it is difficult to determine whether the results are due to differences in extraversion/introversion or emotionality/unstability. Also, it is not clear how emotionality (neuroticism) is related to anxiety. Finally, it may be wrong, as Pichot (1969) argues, to equate a disposition to anxiety with pathological anxiety. It may be that 'anxiety disposition' is a proneness to respond to real danger maladaptively, and that anxiety states are the result of nonobjective danger, coming from psychological conflicts for example (see discussion below of Spielberger's work on state and trait anxiety).

Some light is thrown on this area of study by Cattell (e.g. 1963), who suggests that anxiety is an underlying state which is reflected in many ways, introspective, behavioural, and physiological, 'typical' measures for each of which he has developed. Whichever way he collects his data, they suggest, through factor analysis, that they depend on one main factor which can best be labelled anxiety. He argues in fact that factor analytic studies separate anxiety from neuroticism and stress reactions.

Anxiety and psychophysiology

Reviews of work on the psychophysiological measurement of anxiety may be seen in B. Martin (1961), I. Martin (1960), and Lader (1969b). There have been two main approaches. (1) Stimulation has been used to induce anxiety in normal subjects or psychiatric patients. (2) Differences have been measured between the anxious and the normal. Again, this implies two views of anxiety: as predisposition, or as a chronic, perhaps morbid, state.

The best results in this area come from cardiovascular measures. For example, in patients with anxiety states there is a general rise in heart rate (e.g. Lader and Wing 1966), although sometimes blood pressure has also been shown to rise (e.g. Malmo and Shagass 1952). Large increases in the flow of blood to the forearms often accompany emotional stress (e.g. Kelly 1966; 1967; Kelly and Walter 1968). Other standard psychophysiological measures such as PGR and EMG have not been especially productive.

Lader (1969a) points to one important problem in this area: that of reactivity. If the resting levels of various physiological measures are studied, there is no consistent relationship between anxious patients and normal subjects. Add stimulation and the differences become obvious, but tend to go in *both* directions. Anxious patients are sometimes more reactive than controls and sometimes less, although they do adapt more slowly to the experimental situation than normal subjects (e.g. Martin 1956; Kelly 1966). Further, Lader (1969) suggests that anxiety can be seen as one of many states that can be distinguished as arousal becomes more intense. So, psychophysiological measures reflect the level of arousal and therefore the intensity of the emotion. But, of course, he is forced to say that there are no *definite* physiological patterns yet delineated for the different emotions.

Finally, Lader provides four reasons for the relative unimportance of psychophysiological measures of anxiety to psychiatric considerations. (1) In such studies the groupings of subjects used have been so broad as to render meaningfulness suspect, for example 'neurotics'. (2) Methodology has been poor. (3) There are intrinsic limitations to the measurement techniques which have been used. (4) It is not *anxiety* which has been measured. The last, of course, is the most cogent criticism; it rests on the argument that a high level of physiological reactivity is not necessarily an indicator of anxiety. The increased physiological activity may be a secondary reaction to increased physiological needs and/or high arousal may accompany other states of intense emotion.

Causation of anxiety

Leaving aside for the moment theories of anxiety, there are many accounts which have been given of its possible causation. Three distinct views will be mentioned briefly in this section.

Anxiety and affection

Bowlby (1961; 1969) discusses the role of affectional bonds, particularly between mother and child, in the formation of pathological anxiety. He argues that two sorts of behaviour are related to subjective feelings of anxiety: escape and attachment. Escape is the result of sudden, strange events; attachment occurs when the members of a 'bonded pair' become separated from one another. Without discussing all the evidence, it can be said with reasonable conviction that some children who experience an unsettled early home life are far more anxious than control children who have had more settled home lives. Also, they tend to be more aggressive and antisocial. Such separation anxiety only becomes pathological when it is extreme, although it is difficult to define what 'extreme' is in this context. Bowlby argues that such extreme reactions result from long or repeated periods of separation in strange surroundings.

Anxiety and genetics

Slater and Shields (1969) provide a review of studies designed to assess genetic influences on anxiety. Such studies range from selective breeding in animals (e.g. Broadhurst 1967) to family studies (e.g. Cohen 1951) and twin studies (e.g. Lader and Wing 1966; Slater and Shields 1969; Vandenberg 1967). They find, for example, that about 15 per cent of the parents and siblings of anxiety neurotics are also anxious, and that 50 per cent of the co-twins of anxiety neurotics are similarly diagnosed. However, only the usual conclusions can be drawn; namely, that a predisposition to anxiety is best accounted for by an interaction between hereditary and environmental factors.

Experimental neurosis

The learning theory approach to anxiety has already been described. One specific form which this takes is that of work on experimental neurosis (see Kimble 1961; Lazarus 1972; and Wolpe 1961; 1966 for reviews). The basic question is that if neurosis (and hence anxiety) is learned, then how does this learning occur? In answer to this, Wolpe, for example, suggests that neurosis develops through simple conditioning.

Wolpe's view depends very much on the early demonstrations of so-called experimental neurosis in animals by Pavlov (1928), Liddell (1944), and Masserman (1943). These demonstrations led to the development of two methods for producing the effects. (1) Subjecting animals to ambivalent stimuli when they are under the influence of a powerful drive. Pavlov, for example, in a conditioning study made a circle a positive stimulus and an ellipse a negative stimulus. When he altered the semi-axes of the ellipse so that they more and more approximated circularity, his dogs responded with what can be described as generalized anxiety. (2) Presenting animals with aversive stimuli in confined places.

Wolpe argues that if work on experimental neurosis can be extrapolated to the development of neuroses in humans under 'natural' conditions, they will have to show three common features of learning. (1) Neurotic behaviour will be similar to that seen in the precipitating situation. (2) The neurotic response will occur in the presence of the original stimulus. (3) There will be stimulus generalization. Each of these features was shown in Wolpe's (1966) work on neurotic cats. From the human viewpoint, anxiety is thought to be important in any neurosis. The starting point for a neurosis is usually regarded as a single or recurrent anxiety-producing event or a chronic anxiety situation. The stimuli present at this time are those most likely to become conditioned to neurotic anxiety responses. Also, stimulus generalization is clearly evident in neurotic anxiety.

Here then are three representative examples of some of the hypotheses which have been put forward to account for the causation of anxiety. They differ markedly from one another and each has its limitations. However, the evidence for each is sufficient to suggest that they have some force. Indeed, the idea of experimental neurosis has led to the development of the very important therapeutic technique of desensitization (see later). Anxiety is a complex topic and is likely to have complex causes.

Some theories of anxiety

The three theories of anxiety to be summarized below have been chosen because they seem to be representative of the general field, but it must be added that this is according to my own interpretations, which, in such a vast area of study, are bound to be somewhat arbitrary. For more comprehensive reviews see: Fischer (1970); Hoch and Zubin (1950); Lader (1969); Lazarus *et al.* (1952); Malmo (1957); Spence (1958); Spielberger (1966); Taylor (1956). Also, although a natural starting point for a theoretical consideration of anxiety is with Freud's distinction between objective anxiety and neurotic anxiety, this has been omitted in favour of some more recent conceptualizations.

One of the most extensive theories of anxiety to emerge in recent years is that of *Epstein* (1967). He bases his ideas on a series of investigations involving parachutists. On the days of their jumps he took three measures from novice and experienced parachutists: (1) physiological reactions to parachute-relevant words in word-association tests; (2) subjective ratings of fear; and (3) physiological reactions at all stages of aircraft ascent. His general, and very consistent, findings were that novices show a steep monotonic gradient of both expressed fear and physiological arousal as a function of time or of the four levels of parachute-relevant stimuli in the word-association tests. Experienced jumpers, on the other hand, provided inverted V-shaped curves relating fear and arousal to time and relevant cues; with increasing experience, the peak of these curves nears the remote end of the dimension. These findings were established in both cross-sectional and longitudinal studies. It was also noted that differential functional relationships obtained for physiological arousal and self-reported fear. Rising fear and its inhibition regularly preceded rising physiological arousal and its inhibition.

These results led Epstein to put forward a general theory of anxiety, or, more properly, of the mastery of anxiety. He proposed that two developments accompany any increasing experience with some threatening stimulus: (1) a generalization gradient of anxiety heightens, steepens, or broadens; (2) an inhibition gradient develops and becomes increasingly steeper than the anxiety gradient. Epstein also argues that psychological and physiological inhibitory reactions are organized into a system of defence in depth. He suggests that there are three lines of defence, each of which allows an organism to maintain an appropriate level of arousal: (1) fear and its inhibition; (2) physiological arousal and its psychological inhibition; and (3) physiologically mediated (i.e. reflexive) inhibition.

Epstein goes on to a comparative analysis of fear, arousal, and anxiety. Briefly, he views fear as an avoidance motive and arousal as a nonspecific excitation which underlines all motives and reactions. Anxiety is an undirected arousal state which follows the perception of danger. He characterizes it as extremely noxious and as therefore often channelled into direct motives (fear), so allowing the possibility of action. This is clearly an adaptive function, implying as it does an increased likelihood of direct action as the situation (threat) worsens.

Epstein regards these ideas as resulting in a system for keeping high arousal within reasonable limits. He sees this as part of a general system for modulating the *intensity* of all stimulation. As a theoretical substrate for this view, he provides a set of postulates. These relate excitation and inhibition to stimulus intensity, the time since stimuli were presented, and the numbers and rate of stimulus inputs. Although these postulates are very speculative, Epstein believes that they apply to a wide range of phenomena (for example, the working through of extreme grief, and GSR adaptation). Finally, he suggests that his basic unifying assumption regarding anxiety should qualify as a law of excitatory modulation. This states that '... the gradient of inhibition as a function of increasing (or decreasing), excitation is steeper than the gradient of excitation that it inhibits' (1967, p. 86). He believes that this law describes how the intensity of any stimulation is modified, allowing the organism to function at appropriate (i.e. efficient) levels of arousal.

Clearly, Epstein has made a very broad attempt at theoretical unification in this difficult field. Although many of his ideas are highly speculative, they are also useful in that they lead to testable predictions. His studies with parachutists are interesting, well conducted and informative, and, resting on them as it does, his basic theory of anxiety is more firmly grounded than most. However, in extending his theoretical arguments he strays a long way from his original data. Although it is worthwhile and stimulating, Epstein's 'unified' theory of anxiety perhaps suffers from being a little too grandiose.

In his very useful attempt at theoretical clarification of anxiety, *Spielberger* (1966) suggests that conceptual ambiguity has surrounded the term because it has been typically used in two different ways. (1) As a complex response—a fluctuating state, varying in intensity. (2) As a personality trait, in which there are individual differences. On the basis of factor analytic studies, Cattell and Scheier (1958; 1961) identified two distinct anxiety factors, which they labelled (1) trait anxiety and (2) state anxiety. Trait anxiety refers to stable, individual differences in relatively permanent personality characteristics and state anxiety to a transitory, fluctuating state.

In the field of transitory anxiety, most work seems to have focused on delineating the state and outlining the conditions which may invoke it. Krause (1961) concludes that it can be inferred from six types of evidence: introspective reports, physiological signs, gross behaviours such as bodily posture, speech, etc., task performance, clinical intuition, and responses to stress. However, he suggests that the most important of these is introspective report, since most researchers argue that all one needs to be satisfied that anxiety is present is this plus some physiological or behavioural indices. Martin (1961) describes anxiety as a complex response pattern which should be carefully distinguished from its eliciting internal or external stimuli. This concentrates attention on physiological/behavioural patterns which distinguish anxiety/fear from other emotions. This formulation also carries the implication that it is important to differentiate anxiety from the cognitions and behaviours which are learnt to reduce it.

Work on personality anxiety has mainly centred around subjects chosen because they differ in measured anxiety level. For example, patients with high chronic anxiety have been compared with nonanxious controls in stressful and nonstressful conditions. Using this method of investigation, Malmo (1950; 1957; 1959) has concluded that the chronically anxious show much more reactivity and variability than normals, irrespective of stress. Also, many questionnaire-based studies have been carried out on normal populations. Recent instances of these (for example Spielberger and Smith 1966) suggest that subjects with high manifest anxiety scale scores have higher than average responses in situations involving some stress, but not otherwise. Trait anxiety may therefore be measuring anxiety-proneness. However, in more general terms, state anxiety is seen as an empirical reaction occurring *now* at some given intensity. Trait anxiety is a latent disposition for a certain type of reaction if this is cued by the necessarily stressful stimuli.

Spielberger (1966) proposes an interesting trait–state conceptualization of anxiety. He suggests that anxiety as a state is characterized by subjective, conscious feelings of apprehension and tension, with ANS rousal. Anxiety as a personality trait is more like a motive or an acquired behavioural disposition, predisposing the perception of a threatening environment and also predisposing disproportionate responses to these threatening situations. He suggests further that the arousal of anxiety states involves a series of events. (1) An external stimulus or internal cue. (2) If there is a cognitive appraisal of danger or threat, then an anxiety state develops. (3) The sensory and cognitive feedback may make the anxiety state act as a signal which initiates a behaviour sequence to deal with the danger or avoid it. (4) Also, cognitive or motivational defence processes have been effective in reducing past anxiety states by altering appraisals. (There are clear similarities between this view of anxiety and Arnold's, for example 1960, more general view of emotion.) Anxiety traits, on the other hand, reflect residues of past experiences which have determined individual differences in anxiety-proneness, the most important aspect of this probably being during childhood and involving parent/child punishment situations. Finally, he suggests that anxiety-trait level will only affect some anxiety-state responses, depending on the stressfulness of the situation.

Spielberger's ideas have been described in some detail since they represent a worthwhile attempt at synthesis in a very woolly theoretical field. They gain impetus because they were suggested by two distinctly developed areas of enquiry. Even so, they are speculative and the lack of a general definition is very apparent. Also, whether or not we are considering transient anxiety as well as anxiety as a more permanent characteristic, the status of the concept remains obscure. We cannot say if it is best to regard it as a state of the organism or as a set of physiological and behavioural responses. If we define it in terms of responses, then it is difficult to say whether it is best left there or whether these responses should be seen as symptomatic of some underlying (causal) condition. Also, the distinction between 'normal' and pathological anxiety remains hidden. The differentiation implicit in much of the foregoing discussion is one of degree;

the more extreme forms of transitory or personality anxiety are considered abnormal. The difficulties with this viewpoint are: (1) the arbitrariness involved in drawing the demarcation line; (2) the question of whether or not different determinants might underlie normal and abnormal anxiety.

In his general text on various theoretical considerations of emotion, *Mandler* (1976) puts forward the final theoretical analysis of anxiety to be considered here. He suggests that anxiety is a cyclical distress experienced by the newly born human infant; a fundamental distress, the crucial aspect of which is the perception of a variable and intense autonomic visceral activity. The distress is not necessarily stopped by escape or avoidance; and at times it even reverberates, signalling more distress. There is *no* specific event antecedent to such distress, according to Mandler.

Secondly, Mandler suggests that anxiety is sometimes controlled by specific inhibitors, which eventually leads to the possibility that any organized activity will ward off the distress involved in anxiety. Thus whenever the individual is helpless, anxiety results. This brings Mandler to the concept which has been central to his ideas for many years, that of interruption. Given the foregoing, then it follows that any situation that interrupts, or threatens an interruption of, organized sequences of responses and which does not offer any alternative responses will produce anxiety. He also argues that broad social and cultural variables can influence anxiety in four ways. (1) By providing people with organized sequences of responses that are very likely to be interrupted. (2) By interrupting organized response sequences. (3) By not providing alternative response sequences. (4) By providing inappropriate alternatives to interrupted sequences.

In summary, then, Mandler is hypothesizing that anxiety has its ontogeny in the original distress experienced by the new-born. This has no antecedents but can be inhibited by specific responses such as sucking and rocking. Later these give way to any organized sequences of behaviour. Then interrupted sequences of behaviour lead the organism to be helpless, which in turn alters arousal to anxiety, although interruption is only one condition which might produce helplessness. Mandler's general point here is that disorganization and helplessness may well result in the same emotional state. Finally, if helplessness is extreme and ongoing, it may turn into hopelessness and depression. Clearly, Seligman's (1975) ideas are directly related to Mandler's (see below), although he is concerned with learned helplessness, which Mandler views as an antecedent of the unattainability of a desired state.

Anxiety—conclusions

From this review of some of the research and theory into anxiety it must be concluded that much of the work is not of high standard. It tends to be descriptive rather than explanatory, with the descriptions themselves being made at many different levels. It is not possible to give a precise definition of anxiety nor to distinguish normal anxiety from pathological anxiety. This is simply a reflection of the general field. There is a vast literature on anxiety, the surface of which has been barely scratched here, and it represents work carried out from many standpoints and according to many whims, idiosyncracies, and personal commitments to particular viewpoints.

It may be that, as Izard (1972) points out, those interested in abnormal emotions have not conceptualized conditions such as anxiety adequately. They have tended to treat them as global undifferentiated concepts, possibly because their main source of data has come from disturbed individuals, in whom negative emotion is so predominant, or so confines them, that it seems undifferentiated. It would seem that anxiety is far too complex to be treated as an entity. Izard argues that it is an admixture of at least fear, distress, shame (shyness, guilt), and interest, all of which in his terms are differentiable emotional states. Perhaps it should be dealt with as such.

DEPRESSION

Depression has been chosen as the other main abnormal emotional condition to discuss in this chapter since, like anxiety, it is relatively common, and also because it can take many forms, sometimes being categorized with the neuroses and sometimes with the psychoses. Again like anxiety, it is clearly a very complex emotional disorder, but also one which is experienced by all of us in mild form as part of everyday life. The discussion which follows relies very much on the cogent analyses made by Beck (1967) and Becker (1974), to whom the reader is referred for a much fuller exposition.

Description and classification

Although depression is exacerbated by many other conditions such as hypochondriasis and anxiety, it commonly has five sets of characteristics. (1) A sad, apathetic mood. (2) A negative self-concept involving self-reproach, self-blame, and so on. (3) A desire to avoid other people. (4) A loss of sleep, appetite, and sexual desire. (5) A change in activity level, which may take the form of agitation, but more usually involves lethargy.

Beyond these typical characteristics attempts have been made to classify depression further. For example, a comon distinction is drawn between psychotic and neurotic depression. This is both a matter of degree—psychotic depression is more extreme in all characteristics than is neurotic depression—and kind—psychotic depression is also characterized by delusions. The second common distinction is between endogenous and exogenous depression, the former being thought to be caused by a physiological malfunction and the latter environmentally. As might be imagined, it is often difficult to make this distinction with any confidence. In fact, the general question of the diagnosis of depression is awkward. The usual example is of a man whose wife has died. If he immediately shows the characteristics described above, this is viewed as normal grief; if he still has them two years later, then it is depression. As ever, there is the problem of where the line is drawn.

Mendel (1970) took up some of these problems of whether or not to diagnose depression as abnormal. He points out that reported links between life events and depression might not provide causal links but may only be correlational. Typically, depression is seen to result from illness or a worsening of abilities. Rather than the direct causal explanation, environmental stress may be interacting with underlying predispositions. So since Mendel, the terms endogenous and exogenous depression have been applied to different patterns of reaction. Endogenous depression is seen as more severe than exogenous, being particularly characterized by slowed motor responses, a very deep depression, a lack of reactivity, a general loss of interest, insomnia in the middle of the night, and a lack of self-pity—conditions which do not characterize so-called exogenous, or environmentally generated, depression.

Theories of depression

It will be clear from the following that theories of depression once again reflect the usual ways in which emotion in general has been viewed. They can be most easily broken down into psychoanalytic, cognitive, physiological, and behavioural (or at least based on learning theory).

1. *Psychoanalytic.* The psychoanalytic theories of depression are best exemplified by Freud. He suggested that if a child's oral needs are over or under satisfied, then he may develop an excessive dependency for self-esteem. Then, if he loses a loved person, he introjects the lost person into himself with full identification. As some of his feelings towards the loved person will have been negative, so he now comes to hate and be angry with himself. At the same time he resentfully views the loss as a desertion because he feels guilty at the sins he committed against him. Then he mourns, to separate the self from the lost person. In overdependents this can develop into self-abuse and self-blame and lead to depression. The bonds are never lost and self-castigation continues, as does self-anger. So, Freud sees depression as anger turned against the self.

Of course, there are many criticisms that can be made of such a loose theory. For example: what causes depression in those who have not lost a loved one? why is love not turned inwards as well as anger? where is the evidence that people interpret the death of someone as rejection? how much is too little or too much gratification at the oral stage? It is a theory with no good evidence.

2. *Cognitive.* Cognitive theories of depression can be exemplified by Beck (1967), whose starting point is that thoughts and beliefs cause emotional states. He argues that people become depressed through making a logical error; they distort events into self-blame. An event which is normally seen as just irritating (e.g. spilling a drink) is seen as another example of the utter hopelessness of life. So, the depressed person only draws illogical conclusions about himself.

Beck describes such illogicalities as 'schemata'. So, the depressed person interprets all events from the schema of self-depreciation and self-blame. Beck describes him as making four types of logical error. (1) Arbitrary inference, where there is no evidence for a conclusion drawn; (I am useless because the shop was closed when I went to buy something). (2) Selective abstraction, in which a conclusion is drawn from only one element of the many possible; (it is my fault that the firm I work for is full of unintelligent people). (3) Over-generalization, or the making of a massive conclusion from a trivial starting point; (I am completely thick because I did not understand that one point). (4) Magnification and minimization, which simply involve errors in judging performance; (I told one white lie and completely lost all integrity).

From Beck's viewpoint, then, emotional reactions come from cognitions, and the interpretations of the world made by depressed persons do not accord with reality. He provides some evidence that depressives do indeed think in this way, but the problem with this is that it is correlational. To endorse his thesis he must also show that the cognitive errors which depressives appear to make are *not* the result of their emotional disturbance.

3. *Physiological.* The basic point underlying physiological theories of depression is that if a genetic basis can be proved for the predisposition to depression then physiology must be an important link in this. The evidence on this point is only suggestive. For example, Rosenthal (1970) showed that approximately two-thirds of monozygotic pairs are concordant for manic depression in comparison with only about one-sixth in dizygotic pairs.

Nevertheless, two main types of physiological theory of depression have been put forward. The first is argued on the basis that there is a disturbance in the electrolyte metabolism of depressed patients. Sodium and potassium chlorides are particularly important in the maintenance of potential and the control of excitability in the nervous system. Normally there is more sodium outside the neuron and more potassium inside it, but in depressed patients this distribution is disturbed.

The second physiologically based theory views depression as resulting from an inhibition of neural transmission. This is thought to occur in the SNS and to involve its neural transmitter—norepinephrine.

There are a number of lines of evidence in support of these two theories which are quite opposed. The major problem is that it is not known how the psychological and physiological factors in depression are causally linked.

4. *Learning.* The main idea behind the various learning theories of depression is that it is a condition which is mainly characterized by a reduction in activity which occurs when a large and accustomed reinforcement is withdrawn. There is no recourse to concepts such as unconscious mourning. Often it is argued that the depressed behaviour itself may be reinforced, by attention and sympathy.

Lewinsohn (1975) makes three assumptions in his behavioural analysis of depression. (1) Feelings of depression can be elicited when there is little rein-forcement. (2) This reduces activity even more, resulting in even fewer reinforce-ments. (3) The amount of positive reinforcement depends on: the number of potential reinforcers available as a function of age, sex, attractiveness, and so on, the number available through a particular environment, and the individual's repertoire of behaviour that can gain reinforcement (such as verbal skills). Thus Lewinsohn's idea of depression is very much that of a vicious circle, but one about which data would be very difficult to collect for practical reasons. However, the central hypothesis that depression involves reduced reinforcement is fairly well substantiated.

Along similar lines, Seligman (1975) has recently put forward the view, which is already becoming influential, of depression as learned helplessness. This is based on seeing anxiety as the initial response to stressful situations, which, if a person comes to believe them uncontrollable, leads to the anxiety being replaced by depression. In a typical experiment of a series to test this hypothesis, Seligman gives dogs severe inescapable shocks and then puts these and unshocked dogs in an avoidance apparatus. Those without previous experience with shock soon learn to avoid, whereas the previously shocked animals give up and seem to passively accept the shocks in the new situation. Seligman describes this as a sense of helplessness acquired in the presence of uncontrollable stimuli affecting behaviour in other situations in which similar stimuli *can* be controlled.

Thus learned helplessness in animals provides a model of depression in man, there being remarkable similarities between animal and human data on the symptoms of the two conditions. This inevitably leads to an examination of common causes, which is more difficult since there has to be a comparison of data derived experimentally in dogs and on the basis of clinical observations in humans. However, it is commonly remarked that one of the aspects of human depression is that the patient seems unable to control events; he seems unable to act to reduce his suffering or to obtain gratification.

Clearly, Seligman is only attempting to account for depression which is reactive to environmental stress and which takes the form of lethargy rather than agitation. This is an obvious limitation of the learned helplessness hypothesis. Also, there is a major difference between this view and that which regards depression as the result of reduced reinforcement. The latter view is noncognitive, simply regarding behaviour as a function of reward, with mood altering as a function of behaviour. The learned helplessness hypothesis highlights an individual's *perception* of the degree to which he is in control of the environment, and hence has an important cognitive element.

Conclusions

The only conclusions which can be drawn from this brief overview of depression are that it involves abnormal extremes of mood and emotion and that it is possible to provide theories about it ranging from the psychoanalytic to the behavioural and physiological. Which type of theory is likely to lead to a greater understanding is at the moment a matter of conjecture and individual preference, although it seems quite clear that Seligman's views will continue to be influential, at least with respect to reactive depression.

THEORIES AND MODELS

In this section two rather broad theories will be discussed. The first, that of Gellhorn and Loufbourrow, represents the only general theory of abnormal emotion to be found in the literature. The second is Eysenck's recent learning theory model of the neuroses, which is included for its freshness of approach and its interesting implications.

Gellhorn and Loufbourrow

Initially, Gellhorn and Loufbourrow (1963) review fields such as experimental neurosis, sensory deprivation (for example Solomon *et al.* 1961), and stress. In each case they argue that the hypothalamus is crucially involved. For example, they suggest that the hypothalamus is unable to cope with the reduced sensory input characteristic of sensory deprivation or that prolonged stress produces hypothalamic changes which may ultimately prove pathological. They maintain that in neurosis and experimental neurosis the two divisions of the hypothalamus are simultaneously activated; this produces autonomic imbalance, which in turn leads to neurosis. The premorbid balance determines the extent of the reaction, in some cases there being no neurosis at all. They suggest that such effects occur following exposure to severe and unexpected pain, 'emotional excitement', particularly where life is threatened, and strong conflicts. Each of these will change behaviour, via their effect on the hypothalamus; the autonomic changes may persist for years, with the behavioural aspects varying from stuporous to manic, convulsive to compulsive.

Gellhorn and Loufbourrow support the role of the hypothalamus in emotion by their analysis of the physiological mechanisms involved in such states as hypertension, peptic ulcers, nausea, and fever. They believe that all evidence points to the importance of the hypothalamically-controlled autonomic balance. For example, the SNS is predominant in sympathotonics, so disposing hypertension. Gellhorn and Loufbourrow argue that the experience of different moods is the reflection of various states which exist between the extremes of hypothalamic action on the cortex, from emotional excitement (sympathetic—ergotropic) to sleep (parasympathetic—trophotropic). Also involved are positive feedback systems, such that if the skeletal muscles are somehow relaxed, then emotional reactivity and possibly neurotic symptoms will be reduced (as in some aspects of behaviour therapy). Finally, they suggest that the physiological and pathological states of altered hypothalamic balance are characterized by changes in autonomic reactivity and by changes in the whole personality. These effects will result partially from altered hypothalamic–cortical discharges. This picture is complicated further by the influence of the hypothalamus on the endocrine system.

Gellhorn and Loufbourrow extend their argument with the suggestion that there is an interrelationship between emotional disturbance, autonomic changes, and behaviour disorder. At this point their thesis weakens. They maintain, for example, that the fact that many investigators have emphasized the emotional aspects of psychoses and neuroses also points indirectly to the hypothalamus. Also, they suggest that perception depends on emotion and hence on the various links which exist between the hypothalamus and cortex. Anxiety modifies perceptual thresholds and perceptions are distorted in psychoses and neuroses. They argue that psychosis is characterized by two symptoms, which again point to the hypothalamus. (1) The psychotic will often not react to physical pain—the hypothalamus is pain-sensitive. (2) The catatonic schizophrenic state known as waxy fexibility can be produced by bilateral hypothalamic lesions (Ranson 1939).

In outlining the possible role of the hypothalamus and emotional responsiveness in the functional mental disorders, Gellhorn and Loufbourrow stress Walther's (1956) idea of the autonomic–affective syndrome, which shows fluctuations in mood, restlessness, anxiety, and various autonomic disturbances. They argue that this syndrome is the response of a labile hypothalamic system to acute emotional stimuli and bodily stress and that a gradually developing imbalance from similar circumstances will produce hypertension or gastric ulcers. Walther also observed the autonomic–affective syndrome to precede functional psychoses and to occur transitorily during remission from a psychosis and on awakening from an insulin coma. This all supports the idea that 'mood' is determined by the state of the hypothalamus and its autonomic balance. Mood is determined by the hypothalamic–cortical discharge, and by the rate of secretion of various hormones.

Gellhorn and Loufbourrow's theory is best illustrated by a brief description of their analysis of battle fatigue and abreaction. They suggest that in combat fear is the first reaction. Those who are exposed to such fear for long periods of time and are unable to conquer it react with nervous fatigue, irritability, and tenseness—an overreaction. They then become emotionally exhausted, dull, listless, apathetic, anxious, and depressed. Sargant (1957) draws the parallel between this change from overreactivity to emotional exhaustion and some of the phenomena seen in experimental neurosis. Prolonged excitation of the SNS leads to a basic change in autonomic reactivity—the usual level of sympathetic dominance is increased. If this goes too far, there is a reversal in autonomic balance and the general emotional state swings.

Abreaction involves reviving a memory of supposedly repressed unpleasant experiences and expressing the emotions related to them. This is believed to relieve the pressure on the personality: a release of emotions through reliving the experience. It is usually brought about by the administration of cortical depressants. Again, there is strong emotional excitement, then exhaustion, and then finally the disturbances disappear. Gellhorn and Loufbourrow suggest that the hypothalamic action which typifies intense excitement is enhanced by a cortical depressant, since this releases the hypothalamus from cortical inhibition. After an abreaction there is some evidence for a physiological oscillation until the balance is restored; this is supported by the alternating laughter and crying which is seen at this stage. Thus, to Gellhorn and Loufbourrow, an abreaction consists of an intensive hypothalamic–cortical discharge, lessened hypothalamic–cortical interactions, and the reestablishment of normal relations and excitability.

This has only been a brief description of some of Gellhorn and Loufbourrow's (1963) fundamental arguments. They range far wider than it is possible to show here. However, whatever the topic they touch on, it is with the same guiding principle: the conviction that the hypothalamus, its interactions with the cortex, and the balance between its ergotropic and trophotropic systems are crucial to all aspects of emotion, particularly pathological emotion. At times they become highly speculative, but nevertheless provide a reasonably solid theoretical starting point for the study of pathological emotion.

Eysenck

Eysenck's (1976) theory is narrower than that of Gellhorn and Loufbourrow, being restricted to a consideration of the neuroses. To give justice to its description, it is first necessary to summarize the analysis he makes of the work of Watson and Mowrer. Eysenck points to three basic criticisms which can be levelled against Watson's view of neuroses as CERs. (1) The only study on which it was based was the famous one with Raynor (see Chapter 6), which has never been replicated. No-one has attempted to take genetic influences into account. (2) Eysenck points out that many neuroses do not develop from a single traumatic event. (3) There is direct evidence for strong fears other than those mentioned by Watson.

However, Eysenck suggests that these criticisms can be dealt with by substituting frustration for pain, the CER model then possibly pointing to the causation of neurosis. Again, though, he raises two objections. (1) Unreinforced conditioned responses extinguish; so then should neurotic reactions. It appears, though, that many neuroses do not extinguish. In this regard Mowrer's two-factor theory is of some help, in which the original conditioning can be viewed as 'protected' by the second stage of instrumental conditioning, in which relief from anxiety produced by the avoidance of the CS leads to a conditioned avoidance reaction. However, this still cannot account for all neuroses and the sometimes massive resistance to extinction. (2) Eysenck points out that there have been several attempts to explain the problems of the absence of extinction in neurotic behaviours, but that even if these were successful they could not account for the commonly observed enhancement effect in which a CS produces *more* and *more* anxiety with no reinforcement. Eventually, under these conditions, the CRs are *stronger* than the original URs.

These difficulties lead Eysenck on to his incubation model of neurosis. He argues that there are two possible outcomes of the presentation of a CS alone. The CR might extinguish or might be enhanced, the latter being an incubation of the anxiety or fear response. He believes it necessary to postulate two classes of CR which lead to these responses—those with drive properties and those without. Those which do not produce drive extinguish, and those which do lead to enhancement (incubation). Eysenck is not arguing that a CS with drive properties (e.g. anxiety) is reinforced without the US. Rather, he is arguing that the US produces the anxiety originally, and the CS does not. Pairing the two leads to identical effects; both produce anxiety. Hence a positive feedback cycle develops, the CS-only reinforcing itself and incrementing the CR.

Eysenck points out that there is much experimental evidence in support of this theory, both from animal studies and from those with neurotic humans. These also point to the time and duration of the CS-only presentation as an important parameter in determining whether extinction or enhancement will ensue. He also argues that important sources of influence are personality (particularly extraversion/introversion and neuroticism, with their genetic basis and implications for conditioning), and the strength of the UR.

However, Eysenck also points out that incubation plus individual differences may still not be enough to account for all neurosis, and suggests that Seligman's (1971) idea of preparedness may give the final link. This suggests that whilst certain fears may not be innate, phobias are likely to be highly prepared to be learned by humans. If this is so, they are also likely to be selective (to particular CSs), resistant to extinction, easily learned, and probably noncognitive. Preparedness *may* interact with incubation.

It is easiest to finalize Eysenck's theory by presenting a brief summary of the conclusions he draws from it. (1) Maladaptive, unreasoning fears which can be innate or learned through modelling sensitize a person to certain types of stimuli and facilitate the conditioning of fear to these (preparedness). (2) The main process of such learning is classical conditioning, traumatic or repeated presentations of CS and US. (3) The main US in human conditioning is not pain but frustration. (4) CRs may extinguish with nonreinforcement (CS-only). (5) Sometimes CS-only leads to incubation or the enhancement of the response, more frequently the greater the CR—this is neurosis. (6) Incubation only occurs in CSs which have drive properties, which through positive feedback makes it functionally equivalent to the US. (7) The prime examples of CRs with drives linked to CSs are fear and anxiety (and possibly sex). (8) The most favourable conditions for CS-only leading to incubation are: short presentations of strong USs, high N versus low N scores, and introverts versus extraverts. (9) CRs which develop from this process are stronger than the original URs and allow for the slow growth of neurosis. (10) The incubation model of neurosis is not open to the objections which can be made to the other learning models of neurosis.

THERAPY

In the context of abnormal emotion it is important to make mention of two types of therapy or therapeutic programme. The first is concerned specifically with neurotic anxiety and has been developed from the learning theory approach to this. The second is that which Izard (1972) has developed on the basis of his theory of and research into emotion. Since this has wider implications, it will be discussed in greater detail.

Therapy for neurotic anxiety

To return briefly to experimental neurosis, Wolpe (1966) argues that neurotic anxiety is very persistent, even though in the long term it is maladaptive and in the short term it is unpleasant. For example, if the phobic patient is forced into contact with the feared object he does not improve and may in fact worsen—the neurosis may even spread in this way. However, it can easily be eliminated by counterconditioning: presenting the anxiety-invoking stimuli when anxiety-inhibiting responses are present. To return to the animal studies, Masserman, using cats, conditioned anxiety to a buzzer. They were then made hungry and required to eat food pellets 40 feet away from the original situation. Anxiety gradually disappeared. Then, by degrees, the distance was diminished. Food-approach responses systematically weakened the anxiety. In humans many responses other than eating have been used as reciprocal inhibitors of anxiety (see Wolpe and Lazarus 1966). Wolpe (1966) describes three of the more common responses.

1. *Assertive* responses involve the overt expression of feelings other than anxiety. The therapist encourages the person to be assertive in the appropriate situations; each assertion reduces the anxiety a little, leading to easier assertion the next time, and so on.

2. *Sexual* responses are used mainly against neurotic reactions to sex, often impotence or premature ejaculation for example. The patient is persuaded to restrict his sexual advances to the point in time where he experiences minimal anxiety. He only allows himself to move on to the next point when the anxiety is entirely gone. Again there is a slow build-up, but of course this technique usually requires the aid of another person (or persons).

3. The idea of *deep relaxation* is probably the most important in this context; it began with Jacobson (1938; 1939; 1940). If a person is taught to relax deeply, then this involves him in ANS responses which are the opposite to those seen in anxiety. Bodily processes are at rest, rather than mobilized for some nebulous action. Clearly, these two states cannot be simultaneously evident, i.e. the PNS and SNS cannot be simultaneously dominant. Relaxation has been mainly used in the treatment of phobias. Wolpe (for example 1961) introduced the notion of *systematic desensitization*. This requires the construction of a hierarchy of situations which are increasingly threatening to the individual. Over the course of about one and a half hours of 15-minute sessions, the deeply relaxed patient is asked to imagine these situations. The weakest scene is presented first and repeated until it is reported that no anxiety is experienced while it is being thought of. The hierarchy is gradually worked through in this way. With any one patient, several hierarchies may be involved.

The learning theory approach to neurotic anxiety has produced an interesting therapeutic technique, but what of its success? Eysenck (1965) suggests that *any* therapy is successful in about 40 per cent of cases. Using techniques such as have just been described, Lazarus (1963; 1965) and Wolpe (1958) have achieved remission in 90 per cent of unselected neurotics. Although this is a very promising result and Wolpe asserts that the effects are lasting and that there is no symptom substitution, it has been largely confirmed to specific phobias; it has not been successful in cases of general anxiety neuroses. Perhaps Eysenck (1976—described earlier) has provided the reason for this lack of success.

A general therapeutic programme

On the basis of his own theory and evidence, Izard (1972) has developed a therapeutic programme which is concerned centrally with emotion. A number of fundamental principles lead him to suggest a new approach to psychotherapy. The principles are as follows, and have mainly been mentioned earlier in this text. (1) Fundamental emotions are innate and universal. (2) Fundamental emotions are recognized and labelled consistently by most people in most cultures. (3) Fundamental emotions provide people with the capacity for a common set of subjective experiences and expressions. (4) Emotional expressions have special communication value since thay are universally recognizable. (5) This communication enhances understanding of subjective experiences and helps in the development of a therapist–client relationship. (6) The experiences and expressions of the fundamental emotions form the basis for understanding complex emotions, cognitions, and actions. (7) Fundamental emotions generate cognitive labels which translate into a common set of meanings.

Izard also analyses typical therapist–client relationships. He characterizes an effective relationship as involving trust and warmth, interest and concern, emotional expression and labelling, an analysis of the role of each emotion in the functioning of the personality, as action-oriented and problem-solving, and as viewing psychotherapy as work, especially in emotion. On the other hand, he sees a poor therapist–client relationship as involving overdependence, morbid curiosity and sexual entanglement, unregulated emotional outbursts, verbalized empathy, intellectuallization, and as seeing psychotherapy as merely a passive tranquilizing.

According to Izard, when patients are in the therapeutic situation they do not tend to characterize their life patterns by speaking of discrete emotions; they normally use general terms and descriptions. He suggests that the aim should therefore be to make this vagueness into discrete emotions. To this end the therapist should administer certain measures of emotion and then develop a hierarchy of situations for each emotion involved in the various problems of adjustment experienced by the patient. If the discrete emotions are not generally available, then hierarchies involving stress broadly conceived might be used instead.

Having made such analyses, the therapist should put the patient through a series of exercises which involve relaxation, the visualization of important life situations, and an attention to international emotional signals. He should also check the involvement of the striate muscles and viscera (with psychophysiological measures) and persuade the patient to imagine increasingly difficult situations. Izard feels that this procedure would allow a delineation to be made of whatever discrete emotions were involved in the patient's problems. It would also allow him to assess whether or not the patient receives usable signals from the striate muscles.

Moving on to the matter of emotional control, Izard suggests that any component of emotion or subsystem of personality is potentially usable. However, he feels that the best policy is to attempt to use those which relate to the striate muscles, particularly those concerned with facial expression and posture, since these can initiate, enhance, inhibit, or truncate an emotion. One possibility, for example, is to generate one emotion which will inhibit another. He suggests two ways in which this might be achieved. (1) Selective relaxation to inhibit unwanted aspects of expression. (2) Role-playing or therapist–client interactions. He also mentions the techniques described above of counter-conditioning, self-assertion, and desensitization as useful adjuncts.

There are two alternatives in Izard's view when dealing with a complex condition such as anxiety. It can be analysed into the discrete emotions involved, or it can be treated in a global way with behaviour therapy, although he argues that the latter by itself is not enough. For example, where the emotion process is incomplete or the neuromuscular component is dissociated from it, autonomic conditioning might be necessary.

In particular, Izard sees emotion as an important means of the control of emotion, again, for example, using one emotion to inhibit another. Also, cognitive control may be achieved by imaginal activity. Overall, he argues that it is best to have a combination of neuromuscular, emotional, and cognitive control.

Izard outlines two main principles which normal personalities can use to increase their spontaneity and effectiveness (a point which will be returned to in Chapter 10) and which therapeutic programmes should employ. (1) Each experience of emotion has an inherently adaptive aspect, so the adaptive action involved should be executed. (2) Emotional control can be achieved by the appropriate integration of emotion, cognition, and the motor.

Concerning the integration of emotion, Izard argues that the therapist should work with stressful situations, in an attempt to move towards relief and once again an analysis of what is involved into discrete emotions. The patient should be taught whatever is essential for understanding the natural process of emotion, and also about bodily signals, particularly those which come from the striate muscles. He can use these in the control of his emotions either to relax or to assume postures (facial) other than those which he would normally in a given situation. Alternatively, the patient could be put through the enactment of a series of mildly emotion-provoking situations whilst engaging in progressive relaxation—a procedure which has clear foundations in progressive relaxation and desensitization.

Hence the first stage in therapy is for the patient to develop these skills. Then he should be trained to allow the signals from the striate muscles to impel and guide his actions (both verbal and behavioural). This will inhibit the build-up of tension and so serve an adaptive function. Note that Izard is here advocating training, so he is straightforwardly saying that the use of cues from the striate muscles can be learned.

Izard's general point is that if emotional expression or action is suppressed or postponed, then there is an increased likelihood of maladaptive functioning. Vicious circles are set up which may be exacerbated by repression. Therapy then takes the essential form of enacting more and more emotional situations in appropriate ways.

In his rather radical ideas for emotionally based therapy, Izard is working towards the concept of an optimum personality. He seems to hold a concept of personality and behaviour which is very similar to self-actualization. He views all the subsystems in his theory of personality as being free to interact so as to capitalize on all their various inherently adaptive aspects. But in this free-wheeling system emotion is given the most important role.

In the development of the optimum personality, Izard believes five processes to be involved. (1) Emotional experience. (2) The differentiation in awareness of the discrete emotions. (3) Emotional expression. (4) Action which follows from the inherent adaptiveness of an emotion. (5) The optimal integration of emotion with cognitions and interactions between persons and the person and his environment. To allow Izard his own final word: 'Personality functioning is optimally effective when the person's goal and the cognitive and motor processes constituting the goal-directed activities are congruent with the underlying emotional processes which initiate, sustain and guide the effort'.

CONCLUSIONS

The aim of this chapter has been to give an idea of recent research and thought in the area of abnormal emotion. As pointed out in the introduction, the coverage of material has of necessity been somewhat restricted and, no doubt, a little biased. Anxiety and depression were dealt with in some detail, since they are the sometimes abnormal emotional complexes to which most attention has been given. They typify the field of abnormal emotion in general. If the various problems which surround these fields cannot be solved, then it is unlikely that they will be solved more generally. It is clear that these problems—ranging from definition to explanation—have not yet been solved, although there has been a plethora of work on both topics. Perhaps the main problem is that, like work on the normal emotions, research in this field has been carried on at several different levels at once, with little attempt, other than Izard's, to put them together.

Some conclusions can be drawn. For example, it would seem that there are two sorts of anxiety: (1) trait—enduring, a personality characteristic; (2) state—transient, situational-bound. In the extreme, either of these may be described as abnormal or as having pathological effects. Of course, the delineation of what is 'extreme' is arbitrary. Similarly, there would seem to be two sorts of depression: endogenous and exogenous. Although little headway has been made with the former, Seligman's recent work is valuable in accounting for the latter.

On the theoretical side of the coin, there has been little in the way of general theories of abnormal emotion, Gellhorn and Loufbourrow providing the exception; perhaps this is not surprising with such a broad topic. However, there have been some important theories which are rather more circumscribed in their coverage, Eysenck's incubation theory and, again, Seligman's learned helplessness providing the best examples. This picture is repeated when it comes to therapy, work on the behaviour therapy of neurotic anxiety being well established but somewhat limited in its efficacy, and suggestions by Izard being fresh, interesting, and somewhat radical.

Finally, then, the state of understanding of abnormal emotion is not very profound; the only general conclusions which can be drawn are relatively trivial. Sometimes abnormal emotion springs from what, to the individual, are abnormal and extreme external situations, and sometimes it *seems* to come from within. This is further complicated if one considers that in psychopathology the emotions need not be particularly abnormal—if comparisons are made across individuals it might not even be an extension of normal emotion. It is the interaction between the person and his circumstances which is unusual. This may stem from an abnormal environmental situation, and/or from an abnormal constitution which predisposes extreme reactions to relatively mild stimuli. So-called pathological or abnormal emotion is then little more than a corollary to this. Nevertheless it exists and needs to be dealt with, perhaps along the lines suggested by Izard (1972).

10

Overview

The aims of this final chapter are: (1) to summarize the current position in the various approaches which have been made to the study of emotion; (2) to discuss some of the problems which remain unsolved; (3) to present a possible behaviourally based framework within which any analysis of emotion could be made; (4) to speculate a little about some of the implications of attempts at emotional control.

The search for a physiological substrate to emotion has shown both the CNS and the ANS (plus hormonal and chemical change) to be implicated. However, their relative importance remains unclear. Within the CNS, it is the evolutionarily 'older' parts of the brain (mainly the limbic system) which appear to be necessary to emotion. Their precise function and mechanism of action are still obscure. The indirect measures of psychophysiology have led to some well-conducted research on the ANS. However, the evidence for any physiological response patterning is disappointingly slight. All that can be definitely concluded is that the viscera are necessary to emotion.

There are many reasons for the absence of more precise conclusions at the physiological level. As mentioned in Chapter 1, there is the problem of reductionism. It may be inappropriate, particularly in our present state of knowledge, to attempt a reduction of the study of emotion to the physiological level. Also, of course, there is the more obvious reason that emotion may not have an easily interpretable physiological basis. Two more subsidiary but nevertheless cogent reasons are, firstly, that physiological research into emotion has run ahead of theory. It is comparatively more sophisticated and expert. Secondly, with a few exceptions, there has been little rapprochment with the behavioural approach. It is possible, and indeed likely, that a closer working relationship between these two levels of study would be highly productive.

The more cognitive study of emotion has led to some of the most interesting research in the whole field. However, some of the theorizing which lies behind this research is more open to question. The usual position has been based on a hypothetical interaction between physiological factors and cognition. Schachter's work, which is clearly amongst the most significant in this area, suggests that although there is no physiological response patterning, patterns in emotion occur through cognitive labelling. This is possibly an illuminating point, but the general theorizing which backs it up is too speculative. It is difficult to decide whether or not it is useful to consider possible cognitive elements in emotion (this will be discussed further below). It may be that it provides an appropriate way of conceptualizing the milder aspects of emotion if not the more intense. In any case, it is clear that the most promising ideas are to be found in Izard's far-reaching work. Behavioural research on emotion has been methodologically sounder than any other study of emotion, with the possible exception of work on emotional expression. Definitions have been precise and operations. There has recently been a great proliferation of research within both Hullian and Skinnerian frameworks. However, there are some rather naive, half-explanatory, half-descriptive concepts to be found in this area, 'emotionality' for example. Also, although the behavioural approach has been highly productive of data, it has led to little in the way of grand theory. Of course, it can be argued that such theorizing is unnecessary. However, those with a behavioural approach can be questioned as to whether they are dealing with emotion at all. Data are sometimes gathered in so rarified an atmosphere that they seem far removed from emotion as it is more commonly conceived.

Work on the phenomenology of emotion has been almost entirely concerned with theoretical speculation concerning the nature of emotional experience. Cogent analyses have been made by philosophers, existential psychologists, and, of course, by phenomenological psychologists. The main problem with this approach is not, as might be expected, that of whether or not subjective experience should be assigned a causal role in emotion. Rather, it is one of attempting a rapprochement between phenomenological analysis and the empirical methods of conventional scientific psychology. There is some hope that this might be possible.

Analysis of the course of emotional development falls into two very distinct types. There has been some research with human subjects. Methodologically it has usually been poor, and theoretically it has tended to be speculative and subjective. Research using infrahuman subjects has been more in evidence, probably because of the obvious ethical objections to manipulating the emotions of infants. It has usually taken the form of giving young animals extra or restricted experience and observing the effects of this on adult emotional behaviour. These two very different approaches to emotional development point to surprisingly similar contributory factors. For example, early experience is clearly important to later emotional development, although it interacts with genetic factors. In some species, there is evidence for the importance of critical periods in emotional development. Also, the establishment, maintenance, and possible breaking of (affectional) bonds to both people and places is of prime importance, indicating the possible usefulness of analysis in terms of novelty and strangeness. There is a straightforward need in this area of study for well-conceived and well-conducted investigations with children. However, the problem which it is particularly difficult to overcome is that of artificiality. With children this involves the meaningful manipulation of realistic 'emotional' situations, and with animals it is the usual question of relevance, which appears intensified from the developmental viewpoint.

The topic of the expression and recognition of emotion has recently inspired some interesting research, both psychologically and ethologically. Some of this is promising at the level of observation and description rather than explanation. However, much of the theoretical structure which underlies this research is concerned with possible factors and dimensions of emotional expression. The status of such analysis is awkward to place; it may be that semantic problems are simply being studied indirectly. Of course, the study of the semantics of emotion is important in its own right, but the extent to which it is implicated in problems of expression and recognition remains to be seen. Again, this area of study is plagued by the problem of devising investigations which are representative of real-life emotion. From this viewpoint, photographs, films, and tape-recordings may not be providing adequate material. The expression and recognition of emotion in a social context is self-evidently a very rapid and intricate process in everyday life. At present, we do not understand its determinates.

However, Izard's work has pointed to the extreme importance of emotional expression and he has demonstrated very convincingly the central role which it should be accorded in conceptualizations of emotion.

Although covering a very broad area, the study of abnormal emotion has been less productive of fundamental research than any other aspect of emotion. It is well exemplified by research and ideas concerning anxiety and depression. Both terms have been used in description and explanation, have been given many definitions, and have been studied from numerous viewpoints. In spite of this, it is not possible to draw any firm conclusions about the determinants of these conditions or even about the most productive way in which they might be studied, although Seligman's work on depression is perhaps the exception to this. Also, some of the theoretical contributions by Eysenck to the under-standing of neurosis and by Izard to the possibilities of emotional therapy are well-conceived and far-reaching. In sum, it may be that the study of abnormal emotion should not proceed in any way distinct from the study of 'normal' emotion. Presumably, they each represent an aspect of an individual's inter-action with his environment and might be more parsimoniously regarded as dependent on just one set of determinants.

In drawing together these areas of study and approaches to emotion, the salient feature seems to be that each investigator has focused on one aspect of the subject and tended to go no further. This is also reflected in the many theories of emotion. They are physiological, cognitive, behavioural, or experiential, or sometimes any two of these, but with the exception of Izard's and possibly Mandler's, never cover all aspects. This is also evident in the huge array of research which has developed from these theories. Perhaps because they are biased according to the predilections of their exponents, most theories of emotion are lacking in some way. Some are too narrow, other too broad; some move hardly at all from empirical data, others are too speculative.

A CONCEPTUAL FRAMEWORK

In preparing the second edition of this book my first thought was to omit the present section, feeling that its behavioural bias would not give a true reflection of the current emphases in emotion; these appear to become increasingly 'cognitive'. However, second thoughts made it clear that it still seemed viable as a conceptual framework, within which it is perfectly possible to take account of more cognitive viewpoints. It is a prescription for conceivable research strategies. The aim is not to present a theory or model of emotion, but a framework within which it would seem possible to study emotion in a reasonably systematic way. At best, it can perhaps be regarded as notes towards a definition of emotion.

Any stimulus can have two effects on behaviour. Firstly, it can act as a reinforcing stimulus for whatever behaviour immediately precedes it in time. That is, it makes that behaviour either more or less likely to occur on similar occasions in the future. This is a straightforward instrumental effect. Secondly, the *same* stimulus may elicit some immediate response or set of responses from the organism. It is this second type of response, the simplest form of which is a Pavlovian reflex, which is of interest here and which I would like to define as emotional. Whether such a response is unconditioned or conditioned is immaterial, although perhaps of significance for the course of emotional development. Some stimuli will clearly have built-in, unconditioned effects; others, the majority, will have similar but conditioned effects. From the viewpoint of emotional reactions, it is argued that the intensity or magnitude of these effects is of more significance than whether they are conditioned or unconditioned. If *any* stimulus is regarded as having some effect, albeit a very mild one in some instances, this may reasonably suggest that any aspect of our behaviour or life has some emotional colouring. Intuitively, this would seem plausible.

If emotion is defined in this way, there are a number of implications as to its measurement. Direct measurement might be made at any or all of the usual three levels, behavioural (for example elicited aggression), physiological (for example changes in the ANS), and subjective (for example verbal report of experience and feelings). Also, of course, indirect measures can be taken of the effects of elicited emotion on ongoing instrumental behaviour (for example work stemming from double-runway studies or conditioned emotional responding). Such effects might elevate or depress the ongoing (rate of) behaviour. Either way, this might be enhancing or disrupting performance. In some situations an increased rate or vigour of response is preferable; in others a decreased rate or vigour. In this context 'preferable' means leading to positive stimuli or away from negative stimuli more efficiently, i.e. at less cost to the organism.

The question which should be asked about this formulation is how well the existing facts of emotion can be fitted to it. The general answer, I think, is that they accord quite well. Consider, for example, the somewhat elusive concept of emotionality. In terms of the present idea, this might be defined as an inherited predisposition to respond in particular (emotional) ways to certain stimuli. It refers to what could be called response style. It is mainly a genetically determined factor which ensures that individuals respond differentially to the same stimulus. Extending the argument, emotional development becomes a matter of changing the degree to which particular stimuli have emotional effects and the association (in the Pavlovian sense) of those which have very weak effects with those which have stronger effects. When this process goes wrong, the result may be so-called pathological emotion. For example, there may be 'strong', vigorous, high-probability responses to stimuli which would only elicit 'weak' responses from normal persons. This point of view permits us to avoid the explanatory use of ill-defined concepts such as anxiety. Instead, attention is directed to the determinants of particular responses and types of response, some of which may be conveniently described by terms like anxiety. Any knowledge of abnormal (or, indeed normal) emotion would then accrue from an elucidation of the relationship between emotion-eliciting stimuli and emotional responses, a major part of which would depend on the individual's past history.

The strictly behavioural approach to emotion is clearly in accord with the present definition; it is implicit in work on frustration and elation and CERs. Normally, in this field, emotion has not been studied directly, but rather its *effects* on ongoing instrumental behaviour have been recorded. There is a need for the direct measurement of emotion (physiologically, behaviourally, and, with human subjects, subjectively) in runways, Skinner boxes and their analogues. Similarly, the problem of emotional expression also falls within this proposed framework—it is but one type of emotional response to stimuli which in this case are mainly social. Of more interest, perhaps, is the question of the recognition of emotional expression. I would suggest that this is a quite distinct matter which is best pursued by the social psychologist with whatever techniques he has available. It is taking a measure of emotion as itself a determinant of social behaviour and as such has little to do with the problems of emotion itself, although it may well have therapeutic implications.

A consideration of possible cognitive factors in emotion is a little more difficult to make, since it seems to imply a very different approach to the subject. The main problem is whether or not cognitive or subjective factors are assigned a causal role in emotion; do cognitive appraisals cause emotion? do subjective experiences of emotion lead to its overt expression? These questions might be avoided by studying the stimuli and responses which are involved. For example, in Schachter's original studies, the stimuli provided by his euphoric and angry stooges would have certain emotional effects, and not surprisingly these could be made to depend on an artificial manipulation of the physiological state of the subjects. It is unnecessary to invoke cognitions to account for 'euphoric' and 'angry' stimuli having differential effects. Of course, this is not an attempt to say that cognitions or subjective experiences do not exist, but rather to deny them a necessary function, and also to suggest that there are more productive, less debatable ways of studying emotion. As has already been pointed out, the present framework is a perfectly valid one within which to ask questions about subjective feelings and cognitions, but these are seen as part of emotion itself rather than as underlying conditions. Also, under some circumstances a stimulus (perhaps a mild one) might have some of its emotional effects more cognitively than in any other way. And, as the organism is dynamic rather than static, changed cognitions might affect *subsequent* emotional responses.

Equally, physiological or behavioural changes could affect one another, or cognition, a viewpoint well in accord with Izard's theory.

Giving any stimulus the dual role of strengthening or weakening responses emitted by the organism and eliciting emotional responses has much in common with the original rationalist doctrine. However, it carries no implications about free will or choice. Man is not regarded as striving to overcome his 'baser' emotions with 'purer', rational behaviour. All of his behaviour is simply viewed as categorizable in these two ways. Such a definition allows emotions or emotional reactions to be intense or mild, long or short lived, and disruptive or enhancing in their effects on instrumental (rational?) behaviour. No claim is made for this as a grand theory of emotion. It is a somewhat self-evident way of defining emotion and hence of structuring any study which is made of it. It has two important implications. Firstly, that any theory, and hopefully whenever possible any research, whould take into account *all* of the measures of emotion and also its *effects*. Secondly, it promotes a focusing of attention on the characteristics (qualities) of stimuli and on the relationship between stimulus and response. Although this sounds like a thoroughly behavioural (or even behaviouristic) way of viewing emotion, I would suggest that it is not. The main argument is that our knowledge of emotion should be gleaned from all sources, thus bringing us back to emotion in its everyday richness.

EMOTION CONTROL

The point of this final section is to speculate a little about the possible education of the emotions. Although largely ignored by experimental psychologists, some theorists have been turning their thoughts to it. Certainly it seems to be a topic which has considerable ramifications, especially for therapy in the widest sense of the term.

Leeper (1970) suggests that emotions are perceptions of various life situations. He holds that one implication of this view is that society should give some attention to moving into an age in which we concentrate on the emotions.

Leeper argues that man has passed through two great ages. In the first he learned very slowly the techniques which allowed him to cope with the simple but nevertheless huge problems of physical survival. Having done this, he entered into an age of rapid scientific, technological, and educational advance. In this second age the emphasis in Leeper's view has been placed on the value of objectively based knowledge. The individual has been taught to be self-effacing in the presence of what he has been taught to think of as objective reality. Traditionally, emotions have been seen as obstructing this ideal. Leeper points out that the distinction has been made between intellectual and emotional functioning, and that the latter has been suppressed in favour of the former. If we are reacting emotionally, then we cannot be aware of what is thought to be objective reality.

Within the context of emotion as motivation, Leeper believes that the outcome of the second age of man has been an emphasis on what Leeper terms negative emotional motives such as shame and insecurity, whilst dwelling only on very crude positive emotional motives. He suggests that one way out of this (undesirable) state of affairs is that a third age of man be developed in which due recognition is given to the fact that people experience situations emotionally. Then society, or its educators, would be in a position to concentrate on subtle emotional reactions and place any activities, however simple they might be, on a *positive* emotional basis. Leeper does not suggest how this might be done, but believes that he has taken the first step by pointing out that emotion is not merely a hindrance to objectivity but exists in its own and very significant right.

Peters, (1970), whose basic view of emotion was discussed in Chapter 5, provides a more substantial argument than Leeper in favour of educating the emotions. He regards educating the emotions to be primarily a moral concern. He suggests that from the everyday viewpoint many emotions are also seen as virtues or vices, pity and envy for example. He holds that education implies the introduction of people to knowledge and understanding, to what is valuable, and to the pursuit of truth. Thus, he who is concerned with the education of the emotions inevitably in Peters' view assumes a moral standpoint; he sees some emotions as 'better', more worthwhile, more to be sought after, than others.

Taken at its face value, Peters' argument would seem to imply that emotional education is beyond the scope, or perhaps even the competence, of the psychologist or indeed of the phenomenologist. However, Peters points to two ways in which the psychologist would have something useful to offer. First, on the basis of research, the psychologist should be able to say what people do and what they experience, and hence, to an extent what they are *capable* of doing and experiencing. If, for example, it is decided on the basis of proper research that it is inevitable that people experience anger or rage from time to time (a point which has certainly not been established as yet), then it becomes pointless to try to teach them not to. The emphasis could instead be on training them to be enraged at particular times and with particular people. Second, Peters maintains that those psychologists who are concerned with abnormal behaviour should be in a fair position to make evaluative pronouncements about the various emotions. Some emotions are more appropriate for healthy development than others, some should be avoided as far as is possible, the experience of certain emotions might be seen as basic to a normal development of other emotions, and so on.

Education of appraisals

As was described in Chapter 5, Peters' view of emotion is that it hinges on a process of cognitive appraisal. He suggests that when such appraisals are complex they subsume *belief*. For example, my fear of someone might be based on the belief that he intends to do me some harm. The belief might well be mistaken. Peters therefore argues that one way in which the emotions might be educated is to make certain that people do not make appraisals which are based on mistaken beliefs.

To train people in this way is more easily said than done. Like Arnold, Peters regards emotional appraisals as rapid immediate occurrences, which will naturally make them difficult to handle. Also, if someone is in a particular mood, then this may bias, on false grounds, any appraisal that he makes. Peters' answer to this sets him somewhat against Leeper, in that he suggests that it comes from training in objectivity, which he views in some way synonymous with truth. In a sense, Peters is ducking out of the problem by suggesting that the emotions can be educated by educating rational, objective thought. He believes that it is the psychoanalysts who have taken us furthest along this path. Although he suggests that what the psychoanalysts do can be characterized as a reeducation of the emotions, it can also be seen as an educated suppression of the emotions in favour of what is regarded as more objectively based behaviour.

However, to go along with Peters for the moment, one aspect of the education of appraisals which he deems to be important is *sincerity*. This follows on well from his delineation of the aims of education. If an educator is concerned with knowledge and the pursuit of truth, then he is obviously concerned with sincerity. If people are insincere in their emotions, then the truth is obscured. But Peters makes no prescriptions as to how sincerity in emotion might best be trained.

At this point it is worth mentioning briefly that Arnold (1969) also makes a few suggestions about the education of intuitive, emotional appraisals. She simply holds that it is possible to reduce the intensity of either pleasant or unpleasant emotions and that we do this by the use of imagination, on which, in her terms, our emotional appraisals depend. For example, Arnold believes that we can learn to dwell on only the positive aspects of something which we dislike or which is generally unpleasant to us. Or that we can learn to live without some pleasure which we covet. But Arnold offers no precise directions as to how these ends are, or might be, met.

Education of passivity

Recalling the previous discussion of Peters' view of emotion, a second important element in it is passivity. He believes that emotions overcome us, passively, and that we can therefore do little to stop this. He regards this as being particularly the case with the more primitive appraisals, which overwhelm us completely, thoroughly distorting our perceptions and judgments, even our self-perceptions and self-judgments.

Peters suggests three ways in which education might be applied to these more atavistic emotions. First, use could be made of conditioning or drugs. Peters brackets these together as having the effect of reducing some current condition so that more appropriate educational techniques could be brought into use. However, many psychologists would view conditioning techniques as being directly educational, or that all education could be construed in terms of conditioning.

Second, Peters proposes that a person could be brought to have some insight into his irrational behaviours, which might encourage them to cease. Here, he is in fact referring to what is the avowed aim of much of psychotherapy.

Finally, Peters develops a notion first put forward by Spinoza, namely, that an emotion might best be controlled with another emotion. He suggests that certain appraisals such as that which leads to love or perhaps to empathy make little or no reference to self. If these are developed, then they could well have an overriding function on the other, more primitive, emotions. He argues that to be most effective such appraisals should be developed into settled dispositions or sentiments.

A further way in which passivity in emotion can be controlled, according to Peters, is by developing action patterns to which emotional appraisals can be connected. In this way emotion is turned into motive. Here Peters is suggesting that instead, for example, of being overwhelmed by anger, a man direct his appraisals into a motive which leads to definite action. This implies that positive moral patterns of active emotion should be developed, rather than the vaguely negative one which Peters believes to be currently prevalent.

Peters also raised the interesting question of emotional expression, which he views as a sort of halfway house between the emotion felt and violent action. Thus it is better that we shake and fume and grow red with rage, rather than murder someone. Clearly, much of our social learning is concerned with developing ways of controlling the expression of our emotions, particularly its facial expression, so that it becomes socially acceptable. Here is an obvious way in which emotions can be educated, and yet very little is known about such education. For example, nothing is known of the effects of extreme control, almost suppression, of emotional expression. Does it lead to a reduced capacity to *experience* emotion, or not?

Peters then expresses clear and well thought out ideas on the various ways in which the education of the emotions might take place, and on the general importance of the aim. Naturally enough, however, Peters' views are couched in the terms of his general theory of emotion. This results in his ideas for educating the emotions having little to do with the emotions directly, but being more concerned with the training of the various alternatives to emotional reaction. The one exception to this is when he speaks of the education of emotional expression. This, of course, is a perfectly valid view, but one which can be contested on the grounds that it is a way round the problem, rather than an attempt at direct solution. It is an updating of the traditional contrast between emotion and reason, and a concomitant devaluation of emotion. There would seem to be no need to devalue emotion, but rather to recognize it as an important and significant aspect of human experience and functioning and therefore to work with its education directly. However, in spite of their points of contrast, both Leeper and Peters have provided a good general case for educating the emotions.

Finally, it is clear that the views expressed above are in close accord with Izard's ideas concerning emotional therapy and education, some of which were mentioned in the last chapter. He argues that the typical aim of socialization in our society is to suppress emotional adaptiveness and even to work against an understanding of the emotions. The pressures are to inhibit certain emotions with the aim of increasing the use of the intellect coupled with a hiding of emotional reactions. The implicit thesis seems to be that truth and knowledge come from reason and intellect, with emotion acting solely as a hindrance to sound perception and judgment. Izard suggests that attitudes such as these make it very difficult to develop a fully integrated personality and also make effective therapy for behavioural (emotional) problems very awkward to pursue.

In their various ways and from their different starting points, it may well be that Leeper, Peters, and Izard are right and that it is important to gain an understanding of, and some degree of effective education of, the emotions, rather than simply trying to hide them away. It is hoped that the present text has made a small contribution to this endeavour.

References

Abelson, R. P., and Sermat, V. (1962). 'Multidimensional scaling of facial expressions', *J. exp. Psychol., 63*, 546–54.

Adelman, H. M., and Maatsch, J. L. (1956). 'Learning and extinction based upon frustration, food reward, and exploratory tendency', *J. exp. Psychol., 52*, 311–15.

Alexander, B. K. (1966). *The Effects of Early Peer-deprivation on Juvenile Behavior of Rhesus Monkey.* Unpubl. doctoral dissn. University of Wisconsin (Quoted in Harlow and Harlow 1970.)

Alexander, F. (1950). *Psychosomatic Medicine. Its Principles and Applications.* Norton, New York.

Allerand, A. M. (1967). *Remembrance of Feelings Past: A Study of Phenomenological Genetics.* Unpubl. doctoral thesis. University of Columbia. (Quoted in Davitz 1969.)

Ambrose, J. A. (1961). 'The development of the smiling response in early infancy', in B. M. Foss (Ed.) *Determinants of Infant Behaviour*, Vol. 1. Wiley, New York.

Amsel, A. (1950). 'The combination of a primary appetitional need with primary and secondary emotionally derived needs', *J. exp. Psychol., 40*, 1–14.

Amsel, A. (1958). 'The role of frustrative nonreward in noncontinuous reward situations', *Psychol. Bull., 55*, 102–19.

Amsel, A. (1962). 'Frustrative nonreward in partial reinforcement and discrimination learning: some recent history and a theoretical extension', *Psychol. Rev., 69*, 306–28.

Amsel, A. (1967). 'Partial reinforcement effects on vigor and persistance: Advances in frustration theory derived from a variety of within-subject experiments', in K. W. Spence, J. T. Spence and N. Anderson (Eds.) *The Psychology of Learning and Motivation: Advances in Research and Theory.* Academic Press, New York, London.

Amsel, A., and Cole, K. F. (1953). 'Generalization of fear motivated interference with water intake', *J. exp. Psychol., 46*, 243–7.

Amsel, A., and Malzman, I. (1950). 'The effect upon generalized drive strength of emotionality as inferred from the level of consummatory response', *J. exp. Psychol., 40*, 563–9.

Amsel, A., and Prouty, D. L. (1959). 'Frustrated factors in selective learning with reward and nonreward as discriminanda', *J. exp. Psychol., 57*, 224–30.

Amsel, A., and Roussel, J. (1952). 'Motivational properties of frustration: I. Effect on a running response of the addition of frustration to the motivational complex', *J. exp. Psychol., 43*, 363–8.

Amsel, A., and Ward, J. S. (1954). 'Motivational properties of frustration: II. Frustration drive stimulus and frustration reduction in selective learning', *J. exp. Psychol., 48*, 37–47.

Amsel, A., and Ward, J. S. (1965). 'Frustration and persistence: Resistance to discrimination following prior experience with the discriminanda', *Psychol. Monogr., 79*, (4, Whole No. 597).

Anastasi, A. (1958). 'Heredity, environment and the question "how?"', *Psychol. Rev., 65*, 197–208.

Anderson, D. C., Cole, J., and McVaugh, W. (1968). 'Variations in unsignalled inescapable preshock as determinants of responses to punishment', *J. comp. physiol. Psychol.*, **65**, (3), Part 2.

Annau, Z., and Kamin, L. J. (1961). 'The conditioned emotional response as a function of the intensity of the US, *J. comp. physiol. Psychol.*, **54**, 428–32.

Argyle, M. (1967). *The psychology of Interpersonal Behaviour.* Penguin, Harmondsworth.

Argyle, M. (1969). *Social Interaction.* Methuen, London.

Argyle, M., and Kendon, A. (1967). 'The experimental analysis of social performance', in L. Berkowitz (Ed.) *Adv. in Exp. Soc. Psychol.*, **3**.

Arieti, S. (1970). 'Cognition and feeling', in M. B. Arnold (Ed.) *Feeling and Emotion.* Academic Press, New York, London. 135–43.

Arnold, M. B. (1945). 'Physiological differentiation of emotional states', *Psychol. Rev.*, **52**, 35–48.

Arnold, M. B. (1950). 'An excitatory theory of emotion', in M. L. Reymert (Ed.) *Feelings and Emotions.* McGraw-Hill, New York.

Arnold, M. B. (Ed.) (1060). *Emotion and Personality* (2 volumes). Columbia Univ. Press, New York.

Arnold, M. B. (1968). *The Nature of Emotion: Selected Readings.* Penguin, Baltimore, U.S.A.; Harmondsworth, England.

Arnold, M. B. (1969). 'Human emotion and action', in T. Mischel (Ed.) *Human Action.* Academic Press, New York, London, 167–97.

Arnold, M. B. (1970a). *Feelings and Emotions: The Loyola Symposium.* Academic Press, New York, London.

Arnold, M. B. (1970b). 'Brain function in emotions: A phenomenological analysis', in P. Black (Ed.) *Physiological Correlates of Emotion.* Academic Press, New York, London.

Aronfreed, J. (1968). *Conduct and Conscious: The Socialization of Internalized Control over Behavior.* Academic Press, New York.

Austin, J. L. (1961). *Other Minds. Philosophical Papers.* Oxford University Press, 44.

Averill, J. R., Opton, E. M. Jr., and Lazarus, R. S. (1969). 'Cross-cultural studies of psychophysiological responses during stress and emotion', *International journal of Psychology*, **4**, 83–102.

Ax, A. F. (1953). 'The physiological differentiation of fear and anger in humans', *Psychosom. Med.*, **15**, 433–42.

Azrin, N. (1956). 'Some effects of two intermittent schedules of immediate and non-immediate punishment', *J. Psychol.*, **42**, 3–21.

Azrin, N. H., and Hake, D. F. (1969). 'Positive conditioned suppression: Conditioned suppression using positive reinforcers as the unconditioned stimuli', *J. exp. Anal. Beh.*, **12**, 167–73.

Azrin, N. H., and Holz, W. C. (1966). 'Punishment', in W. K. Honig (Ed,) *Operant Behavior: Areas of Research and Application.* Appleton-Century-Crofts, New York, 380–447.

Azrin, N. H., Hutchinson, R. R., and Hake, D. F. (1966). 'Extinction-induced aggression', *J. exp. Anal. Beh.*, **9**, 191–204.

Baccelli, G., Guazzi, M., Libretti, A., and Zanchetti, A. (1965). 'Pressoceptive and chemoceptive aortic reflexes in decorticate and in decerebrate cats', *Amer. J. Physiol.*, **208**, 708, 14.

Bannister, D., and Fransella, F. (1971). *Inquiring Man.* Penguin, Harmondsworth, Middlesex.

Bannister, D., and Mair, J. M. M. (1968). *The Evaluation of Personal Constructs.* Academic Press, New York, London.

Bard, P. (1928). 'A diencephalic mechanism for the expression of rage with special reference to the sympathetic nervous system', *Amer. J. Physiol.*, **84**, 490–515.

Bard, P. (1929). 'The central representation of the sympathetic nervous system as indicated by certain physiologic observations', *Arch. Neurol. Psychiat.*, **22**, 230–46.

Bard, P. (1934). 'Emotion 1. The Neuro-humanol basis of emotional reactions', in C. Murchison (Ed.) *Handbook of General Experimental Psychology*. Clark University Press, Worcester.

Bard, P. (1950). 'Central nervous mechanisms for the expression of anger in animals', in M. L. Reymert (Ed.) *Feelings and Emotions: The Mooseheart Symposium*. McGraw-Hill, New York, 211–37.

Bard, P., and Mountcastle, V. B. (1948). 'Some forebrain mechanisms involved in expression of rage with special reference to suppression of angry behaviour', Research Publication, *Assoc. Res. nerv. ment. Dis.*, **27**, 362–404.

Barker, R., Dembo, T., and Lewin, K. (1941). 'Frustration and regression: an experiment with young children', *University of Iowa Studies in Child Welfare*, **18**, No. 1.

Baron, A. (1963). 'Differential effects of fear on anxiety in novel and familiar environments', *Psychol. Rep.*, **13**, 251–7.

Baron, A., and Antonitis, J. J. (1961). 'Punishment and shock as determinants of barpressing behaviour', *J. comp. Physiol. Psychol.*, **54**, 716–20.

Barry, H. III, Wagner, A. R., and Miller, N. E. (1962). 'Effects of alcohol and amobarbital on performance inhibited by experimental extinction', *J. comp. physiol. Psychol.*, **55**, 464–8.

Beatty, W. W., and Schwartzbaum, J. S. (1967). 'Enhanced reactivity to quinine and saccharine solutions following septal lesions in the rat', *Psychon. Sci.*, **8**, 483–4.

Beatty, W. W., and Schwartzbaum, J. S. (1968). 'Consummatory behavior for sucrose following septal lesions in the rat', *J. comp. physiol. Psychol.*, **65**, 93–102.

Beck, A. T. (1967). *Depression: Clinical, Experimental and Theoretical Aspects*. Harper & Row, New York.

Becker, H. S. (1953). 'Becoming a marihuana user', *Amer. J. Sociol.*, **59**, 235–42.

Becker, J. (1974). *Depression: Theory and Research*. Halstead Press. Wiley, New York, London.

Belanger, D., and Feldman, S. M. (1962). 'Effects of water deprivation upon heart rate and instrumental activity in the rat', *J. comp. physiol. Psychol.*, **55**, 220–5.

Beldoch, M. (1964). 'Sensitivity to expression of emotional meaning in three modes of communication', in J. L. Davitz (Ed.) *The Communication of Emotional Meaning*. McGraw-Hill, New York, 31–42.

Berkowitz, L. (1962). *Aggression: A Social Psychological Analysis*. McGraw-Hill, New York.

Bevan, W., Bell, C., and Lankford, H. G. (1967). 'The residual effect of shock upon barpressing for water', *Psychol. Rec.*, **17**, 23–8.

Billingsea, F. Y. (1942). 'Intercorrelational analysis of certain behavior salients in the rat', *J. comp. Psychol.*, **34**, 203–11.

Bindra, D. (1959). *Motivation: A Systematic Reinterpretation*. Ronald Press, New York.

Bindra, D. (1968). 'A neuropsychological interpretation of the effects of drive and incentive-motivation on general activity and instrumental behavior', *Psychol. Rev.*, **75**, 1–22.

Bindra, D. (1969). 'A unified interpretation of emotion and motivation', *Ann. New York. Acad. Sci.*, **159**, 1071–83.

Bindra, D. (1970). 'Emotion and behaviour theory: Current research in historical perspective', in P. Black (Ed.) *Physiological Correlates of Emotion*. Academic Press, New York, London.

Blackman, D. (1966). 'Response rate and conditioned suppression', *Psychol. Rep.*, **19**, 687–93.

Blackman, D. (1967). 'Effects of response pacing on conditioned suppression', *Quart. J. exp. Psychol.*, **19**, 170–4.

Blackman, D. (1968a). 'Conditioned suppression as a function of the behavioral baseline', *J. exp. Anal. Beh.,* **11**, 53–61.

Blackman, D. (1968b). 'Response rate, reinforcement frequency and conditioned suppression', *J. exp. Anal. Beh.,* **11**, 503–16.

Blau, S. (1964). 'An ear for an eye: Sensory compensation and judgments of affect by the blind', in J. L. Davitz (Ed.) *The Communication of Emotional Meaning.* McGraw-Hill, New York, 113–27.

Block, J. (1954). 'Studies in the phenomenology of emotions', *J. Abnorm. Soc. Psychol.,* **54**, 358–63.

Bloemkolb, D., Defares, P., Van Enckevert, G., and Van Gelderen, M. (1971). 'Cognitive processing of information on varied physiological arousal', *Europ. J. Soc. Psychol.,* **1-1**, 31–46.

Bolles, R. C. (1967). *Theory of Motivation.* Harper & Row, New York.

Bonvallet, M., and Allen, M. B. (1963). 'Prolonged spontaneous and evoked reticular activation following discrete bulbar lesions', *Electroenceph. Clin. Neurophysiol.,* **15**, 969–88.

Bousfield, W. I., and Orbison, W. D. (1952). 'Ontogenesis of emotional behaviour', *Psychol. Rev.,* **59**, 1–7.

Bower, G. H. (1962). 'The influence of graded reductions in reward and prior frustrating events upon the magnitude of the frustration effect', *J. comp. physiol. Psychol.,* **55**, 582–7.

Bower, G., and Grusec, T. (1964). 'Effect of prior Pavlovian discrimination training upon learning an operant discrimination', *J. exp. Anal. Beh.,* **7**, 401–4.

Bowlby, J. (1951). *Maternal Care and Mental Health.* World Health Organisation, Geneva.

Bowlby, J. (1953). 'Critical phases in the development of social responses in man', *New Biology,* Vol. 14, Penguin, London.

Bowlby, J. (1960). 'Separation anxiety', *Internat. J. psychoanal.,* **41**, 1–25.

Bowlby, J. (1961). 'Separation anxiety: a critical review of the literature', *J. child Psychol.,* **15**, 9–52.

Bowlby, J. (1969). 'Psychopathology of anxiety: The role of affectional bonds', in M. H. Lader (Ed.) *Studies of Anxiety.* Headley Bros., Ashford, 80–6.

Brackbill, Y. (1958). 'Extinction of the smiling response in infants as a function of reinforcement schedule', *Child Developm.,* **29**, 115–24.

Brady, J. V. (1955). 'The extinction of a conditioned "fear" response as a function of reinforcement schedules for competing behavior', *J. Psychol.,* **40**, 25–34.

Brady, J. V. (1958a). 'The paleocortex and behavioral motivation', in H. F. Harlow, and C. Woolsey (Eds.) *Biological and Biochemical Bases of Behavior.* University of Wisconsin Press, Madison.

Brady, J. V. (1958b). 'Ulcers in "executive" monkeys', *Scient. Amer.,* **199**, 95–100.

Brady, J. V. (1960). 'Emotional behavior', in J. Field, H. W. Magoun and V. E. Hall (Eds.) *Handbook of Physiology,* Vol. III. Williams & Wilkins, Baltimore.

Brady, J. V. (1961). 'Motivation—emotional factors and inter-cranial self-stimulation', in D. E. Steer (Ed.) *Electrical Stimulation of the Brain.* University of Texas Press, Austin, 413–30.

Brady, J. V. (1962). 'Psychophysiology of emotional behavior', in A. Backrach (Ed.) *Experimental Foundations of Clinical Psychology.* Basic Books, New York.

Brady, J. V. (1963). 'Further comments on the gastro intestinal system and avoidance behaviour', *Psychol. Rep.,* **12**, 742.

Brady, J. V. (1970a). 'Emotion: Some conceptual problems and psychophysiological experiments', in M. B. Arnold (Ed.) *Feelings and Emotions: The Loyola Symposium.* Academic Press, New York, London.

Brady, J. V. (1970b). 'Endocrine and autonomic correlates of emotional behaviour', in P.

Black (Ed.) *Physiological Correlates of Emotion*. Academic Press, New York, London.

Brady, J. V. (1975). 'Towards a behavioral biology of emotion', in L. Levi (Ed.) *Emotions: Their Parameters and Measurement*. Raven Press, New York.

Brady, J. V. and Conrad, D. G. (1960). 'Some effects of limbic system self-stimulation upon conditioned emotional behavior', *J. comp. physiol. Psychol.*, **53**, 128–37.

Brady, J. V., and Hunt, H. F. (1955). 'An experimental approach to the analysis of emotional behavior', *J. Psychol.*, **40**, 313–24.

Brady, J. V., and Nauta, W. J. H. (1953). 'Subcortical mechanisms in emotional behavior: affective changes following septal forebrain lesions in the albino rat', *J. comp. physiol. Psychol.*, **46**, 339–46.

Brady, J. V., and Nauta, W. J. H. (1955). 'Subcortical mechanisms in emotional behavior: The duration of affective changes following septal and labenular lesions in the albino rat', *J. comp. physiol. Psychol.*, **48**, 412–20.

Brannigan, C. R., and Humphries, D. A. (1971). 'Human non-verbal behaviour. A means of communication', in N. Blurton-Jones (Ed.) *Ethological Studies on infant Behaviour*. Cambridge University Press, Cambridge.

Bridges, K. M. B. (1932). *The Social and Emotional Development of the Pre-school Child*. Kegan Paul, London.

Brierley, M. (1937). 'Affects in theory and practice', *Internat. Psychoanal.*, **18**, 256–68 (As quoted in Rapaport 1950).

Broadhurst, P. L. (1957a). 'Determinants of emotionality in the rat: I. Situational factors', *Brit. J. Psychol.*, **48**, 1–12.

Broadhurst, P. L. (1957b). 'Emotionality and the Yerkes–Dodson law', *J. exp. Psychol.*, **54**, 345–52.

Broadhurst, P. L. (1959). 'The interaction of task difficulty and motivation: the Yerkes–Dodson law revived', *Acta Psychol.*, **16**, 321–38.

Broadhurts, P. L. (1960). 'Studies in psychogenetics: applications of biometrical genetics to the inheritance of behaviour', in H. J. Eysenck (Ed.) *Experiments in Personality*, Vol. 1. Routledge & Kegan Paul, London.

Broadhurst, P. L. (1967). 'The biometrical analysis of behavioural inheritance', *Sci. Prog. Oxf.*, **55**, 123–9.

Bronson, G. (1965). 'The hierarchical organization of the central nervous system: implication for learning processes and critical periods in early development', *Behav. Sci.*, **10**, 7–25.

Brown, J. J., and Farber, I. E. (1951). 'Emotions conceptualized as intervening variables—with suggestions toward a theory of frustration', *Psychol. Bull.*, **48**, 465–95.

Brown, J. S. (1961). *The Motivation of Behavior*. McGraw-Hill, New York.

Brown, R. (1965). *Social Psychology*. Free Press, New York.

Brown, R. T., and Wagner, A. R. (1964). 'Resistance to punishment and extinction following training with shock or nonreinforcement', *J. exp. Psychol.*, **68**, 503–7.

Bruell, J. H. (1965). 'Mode of inheritance of response time in mice', *J. comp. physiol. Psychol.*, **60**, 147–8.

Bruell, J. H. (1970). 'Heritabiiity of emotional behaviour', in P. R. Black (Ed.) *Physiological correlates of Emotion*. Academic Press, New York, London, 23–35.

Brunswick, D. (1924). 'The effect of emotional stimuli on the gastro-intestinal tone', *J. comp. Psychol.*, **4**, 19–79.

Bugental, J. F. T. (1966). 'Humanistic psychology and the clinician', in L. E. Able and B. F. Reiss (Eds.) *Progress in Clinical Psychology*, Vol. 7. Grune & Stratton, New York, 223–39.

Bull, N. (1951). 'The attitude theory of emotion', *Nerv. Ment. Dis. Monogr.*, No. 81.

Bures, J., and Buresova, O. (1960). 'The use of Leao's spreading depression in the study of inter-hemispheric transfer of memory traces', *J. comp. physiol. Psychol.*, **53**, 558–65.

Buss, A. H. (1961). *The Psychology of Aggression*. Wiley, New York.

Buss, A. H. (1966). *Psychopathology*. Wiley, New York, London.

Buytedjik, F. J. J. (1950). 'The phenomenological approach to the problem of feelings and emotions', in M. L. Reymert (Ed.) *Feelings and Emotions: the Mooseheart Symposium*, McGraw-Hill, New York, 127–41.

Cannon, W. B. (1915). *Bodily Changes in Panic, Hunger, Fear and Rage*, 2nd edn., 1929. Appleton–Century, New York.

Cannon, W. B. (1927). 'The James–Lange theory of emotion; a critical examination and an alternative theory', *Am. J. Psychol.*, **39**, 106–24.

Cannon, W. B. (1931). 'Again the James–Lange and the thalamic theories of emotions', *Psych. Rev.*, **38**, 281–95.

Cannon, W. B. (1932). *The Wisdom of the Body*, 2nd edn., 1939. Norton, New York.

Cannon, W. B. and Britton, S. W. (1927). 'The influence of emotion on medulliadrenal secretion', *Amer. J. Physiol.*, **79**, 433–65.

Cantril, H., and Hunt, W. A. (1932). 'Emotional effects produced by the injection of adrenaline', *Amer. J. Psychol.*, **44**, 300–7.

Carlton, P. L., and Didamo, P. (1960). 'Some notes on the conditioned suppression', *J. exp. Anal. Beh.*, **3**, 255–8.

Cattell, R. B. (1963). 'The nature and measurement of anxiety', *Scient. Amer.*, March. See *Contemporary Psychol.*, 1971. W. A. Freeman, New York, 358–65.

Cattell, R. B., and Scheier, I. H. (1958). 'The nature of anxiety: A review of thirteen multivariate analyses comprising 814 variables', *Psychol. Rep.*, **4**, 351–88.

Cattell, R. B., and Scheier, I. H. (1961). *The Meaning and Measurement of Neuroticism and Anxiety*. Ronald Press, New York.

Child, I. L., and Waterhouse, I. K. (1952). 'Frustration and the quality of performance: I. A critique of the Barker, Dembo and Lewin experiment', *Psychol. Rev.*, **59**, 351–62.

Child, I. L., and Waterhouse, I. K. (1953). 'Frustration and the quality of performance: II. A theoretical statement', *Psychol. Rev.*, **60**, 127–39.

Church, M. (1969). Unpublished study described in Wagner (1969).

CIBA Foundation Symposium 8. (1972). *Physiology, Emotion and Psychosomatic Illness*. Elsevier. Excerpta Medica, Amsterdam, London.

Cline, M. G. (1956). 'The influence of social context on the perception of faces', *J. Pers.*, **25**, 142–58.

Cohen, M. E. (1951). 'The high familial prevalence of neurocirculatory asthenia (anxiety neurosis, effort syndrome)', *Amer. J. hum. Genet.*, **3**, 126–58.

Cohen, P. S. (1967). 'Response suppression as a function of intensity and delay of response-contingent shock'. Paper read at Eastern Psychological Association Meeting (Described by Lyon 1968.)

Coleman, J. (1949). 'Facial expression of emotion', *Psychol. Monogr.*, **63**, 1.

Coles, M. G. H. (1970). 'Individual differences in relation to attention and arousal'. Unpubl. Ph.D. thesis. University of Exeter.

Coulson, G., and Walsh, M. (1968). 'Facilitation of avoidance responding in white rats during a stimulus preceding food', *Psychol. Rep.*, **22**, 1277–84.

Dana, C. L. (1921). 'The anatomic seat of the emotions: a discussion of the James–Lange theory', *Arch. Neurol. Psychiat.*, **6**, 634–9.

Darrow, C. W. (1947). 'Psychological and psychophysiological significance of the electroencephalogram', *Psychol. Rev.*, **54**, 157–68.

Darrow, C. W. (1950). 'Neurophysiological effect of emotion on the brain', in M. L. Reymert (Ed.) *Feelings and Emotions: The Mooseheart Symposium*. McGraw-Hill, New York.

Darrow, C. W., Pathman, J., and Kronenberg, G. (1946). 'Level of autonomic activity and electrocephalogram', *J. exp. Psychol.*, **36**, 355–65.

Darwin, C. R. (1872). *The Expression of Emotions in Man and Animals*. Murray, London.

Davis, H. (1968). 'Conditioned suppression: a survey of the literature', *Psychon. Monogr. Supp.*, **2**, (Whole No. 30).

Davison, G. C. (1968). 'Systematic desensitization as a counter conditioning process', *J. abnorm. Psychol.,* **73**, 91–9.

Davitz, J. L. (1964). *The Communication of Emotional Meaning.* McGraw-Hill, New York.

Davitz, J. L. (1964). 'Personality, perceptual and cognitive correlates of emotional sensitivity', in J. L. Davitz (Ed.) *The Communication of Emotional Meaning.* McGraw-Hill, New York, 57–68.

Davitz, J. R. (1969). *The Language of Emotion.* Academic Press, New York, London.

Davitz, J. R. (1970). 'A dictionary and grammar of emotion', in M. L. Arnold (Ed.) *Feelings and Emotion: The Loyola Symposium.* Academic Press, New York, London, 251–58.

Davitz, J., and Davitz, L. (1959a). 'The communication of feelings by content free speech', *J. Communication,* **9**, 6–13.

Davitz, J., and Davitz, L. (1959b). 'Correlates of accuracy in the communication of feelings', *J. Communication,* **9**, 110–17.

Deaux, E., and Kakolewski, J. W. (1970). 'Emotionally induced increases in effective osmotic pressure and subsequent thirst', *Science,* **169**, 1226–8.

Delgado, J. M. R. (1970). 'modulation of emotions by cerebral radio stimulation', in P. Black (Ed.) *Physiological Correlates of Emotion.* Academic Press, New York, London.

Delgado, J. M. R., Roberts, W. W., and Miller, N. E. (1954). 'Learning motivated by electrical stimulation of the brain', *Amer. J. Physiol.,* **179**, 587–93.

Denenberg, V. H. (1964). 'Critical periods, stimulus input, and emotional reactivity: A theory of infantile stimulation', *Psychol. Rev.,* **71**, 335–51.

Denenberg, V. H., and Kline, N. J. (1964). 'Stimulus intensity vs. critical periods: A test of two hypotheses concerning infantile stimulation', *Canad. J. Psychol.,* **18**, 1–5.

Denenberg, V. H., and Morton, J. R. C. (1962). 'Effects of environmental complexity and social groupings upon modification of emotional behaviour', *J. comp. physiol. Psychol.,* **55**, 242–6.

Denenberg, V. H., and Smith, S. A. (1963). 'Effects of infantile stimulation and age upon behavior', *J. comp. physiol. Psychol.,* **56**, 307–12.

Dennis, W. (1935). 'Experimental test of two theories of social smiling in infants', *J. soc. Psychol.,* **6**, 214–23.

De Toledo, L., and Black, A. H. (1966). 'Heart rate: Changes during conditioned suppression in rats', *Science,* **152**, 1404–6.

Dittman, A. T. (1962). 'The relationship between body movements and mood in interviews', *J. consult. Psychol.,* **26**, 48.

Dittman, A. T., Parloff, M. B., and Boomer, D. S. (1965). 'Facial and bodily expression: A study of receptivity of emotional cues', *Psychiatry,* **28**, 239–44.

Dollard, J., Doob, L. W., Miller, N. E., Mowrer, O. H., and Sears, R. R. (1939). *Frustration and Aggression.* Yale University Press, New Haven.

Douglas, K. J. (1967). 'The hippocampus and behaviour', *Psychol. Bull.,* **67**, 416–22.

Drever, J. (1952). *A Dictionary of Psychology.* Penguin, Harmondsworth.

Ducharme, R., and Belanger, D. (1961). 'Influence d'une stimulation electrique sur le niveau d'activation et la performance', *Canad, J. Psychol.,* **15**, 61–8.

Duffy, E. (1934). 'Emotion: An example of the need for reorientation in psychology', *Psychol. Rev.,* **41**, 184–98.

Duffy, E. (1941). 'An explanation of "emotional" phenomena without the use of the concept "emotion"', *J. gen. Psychol.,* **25**, 283–93.

Duffy, E. (1951). 'The concept of energy mobilization', *Psychol. Rev.,* **58**, 30–40.

Duffy, E. (1962). *Activation and Behaviour.* Wiley, New York, London.

Dusser de Barenne, J. G. (1920). 'Recherches experimentales sur les fonctions du système nerveux central, failes en particulier sur deux chats dont le neopallium a été enlevé', *Arch. Neurol. Physiol.,* **4**, 31–123.

Easterbrook, J. A. (1959). 'The effect of emotion on cue utilization and the organization of behaviour', *Psychol. Rev., 66,* 183–201.

Eibl-Eisbesfeldt, I. (1970). *Ethology — The Biology of Behaviour.* Holt, Rinehart & Winston, New York, London.

Ekman, P. (1965a). 'Communication through nonverbal behaviour: A source of information about interpersonal relationhips', in S. S. Tomkins and C. E. Izard (Eds.) *Affect, Cognition, and Personality.* Springer, New York, 390–442.

Ekman, P. (1965b). 'Differential communications of affect by head and body cues', *J. pers. soc. Psychol., 2,* 726–35.

Ekman, P., and Friesen, W. V. (1967a). 'Head and body cues in the judgement of emotion: a reformulation', *Percept. Mot. Sk., 24,* 711.

Ekman, P., and Friesen, W. V. (1967b). 'Nonverbal behavior in psycholtherapy research', in J. Schlein (Ed.) *Research in Psychotherapy,* Vol. 3. A.P.A., Washington.

Ekman, P., and Friesen, W. V. (1969). 'Non-verbal leakage and clues to deception', *Psychiatry, 32,* 88–106.

Ekman, P., Friesen, W. V., and Ellsworth, P. (1972). *Emotion in the Human Face.* Pergamon, New York, Oxford.

Ellis, N. R. (1957). 'The immediate effect of emotionality upon behavior strength', *J. exp. Psychol., 54,* 339–44.

Elshout, J. J. (1967). 'Computation of factor scores by complete regression', *Technical Reports,* Psychology Laboratory, Amsterdam University. (Quoted in Frijda 1969.)

Epstein, S. (1967). 'Toward a unified theory of anxiety', *Prog. exp. re. pers., 4,* 1–89. Academic Press, New York.

Estes, W. K. (1948). 'Discrimination conditioning: II. Effects of a Pavlovian conditioned stimulus upon a subsequently established operant response', *J. exp. Psychol., 38,* 173–7.

Estes, W. K. (1969). 'Outline of a theory of punishment', in B. A. Campbell and R. M. Church (Eds.) *Punishment and Aversive Behavior.* Appleton-Century-Crofts, New York, 57–82.

Estes, W. K., and Skinner, B. F. (1941). 'Some quantitative properties of anxiety', *J. exp. Psychol., 29,* 390–400.

Ewart, E. (1970). 'The attitudinal character of emotion', in M. L. Arnold (Ed.) *Feelings and Emotion: The Loyola Symposium.* Academic Press, New York, London.

Eysenck, H. J. (Ed.) (1964). *Experiments in Motivation.* Pergamon, Oxford.

Eysenck, H. J. (1965). 'The effects of psychotherapy', *Internat. j. Psychiat.. 1,* 99–142.

Eysenck, H. J. (1967). *The Biological Basis of Personality.* Springfield, Illinois.

Eysenck, H. J., (1969). 'Psychological aspects of anxiety', in M. H. Lader (Ed.) *Studies of Anxiety.* Headley Bros., Ashford, 7–20.

Eysenck, H. J. (1976). The learning theory model of neurosis — a new approach. *Behaviour research and therapy, 14,* 251–267.

Farmer, C. (1967). *Words and Feelings: A Developmental Study of the Language of Emotion in Children.* Unpubl. doctoral thesis. University of Colombia. (Quoted in Davitz 1969.)

Federn, P. (1933). 'Die Ich besetzung bie den Fehlleistungen', *Imago,* 19, 312–38, 433–53. (As quoted by Rapaport 1950.)

Federn, P. (1936). 'Zur Unterscheiding des gesunden und krankhaften', *Narzimus,* 22 5–39. (As quoted by Rapaport 1950.)

Fehr, F. S., and Stern, J. A. (1970). 'Peripheral physiological variables and emotion: The James–Lange theory revisited', *Psychol. Bull., 74,* 411–24.

Felecky, A. M. (1914). 'The expression of emotion', *Psychol. Rev., 21,* 33–41.

Felecky, A. M. (1916). 'The influence of emotions on respiration', *J. exp. Psychol., 1,* 218–41.

Ferrier, D. (1875). The Gornian Lecture. 'Experiments on the brain of monkeys' (second series), *Phil. Trans., 165,* 433–88.

Ferster, G. B. (1958). 'Control of behavior in chimpanzees and pigeons by time out from positive reinforcement', *Psychol. Monogr.*, **72**, 8. (Whole No. 461.)

Festinger, L. (1954). 'A theory of social comparison processes', Human Relations, 7 114–40.

Festinger, L. (1957). *A Theory of Cognitive Dissonance.* Row, Peterson, Evanston, Ill.

Fischer, W. F. (1970). *Theories of Anxiety.* Harper & Row, New York.

Flores d'Arcais. (1961). 'Forming impressions of personality in situations of contrast between verbal and minoric expressions', *Acta Psychol.*, **19**, 494–5.

Folkins, C. H. (1970). 'Temporal factors and the cognitive mediators of stress reaction', *J. person. soc. Psychol.*, **14**, 172–83.

Freeman, G. L. (1948). *Physiological Psychology.* Van Nostrand, New York.

Frijda, N. H. (1953). 'The understanding of facial expression of emotion', *Acta Psychol.*, **9**, 294–362.

Frijda, N. H. (1956). *Het Bergrijpen van Gelaatsexpressies.* Van Oorschot, Amsterdam.

Frijda, N. H. (1958). 'Facial expression and situational cues', *J. abnorm. soc. Psychol.*, **57**, 149–54.

Frijda, N. H. (1969). 'Recognition of emotion', in L. Berkowitz (Ed.) *Advances in Experimental Social Psychology*, **4**, 167–223.

Frijda, N. H. (1970). 'Emotion and recognition of emotion', in M. L. Arnold (Ed.) *Feelings and Emotions: The Loyola Symposium.* Academic Press, New York, London, 241–50.

Frijda, N. H., and Philipszoon, E. (1963). 'Dimensions of recognition of emotion', *J. abnorm. soc. Psychol.*, **66**, 45–51.

Frisch, K. V. (1950). *Bees — Their Vision, Chemical Senses and Language.* Cornell University Press, New York.

Frisch, K. V. (1968). 'Honey bees: Do they use direction and distance information provided by their dancers?', *Science*, **158**, 1072–6.

Frois-Wittman, J. (1930). 'The judgement of facial expression', *J. exp. Psychol.*, **13**, 113–51.

Fulton, J. F. (1951). *Frontal Lobotomy and Affective Behaviour.* Norton, New York. (As quoted by Arnold 1960.)

Fulton, J. F., Pribram, K. H., Stevenson, J. A. F., and Wall, P. D. (1949). 'Interrelations between orbital gyrus, insula, temporal tip, and anterior cingulate', *Trans. Amer. neurol. Assoc.*, **74**, 175–9.

Funkenstein, D. H., King, S. H., and Drolette, M. E. (1957). *Mastery of Stress.* Harvard University Press, Cambridge, Mass.

Geller, I. (1960). 'The acquisition and extinction of conditioned suppression as a function of the base-line reinforcer', *J. exp. anal. Behav.*, **3**, 235–40.

Gellhorn, E. (1964). 'Motion and emotion: The role of proprioception in the physiology and pathology of the emotions', *Psychol. Rev.*, **71**, 457–72.

Gellhorn, E. (1968). *Biological Foundations of Emotion.* Scott, Foresman, Glenview, Ill.

Gellhorn, E., and Loufbourrow, G. N. (1963). *Emotions and Emotional Disorders.* Hoeber, New York.

Giorgi, A., (1970). *Psychology as a Human Science: A Phenomenologically Based Approach.* Harper & Row, New York.

Gladstones, W H. (1962). 'A multidimensional study of facial expression of emotion', *Austral. J. Psychol.*, **14**, 95–100.

Glickman, S. E., and Schiff, B. B. (1967). 'A biological theory of reinforcement', *Psychol. Rev.*, **74**, 81–109.

Goldman, R., Jaffa, M., and Schachier, S. (1968). 'Yom kippur, Air France, dormitory food and the eating behavior of obese and normal persons', *J. person. soc. Psychol.*, **10**, 117–23.

Goldstein, D., Fink, D., and Mettee, D. R. (1972). 'Cognition of arousal and actual arousal as determinants of emotion', *Journal of Personality and Social Psychology*, **21**, 41–51.

Goldstein, K. (1951). 'On emotions: considerations from the organismic point of view', *Journal of Psychology*, **31**, 37–49.

Goldstein, M. L. (1968). 'Physiological theories of emotion: A critical historical review from the standpoint of behavior theory', *Psychol. Bull.*, **69**, 23–40.

Goltz, F. (1892). 'Der Hund ohne Grosshirn', *Pflüg. Arch. ges Physiol.*, **51**, 570–614.

Goodenough, F. L. (1932). 'Expression of the emotions in a blind–deaf child', *J. abnorm. soc. Psychol.*, **27**, 328–33.

Gray, J. A. (1970). 'The psychophysiological basis of introversion-extraversion', *Behavior Research and Therapy*, **8**, 249–66.

Gray, J. A. (1971). *The Psychology of Fear and Stress*. Weidenfeld & Nicolson, London.

Grinker, R. R. Sr. (1953). *Psychosomatic Research*. Norton, New York.

Grinker, R. R. Sr. (1966). 'The psychosomatic aspects of anxiety', in G. D. Spielberger (Ed.) *Anxiety and Behavior*. Academic Press, New York, London, 129–42.

Grinker, R. R. Sr., Miller, J., Sabshin, M. A., Nunn, R., and Nunnally, J. C. (1961). *The Phenomena of Depressions*. Harper (Hoeber), New York.

Grinker, R. R. Sr., and Spiegel, J. P. (1945). *Men under Stress*. Blakiston, Philadelphia. 1961, McGraw-Hill, New York.

Grossman, S. P. (1963). 'Chemically induced epileptiform seizures in the cat', *Science*, **142**, 409–11.

Grossman, S. P. (1964). 'Effects of chemical stimulation of the septal areas on motivation', *J. comp. physiol. Psychol.*, **58**, 194–200.

Grossman, S. P. (1967). *Physiological Psychology*. Wiley, New York, London.

Grossman, S. P. (1970). 'Modification of emotional behaviour by intercranial administration of chemicals', in P. Black (Ed.) *Physiological Correlates of Emotion*. Academic Press, New York, London.

Grusec, J. (1966). 'Some antecedents of self-criticism', *J. pers. soc. Psychol.*, **4**, 244–52.

Guhl, A. M., Craig, J. V., and Mueller, C. D. (1960). 'Selective breeding for aggressiveness in chickens', *Poultry Science*, **39**, 970–80. (Quoted in Bruell 1970.)

Haggard, E. A., and Isaacs, F. S. (1966). 'Micromomentary facial expressions as indicators of ego mechanisms in psychotherapy', in L. A. Gottschak and A. H. Averback (Eds.) *Methods of Research in Psychotherapy*. Appleton-Century-Crofts, New York, 151–92.

Hale, E. D., and Schein, M. W. (1962). 'The behaviour of turkeys', in E. S. E. Hafez (Ed.) *The Behaviour of Domestic Animals*. Bailliere, Tindall & Cox, London.

Hall, C. S. (1934a). 'Emotional behavior in the rat: I. Defecation and urination as measures of individual differences in emotionality', *J. comp. Psychol.*, **18**, 385–403.

Hall, C. S. (1934b). 'Drive and emotionality: factors associated with adjustment in the rat', *J. comp. Psychol.*, **17**, 89–108.

Hall, C. S. (1941). 'Temperament: a survey of animal studies', *Psychol. Bull.*, **38**, 909–43.

Hall, C. S. (1951). 'The genetics of behavior', in S. S. Stevens (Ed.) *Handbook of Experimental Psychology*. Wiley, New York.

Hammond, L. J. (1966). 'Increased responding to CS in differential CER', *Psychon. Sci.*, **5**, 337–8.

Hammond, L. J. (1967). 'A traditional demonstration of the active properties of Pavlovian inhibition using differential CER', *Psychon. Sci.*, **9**, 65–6.

Hammond, L. J. (1968). 'Retardation of fear acquisition by a previously inhibitory CS', *J. comp. physiol. Psychol.*, **66**, 756–9.

Hammond, L. J. (1970). 'Conditioned emotional states', in P. Black (Ed.) *Physiological Correlates of Emotion*. Academic Press, New York, London, 245–59.

Harlow, H. F., and Harlow, M. K. (1962). 'Social deprivation in monkeys', *Sci. Amer.*, **207**, 136–46.

Harlow, H. F., and Harlow, M. K. (1970). 'Developmental aspects of emotional behaviour', in P. R. Black (Ed.) *Physiological Correlates of Emotion*. Academic Press, New York, London, 37–58.

Harlow, H. F., and Stagner, R. (1933). 'Psychology of feelings and emotions. II. Theory of emotions', *Psychol. Rev.*, **40**, 184–94.

Harlow, H. F., and Zimmerman, R. R. (1959). 'Affectional patterns in the infant monkey', *Science*, **130**, 421–32.

Harris, V. A., and Katkin, E. S. (1975). 'Primary and secondary emotional behaviour: An analysis of the role of autonomic feedback on affect, arousal and attribution', *Psychological Bulletin*, **82**, 6, 904–916.

Harrower, M., and Grinker, R. R. Snr. (1946). 'The stress tolerance test: preliminary experiments with a new projective technique utilizing both meaningful and meaningless stimuli', *Psychosom. Med.*, **8**, 3–15.

Harvey, J. A., Jacobson, L. E., and Hunt, H. F. (1961). 'Long-term effects of lesions in the peptal forebrain on acquisition and retention of conditioned fear', *Amer. Psychol.*, **16**, 449.

Head, H. (1921). 'Release of function in the nervous system', *Proc. Roy. Soc.*, **926**, 184. (As cited in Cannon 1927.)

Hearst, E. (1969). 'Aversive conditioning and external stimulus control', in B. A. Campbell, and M. R. Church (Eds.) *Punishment and Aversive Behavior*. Appleton-Century-Crofts, New York, 235–77.

Hebb, D. O. (1949). *The Organization of Behaviour*. Wiley, New York.

Hebb, D. O. (1955). 'Drives and the CNS (conceptual nervous system)', *Psychol. Rev.*, **62**, 243–54.

Henton, W. W., and Brady, J. V. (1970). 'Operant acceleration during a pre-reward stimulus', *J. exp. anal. Behav.*, **13**, 205–9.

Herrnstein, R. J. (1955). 'Behavioral consequences of the removal of a discriminative stimulus associated with variable-interval reinforcement'. Unpubl. Ph.D. Thesis. Harvard University.

Herrnstein, R. J., and Morse, W. H. (1957). 'Some effects of response independent positive reinforcement on maintained operant behavior', *J. comp. physiol. Psychol.*, **50**, 461–7.

Hess, E. H. (1959). 'The relationship between imprinting and motivation', in M. R. Jones (Ed.) *Nebraska Symposium on Motivation*. University of Nebraska Press, Lincoln, Neb.

Hess, E. H. (1962a). 'Ethology: an approach toward the complete analysis of behavior', in *New Directions in Psychology*, Vol. 1. Holt, Rinehart & Winston, New York.

Hess, E. H. (1962b). 'Imprinting and the "critical period" concept', in E. L. Bliss (Ed.) *Roots of Behavior*. Harper & Bros., New York.

Hess, W. R. (1936). 'Hypothalamus und die Zentien des autonomen nerveu systems: Physiologie', *Arch. Physhiat. Nerveuk*, **104**, 548–57.

Hess, W. R. (1949). *Das Zeisdenhirn: Syndrome Lokalizationen, Funktionen*. Schwabe, Basel.

Hess, W. R. (1954). *Diencephalon: Autonomic and Extrapyramidal Functions*. Grune & Stratton, New York.

Hillman, J. (1960). *Emotion*. Routledge & Kegan Paul, London.

Hillman, J. (1970). 'C. G. Jung's contributions to "Feelings and emotions": Synopsis and implications', in M. B. Arnold (Ed.) *Feelings and Emotions*. Academic Press, New York, London, 125–34.

Hinde, R. A. (1955). 'The following response of moorhens and coots', *Brit. J. Anim. Behav.*, **3** 121–2.

Hinde, R. A., Thorpe, W. H., and Vince, M. A. (1956). 'The following response of young coots and moorhens', *Behav.*, **11**, 214–42.

Hirschman, R. D. (1975). 'Cross modal effects of anticipatory bogus heart rate feedback in a negative emotional context', *Journal of Personality and Social Psychology*, **31**, 13–19.

Hoch, P. H., and Zubin, J. (Eds.) (1950). *Anxiety*. Grune & Stratton, New York.

Hoffman, H. S. (1969). 'Stimulus factors in conditioned suppression', in B. A. Campbell and R. M. Church (Eds.) *Punishment and Aversive Behavior*. Appleton-Century-Crofts, New York, 185–234.

Hoffman, H. S., and Fleshler, M. (1961). 'Stimulus factors in aversive controls: the generalization of conditioned suppression', *J. exp. anal. Beh.*, **4**, 371–8.

Hoffman, H. S., and Fleshler, M. (1965). 'Stimulus aspects of aversive controls: The effects of response contingent shock', *J. Exp. anal. Beh.*, **8**, 89–96.

Hoffman, H. S., Selekman, W. L., and Fleshler, M. (1966). 'Stimulus aspects of aversive controls: long-term effects of suppression procedures', *J. exp anal. Beh.*, **9**, 659–662.

Hohmann, G. W. (1962). 'The effects of dysfunctions of the autonomic nervous system on experienced feelings and emotions'. Paper read at Conference on Emotions and feelings at New School for Social Research, New York. (Quoted by Schachter 1964.)

Hohmann, G. W. (1966). 'Some effects of spinal cord lesions on experienced emotional feelings', *Psychophys.*, **3**, 143–56.

Hull, C. L. (1943). *Principles of Behavior*. Appleton-Century-Crofts, New York.

Hunt, H. F., and Brady, J. V. (1951). 'Some effects of electro-convulsive shock on a conditioned emotional response ("anxiety")', *J. comp. physiol. Psychol.*, **44**, 88–98.

Hunt, H. F., and Brady, J. V. (1955). 'Some effects of punishment and intercurrent anxiety on a simple operant', *J. comp. physiol. Psychol.*, **48**, 305–10.

Hunt, H. F., and Otis, L. S. (1953). 'Conditioned and unconditioned emotional defection in the rat', *J. comp. physiol. Psychol.*, **46**, 378–82.

Husserl, E. (1913). *Ideas* (1962 edition). Collier, New York.

Hyde, T. S., Trappold, M. A., and Gross, D. M. (1968). 'Facilitative effect of a CS for re-inforcement upon instrumental responding as a function of reinforcement magnitude: A test of incentive–motivation theory', *J. exp. Psychol.*, **73**, 423–8.

Isaacson, R. L., Douglas, R. J., and Moore, R. Y. (1961. 'The effect of radial hippo-campal ablation on acquisition of avoidance responses', *J. comp. physiol. Psychol.*, **54**, 625–8.

Isaacson, R. L., and Wickelgren, W. D. (1962). 'Hippocampal ablation and passive avoidance', *Science*, **138**, 1104–6.

Israel, N. R. (1969). 'Levelling-sharpening and anticipatory cardiac response', *Psychosomatic Medicine*, **31**, 499–509.

Izard, C. E. (1960). 'Personality similarity and friendship', *J. abnorm. soc. Psychol.*, **61**, 47–51.

Izard, C. E. (1964). 'The effects of role-played emotion on affective reactions, intellectual functioning and evaluative ratings of the actress', *J. clin. Psychol.*, **20**, 444–6.

Izard, C. E. (1965). 'Personal growth through experience', in S. S. Tomkins, and C. E. Izard (Eds.) *Affect, Cognition and Personality*. Springer, New York, 200–41.

Izard, C. E. (1972). *The Face of Emotion*. Appleton-Century-Crofts, New York.

Izard, C. E., Randall, D., Nagler, S., and Fox, J. (1965a). 'The effects of affective picture stimuli on learning, perception and the affective value of previously neutral symbols', in S. S. Tomkins and C. E. Izard (Eds.), *Affect, Cognition and Personality*. Springer, New York, 42–70.

Izard, C. E., and Tomkins, S. S. (1966). 'Affect and behavior: Anxiety as negative affect', in G. D. Spielberger (Ed.) *Anxiety and Behavior*. Academic Press, New York, London.

Izard, C. E., Wehmer, G. M., Livsey, W., and Jennings, J. R. (1965b). 'Affect, awareness and performance', in S. S. Tomkins and C. E. Izard (Eds.) *Affect, Cognition and Personality*. Springer, New York, 2–41.

Jaanus, H. (1966). *Het Aspect Activiteit by de Beoordeling van Gelaatexpressies*. M.A. Thesis. Amsterdam University. (Quoted in Frijda 1969.)

Jacobson, E. (1932). 'The electrophysiology of mental activities', *Amer. J. Psychol.*, **44**, 677–94.

Jacobson, E. (1938). *Progressive Relaxation*. University of Chicago Press, Chicago.

276

Jacobson, E. (1939). 'Variation of pulse rate with skeletal muscle tension and relaxation', *Annals intenat. Med.*, **12**, 1194.

Jacobson, E. (1940). 'Variations of blood pressure with skeletal muscle tension and relaxation', *Annals internal. Med.*, **13**, 1619.

Jacobson, E. (1951). 'Muscular tension and the estimation of effort', *Amer. J. Psychol.*, **64**, 112–17.

James, W. (1884). 'What is an emotion?', *Mind*, **9**, 188–205.

Jeness, A. F. (1932a). 'Differences in the recognition of facial expressions', *J. genet. Psychol.*, **7**, 192–6.

Jeness, A. F. (1932b). 'The effect of coaching subjects in the recognition of facial expressions', *J. genet. Psychol.*, **7**, 163–78.

Jeness, A. F. (1932c). 'The recognition of facial expressions of emotion', *Psychol. Bull.*, **29**, 324–50.

Johnson, D. L. (1967). 'Honeybees: Do they use the direction information contained in their dance manoeuvre?', *Science*, **155**, 844–7.

Jones, H. E. (1950). 'The study of patterns of emotional expressions', in M. L. Reymert (Ed.) *Feelings and Emotions.* McGraw-Hill, New York.

Jorgensen, E. C., and Howell, R. J. (1969). 'Judged imposed emotional behaviour', *Psychotheraphy: Theory, Research and Practice*, **6**, (3), 161–165.

Kamin, L. J. (1961). 'Trace conditioning of the conditioned emotional response', *J. comp. physiol. Psychol.*, **54**, 149–53.

Kamin, L. J. (1965). 'Temporal and intensity characteristics of the condition stimulus', in W. E. Prokasy (Ed.) *Classical Conditioning.* Appleton-Century-Crofts, New York, 118–47.

Kamin, L. J., Brimer, C. J., and Black, A. H. (1963). 'Conditioned suppression as a monitor of fear of the CS in the course of avoidance training', *J. comp. physiol. Psychol.*, **56**, 202–5.

Kamiya, J. (1969). 'Operant control of the EEG alpha rhythm and some of its related effects on consciousness', in C. Tait (Ed.) *Altered States of Consciousness.* Wiley, New York.

Karabenick, S. A. (1969). 'Effects of reward increase and reduction in the double runway', *J. exp. Psychol.*, **82**, 79–87.

Karas, G. G., and Denenberg, V. H. (1961). 'The effects of duration and distribution of infantile experience on adult learning', *J. comp. physiol. Psychol.*, **54**, 170–4.

Karsten, L. (1965). 'Dimensies van de Gelaatsexpressie: Ein Replicatie met de Marjorie Lightfoot photos', M.A. Thesis. Amsterdam University. (Quoted by Frijda 1969.)

Katkin, E. S., and Murray, E. N. (1968). 'Instrumental conditioning of autonomically mediated behavior', *Psychol. Bull.*, **70**, 52–68.

Kaufman, A., Baron, A., and Kopp, R. E. (1966). 'Some effects of instructions on human operant behavior', *Psychon. monogr. supp.*, **1**, 243–50.

Kelly, A. H., Beaton, L. E., and Magoun, H. W. (1946). 'A mid-brain mechanism for facio-vocal activity', *J. Neurophysiol.*, **9**, 181–9.

Kelly, D. H. W. (1966). 'Measurement of anxiety by forearm blood flow', *Brit. J. Psychiat.*, **112**, 789–98.

Kelly, D. H. W. (1967). 'The technique of forearm plethysmography for assessing anxiety', *J. psychosom. Res.*, **10**, 373–82.

Kelly, D. H. W., and Walter, C. J. S. (1968). 'The relationship between clinical diagnosis and anxiety, assessed by forearm blood flow and other measurements', *Brit. J. Psychiat.*, **114**, 611–26.

Kelly, G. A. (1955). *The Psychology of Personal Constructs*, Vol. 1 and 2. Norton, New York.

Kelsey, J. E., and Grossman, S. P. (1969). 'Cholinmergic blockade and lesions in the ventromedial septum of the rat', *Physiol. Beh.*, **4**, 837–45.

Kennard, M. A. (1955). 'Effect of bilateral ablation of cingulate area on behavior of cats', *J. Neurophysiol.*, **18**, 159–69.

Kety, S. S. (1966). 'Catecholamines in neuropsychiatric state', *Pharmacol. Rev.*, **18**, 787–98.

Kety, S. S. (1970). 'Neurochemical aspects of emotional behaviour', in P. Black (Ed.) *Physiological Correlates of Emotion*. Academic Press, New York, London.

Kimble, G. A. (1961). *Hilgard and Marquis' Conditioning and Learning*. Methuen, London.

King, F. A. (1958). 'Effects of septal and amygdaloid lesions on emotional behavior and conditioned avoidance responses in the rat', *J. nerv. ment. Dis.*, **126**, 57–63.

Klages, L. (1950). 'The life of feeling'. Excerpts from *Grundlegung der Wissenschaft rom Ausdruck*, Bouvrer, 1950. 6th Edn. 1964. Transl. by M. B. Arnold in *The Nature of Emotion* (1968) (Ed. Arnold). Penguin, Harmondsworth.

Klüver, H., and Bucy, P. C. (1937). ' "Psychic blindness" and other symptoms following bilateral temporal lobectomy in rhesus monkeys', *Amer. J. Physiol.*, **119**, 352–3.

Klüver, H., and Bucy, P. C. (1938). 'An analysis of certain effects of bilateral temporal lobectomy in the rhesus monkey, with special reference to "psychic blindness" ', *J. Psychol.*, **5**, 33–54.

Klüver, H., and Bucy, P. C. (1939). 'Preliminary analysis of functions of the temporal lobe in monkeys', *A.M.A. Arch. Neuros. Psychiat.*, **42**, 979–1000.

Knapp, P. H. (1963) (Ed.) *Expression of the Emotions in Man*. International University Press, New York.

Koehler, O. (1954). 'Das Lächeln ab angerborene Ausdrucksbewegung', *Zeitschr. menscht. Vererb-u. Konstitutionslehre*, **32**, 390–8. (Quoted in Schneirla 1959.)

Krause, M. S. (1961). 'The measurement of transitory anxiety', *Psychol. Rev.*, **68**, 178–89.

Krieckhaus, E. E., Simmon, H. J., Thomas, G. J., and Kenyon, J. (1964). 'Septal lesions enhance shock avoidance behavior in the rat', *Exp. Neurol.*, **9**, 107–13.

Krueger, F. (1928). 'The essence of feeling'. Abridged from 'Das Wesen der Gerfühle', *Arch. f. d. ges Psychol.*, **65**, 91–128. Transl. by M. B. Arnold in *The Nature of Emotion* (1968) (Ed. Arnold). Penguin, Harmondsworth.

Lacey, J. I. (1950). 'Individual differences in somatic response patterns', *J. comp. physiol. Psychol.*, **43**, 338–50.

Lacey, J. I. (1956). 'The evaluation of autonomic responses toward a general solution', *Annals N.Y. Acad. Sci.*, **67**, 123–63.

Lacey, J. I., and Lacey, B. C. (1958). 'Verification and extension of the principle of autonomic response stereotypy', *Amer. J. Psychol.*, **71**, 50–73.

Lacey, J. I., and Lacey, B. C. (1970). 'Some autonomic–central nervous system inter-relationships', in P. Black (Ed.) *Physiological Correlates of Emotion*. Academic Press, New York, London.

Lacey, J. I., Kagan, J., Lacey, B. C., and Moss, H. A. (1963). 'The visceral level: Situational determinants and behavioural correlates of autonomic response patterns', in P. H. Knapp (Ed.) *Expressions of the Emotions in Man*. International University Press, New York.

Lader, M. H. (1967). 'Palmer skin conductance measures in anxiety and phobic states', *J. Psychosom. Res.*, **11**, 271–81.

Lader, M. H. (1969a). 'Psychophysiological aspects of anxiety', in M. H. Lader (Ed.) *Studies of Anxiety*. Headley Bros., Ashford, 53–61.

Lader, M. H. (1969b). (Ed.) *Studies of Anxiety*. Headley Bros., Ashford, for the World Psychiatric Association and the Royal Medico-Psychological Association.

Lader, M.H. (1972). 'Psychophysiological research and psychosomatic medicine', in CIBA Foundation Symposium 8, 297–311.

Lader, M. H., and Wing, L. (1964). 'Habituation of the psychogalvanic reflex in patients with anxiety states and in normal subjects', *J. neurol. neurosurg. Psychiat.*, **27**, 210–18.

Lader, M. H., and Wing, L. (1966). *Physiological Measure, Sedative Drugs and Morbid Anxiety*. Oxford University Press, London.

278

Landis, C. (1925). 'Studies of emotional reactions IV: Metabolic rate', *Amer. J. Physiol.*, **74**, 188–203.

Landis, C. (1929). 'The interpretation of facial expression in emotion', *J. genet. Psychol.*, **2**, 59–72.

Landis, C. (1932). 'An attempt to measure emotional traits in juvenile delinquency', in K. S. Lashley *et al.* (Eds.) *Studies in the Dynamics of Behavior*. University of Chicago Press, Chicago.

Landis, C., and Hunt, W. Z. (1932), 'Adrenalin and emotion', *Psychol. Rev.*, **39**, 467–85.

Lange, C. G. (1885). *The Emotions*. Eng. transl. publ. 1922. Williams & Wilkins, Baltimore.

Latane, B., and Schachter, S. (1962). 'Adrenaline and avoidance learning', *J. comp. physiol. Psychol.*, **65**, 369–72.

Lawson, R. (1965). *Frustration*. Macmillan, New York.

Lawson, R., and Marx, M. H. (1958). 'Frustration: Theory and experiment', *Genetic Psychol. Monogr.*, **57**, 393–464.

Lazarus, A. A. (1963). 'The results of behavior therapy in 126 cases of severe neuroses', *Behav. res. Ther.*, **1**, 69–79.

Lazarus, A. A. (1965), 'A preliminary report on the use of directed muscular activity in counter-conditioning', *Behav. res. Ther.*, **2**, 301–3.

Lazarus, A. A. (1972). *Behavior Therapy and Beyond*. McGraw-Hill, New York.

Lazarus, R. S. (1966). *Psychological Stress and the Coping Process*. McGraw-Hill, New York.

Lazarus, R. S. (1968). 'Emotions and adaptation: Conceptual and empirical relations', in W. J. Arnold (Ed.) *Nebraska Symposium on Motivation*. University of Nebraska Press, Lincoln, Nebraska.

Lazarus, R. S., Averill, J. R., and Opton, E. M. Jr. (1970). 'Towards a cognitive theory of emotion', in M. B. Arnold (Ed.) *Feelings and Emotions: The Loyola Symposium*. Academic Press, New York, London, 207–32.

Lazarus, R. S., Deese, J., and Osler, S. F. (1952). 'The effects of psychological stress upon performance', *Psychol. Bull.*, **49**, 293–317.

Lazarus, R. S., and Opton, E. M. Jr. (1966). 'The study of psychological stress: A summary of theoretical formulations and experimental findings', in C. D. Spielberger (Ed.) *Anxiety and Behavior*. Academic Press, New York, 225–62.

Lazarus, R. S., Opton, E. M. Jr., Nomikos, M. S., and Rankin, N. O. (1965). 'The principle of short-circuiting of threat: Further evidence', *J. Person.*, **33**, 622–35.

Lazarus, R. S., Spiesman, J. C.,, Mordkoff, A. M., and Davison, L. A. (1962). 'A laboratory study of psychological stress produced by a motion picture film', *Psychol. Monogr.*, **76**, No. 34. (Whole No. 553).

Lazarus, R. S., Tomita, M., Opton, E. Jr., and Kodama, M. (1966). 'A cross-cultural study of stress-reduction patterns in Japan', *J. person. soc. Psychol.*, **4**, 622–33.

Leeper, R. W. (1948). 'A motivational theory of emotion to replace "emotion as disorganized response"', *Psychol. Rev.*, **55**, 5–21.

Leeper, R. W. (1962a). 'The motivational theory of emotion', in C. L. Stacey and M. F. De Martino (Eds.) *Understanding Human Motivation*. Howard Allen, Cleveland, Ohio, 657–65.

Leeper, R. W. (1962b). 'Learning and the fields of perception, motivation and personality', in S. Koch (Ed.) *Psychology: a Study of a Science*, Vol. 5. McGraw-Hill, New York, 365–487.

Leeper, R. W. (1965). 'Some needed developments in the motivational theory of emotions', in D. Levine (Ed.) *Nebraska Symposium on Motivation*. University of Nebraska Press, Lincoln, Nebraska, 25–122.

Leeper, R. W. (1970). 'Feelings and emotions', in M. D. Arnold (Ed.) *Feelings and Emotions: The Loyola Symposium*. Academic Press, New York, London, 151–68.

Leitenberg, H. (1965). 'Is time-out from positive reinforcement an aversive event? A review of the experimental evidence', *Psychol. Bull.*, **64**, 428–41.

Leitenberg, H. (1966). 'Conditioned acceleration and conditioned suppression in pigeons', *J. exp. anal. Behav.*, **9**, 205–12.

Leitenberg, H., Bertsch, G., and Coughlin, R. (1968). ' "Time-out from positive reinforcement" as the UCS in a CER paradigm with rats', *Psychon. Sci.*, **13**, 3–4.

Leventhal, H. (1974). 'Emotions: A basic problem for social psychology', in C. Nemeth (Ed.) *Social Psychology: Classic and Contemporary Integrations*. Rand-McNally, Chicago, 1–51.

Levine, S. (1956). 'A further study of infantile handling and adult avoidance learning', *J. Pers.*, **25**, 70–80.

Levine, S. (1957). 'Infantile experience and consummatory behavior in adulthood', *J. comp. physiol. Psychol.*, **50**, 609–12.

Levine, S. (1958). 'Noxious stimulation in infant and adult rats and consummatory behavior', *J. comp. physiol. Psychol.*, **51**, 230–3.

Levine, S. (1959). 'Differential emotionality at weaning as a function of infantile stimulation', *Canad. J. Psychol.*, **13**, 243–7.

Levine, S. (1962). 'Psychophysiological effects of infantile stimulation', in E. L. Bliss (Ed.) *Roots of Behavior*. Harper & Bros., New York.

Levine, S. (1965). 'Water consumption: Emotionally produced facilitation or suppression?', *Psychon. Sci.*, **3**, 105–6.

Levine, S., and Lewis, G. W. (1959). 'Critical periods and the effects of infantile experience on the maturation of a stress response', *Science*, **129**, 42–3.

Levitt, E. A. (1964). 'The relationship between abilities to express emotional meanings vocally and facially', in J. L. Davitz (Ed.) *The Communication of Emotional Meaning*. McGraw-Hill, New York.

Levy, P. K. (1964). 'The ability to express and perceive vocal communications of feeling', in J. L. Davitz (Ed.) *The Communication of Emotional Meaning*. McGraw-Hill, New York, 43–55.

Lewinsohn, P. H. (1975). 'A behavioral approach to depression', in R. J. Friedman and M. M. Katz (Eds.) *The Psychology of Depression: Contemporary Theory and Research*. Winston-Wiley, Washington.

Liddell, R. D. (1944). 'Conditioned reflex method and experimental neurosis', in J. McV. Hunt (Ed.) *Personality and the Behavior Disorders*. Ronald Press, New York, 389–412.

Lindholm, B. W. (1962). 'Critical periods and the effects of early shock on later behavior in the white rat', *J. comp. physiol. Psychol.*, **55**, 597–9.

Lindsley, D. B. (1950). 'Emotions and the electroencephalogram', in M. L. Reymert (Ed.) *Feelings and Emotions: The Mooseheart Symposium*. McGraw-Hill, New York.

Lindsley, D. B. (1951). 'Emotion', in S. S. Stevens (Ed.) *Handbook of Experimental Psychology*. Wiley, New York, 473–516.

Lindsley, D. B. (1957). 'Psychophysiology and motivation', in M. R. Jones (Ed.) *Nebraska Symposium on Motivation*. University of Nebraska Press, Lincoln, Nebraska, 44–105.

Lindsley, D. B. (1970). 'The role of nonspecific reticulothalamocortical systems in emotion', in P. Black (Ed.) *Physiological Correlates of Emotion*. Academic Press, New York, London.

Longo, N., Klempay, S., and Bitterman, M. E. (1964). 'Classical appetitive conditioning in the pigeon', *Psychon. Sci.*, **1**, 19–20.

Louch, A. R. (1966). *Explanation and Human Action*. Blackwell, Oxford.

Lubar, J. F. (1964). 'Effects of medial cortical lesions on the avoidance behavior of a cat', *J. comp. physiol. Psychol.*, **58**, 34–6.

Luchins, A. S. (1958). 'Definitiveness of impression and primacy in communications', *J. soc. Psychol.*, **48**, 275–90.

Lykken, D. T. (1957). 'A study of anxiety in the sociopathic personality', *J. abnorm. soc. Psychol.*, **55**, 6–10.

Lyon, D. O. (1963). 'Frequency of reinforcement as a parameter of conditioned suppression', *J. exp. anal. Behav.*, **6**, 95–8.

Lyon, D. O. (1964). 'Some notes on conditioned suppression and reinforcement schedules', *J. exp. anal. Behav.*, **7**, 289–91.

Lyon, D. O. (1968). 'Conditioned suppression: Operant variables and aversive control', *Psychol. Rec.*, **18**, 317–38.

Lyon, D. O., and Felton, M. (1966a). 'Conditioned suppression and variable ratio reinforcement', *J. exp. anal. Behav.*, **9**, 245–8.

Lyon, D. O., and Felton, M. (1966b). 'Conditioned suppression and fixed ratio schedule of reinforcement', *Psychol. Rec.*, **16**, 433–40.

Mahl, G. F. (1950). 'Anxiety, HCL secretion, and peptic ulcer etiology', *Psychosom. Med.*, **12**, 158–69.

Maier, N. R. F. (1949). *Frustration*. McGraw-Hill, New York.

Maierm N. R. F. (1956). 'Frustration theory: restatement and extension', *Psychol. Rev.*, **63**, 370–88.

Malmo, R. B. (1950). 'Experimental studies of mental patients under stress', in M. Reymert (Ed.) *Feelings and Emotions*. McGraw-Hill, New York, 169–80.

Malmo, R. B. (1957). 'Anxiety and behavioural arousal', *Psychol. Rev.*, **64**, 276–87.

Malmo, R. B. (1959). 'Activation: a neuropsychological dimension', *Psychol. Bull.*, **66**, 367–86.

Malmo, R. B., and Heslam, R. M. (1951). 'Blood pressure response to repeated brief stress in psychoneurosis: a study of adaptation', *Canad. J. Psychol.*, **5**, 167–79.

Malmo, R. B., and Shagass, C. (1952). 'Studies of blood pressure in psychiatric patients under stress', *Psychosom. Med.*, **13**, 82–93.

Mandler, G. (1962). 'Emotion', in *New Directions in Psychology*, **1**. Holt, Rinehart & Winston, New York, 269–353.

Mandler, G. (1976). *Mind and Emotion*. Wiley, New York, London.

Maranon, G. (1924). 'Contribution a l'étude de l'action emotive de l'adreoline', *Revue Franc d)Endocrin*, **21**, 301–25. (As quoted in Fehr and Stern 1970.)

Martin, B. (1961). 'The assessment of anxiety by physiological behavioral measures', *Psychol. Bull.*, **58**, 234–55.

Martin, I. (1956). 'Levels of muscle activity in psychiatric patients', *Acta Psychol.*, **12**, 326–41.

Martin, I. (1960). 'Somatic reactivity', in H. J. Eysenck (Ed.) *Handbook of Abnormal Psychology*. University of London Press, London.

Marx, M. H. (1956). 'Some relations between frustration and drive', in M. R. Jones (Ed.), *Nebraska Symposium on Motivation*, University of Nebraska Press, Lincoln, Nebraska.

Marzocco, F. N. (1951). *Frustration Effect as a Function of Drive Level, Habit Strength, and Distribution of Trials During Extinction*. Unpubl. Ph.D. thesis. State University of Iowa. (Cited by Brown, J. S., 1961.) *The Motivation of Behavior*. McGraw-Hill, New York.

Maslow, A. H. (1972). *The Farther Reaches of Human Nature*. Penguin, Harmondsworth, Middx.

Masserman, J. H. (1943). *Behavior and Neurosis*. University of Chicago Press, Chicago.

May, H. S. (1938). 'A study of emotional expression among Chinese and Americans'. Unpubl. master thesis. Colombia University. (Quoted in Davitz 1964.)

Mayer-Gross, W., Slater, E., and Roth, M. *See* Slater and Roth (1969).

Meltzer, D., and Brahlek, J. A. (1970). 'Conditioned suppression and conditioned enhancement with the same positive UCS: an effect of CS duration', *J. exp. anal. Behav.*, **13**, 67–73.

Melzack, R. (1952). 'Irrational fears in the dog', *Canad. J. Psychol.*, **6**, 141–7.

Melzack, R., and Casey, K. L. (1970). 'The affective dimension of pain', in M. B. Arnold (Ed.) *Feelings and Emotions: The Loyola Symposium*. Academic Press, New York, London.

Melzack, R., Penick, E., and Beckett, A. (1959. 'The problem of "innate fear" of the hawk shape: An experimental study with mallard ducks', *J. comp. physiol. Psychol.*, **52**, 694–8.

Mendel, S. J. (1970). *Concepts of Depression*. Wiley, New York, London.

Meyer, P. A., and McHose, J. H. (1968). 'Facilitative effects of reward increase: An apparent "elation effect" ', *Psychon. Sci.*, **13**, 165–6.

Michotte, A. E. (1950). 'The emotions as functional connections', in M. L. Reymert (Ed.) *Feelings and Emotions: The Mooseheart Symposium*. McGraw-Hill, New York.

Miczek, K. A., and Grossman, s. (1971). 'Positive conditioned suppression: effects of CS duration', *J. exp. anal. Behav.*, **15**, 243–7.

Millenson, J. R. (1967). *Principles of Behavioural Analysis*. Macmillan, New York; Collier-Macmillan, London.

Millenson, J. R., and de Villiers, P. A. (1971). 'Motivational properties of conditioned anxiety', in R. M. Gilber and J. R. Millenson (Eds.) *Reinforcement Processes: Schedule Induced and Schedule Dependent Effects*. Academic Press, New York, London.

Miller, G. A., Galanter, E. H., and Pribram, K. H. (1960). *Plans and the Structure of Behaviour*. Holt, New York.

Miller, N. E. (1948). 'Studies of fear as an acquirable drive: I. Fear as motivation and fear-reduction as reinforcement in the learning of new responses', *J. exp. Psychol.*, **38**, 89–101.

Miller, N. E. (1951). 'Learning drives and rewards', in S. S. Stevens (Ed.) *Handbook of Experimental Psychology*. Wiley, New York.

Miller, N. E. (1958). 'Central stimulation and other new approaches to motivation and reward', *Amer. Psychol.*, **13**, 100–8.

Miller, N. E. (1959). 'Liberalization of basic S–R concepts: Extensions to conflict behavior, motivation and social learning', in S. Koch (Ed.) *Psychology: A Study of a Science*, Vol. 2. McGraw-Hill, New York.

Miller, N. E. (1960). 'Learning resistance to pain and fear: effects of overlearning, exposure, and rewarded exposure in context', *J. exp. Psychol.*, **60**, 137–45.

Miller, N. E. (1969). 'Learning of visceral and glandular responses', *Science*, **163**, 434–45.

Miller, N. E., and Stevenson, S. S. (1936). 'Agitated behavior of rats during experimental extinction and a curve of spontaneous recovery', *J. comp. Psychol*, **21**, 205–31.

Miller, R. E., Banks, J. H., and Kuwahara, H. (1966). 'The communication of affects in monkeys: cooperative reward conditioning', *J. genet. Psychol.*, **108**, 121–34.

Miller, R. E., Banks, J. H., and Ogawa, N. (1962). 'Communication of affect in "cooperative conditioning" of rhesus monkeys', *J. comp. physiol. Psychol.*, **5**, 343–8.

Miller, R. E., Banks, J. H., and Ogawa, N. (1963). 'Role of facial expression in "cooperative-avoidance conditioning" in monkeys', *J. abnorm. soc. Psychol.*, **67**, 24–30.

Miller, R. E., Murphy, J. V., and Mirsky, I. A. (1959a). 'Non-verbal communication of affect', *J. clin. Psychol.*, **15**, 155–8.

Miller, R. E., Murphy, J. V., and Mirsky, I. A. (1959b). 'The relevance of facial expression and posture as cues in the communication of affect between monkeys', *Arch. gen. Psychiat.*, **1**, 480–8.

Mirsky, A. F. (1960). 'Studies of the effects of brain lesions on social behavior in *Macaca mulatta*: methodological and theoretical consideration', *Ann. N.Y. Acad. Sci.*, **85**, 785–94.

Mirsky, I. A. (1958). 'Physiologic, psychologic and social determinants in the etiology of duodenal ulcer', *Amer. J. Digest. Diseases*, **3**, 285–314.

282

Mirsky, I. A., Miller, R. E., and Murphy, J. V. (1958). 'The communication of affect in rhesus monkeys: I. An experimental method', *J. Amer. Psychol. Ass.*, **6**, 433–41.

Moltz, H. (1960). 'Imprinting: empirical basis and theoretical significance', *Psychol Bull.*, **57**, 291–314.

Moltz, H., Rosenblum, L., and Halikas, N. (1959). 'Imprinting and level of anxiety', *J comp. physiol. Psychol.*, **52**, 240–4.

Morse, W. E., and Skinner, B. F. (1958). 'Some factors involved in the stimulus control o operant behavior', *J. exp. anal. Behav.*, **1**, 103–7.

Moruzzi, G., and Magoun, H. W. (1949). 'Brain stem reticular formation and activation of the EEG', *Electroenceph. and Clin. Neurophys.*, **1**, 455–73.

Mowrer, O. H. (1939). 'A stimulus–suspense analysis of anxiety and its role as a reinforc ing agent', *Psychol. Rev.*, **46**, 533–65.

Mowrer, O. H. (1959). *Learning Theory and Personality Dynamics.* Ronald Press, New York.

Mowrer, O. H. (1960a). *Learning Theory and Behavior.* Wiley, New York.

Mowrer, O. H. (1960b). *Learning Theory and the Symbolic Processes.* Wiley, New York.

Moyer, K. E. (1965). 'Effect of experience with emotion provoking stimuli on water con sumption in the rat', *Psychon. Sci.*, **2**, 251–2.

Moyer, K. E., and Benninger, R. (1963). 'Effect on environmental change and electric shock on water consumption in the rat', *Psychol. Rep.*, **13**, 179–85.

Munn, N. L. (1946). *Psychology: The Fundamentals of Human Adjustment.* Houghton and Mifflin, Boston.

Murphy, J. V., Miller, R. E., and Mirsky, I. A. (1955). 'Interanimal conditioning in the monkey', *J. comp. physiol. Psychol.*, **48**, 211–4.

Myer, J. S. (1971). 'Some effects of noncontingent aversive stimulation', in *Aversive Conditioning and Learning.* Academic Press, New York, London, 469–536.

MacLean, P. D. (1949). 'Psychosomatic disease and the "visceral brain"', *Psychosom Med.*, **III**, 338–53.

MacLean, P. D. (1945). 'The limbic system and its hippocampal formation: studies in animals and their possible application to man', *J. Neurosurg.*, **II**, 29–44.

MacLean, P. D. (1957). 'Chemical and electrical stimulation of hippocampus in unrestrained animals. II: Behavioral findings', *Arch. Neurol. Psychiat.*, **78**, 128–42.

MacLean, P. D. (1970). 'The limbic brain in relation to the psychoses', in P. D. Black (Ed.) *Physiological Correlates of Emotion.* Academic Press, New York, London.

McCleary, R. A. (1961). 'Response specificity in the behavioral effects of limbic system lesions in the cat', *J. comp. physiol. Psychol.*, **54**, 605–13.

McCleary, R. A. (1966). 'Response-modulating functions of the limbic system: Initiation and suppression', *Prog. physiol. Psychol.*, **1**, 209–72.

McCleary, R. A., Jones, C., and Ursin, H. (1965). 'Avoidance and retention deficits in septal cats', *Psychon. Sci.*, **2**, 85–6.

McDougall, W. (1910). *Introduction to Social Psychology.* Luce, Boston.

McDougall, W. (1923). *Outline of Psychology.* Scribner, New York.

McDougall, W. (1928). 'Emotion and feeling distinguished', in M. L. Reymert (Ed. *Feelings and Emotions.* Clark University Press, Worcester, Massachusetts.

McHose, J. H. (1963). 'Effect of continued nonreinforcement on the frustration effect', *J exp. Psychol.*, **65**, 444–50.

Nash, J. (1970). *Developmental Psychology: A Psychological Approach.* Prentice Hall New Jersey.

Nisbett, R. E. (1968). 'Taste, deprivation, and weight determinants of eating behavior', *J person. soc. Psychol.*, **16**, 107—16.

Nisbett, R. E., and Schachter, S. (1966). 'Cognitive manipulation of gain', *J. exp. soc Psychol.*, **2**, 227–36.

Nowlis, V. (1953). 'The development and modification of motivational systems in personality', in M. R. Jones (Ed.) *Current Theory and Research in Motivation* University of Nebraska Press, Lincoln, Nebraska.

Nowlis, V. (1959). 'The experimental analysis of mood' (Abstract), XVth International Congress of Psychology. *Acta Psychol.*, **15**, 426.

Nowlis, V. (1963). 'The concept of mood', in S. M. Farber and R. H. L. Wilson (Eds.) *Conflict and Creativity.* McGraw-Hill, New York.

Nowlis, V. (1965). 'Research with the mood adjective check list', in S. S. Tomkins and C. E. Izard (Eds.) *Affect, Cognition and Personality.* Springer, New York.

Nowlis, V. (1970). 'Mood: Behavior and Experience', in M. B. Arnold (Ed.) *Feelings and Emotions: The Loyola Symposium.* Academic Press, New York, London, 261-72.

Nowlis, V., and Nowlis, H. H. (1956). 'The description and analysis of moods', *Ann. N.Y. Acad. Sci.*, **65**, 345-55.

Oakley, D. A., and Russell, I. S. (1968). 'Mass action and Pavlovian conditioning', *Psychon. Sci.*, **12**, 91-2.

O'Kelly, L. I. (1940). 'The validity of defecation as a measure of emotionality in the rat', *J. gen. Psychol.*, **23**, 75-87.

Olds, J. (1955). 'Physiological mechanisms of reward', in M. R. Jones (Ed.) *Nebraska Symposium on Motivation.* University of Nebraska Press, Lincoln, Nebraska.

Olds, J. (1958). 'Self-stimulation of the brain', *Science*, **127**, 315-24.

Olds, J., and Milner, P. (1954). 'Positive reinforcement produced by electrical stimulation of the septal area and other regions of the rat brain', *J. comp. physiol. Psychol.*, **47**, 419-27.

Orbach, J., Milner, B., and Rasmussen, T. (1960). 'Learning and retention in monkeys after amygdalahippocampal resection', *Arch. Neurol.* (Chicago), 3, 230-51.

Osgood, C. E. (1952). 'The nature and measurement of meaning', *Psychol. Bull.*, **49**, 197-237.

Osgood, C. E. (1955). 'Fidelity and reliability', in H. Quastler, *Information Theory in Psychology.* Free Press, Glencoe, 374-84.

Osgood, C. E. (1966). 'Dimensionality of the semantic space for communication via facial expressions', *Scand. J. Psychol.*, **7**, 1-30.

Papez, J. W. (1937). 'A proposed mechanism of emotion', *Arch. neurol. Psychiat.*, **38**, 725-43.

Papez, J. W. (1939). 'Cerebral mechanisms', *Research publication, Association for Research in Nervous and Mental Disorders*, **89**, 145-59.

Pare, W. P. (1965). 'Stress and consummatory behavior in the albino rat', *Psychol. Rep.*, **16**, 399-405.

Parke, R. D., and Walters, R. H. (1967). 'Some factors influencing the efficacy of punishment training for inducing response inhibition. Experiment 2', *Monogr. Soc. Res. Child. Developm.*, **32**, No. 1.

Pavlov, I. P. (1928). *Conditioned Reflexes.* Trans. and ed. G. V. Anup. Oxford University Press, London, New York.

Peckham, R. H., and Amsel, A. (1967). 'Within-subject demonstration of a relationship between frustration and magnitude of reward in a differential magnitude of reward discrimination', *J. exp. Psychol.*, **73**, 187-95.

Peiper, A. (1926). 'Untersuchungen über die Reaktionzeit ein Sanglingsalter: II. Reaktionzeit auf Schmerzreiz', *Monatschr. Kinderheilk*, **32**, 136-43. (Quoted in Schneirla 1959.)

Persky, H., Gamm, S. R., and Grinker, R. R. Sr. (1952). 'Correlation between fluctuation of free anxiety and quantity of hippuric acid secretion', *Psychosom. Med.*, **14**, 34-40.

Persky, H., Grinker, R. R. Sr., and Mirsky, J. A. (1950). 'Excretion of hippuric acid in subjects with free anxiety', *J. clin. Invest.*, **29**, 110-14.

Peters, R. S. (1969). 'Motivation, emotion and the conceptual schemes of common sense', in T. Mischel (Ed.) *Human Action.* Academic Press, New York, London, 135-65.

Peters, R. S. (1970). 'The education of the emotions', in M. B. Arnold (Ed.) *Feelings and Emotions: The Loyola Symposium.* Academic Press, New York, London, 187-204.

Pichot, P. (1969). 'Discussion of "Biological aspects of anxiety"', in M. L. Lader (Ed.) *Studies of Anxiety.* Headley Bros., Ashford, 26-7.

284

Pliskoff, S. (1961). 'Rate-change effects during a pre-schedule-change stimulus', *J. exp. anal. Behav.*, **4**, 383–6.

Pliskoff, S. (1963). 'Rate-change effects with equal potential reinforcements during the "warming" stimulus', *J. exp. anal. Behav.*, **6**, 557–62.

Plutchik, R. (1954). 'The role of muscular tension in maladjustment', *J. Gen. Psychol.*, **50**, 45–62.

Plutchik, R. (1962). *The Emotions: Facts, Theories and a New Model*. Randon House, New York.

Plutchik, R. (1965). 'What is an emotion?', *J. Psychol.*, **61**, 295–303.

Plutchik, R. (1966). 'Emotions as adaptive reactions: Implications for therapy', *Psychoanalyt. Rev.*, **53**, 105–10.

Plutchik, R. (1970). 'Emotions, evolution and adaptive processes', in M. D. Arnold (Ed.) *Feelings and Emotions: The Loyola Symposium*. Academic Press, New York, London, 3–24.

Plutchik, R., and Ax, A. F. (1967). 'A critique of determinants of emotional state by Schachter and Singer', *Psychophysiology*, **4**, (1), 79–82.

Polack, I., Rubenstein, H., and Horowitz, A. (1960). 'Communication of verbal modes of expression', *Language and Speech*, **3**, 121–30.

Pradines, M. (1958). *Traite de Psychologie*, 6th Edn., Vol. 1. Presses Universitaires de France. Transl. by Y. Begin and M. B. Arnold. Excerpts reprinted in M. B. Arnold (Ed.) (1968) *The Nature of Emotion*. Penguin, Harmondsworth, 189–200.

Pribram, K. H. (1970). 'Feelings as monitors', In M. B. Arnold (Ed.) *Feelings and Emotions: The Loyola Symposium*. Academic Press, New York, London, 41–53.

Pribram, K. H., and Fulton, J. F. (1954). 'An experimental critique of the effects of anterior cingulate ablations in monkey', *Brain*, **77**, 34–44.

Pribram, K. H., Mishkin, M., Rosvold, H. E., and Kaplan, S. J. (1952). 'Effects on delayed response performance of lesions of dorsolateral and ventromedial frontal cortex of baboons', *J. comp. physiol. Psychol.*, **45**, 565–75.

Pribram, K. H., and Weiskrantz, L. A. (1957). 'A comparison of the effects of medial and lateral cerebral resections on conditioned avoidance behavior of monkeys', *J. comp. physiol. Psychol.*, **50**, 74–80.

Prytula, R. E., and Braund, W. G. (1970). 'Sucrose pellets incentive shifts in the double alley', *Psychol. Rep.*, **27**, 391–7.

Ranson, S. W. (1939). 'Somnolence caused by hypothalamic lesions in the monkey', *Arch. Neurol. Psychiat.*, **41**, 1–23.

Ranson, S. W., and Magoun, H. W. (1939). 'The hypothalamus', *Ergebn. Physiol.*, **41**, 56–163.

Rapaport, D. (1950). *Emotions and Memory*. International Universities Press, New York.

Reis, D. J., and Fuxe, K. (1969). 'Brain norepinephrine: Evidence that neuronal release is essential for sham rage behavior following brain-stem transection in the cat', *Proceedings of the National Academy of Sciences of the United States of America*, **64**, 108–12. (Quoted by Kety 1970.)

Remington, R. E., and Strongman, K. T. (1970). 'Instruction-dependent facilitation during a pretimeout stimulus in human subjects', *Psychon. Sci.*, **20**, 348–9.

Remington, R. E., and Strongman, K. T. (1972a). 'Operant facilitation during a pre-reward stimulus: differential effects in human subjects', *Brit. j. Psychol.*, **63**, 237–42.

Remington, R. E., and Strongman, K. T. (1972b). 'Baseline dependent facilitation. Effects of a prereward stimulus', *Brit. j. Psychol.*, **53**, 575–82.

Rescorla, R. '1967). 'Pavlovian conditioning and its proper control procedures', *Psychol. Rev.*, **74**, 71–80.

Rescorla, R. A. (1968). 'Probability of shock in the presence and absence of CS in fear conditioning', *J. comp. physiol. Psychol.*, **66**, 1–5.

Rescorla, R. A. (1969). 'Conditioned inhibition of fear resulting from negative CS–US contingencies', *J. comp. physiol. Psychol.*, **67**, 504–9.

Rescorla, R. A., and Lolordo, V. M. (1965). 'Inhibition of avoidance behavior', *J. comp. physiol. Psychol.*, **59**, 406–12.

Rescorla, R. A., and Solomon, R. L. (1967). 'Two-process learning: Relationships between Pavlovian conditioning and instrumental learning', *Psychol. Rev.*, **74**, 151–82.

Reynolds, G. S. (1961). 'Behavioral contrast', *J. exp. anal. Behav.*, **4**, 57–71.

Rodnick, E. H., and Garmezy, N. (1957). 'An experimental approach to the study of motivation in schizophrenia', in M. R. Jones (Ed.) *Nebraska Symposium on Motivation*. University of Nebraska Press, Lincoln, Nebraska, 109–84.

Rogers, E. R. (1961). *On Becoming a Person*. Houghton Mifflin, Boston.

Rosenthal, D. (1970). *Genetic Theory and Abnormal Behaviour*. McGraw-Hill, New York.

Rosenzweig, S. (1934). 'Types of reaction to frustration: an heuristic classification', *J. abnorm. soc. Psychol.*, **29**, 298–300.

Rosenzweig, S. (1938). 'A general outline of frustration', *Char. person.*, 7, 151–60.

Rosenzweig, S. (1944). 'An outline of frustration theory', in J. McV. Hunt (Ed.) *Personality and the Behavior Disorders*. Ronald Press, New York.

Ross, G. S., Hodos, W., and Brady, J. V. (1962). 'Electroencephalographic correlates of temporally spaced responding and avoidance behavior', *J. exp. anal. Behav.*, **5**, 467–72.

Ross, R. B., and Russell, I. S. (1967). 'Subcortical storage of classical conditioning', *Nature*, **214**, 5084, 210–11.

Ruckmick, C. A. (1936). *The Psychology of Feeling and Emotion*. McGraw-Hill, New York.

Russell, I. S. (1967). 'Animal learning and memory', in D. Richter (Ed.) *Aspects of Learning and Memory*. Heinemann, London.

Ryan, T. J., and Watson, P. (1968). 'Frustrative nonreward theory applied to children's behavior', *Psychol. Bull.*, **69**, 111–25.

Rylander, G. (1939). *Personality Changes after Operations on the Frontal Lobes. A Clinical Study of 32 Cases*. Munksgaard, Copenhagen.

Rylander, G. (1948). 'Personality analysis before and after frontal lobotomy', *Res. Pub. Assoc. res. nerv. ment. Dis.*, **27**, 691–705.

Ryle, G. (1948). *The Concept of Mind*. Hutchinson, London.

Salzen, E. A. (1962). 'Imprinting and fear', *Symp. Zoo. Soc. London*, No. 8, 197–217.

Salzen, E. A. (1963). 'Visual stimuli eliciting the smiling response in the human infant', *J. genet. Psychol.*, **102**, 51–4.

Salzen, E. A., and Tomlin, F. J. (1963). 'The effect of cold on the following response of domestic fowl', *Anim. Behav.*, 7, 172–9.

Sargant, W. (1957). *Battle for the Mind*. Heinemann, London.

Sarte, J. P. (1948). *The Emotions*. Philosophical Library, New York.

Sawrey, W. J., and Weisz, J. D. (1956). 'An experimental method of producing gastric ulcers', *J. comp. physiol. Psychol.*, **49**, 269–70.

Schachter, S. (1957). 'Pain, fear and anger in hypertensives and a psychophysiologic study', *Psychosom. Med.*, **19**, 17–29.

Schachter, S. (1959). *The Psychology of Affiliation*. Stamford University Press, Stamford, California.

Schachter, S. (1964). 'The interaction of cognitive and physiological determinants of emotional state', in L. Berkowitz (Ed.) *Advances in Experimental Social Psychology*, Vol. 1. Academic Press, New York, 49–80.

Schachter, S. (1965). 'A cognitive–physiological view of emotion', in Klineberg and Christie (Eds.) *Perspectives in Social Psychology*. Holt, Rinehart & Winston, New York, 75–105.

Schachter, S. (1967). 'Cognitive effects on bodily functioning: Studies of obesity and eating', in D. C. Glass (Ed.) *Neurophysiology and Emotion*. Rockefeller University Press and Russell Sage Foundation, New York.

Schacter, S. (1970). 'The assumption of identity and peripherilist–centralist controversies in motivation and emotion', in M. B. Arnold (Ed.) *Feelings and Emotion: The Loyola Symposium.* Academic Press, New York, London.

Schachter, S. (1972). *Emotion, Obesity and Crime.* Academic Press, New York.

Schachter, S., Goldman, R., and Gordon, A. (1968). 'Effects of fear, food deprivation and obesity on eating', *J. pers. soc. Psychol.,* **10**, 91–7.

Schachter, S., and Gross, L. P. (1968). 'Manipulated time and eating behavior', *J. pers. soc. Psychol.,* **10**, 98–106.

Schachter, S., and Latane, B. (1964). 'Crime, cognition and the autonomic nervous system', in D. Levine (Ed.) *Nebraska Symposium on Motivation.* University of Nebraska Press, Lincoln, Nebraksa, 221–73.

Schachter, S., and Singer, J. (1962). 'Cognitive, social and physiological determinants of emotional state', *Psychol. Rev.,* **69**, 378–99.

Schachter, S., and Wheeler, L. (1962). 'Epineprine, chlorpromizine and amusement'. *J. abnorm. soc. Psychol.,* **65**, :21–8.

Schaffer, H. R. (1958). 'Objective observations of personality development in early infancy', *Brit. J. Med. Psychol.,* **31**, 174–83.

Schaller, G. B., and Emlen, J. T. (1962). 'The ontogeny of avoidance behaviour in some precocial birds', *Anim. Behav.,* **10**, 370–81.

Schlosberg, H. (1952). 'The description of facial expression in terms of two dimensions', *J. exp. Psychol.,* **44**, 229–37.

Schlosberg, H. (1954). 'Three dimensions of emotion', *Psychol Rev.,* **61**, 81–8.

Schneirla, T. C. (1959). 'An evolutionary and developmental theory of biphasic processes underlying approach and withdrawal', in M. R. Jones (Ed.) *Nebraska Symposium on Motivation.* University of Nebraska Press, Lincoln, Nebraska, 1–42.

Schneirla, T. C. (1965). 'Aspects of stimulation and organization in approach/withdrawal processes underlying vertebrate behavioral development', in Lehrman, Hinde and Shaw (Eds.) *Advances in the Study of Behavior.* I. Academic Press, New York.

Schreiner, L. H., and Kling, A. (1953). 'Behavioral changes following injury in the cat', *J. Neurophys.,* **16**, 643–59.

Schwartzbaum, J. S. (1965). 'Discrimination behavior after amygdalectomy in monkeys: Visual and somesthetic learning and perceptual capacity', *J. comp. physiol. Psychol.,* **60**, 314–19.

Schwartzbaum, J. S. (1960). 'Changes in reinforcing properties of stimuli following ablation of the amygdaloid complex in monkeys', *J. comp. physiol. Psychol.,* **53**, 388–95.

Schwartzbaum, J. S., Green, R. H., Beatty, W. W., and Thompson, B. 'Acquisition of avoidance behavior following septal lesions in the rat', *J. comp. physiol. Psychol.,* **63**, 95–104.

Scott, J. P. (1962). 'Critical periods in behavioral development', *Science,* **138**, 949–58.

Scott, J. P. (1967). 'The process of primary socialization in the dog', in G. Newton and S. Levine (Eds.) *Early Experience and Behavior.* Thomas, Springfield, U.S.A.

Scott, J. P. (1968). *Early Experience and the Organization of Behavior.* Wadsworth, California, U.S.A.

Scott, J. P., and Fuller, J. L. (1965). *Genetics and the Social Behavior of the Dog.* University of Chicago Press, Chicago.

Sears, R. R. (1950). 'Relation of fantasy aggression to interpersonal aggression', *Child Dev.,* **21**, 5–6.

Sears, R. R., Maccoby, E. E., and Levin, H. (1957). *Patterns of Child Rearing.* Row, Peterson, Evanston, Illinois.

Seligman, M. E. P. (1971). 'Phobias and preparedness', *Behaviour therapy,* **2**, 307–320.

Seligman, M. E. P. (1975). *Helplessness.* Freeman, San Francisco.

Severin, F. T. (1973). *Discovering Man in Psychology.* McGraw-Hill, New York.

Seward, J. P., Pereboom, A. C., Burler, B., and Jones, R. B. (1957). 'The role of pre-feeding in an apparent frustration effect', *J. exp. Psychol.*, **54**, 445–50.

Shepard, R. N. (1963). 'The analysis of proximities: multidimensional scaling with an unknown distance function', *Psychometrica*, **27**, 125–40.

Sherrington, C. S. (1900). 'Experiments on the value of vascular and visceral factors for the genesis of emotion', *Proc. Roy. Soc. (London)*, **66**, 390–403.

Sidman, M. (1960). 'Normal sources of pathological behavior', *Science*, **132**, 61–8.

Siegal, P. S., and Brantley, J. J. (1951). 'The relationship of emotionality to the consummatory response of eating', *J. exp. Psychol.*, **42**, 304–6.

Siegel, P. S., and Siegel, H. S. (1949). 'The effect of emotionality on the water intake of the rat', *J. comp. physiol. Psychol.*, **42**, 12–16.

Siegel, P. S., and Sparks, D. L. (1961). 'Irrelevant aversive stimulation as an activator of an appetitional response: a replication', *Psychol. Rep.*, **9**, 700.

Siminov, P. V. (1970). 'The information theory of emotion', in M. B. Arnold (Ed.) *Feelings and Emotions: The Loyola Symposium*. Academic Press, New York. London, 145–9. (From an original report at the Congress of Psychology, Moscow, 1966.)

Singer, J. L. (1961). 'The effects of epinephrine, chlorpromazine and dibenzyline upon the fright responses of rats under stress and nonstress conditions'. Unpubl. doctoral diss. University of Minnesota. (Quoted by Schachter 1964; 1965.)

Singer, J. L. (Ed.) (1971). *The Control of Aggression and Violence*. Academic Press, New York, London.

Singer, R. D., and Singer, A. (1969). *Psychological Development in Children*. W. S. Saunders, Philadelphia, London.

Skinner, B. F. (1938). *The Behavior of Organisms*. Appleton-Century-Crofts, New York.

Skinner, B. F. (1953). *Science and Human Behavior*. Macmillan, New York.

Skinner, B. F. (1957). *Verbal Behavior*. Appleton-Century-Crofts, New York.

Slater, E., and Roth, M. (1969). *Mayer-Gross, Slater and Roth; Clinical Psychiatry*, 3rd Edn. Bailliere, Tindall & Cassell, London.

Slater, E., and Shields, J. (1969). 'Genetical aspects of anxiety', in M. H. Lader (Ed.) *Studies of Anxiety*. Headley Bros., Ashford, 62–71.

Sluckin, W. (1960). 'Towards a theory of filial responses', *Bull. Brit. psychol. Soc. No. 40*, 5A.

Sluckin, W. (1964). *Imprinting and Early Learning*. Methuen, London.

Smith, W. K. (1950). 'Non-olfactory functions of the pyriform-amygdaloid-hippocampal complex', *Fed. Proc.*, **9**, 118.

Solomon, P., Kubzansky, P. E., Leiderman, P. H., Mendelson, J. H., Trumbull, R., and Wexler, D. (1961). *Sensory Deprivation*. Harvard University Press, Cambridge.

Soskin, W. F., and Kaufman, P. E. (1961). 'Judgment of emotion in word-free speech samples', *J. Communic.*, **11**, 73–80.

Spence, K. W. (1956). *Behavior Theory and Conditioning*. Yale University Press, New Haven.

Spence, K. W. (1958). 'A theory of emotionally based drive (D) and its relation to performance in simple learning situations', *Amer. Psychol.*, **13**, 131–41.

Spielberger, C. D. (1966). 'Theory and research on anxiety', in Spielberger (Ed.) *Anxiety and Behavior*. Academic Press, New York, London, 3–20.

Spielberger, C. D. (Ed.) (1966). *Anxiety and Behavior*. Academic Press, New York, London.

Spielberger, C. D., and Smith, L. H. (1966), 'Anxiety (drive); stress and serial-position effect in serial-verbal learning', *J. exp. Psychol.*, **72**, 589–95.

Spiesman, J. C., Lazarus, R. S., Mordkoff, A. M., and Davidson, L. A. (1964). 'The experimental reduction of stress based on ego-defence theory', *J. abnorm. soc. Psychol.*, **68**, 367–80.

288

Spitz, R. A., and Wolf, K. (1946). 'Anaclitic depressions', *Psychoanal. Stud. of Child.*, **2**, 313–42.

Staddon, J. E. R., and Innis, N. K. (1966). 'An effect analogous to "frustration" on interval reinforcement schedules', *Psychon. Sci.*, **4**, 287–8.

Staddon, J. E. R., and Innis, N. K. (1969). 'Reinforcement omission on fixed-interval schedules', *J. exp. anal. Behav.*, **12**, 689–700.

Stanley-Jones, D. (1970). 'The biological origin of love and hate', in M. B. Arnold (Ed.) *Feelings and Emotions: The Loyola Symposium*. Academic Press, New York, London.

Stein, L., Sidman, M., and Brady, J. V. (1958). 'Some effects of two temporal variables on conditioned suppression', *J. exp. anal. Behav.*, **1**, 154–62.

Stern, R. M., Botto, R. W., and Herrick, C. D. (1972). 'Behavioural and physiological effects of false heartrate feedback: A modification and extension', *Psychophysiology*, **9**, 21–29.

Stern, R. M., and Kaplan, B. E. (1967), 'Galvanic skin response: Voluntary control and externalization', *J. Psychosom. Res.*, **10**, 349–53.

Sternbach, R. A. (1966). *Principles of Psychophysiology*. Academic Press, New York, London.

Sterritt, G. M. (1962), 'Inhibition and facilitation of eating by electric shock', *J. comp. physiol. Psychol.*, **55**, 226–9.

Stotland, E. (1969). 'Exploratory investigations of empathy', in L. Berkowitz (Ed.) *Advances in Experimental Social Psychology*, **4**, 271–314.

Stoyva, J., and Kamiya, J. (1968). 'Electrophysiological studies of dreaming as the prototype of a new strategy in the study of consciousness', *Psychol. Rev.*, **75**, 192–205.

Strasser, S. (1970). 'Feeling as a basis of knowing and recognising the other as an ego', in M. B. Arnold (Ed.) *Feelings and Emotions: The Loyola Symposium*. Academic Press, New York, London.

Stringer, P. (1967). 'Cluster analysis of nonverbal judgments of facial expression', *Brit. J. Math. Stat. Psychol.*, **20**, 71–9.

Strongman, K. T. (1965). 'The effect of anxiety on food intake in the rat', *Quart. J. exp. Psychol.*, **17**, 255–60.

Strongman, K. T. (1967). 'The effect of prior exposure to shock on a visual discrimination by rats', *Canad. J. Psychol,*, **21**, 57–68.

Strongman, K. T. (1969). 'Analysing emotional behavior', *New Scient.*, Aug., 242–343.

Strongman, K. T. (1970). 'Communicating with the eyes', *Science Journal*, **6**, 47–53.

Strongman, K. T., and Champness, B. G. (1968). 'Dominance hierarchies and conflict in eye contact', *Acta Psychol.*, **28**, 376–86.

Strongman, K. T., Coles, M. G. H., Remington, R. E., and Wookey, P. E. (1970). 'The effect of shock duration and intensity on the ingestion of food of varying palatibility', *Quart. J. exp. Psychol.*, **22**, 521–5.

Strongman, K. T., and Wookey, P. E. (1969). 'Frustrative reward', *J. exp. Psychol.*, **82**, 183–4.

Strongman, K. T., Wookey, P. E., and Remington, R. E. (1971). 'Elation', *Brit. J. Psychol.*, **62**, 481–92.

Tart, C. (1969). *Altered States of Consciousness*. Wiley, New York.

Tart, G. T. (1972). 'States of consciousness and state-specific sciences', *Science*, **176**, 1203–1210.

Taylor, J. A. (1956). 'Drive theory and manifest anxiety', *Psychol. Bull.*, **53**, 303–20.

Thierry, A. M., Javoy, F., Glowinski, J., and Ketty, S. S. (1968). 'Effects of stress on the metabolism of noxepinephrine, dopamine and serotonin in the central nervous system of the rat. I. Modification of noxepinephrine turnover', *J. Pharmacol. exp. Therap.*, **163**, 163–71. (Quoted by Kety 1970.)

Thompson, D. F., and Meltzer, L. (1964). 'Communication of emotional intent by facial expression', *J. abnorm. soc. Psychol.*, **68**, 129–35.

Thompson, J. (1941). 'Development of facial expression of emotion in blind and seeing children', *Arch. Psychol.*, **37**, No. 264.

Thorpe, W. H. (1956). *Learning and Instinct in Animals.* Harvard University Press, Cambridge, Mass.

Tobach, E., and Schneirla, T. C. (1962). 'Eliminative responses in mice and rats and the problem of "emotionality" ', in E. L. Bliss (Ed.) *Root of Behavior.* Harper, New York.

Tomkins, S. S. (1962). *Affect, Imagery and Consciousness: Vol. 1. The Positive Affects.* Springer, New York.

Tomkins, S. S. (1963). *Affect, Imagery and Consciousness: Vol. 11. The Negative Affects.* Springer, New York.

Tomkins, S. S., and McCarter, R. (1964). 'What and where are the primary affects? Some evidence for a theory', *Percept. Mot. Sk.*, **18**, 119–58.

Trenholme, I., Baron, A., and Kaufman, A. (1969). 'Effects of signated time-out from and loss of monetary reinforcement on human operant behavior', *Psychon. Sci.*, **15**, 295–6.

Triandis, H. G., and Lamber, W. W. (1958). 'A restatement and test of Schlosberg's theory of emotions, with two kinds of subjects from Greece', *J. abnorm. soc. Psychol.*, **56**, 321–8.

Tryon, R. C., Tryon, C. M., and Kuznets, G. (1941). 'Studies in individual differences in maze ability: IX Ratings of hiding, avoidance, escape and vocalization responses', *J. comp. Psychol.*, **32**, 407–35.

Turner, M. B. (1967). *Philosophy and the Science of Behaviour.* Appleton-Century-Crofts, New York.

Valenstein, E. S. (1959). 'The effect of reserpine on the continued emotional response in the guinea pig', *J. exp. anal. Behav.*, **2**, 219–25.

Valentive, C. W. (1930). 'The innate bases of fear', Journal of Genetic Psychology, **37**, 394–419.

Valins, S. (1963). *Psychopathy and Physiological Reactivity under Stress.* Unpubl. Masters thesis. Colombia University. (Quoted in Schachter and Latane 1964.)

Valins, S. (1966). 'Cognitive effects of false heart-rate feedback', *J. person. soc. Psychol.*, **4**, 400–8.

Valins, S. (1967a). 'Emotionality and information concerning internal reactions', *J. person, soc. Psychol.*, **6**, 458–63.

Valins, S. (1967b). 'Emotionality and autonomic reactivity', *J. exp. res. Pers.*, **2**, 41–8.

Valins, S. (1968). *Persistent Effects of Information Concerning Internal Reactions: Ineffectiveness of Debriefing.* Unpubl. manusc. (Quoted in Valins 1970.)

Valins, S. (1970). 'The perception and labeling of bodily changes as determinants of emotional behavior', in P. Black (Ed.) *Physiological Correlates of Emotion.* Academic Press, New York, London, 229–43.

Valins, S., and Ray, A. A. 'Effects of cognitive desensitization on avoidance behavior', *J. person. soc. Psychol.*, **7**, 345–50.

Vandenberg, S. G. (1967). 'Hereditary factors in normal personality traits (as measured by inventories)', in Wortis (Ed.) *Recent Advances in Biological Psychiatry.* Vol. 9. Plenum Press, New York.

Vine, I. (1970). 'Communication by facial-visual signals', in J. H. Crook (Ed.) *Social Behaviour in Birds and Mammals.* Academic Press, New York, London, 279–354.

Wagner, A. R. (1959). 'The role of reinforcement and nonreinforcement in an "apparent frustration effect" ', *J. exp. Psychol.*, **57**, 130–6.

Wagner, A. R. (1963). 'Conditioned frustration as a learned drive', *J. exp. Psychol.*, **66**, 142–8.

Wagner, A. R. (1966). 'Frustration and punishment', in R. N. Haber (Ed.) *Current Research in Motivation.* Holt, Rinehart & Winston, New York, 229–39.

Wagner, A. R. (1969). 'Frustrative nonreward: A variety of punishment', in B. A.

Campbell and R. M. Church (Eds.) *Punishments and Aversive Behavior.* Appleton-Century-Crofts, New York, 157–81.

Walker, A. E., Thompson, A. F., and McQueen, J. D. (1953), 'Behavior and the temporal rhinecephalon in the monkey', *Bull. Johns Hopk. Hosp.*, **93**, 65–93.

Walsh, R. N., and Cummins, R. A. (1976). 'The open-field test: a critical review', *Psychological Bulletin*, **83**, 3, 482–504.

Walter, W. G., Cooper, R., Aldridge, V. J., McCallum, W. C., and Winter, A. L. (1964). 'Contingent negative variation: An electric sign of sensorimotor association and expectancy in the human brain', *Nature*, **203**, 380–4.

Walther, R. (1956). *Das vegetative-affektive syndrom und seine Bedeut fur die Psychiatrie.* Berlin, VE3 Verlog. (Quoted in Gellhorn and Loufbourrow 1963.)

Warries, E. (1963). *Sitantie en expressie.* M. A. Thesis. Amsterdam University. (Quoted in Frijda 1969.)

Watson, J. B. (1929). *Psychology. From the Standpoint of a Behaviourist.* (3rd Ed. Rev.). J. B. Lipincott, Philadelphia, London.

Watson, J. B. (1930). *Behaviorism,* (Rev. ed.). University of Chicago Press, Chicago.

Watson, J. B., and Rayner, R. (1920). 'Conditioned emotional reactions', *J. Exp. Psychol,* **3**, 1–14.

Webb, W. B., and Goodman, J. J. (1958). 'Activating role of an irrelevant drive in absence of the relevant drive', *Psychol. Rep.,* **4**, 235–8.

Weisberger, C. A. (1956). 'Accuracy in judging emotional expressions as related to college entrance', *J. Psychol.,* **44**, 233–9.

Weiskrantz, L. (1968). 'Emotion', in L. Weiskrantz (Ed.) *Analysis of Behavioural Change.* Harper & Row, New York, London, 50–90.

Weiss, K. M. (1968). 'Some effects of the conditioned suppression paradigm on operant discrimination performance', *J. exp. anal. Behav.,* **11**, 767–75.

Weiss, K. M. (1969). *Experimental Analysis of Emotional Behaviour.* Unpubl. Ph.D. Thesis, University of Exeter.

Wenger, M. A. (1950). 'Emotion as visceral action: An extension of Lange's theory', in M. L. Reymert (Ed.) *Feelings and Emotions: The Mooseheart symposium.* McGraw-Hill, New York.

Wenner, A. M. (1967). 'Honeybees: Do they use the distance information contained in their dance manoeuvre?', *Science,* **155**, 847–9.

West, L. J., and Farber, I. E. (1960). 'The role of pain in emotional development', in *Explorations in the Physiology of Emotions.* L. J. West and M. Greenblak (Eds.) *Psych. res. reps. of the Amer. Psychiat. Assoc.,* **12**, 119–26.

Wike, E. L. (1966). *Secondary Reinforcement: Selected Experiments.* Harper, New York.

Wilton, R. N., and Strongman, K. T. (1967), 'Extinction performance as a function of reinforcement magnitude and number of training trials', *Psychol. Rep.,* **20**, 235–8.

Wilton, R. N., Strongman, K. T., and Nerenberg, A. (1969). 'Some effects of frustration in a free responding operant situation', *Quart. j. exp. Psychol.,* **XXI**, 367–80.

Wolf, S., and Wolff, H. G. (1947). *Human Gastric Function.* Oxford University Press, New York, Oxford.

Wolpe, J. (1952). 'Experimental neurosis as learned behaviour', *Brit. J. Psychol.,* **43**, 243–68.

Wolpe, J. (1958). *Psychotherapy by Reciprocal Inhibition.* Stamford University Press, Stamford.

Wolpe, J. (1961). 'The systematic desensitization treatment of neuroses', *J. nerv. ment. Dis.,* **112**, 189–203.

Wolpe, J. (1966). 'The conditioning and deconditioning of neurotic anxiety', in C. D. Spielberger (Ed.) *Anxiety and Behavior.* Academic Press, New York, London, 179–90.

Wolpe, J., and Lazarus, A. A. (1966). *Behavior Therapy Techniches.* Pergamon, London.

Woodworth, R. S. (1938). *Experimental Psychology*. Holt, New York.

Woodworth, R. S., and Schlosberg, H. (1955). *Experimental Psychology* (Rev. ed.). Holt, New York.

Wookey, P. E., and Strongman, K. T. (1971). 'Emotional and instrumental effects of reward shift', *Psychol. Rec.*, **21**, 181-9.

Wookey, P. E., and Strongman, K. T. (1972). 'Quantitative reward shift in the double runway', *Brit. J. Psychol.*, **63**, 401-5.

Wrightsman, L. S. (1960). 'Effects of waiting with others on changes in level of felt anxiety', *J. abnorm. soc. Psychol.*, **61**, 216-22.

Wynne, L. C., and Solomon, R. L. (1955). 'Traumatic avoidance learning: acquisition and extinction in dogs deprived of normal peripheral autonomic functioning', *Genet. Psychol. Monogr.*, **52**, 241-84.

Yarrow, L. J. (1961). 'Maternal deprivation: toward an empirical and conceptual re-evaluation', *Psychol. Bull.*, **58**, 459-90.

Yarrow, L. J. (1964). 'Separation from parents during early childhood', in M. L. Hoffman, and L. W. Hoffman (Eds.) *Review of Child Development Research*. Russel Sage Foundation, New York.

Yates, A. J. (1962). *Frustration and Conflict*. Wiley, New York.

Yerkes, R. M., and Dobson, J. D. (1908). 'The relation of strength of stimulus to rapidity of habit-formation', *J. comp. neurol. Psychol.*, **18**, 459-82.

Young, P. T. (1961). *Motivation and Emotion*. Wiley, New York, London.

Author Index

296

Subject Index